Light from the Ashes

Light from the Ashes

Social Science Careers of Young Holocaust Refugees and Survivors

Peter Suedfeld, *Editor*

Ann Arbor
THE UNIVERSITY OF MICHIGAN PRESS

Copyright © by the University of Michigan 2001
All rights reserved
Published in the United States of America by
The University of Michigan Press
Manufactured in the United States of America
⊗ Printed on acid-free paper

2004   2003   2002   2001   4   3   2   1

A CIP catalog record for this book is available from the British Library.

Library of Congress Cataloging-in-Publication Data

Light from the ashes : social science careers of young Holocaust
    refugees and survivors / Peter Suedfeld, editor.
        p.   cm.
    Includes bibliographical references and index.
    ISBN 0-472-09745-8 (cloth : alk. paper) — ISBN 0-472-06745-1
(pbk. : alk. paper)
    1. Jewish children in the Holocaust—Biography.   2. Holocaust
survivors—Biography.   3. Holocaust, Jewish (1939–1945)—Personal
narratives.   4. Jewish social scientists—Biography.   I. Suedfeld,
Peter, 1935–
DS804.48 .L55   2000
940.53'18'0922—dc21   00-011815

We dedicate this book to all children, past, present, and future, whose lives are violently ended or disrupted by war; to the nations, organizations, families, and individuals who—in the past, present, or future—dedicate themselves to rescuing, sheltering, and nurturing such children; and to the memory of Mary Engel, our friend and colleague.

Preface

Peter Suedfeld

The idea for this book emerged from a symposium at the annual meeting of the International Society of Political Psychology (ISPP), held in Vancouver, British Columbia, in the summer of 1996. I was in the midst of a period of reminiscence and introspection, tracing possible relationships between my experiences as a Jewish child hidden with Christian identity documents in Budapest during World War II and my subsequent private life and scientific career. During the previous few years, I had become aware for the first time of several colleagues in the social sciences who also had had their childhoods disrupted by Nazi persecution; a few had consciously associated that set of events with their later pursuits, but most— like me up to very recently—had never thought about such a connection.

In organizing the symposium, I asked several of these colleagues to participate. My request was for them to think about the paths of influence that led from childhood persecution and upheaval to the adult choice of profession and research focus and to be prepared to discuss both their personal and professional autobiographies openly at the conference. This was a difficult task for all of us. I, in fact, tried to shirk it by merely chairing the symposium and not actually talking about my own introspections, a strategy that in the event was foiled by the insistence of the panel and the audience.

The session was a huge success. The presentations were revealing and touching, the analyses insightful and enlightening. The room was packed; for the first time ever at a scientific meeting, I saw members of the audience in tears as eminent colleagues and longtime friends revealed aspects of their histories and personalities they had never before mentioned. Some told me later that it had been the most important session they had ever attended, and the presenters themselves felt that it had been a major event. Several people in the audience approached me, then or later, to tell me that they too were refugees from or survivors of the Holocaust.

It was this last experience that led me to organize this book, in which social scientists who had been children or young adolescents under Nazi domination could explore how early trauma and adult career meshed with each other. As the plan unfolded, colleagues suggested other names. I eventually decided that the book should focus on individuals who were engaged in research but not exclusively or primarily research about the Holocaust itself; who represented a range of disciplines and subdisciplines within the social and behavioral sciences; and who had made their postwar life in different countries. However, because fluency in writing English was a necessity and because the identification of appropriate people was done through expanding circles of personal acquaintance, the list ended up with some bias toward scholars working in North America and toward psychologists.

When around two dozen prospective participants were identified, I wrote to each, explaining the nature and goal of the book and inviting them to participate. Not all of those who were invited are represented in the book. One was too ill to write a chapter; a couple had just published autobiographies and did not want to write another one, even one with a specific and different focus; and two, both of them friends and eminent colleagues of mine, did not want to confront or to publicly dissect the theme as it applied to their own life. The rest of us could empathize with this reluctance; we, too, had avoided such a task for decades after the war and even now were stressed by undertaking it.

The Greek origin of the word *holocaust,* meaning a sacrificial offering that is consumed by flames, is very different from the Hebrew word *Shoah,* a catastrophe or major disaster. However, both words have entered common usage as a reference to the Nazi persecutions and mass murders, specifically the attempt to annihilate the Jewish people, and are often used interchangeably.[1] A number of writers and survivor groups have carried the burnt sacrifice metaphor further to refer to the consequences and aftermath of the Holocaust in terms of ashes. I chose *Light from the Ashes* for the title because I believe, and I think the chapters in this book confirm, that reflecting upon the events of the Holocaust can be illuminating. For those involved in producing the book, it has led to greater self-knowledge; for our readers, we hope it will be a contribution to Holocaust literature and to the psychology of science.

NOTE

1. I thank René Goldman for bringing the difference to my attention.

Contents

Introduction: Shaped by the Past, Shaping the Future

Peter Suedfeld

Shaping a Life of Work

Most people spend a large proportion of their life in work. For many, there is little or no personal choice in what that work is. The environment may dictate, or society demand, that women grow vegetables, gather berries, and take care of the family home; or that men be cattle herders and warriors; or that members of a particular caste become merchants or rulers. Others have a choice, but the cards are stacked in a particular way: they inherit a family business, they are expected to follow a family tradition of entering certain professions, or they face social barriers in trying to get an education or enter certain pursuits. In most cases, there are at least subtle pressures—ambitions and expectations, as well as limits, communicated by one's parents, other relatives, teachers, peers, and society.

The psychologically interesting situation is when the individual does have a wide range of possibilities. Sometimes, a cool cost-benefit analysis is recommended as the basis for choosing an occupation (Janis and Mann 1977); but more often, the decision is shaped by personality factors, aptitudes, motives, and fortuitous circumstances of which the chooser may not be fully aware (Feist and Gorman 1998).

Some events can redirect a person's occupational life through a drastic change in the social and geographic environment. In their youth, the contributors to this book all lived through a wrenching change in family and societal influences. The smooth and predictable course of their lives was moved into completely new paths by Nazi persecution during World

War II; they lost many or all of their close relatives, family possessions, and even their homeland. They selected their careers in the context of a newly acquired language, culture, and citizenship. Thus, they had a higher degree of uncertainty (and of free choice) in choosing an occupational direction than they might have had otherwise. When I invited them to contribute, I asked them to analyze how their wartime experiences had influenced that choice.

All of the contributors had decided to specialize in one of the social/ behavioral sciences. Because this was what is euphemistically called an "opportunity sample"—that is, people I knew personally who recommended others—there is a preponderance of psychologists. Nevertheless, the group's scientific foci include a tremendous range of topics, from the study of ancient cultures and the explanation of current political trends to the elucidation of how the brain is involved in thought and action. One concentration that will not be found in the volume is a primary interest in Holocaust-related studies: there would be no mystery in explaining the connection between a childhood marked by the Holocaust and an adulthood devoted to examining it—and no excitement in finding such a connection. Therefore, although some of the contributors (including me) have done some research relevant to the Holocaust, none has been a specialist in that area.

All of the authors are active researchers, rather than (or as well as) being teachers or applied practitioners. Not content with transmitting knowledge, or putting it to use to solve practical problems, they have addressed themselves to discovering facts no one has known before and to explaining, in ways previously unimagined, what those facts mean. These activities have the potential of influencing the future conditions of humankind by increasing our knowledge and understanding of the world in which we live.

What motivates people to devote their lives to such an enterprise? If you ask scientists themselves, the answers usually include something about the excitement of research, the satisfaction of adding to the storehouse of human knowledge, the important possibility of finding ways to solve some of humanity's problems. It is also true that science can provide a comfortable, secure, and respected place in society, one where intelligence, creativity, and hard work can lead not only to acceptance but to acclaim.

Such explanations do not seem to answer all the questions, though. After all, many professions have equally positive spiritual and material payoffs. Why pick scientific research, why a social science, and why the specific social science and the even more specific area within the discipline? Here, we enter a largely unexplored realm. People may be able to recall how one or more of these decisions was made, but they usually have not reflected deeply on why they chose, stayed with, abandoned, or altered their lines of thinking and research. Even when they do consider such issues, they are likely to base their explanations on the immediate circumstances at the time. They rarely trace the connections between their professional choices and the experiences of early life that may be the deep sources of preferences and aversions, of values and ambitions.

I have asked the contributors to this book to do just that: to recall in some detail relevant and important events in their childhoods and to trace how those experiences may have led them to the paths that they have followed professionally and to the places where they now are. As I mentioned earlier, the childhood or adolescence of each author underwent drastic upheaval because of the Nazi persecutions of 1933–1945. Most were Jewish children, living in Europe, who either fled from or lived through the Holocaust; two were the offspring of prominent political opponents of the Nazis, whose lives were imperiled by that opposition.

Their backgrounds have dissimilarities, as well as common characteristics, with regard to country of origin, family structure, level of assimilation to the surrounding culture, wealth, and social position. It is these conditions, both the shared and the unique, whose impact on the later foci of scholarship and thought the contributors were asked to describe.

The Flames of Nazi Persecution

The stories and self-analyses that follow represent an unusual look at traumatic experiences and their long-term aftereffects as perceived by a group of trained social scientists. For once, the scholars who examine these consequences are also the people who experienced them; we are writing about ourselves. We were children or adolescents at the time of our encounter with persecution, uprooting, hunger, and death, and we now look back on those times and trace forward how our experiences have shaped our lives and careers.

Everyone familiar with the history of twentieth-century science, medicine, literature, music, politics, social sciences, and other culturally important pursuits is aware of the important contributions made by adult refugees from the Nazi Holocaust. Scores, perhaps hundreds, of accomplished and eminent professionals were saved by their families, friends, and colleagues in Great Britain, the United States, and other safe havens, and these professionals have transformed their fields. The best-known names are probably those of the physical scientists, including an amazing roster of eventual Nobel laureates; but the list also includes eminent contributors to medical science, biology, mathematics, psychology, history, sociology, economics, pedagogy, philosophy, and political science (see, e.g., Ash and Söllner 1996; Kielmansegg, Mewes, and Glaser-Schmidt 1995; Lehmann and Sheehan 1991).

But these were people whose education had been completed in Europe and whose professional careers had at least been launched there. Many of them were already famous and held prestigious positions when the Nazi movement drove them away, while others were younger, promising scholars in early or midcareer. In their countries of refuge, although some were inspired by their experiences to begin new lines of research and generate new theories (e.g., Lewin 1992), most built upon their earlier successes and continued their work without drastic change. Survivors such as Bruno Bettelheim and Victor Frankl also integrated their Holocaust experiences with previously attained scientific training and ways of thinking.

Not so the contributors to this book. Our schooling was interrupted, or not yet begun, when World War II and the Nazi persecution washed over our native lands. We chose our educational and professional paths in countries far from our original homes, in newly learned languages, in cultures that we did not fully understand. Many of us had lost forever not only the family's material resources to guide and help us on our way but also the close family members who normally transmit values and ambitions to the next generation.

Child survivors and refugees, who will of course be the last eyewitnesses of the Holocaust, have always faced unusual conditions. Even more than their older relatives, they were caught up in events that they did not always fully understand; they were seldom consulted about, or even prepared for, the circumstances of their flight, hiding, or internment, which were determined by adults. All depended, as children must, on the help of adults, without which survival was impossible. Strategies of survival varied widely, as will be seen in the overview that follows; although not all of these are represented in the experiences of the authors, most were experienced by one or more contributors.

Some children were sent far away to safety, perhaps never again to see their parents. Others were concealed in secret rooms, underground bunkers, sewers, forests, and other hiding places. Many were in "open hiding," pretending to be other than what they really were, sheltered by

adults who may or may not have known the child's true identity (and in some cases, adults who tried to change it by converting Jewish children to Christianity as the price of rescue). Still others survived in a ghetto or in a concentration camp (not many; most children sent to a camp were murdered at once). Some had more than one of these experiences during the course of the persecution, which went on for periods lasting from twelve years in Germany itself to more than five in Eastern Europe and for shorter periods in the occupied areas of Western Europe and Hungary.

Most of the children who could not flee suffered starvation, cold, inadequate clothing and shelter, deprivation of love and touch, lack of medical attention, and separation from their families; many witnessed other people being tortured and killed. Childhood, with its toys, games, schooling, treats, and celebrations, came to a sudden end: "[T]he bizarre became the ordinary in children's lives; what had been unconscionable and unimaginable were daily occurrences" (Dwork 1991, xxxi).

Refugee children had to adjust to a completely strange world, often with foster parents or in orphanages. Hidden children passing as Christian learned to answer to new names, profess a new religion, remember a false family history. In order to reduce the likelihood of having their circumcision discovered, some Jewish boys spent years dressing as, and pretending that they were, girls. Children hidden by Christian protectors learned also that it was dangerous to express sadness or anger: continued safety depended on the rescuer's goodwill, which in turn could depend on the child's always being "good." Some of these children were abused, physically, emotionally, or sexually, by those who were supposed to be their benefactors; and psychologically, the situation was complicated because those abusers were in fact also benefactors who saved the children's lives. Concealed children, as well as those in ghettos and camps, had to stifle their natural urges to make noise, to run and jump, to explore their world, because such activities could bring them to the attention of the killers. They also learned the survival skills of how to find food and shelter, sometimes in very harsh physical conditions, for themselves and occasionally for others even more helpless than they. All of these situations were risky, and those children who were old enough were aware of the dangers. The death rate tells one part of the story: two-thirds of Europe's Jews, but more than nine-tenths of the children, died during the war (Tec 1986).

After the war, child refugees and survivors faced the loss of family and friends. Many were orphaned and were dependent on the goodwill of remote relatives, or foster families, or institutions. Again, being "good" was important; some of the children were rejected by their new families; others experienced various forms of abuse (Turner 1990). When they returned "home," some encountered lethal anti-Semitism from former neighbors and even from Soviet troops (see, e.g., Gilbert 1996).

An unknown, but probably high, proportion of child survivors was physically weak and ill, as well as showing the signs of developmental anomalies and psychosocial disturbances. Being "unruly" was a common characteristic, and the description is probably an understatement (Kestenberg and Brenner 1996). "Previous familiar anchors—relatives, possessions, home, daily routines, social etiquette, community—had been stripped away. And because they were not yet adults when the war commenced, many of life's lessons had not been learned. They were filled with questions and confronted with suspended answers" (Hass 1995, 100).

Having come through terrible events, the children were discouraged from talking about them. Many survivor parents and caretakers wanted to conceal the fact that they and the children were Jewish in order to avoid possible future persecution. Adult survivors also commonly rejected any attempt by children to discuss their wartime or postliberation experiences, dismissing them as unimportant either because the children would soon forget them or because being in hiding was trivial compared to the adults' sufferings in concentration camps or ghettos. As a result, many children did not even consider themselves to be Holocaust survivors. No organizations existed to bring them together; support and self-help groups excluded them (Fogelman 1993). It may be noted that books about child survivors (e.g., references cited in this chapter) were mostly published during and since the mid-1990's.

The people who belonged to the children's new milieux were no more hospitable to disclosures than were adult survivors. Those who had lived in countries remote from Nazism during the war may have felt guilt or shame or may just have considered the child survivors strange for having such stories to relate. Other children, whose life had been spent in comfort and safety, viewed the survivors either as liars or as objects of fear and revulsion, or at least of discomfort, much as children tend to shun the visibly handicapped. The child survivors' strangeness was aggravated by language difficulties and by ignorance of the cultural icons of childhood: movie stars, sports figures, the games and teachings shared by natives of the country. Injunctions to keep quiet about the war were usually not necessary. The child survivors and refugees themselves wanted nothing more than to fit in, to be perfect exemplars of their new identity: "to be more fluent in English than native-born Canadians, to be great athletes and, through our accomplishments, to be invisible and to blend in" (Krell 1997).

The likelihood that such children would grow up to achieve their desire to fit in must have seemed low at the time. It was assumed that all Holocaust survivors suffered from "survivor syndrome," with symptoms including intrusive thoughts about traumatic experiences, flashbacks, psychosomatic complaints, nightmares and other sleep disorders, irritability, depression, anxiety, and a reduced ability to feel enjoyment or emotion in general. These are essentially the same components as those of the more recently devised diagnostic category "post-traumatic stress disorder (PTSD)" (Niederland 1968).

Recent research has shown that survivors of concentration camps and of hiding report such symptoms in roughly equal proportions (Yehuda et al. 1997), so that even children who were not interned were susceptible. As to those who did survive the camps, psychiatrists assessing the few child survivors of Buchenwald noted their destructiveness, extreme disobedience, and aggressiveness and doubted that they would ever be completely rehabilitated (Hemmendinger 1968); this group of children, incidentally, included Israel Meir Lau, who became Ashkenazic chief rabbi of Israel, and the future Nobel laureate Elie Wiesel.

Life Emerging from the Ashes

Contrary to many trauma theorists, I believe that the consequences of the Holocaust experience are not main effects on personality development. Rather, they are components that have interacted with inborn characteristics and with other, lifelong, experiential factors based in social circumstances (Elder 1995). The contributors to this volume refer to their wartime experiences to shed light on an immense diversity of later research interests and approaches in addition to a variety of political viewpoints, interpersonal styles, and so on; but of course, there are people who share these orientations who had no direct contact with persecution, and not all survivors of persecution have pursued similar courses.

All attributions of later development to the Holocaust experience are speculative. We do not and cannot know what a person's life path would have been if the Holocaust had not happened. This is especially true of those whose personalities were most malleable at the time; that is, young survivors and refugees. Nor do we know how survivors in general differ from other people, both those who have survived other traumatic experiences and those whose lives have been free of such events. Impressions are all we have. My conversations with child survivors indicate that many consider themselves unusually ambitious and achievement oriented, wanting to fit in and to excel. They also report that they are hypervigilant, overprotective, very sensitive and reactive to slights or insults, and in some ways childlike. Among their other characteristics are a propensity to collect things and a tendency to have trouble throwing things away. This pattern may also include people and activities—for example, wanting to stay in touch with every friend they ever had, adding rather than substituting new research areas or hobbies.

Whatever the exact effects may be, there can be little question that the impact of Nazi oppression left its mark on those who fled or survived it, including those whose stories appear in this book. I am also sure that most, if not all, have experienced some of the symptoms of post-traumatic stress disorder. One crucial question is whether such sequelae pervade their lives; and another is whether symptoms—difficulties, dysfunctions, problems—are the only kind of mark we can find.

The answers to both questions, as indicated in this book and in other recent examinations of survivors, give cause for optimism. The occasional nightmare, episode of anxiety or depression, irrational fear, or psychogenic headache does not disable the survivors. Although numbers are difficult to ascertain, it is obvious that very many child survivors and refugees are psychologically well adjusted, socially integrated, emotionally warm and healthy, professionally successful, and, in general, productive and valuable citizens. This is not to slight those whose physical or psychological injuries have left permanent disabilities; but the viewpoint that such sufferers represent the norm for survivors, and more favorable outcomes the exception, needs to be revised.

Increasingly, researchers are finding and publishing more balanced views of the characteristics and experiences of the survivors' post-Holocaust life. Brenner and Kestenberg (1996, 54) point out that although children suffered more than adults from the chaotic conditions of the Holocaust, they also acquired "premature" strength; other authors refer to resiliency, coping ability, the feeling of having become stronger and more understanding as a result of one's past travails, and successful transitions through life's psychosocial crises (Hass 1995; Kahana et al. 1988; Leon et al. 1981; Lomranz 1995; Suedfeld 1998). Favorable personality characteristics, fortuitous circumstances, elapsed time since the war, and in many cases the act of telling one's story all seem to have made it possible for many survivors to overcome the aftereffects of trauma (Apfel and Simon, 1996).

Some analysts consider such outcomes to be merely a covering up of underlying problems. Hass (1995), for example, entitles the chapter dealing with this topic "The Mask of the Survivor." Others take a more positive, and in my opinion a more valid, view: recent books about survivors have had such subtitles as "Triumph over Adversity" (Gilbert 1996) and "Holocaust Survivors and the Successful Lives They Made in America" (Helmreich 1992).

Obviously, the scientists who have contributed to this book have been able to build coherent lives in spite of whatever sorrow, anger, and anxiety coexist with their successes. But I, for one, am fascinated by the different outcomes they attribute to the influence of their early experiences: a wide range of scientific interests, from the most basic biological processes to the most complex interaction among cultures. The fact that all of these can be credibly explained by tracing them from the Holocaust is evidence either of the complexity of the human psyche or its ability to perceive causality and meaning in almost any sequence of events (cf. Bem 1965; Langer 1991).

The contributors exhibit a wide variety of worldviews: there are religious believers and atheists; liberals and neoconservatives; believers in total disarmament and in military preparedness; those who feel comfortable in present-day Germany and those who retain a permanent aversion to all things German; the peacemakers and the permanently angry. All of us are dedicated to the eradication of racism and other forms of discrimination, but we favor different solutions, from forbidding prejudicial propaganda to maximizing individual freedom.

Thus, the book demonstrates diversity in all of the phases of life that the contributors reveal: their family backgrounds in the years before the war, their experiences during the Nazi era, and their development and careers since then. Several had never before discussed their Holocaust years even with their nearest relatives, much less in public, and found it disturbing and stressful to do so; most had never connected those early times with where they have taken themselves since. As editor of the book, I hope that their efforts were helpful and informative to them as well as to our readers, and I thank them for undertaking this work and seeing it through. Their scientific discoveries and personal insights have shown that the light of knowledge can indeed shine out from the ashes of the Holocaust.

The Organization of the Book

I find it unproductive and demeaning to debate what experiences someone must have lived through in order to be called a survivor of the Holocaust. Merely for the sake of order, I have divided the chapters into three
major, but overlapping, categories. They overlap because children who
escaped (usually with their families) before the outbreak of the war, or
before its end, had experienced various types of persecution similar to
those suffered by the children who remained vulnerable throughout;
and because some of the Jewish families included prominent political
enemies of Nazism, who would have been persecuted even had they
been Christians—just like the Christian political opponents represented
in the book.

The three categories are as follows.

The Survivors: Living through the Holocaust

*Hadassa Black-Gutman, Shlomo Breznitz, Mary Engel, René Goldman, Martin
O. Heisler, Ervin Staub, Peter Suedfeld*

This group of contributors lived in Nazi-ruled countries until they
were liberated by the Allies. Six of the seven individuals in this group
came from Central or Eastern Europe: four from Hungary, and one each
from Czechoslovakia and Poland. The seventh, René Goldman, was born
in Luxembourg of Polish emigrant parents. All seven survived in hiding:
four of them by pretending to be Christian and being concealed among
groups of Christian children, and three in the special "protected" houses
established by some officially neutral, but benevolent, diplomatic mis-
sions in Budapest (whose protection pretty much evaporated during the
closing days of the siege of the city).

The Refugees: Persecution and Escape

*Henry P. David, Herbert C. Kelman, Eric Klinger, Richard Ned Lebow, Gerda
Lederer, Jacob Lomranz, Roberta S. Sigel, Herbert Weingartner*

These contributors had escaped from Nazi-dominated Europe
before the persecution of Jews in their homelands reached the level of
an organized and official project aiming at total annihilation. Eight of
the contributors fall into this category. Seven were born in the heartland
of Nazism: Germany and Austria. They escaped during the period when
the Hitler regime was persecuting Jews but for various reasons was still

considering it an option to engage in what we now call "ethnic cleansing": that is, removing the targets of discrimination from the domain of the Reich (albeit with high levels of brutality and exploitation) rather than killing them all.

The eighth, Richard Ned Lebow, is a special case. He was too young to have any memory of his origins. Only later in life did he encounter evidence that he had probably—not definitely—been a Jewish baby who was saved from the Nazis, smuggled out of Europe, and adopted by an American family. The unusual level of uncertainty about his background makes his experiences unique within our group.

Targets of Political Persecution

Karl W. Butzer, Siegfried Streufert

Two contributors are in this category. Butzer and Streufert came from non-Jewish families in Germany that were targeted by the Hitler regime because their fathers were active and prominent opponents of National Socialism. Although some of our Jewish contributors also had parents who were anti-Nazi political activists, the two in this section would not have been persecuted had they "gone along" with the rulers of the Third Reich.

The last two chapters represent attempts to integrate, interpret, and explain some of the common themes as well as the individual differences revealed by the autobiographical essays. "Loss and Renewal," by Paul Marcus, reflects his training and background in depth psychology. In my opinion, the chapter offers intriguing ideas concerning some implications of the autobiographies. Marcus has written extensively about Holocaust survivors, from the point of view of a thoughtful scholar who empathizes with his subjects although he did not share their experiences. Consequently, his explicitly provisional explanations of the effects of trauma, of the path from the contributors' childhood catastrophes to their scientific maturity, and of the role of writing as a therapeutic exercise may be more objective and generalizable than the approach of the last chapter.

My "Afterthought" is really that. I had originally intended to end the book with Marcus's analysis, but his chapter sparked so many reactions in my own thinking that I had to add my comments. My own professional background being rooted in social psychology, my closing chapter brings to bear some of the current theories in that area to the question of why the lives of the child survivors and refugees developed in the ways shown in the book. My hypotheses are just as tentative as Marcus's, but together the two discussions may provide a fairly diverse and comprehensive set of suggestions, and perhaps will motivate further thought and even research.

REFERENCES

Apfel, R. J., and B. Simon. 1996. Psychosocial interventions for children of war: The value of a model of resiliency. *Medicine and Global Survival* 3:A2 (on-line serial, <http://www.tiac.net/users/jloretz/MGS.html>).

Ash, M. G., and A. Söllner, eds. 1996. *Forced migration and scientific change: Emigré German-speaking scientists and scholars after 1933.* Washington, DC: Cambridge University Press.

Bem, D. J. 1965. An experimental analysis of self-persuasion. *Journal of Experimental Social Psychology* 1:199–218.

Brenner, I., and J. Kestenberg. 1996. Superego in young child survivors. In *The last witness: The child survivor of the Holocaust,* edited by J. Kestenberg and I. Brenner, 53–67. Washington, DC: American Psychiatric Press.

Dwork, D. 1991. *Children with a star: Jewish youth in Nazi Europe.* New Haven, CT: Yale University Press.

Elder, G. H. Jr. 1995. The life course paradigm: Social change and individual development. In *Examining lives in context: Perspectives on the ecology of human development,* edited by P. Moen, G. H. Elder Jr., and K. Lüscher, 101–39. Washington, DC: American Psychological Association.

Feist, G. J., and M. E. Gorman. 1998. The psychology of science: Review and integration of a nascent discipline. *Review of General Psychology* 2:3–47.

Fogelman, E. 1993. The psychology behind being a hidden child. In *The hidden children: The secret survivors of the Holocaust,* edited by J. Marks, 292–307. New York: Fawcett Columbine.

Gilbert, M. 1996. *The boys: Triumph over adversity.* Vancouver, BC: Douglas and McIntyre.

Hass, A. 1995. *The aftermath: Living with the Holocaust.* Cambridge: Cambridge University Press.

Helmreich, W. B. 1992. *Against all odds: Holocaust survivors and the successful lives they made in America.* New York: Simon and Schuster.

Hemmendinger, J. 1968. *Survivors: Children of the Holocaust.* Bethesda, MD: National Press.

Janis, I. L., and L. Mann. 1977. *Decision making: A psychological analysis of conflict, choice, and commitment.* New York: Free Press.

Kahana, E., B. Kahana, Z. Harel, and T. Rosner. 1988. Coping with extreme trauma. In *Human adaptation to extreme stress: From the Holocaust to Vietnam,* edited by J. P. Wilson, Z. Harel, and B. Kahana, 55–79. New York: Plenum.

Kestenberg, J. S., and I. Brenner. 1996. *The last witness: The child survivor of the Holocaust.* Washington, DC: American Psychiatric Press.

Kielmansegg, P., H. Mewes, and E. Glaser-Schmidt, eds. 1995. *Hannah Arendt and*

Leo Strauss: German emigrés and American political thought after World War II. Washington, DC: Cambridge University Press.

Krell, R. 1997. Psychological reverberations of the Holocaust in the lives of child survivors. The Monna and Otto Weinmann Annual Lecture, U.S. Holocaust Memorial Museum, Washington, DC.

Langer, L. L. 1991. *Holocaust testimonies: The ruins of memory.* New Haven: Yale University Press.

Lehmann, H., and J. Sheehan, eds. 1991. *An interrupted past: German-speaking refugee historians in the United States after 1933.* Washington, DC: Cambridge University Press.

Leon, G., J. N. Butcher, M. Kleinman, A. Goldberg, and M. Almagor. 1981. Survivors of the Holocaust and their children: Current status and adjustment. *Journal of Personality and Social Psychology* 41:503–16.

Lewin, M. 1992. The impact of Kurt Lewin's life on the place of social issues in his work. *Journal of Social Issues* 48:15–29.

Lomranz, J. 1995. Endurance and living: Long-term effects of the Holocaust. In *Extreme stress and communities: Impact and intervention,* edited by S. E. Hobfoll and M. W. deVries, 325–52. Amsterdam: Kluwer.

Niederland, W. G. 1968. Clinical observations on the "survivor syndrome": Symposium on psychic traumatization through social catastrophe. *International Journal of Psychoanalysis* 49:313–15.

Suedfeld, P. 1998. Homo invictus: The indomitable species. *Canadian Psychology* 38:164–73.

Tec, N. 1986. *When light pierced the darkness: Christian rescue of Jews in Nazi-occupied Poland.* New York: Oxford University Press.

Turner, B. 1990. *And the policeman smiled: 10,000 children escape from Nazi Europe.* London: Bloomsbury.

Yehuda, R., J. Schmeidler, L. J. Siever, K. Binder-Brynes, and A. Elkin. 1997. Individual differences in posttraumatic stress disorder symptom profiles in Holocaust survivors in concentration camps or in hiding. *Journal of Traumatic Stress* 10:453–63.

Part 1

The Survivors
Living through the Holocaust

Crossing the Borders of Difference

Hadassa Black-Gutman

Biographical Note

Dr. Hadassa (Dasia) Black-Gutman received her Ph.D. from the University of New South Wales. She is now a research associate at the Australian Catholic University, where until 1998 she was senior lecturer in education. She has held visiting appointments at the University of Cambridge and McGill University. Her research interests and publications have focused on the development of racist attitudes in children, measuring equal opportunity climate at universities, and the development of identity in Aboriginal children. She has developed and published multimedia material on child development with special relevance to  *Aboriginal teachers and has taught Aboriginal student teachers in outlying communities. Dr. Black-Gutman has been most active as a media presenter and community educator on race relations, especially on their impact on children, and has been a consultant and an invited contributor to major government-initiated national reviews related to equal opportunity, immigration, youth and racial tolerance at corporate and community levels. She also practices as a child and family psychologist, runs workshops, and counsels second and third generation Holocaust survivors. She is the proud grandmother of five grandchildren.*

Introduction

"This is the tip of a mountain of sadness," a therapist of great wisdom said to me during my training session with him in December 1996. "There has been much tragedy in your life and there is all this sadness." Following a strong impulse, I had traveled all the way from Australia to a beautiful, wild, and rather isolated part of coastal California to participate in an intensive training program on the psychology of selves and voice dialogue therapy. But I did not want to hear what he was saying. I had devoted so much of my life's energy to repairing the damage of my early childhood experiences. I ran, I worked, I achieved, I brought up a family, I disciplined myself consistently and with apparent ease, so what was this sadness all about? With some vehemence I responded that life was too precious to waste time being sad. More than that, I insisted on being happy just like any "normal" person. Yet, the sadness also insisted on making itself known to me. When I returned to Australia I found a note waiting for me from Peter Suedfeld, inviting me to contribute to *Light from the Ashes*. The time had come to go into that mountain and explore its lights and shadows.

Childhood

I was born to Schulem Schachne Braun Kahane and Chana Mirel, a year before the outbreak of war, in Rzeszów, Poland. My parents had come to Rzeszów from Zbarazh, a little town in eastern Galicia on the Ukrainian border, where my paternal family lived. My father had an appointment as professor of Jewish history in a Jewish gymnasium in Rzeszów, having graduated from the Institute of Jewish Studies in Warsaw and having completed his rabbinical studies. He was a religious and learned man, with his "head always in a book." With the invasion of Poland by Germany in September 1939, Rzeszów came under German occupation, as part of the government-general. My parents fled ahead of the German army to the Russian-occupied part of Galicia, to my maternal grandparents' hometown, Mikolince, where we stayed till spring 1942.

My earliest memories are of Mikolince, when I was two to three years old. There was a steep hill outside our house, and in winter bigger girls used to take me down the hill on a sleigh. A faint glimmer of my mother calling me as she stood outside the doorway, hands shading her eyes. Passover was coming. Great excitement. We went to somebody's house, where in a large room people were standing at wooden tables kneading dough and making little holes in it. Matzos. There is a very clear memory of a winter's day, with frost patterns on the windowpane and my father and me sitting together. He was teaching me the Hebrew alphabet, the aleph bet.

Then one day fear struck the house. It was June or July 1941—the Germans were coming. We had to go to the forest to hide and wait. I was scared, terribly scared of the dogs barking at night and hearing the roar, the terrifying roar of the invading Germans' motorcycles. They passed through the town. We came back to the house, but not for long. We were going to rejoin my father's family in Zbarazh. The evening we left, I was not put to bed but was allowed to lie on the sofa, fully dressed, with my doll. It was quiet. The horse-drawn cart arrived and we drove through the night, my father holding me all wrapped up in his arms. The whipping of horses, the stars, the barking of dogs. My father held me tightly.

We arrived in Zbarazh at the beginning of 1942. I was four years old. The so-called final solution entered a new phase, the total destruction of the Jewish people in Europe. In autumn the Zbarazh ghetto was established. The *Aktions* (raids) started. People prepared hiding places (bunkers) in their houses or with Polish Gentiles or fled into the surrounding forests. In each of the Aktions of October and November, one thousand Jews were rounded up and the majority taken to the extermination camp at Belzec. By November 1942 few Jews were visible in the town, which had numbered five thousand Jews before the war.

We were given armbands with blue stars. I don't remember ever going outside the house in the ghetto. I liked sweeping the floor with a little broom in our room and in the hallway where other people lived. My father would take me to the toilet at bedtime, holding me close in his arms. I have only faint memories of my mother.

Another family moved into our room as well. There were a tall man, his wife, and two children. They were nice. After a while the Gestapo took them away. The man came back alone. His wife and children had been killed. He became very ill, lying there for hours staring at the wall, refusing to eat. They made chicken broth for him, but he did not want any food. He died. He was put in the room at the end of the hallway, where he lay covered with a sheet. I kept sneaking in, along with another little girl, to see what a dead body looked like and whether he would move again. He did not.

Everybody was working on building a hideaway in the cellar. One would enter it by lifting what appeared to be a raised step leading from our room to a little balcony. We went down there. The Gestapo were searching our house. We could hear the throwing of furniture, the heavy footsteps. My heart beat wildly with fear. One must keep quiet. Terrible things would happen if you made a sound. Some child was crying. A pause in breathing, nothing happening, a long silence. It was safe to go up again. Another house search by the Gestapo. This time we went to a room on the top story of some house and lay quietly under the beds. The Gestapo marched into the room, looked around, and left.

Sometime in November 1942 my parents arranged for me to be handed over to a Polish Gentile in Tarnopol and take on the identity of an Aryan child, while they stayed in the ghetto and subsequently went into the forests to hide. I never saw them again.

I have no memories of the parting from my parents as they handed me over to my Aryan "parent." What I remember is that my father gave me my favorite toys at the time, a salt and a pepper shaker and a little ball, to take with me. Years later, however, when lying on a sofa recovering from the shock of a horse riding accident, I suddenly had a clear vision of two sets of arms coming from above embracing me. A psychiatrist friend of mine was convinced that it was the memory of my parents' loving farewell that had surfaced. I'd like to think so. The parting is described in the letter that my father sent from the ghetto to "Our dear relatives in America," dated November 30, 1942. The letter was written in epic style in Ivrit (modern Hebrew) and is now deposited in the archives at Yad Vashem in Jerusalem. I shall quote from it, in translation.

> I am forced to see life realistically and I see that we are standing on the threshold of destruction. I am compelled to hide my daughter until the storm passes. It is difficult to describe the sorrow and pain that gnaw at my heart when I see my young daughter unable to understand why she was taken from the arms of her parents. It is my strong hope that you my Uncles Moses, Aaron, Solomon and Meier, and my Aunts Mandle, Rosele and Rochel, will be the saviours and redeemers of the Braun family. Then you will take my daughter from the Gentile family to whom I have given her and bring her up as a daughter of Israel. Also you should know that it is my desire that she build her life in Israel, because who knows as well as we that in all the lands of exile our lives are on a volcano. With reference to my daughter, I again repeat my request as above and just as I participate in the grief of my community, so may God permit us to see the redemption and comfort of the whole community of Israel.

I survived because I was able to pass as an Aryan child. The Polish woman who kept me as one of her children was called Sabina, and her husband was a Czech Jew. He knew my favorite uncle, Simcha, who had been killed and had sent his only valuable, a watch, to be given to me. They had two blond boys younger than me. I was four and a half, and they would have been three and two years old. I was to be called Stasia—a Polish name. My Slavic looks helped. I was repeatedly told that I must never tell anybody what my real name was, as something terrible would happen. We lived on the first floor of a gray apartment building in Tarnopol, the city for this part of Galicia.

While I was living as a Christian Polish child, Sabina's Jewish husband, whose name I do not remember, had to hide whenever visitors came. He would stand for hours between a broom cupboard and a window, hidden by curtains, or lie under the bed. We had to make a noise whenever he would cough or sneeze. But the danger of being discovered was always present. This was especially important when the neighbor next door visited. She was a Nazi informer. I have a clear memory of her discovering and then informing on a Jewish family who were hiding in a ground-floor apartment and our watching as they were taken away by the Gestapo. I knew that I was Jewish but must not say so. From the window of our apartment I could see, from time to time, a whole group of weak, pale people being marched along, and I was upset. They too were Jewish. When I visited Sabina's mother and other places that I only vaguely remember, I was expected to (and would) kneel before a figure of Christ, cross myself, and say the Christian prayers, knowing that I was pretending to be a Catholic girl but really was not. I was forever hungry and remember clearly the occasions when Sabina's little boys were given slices of buttered bread, which I never was given, and they would eat the soft part and leave the crust for me. I now try to impress on my grandchildren that it is just wrong not to eat one's crust.

Two good things stand out in the memories of this painful period. When Sabina and the boys were out, Sabina's husband would make me garlic bread and would teach me the aleph bet. I relished these infrequent intimate moments and can still taste the sublime flavor of dark bread, rubbed with garlic and then fried in chicken fat. I also enjoyed the time I spent with Sabina's mother in a tiny Polish village, where I fed the geese, helped milk the cows, and ran around wildly through meadows and forests, vegetable patches and flowers. These were moments free of oppression.

Sometime toward the end of that period (March 1944?) a man, who might have been someone from my family, came to Tarnopol and told us that my young parents had been murdered somewhere in the vicinity of Mikolince. Who would take care of me? I ran to look for my little ball that I had brought from home.

It must have been spring 1944. Something new was happening. There were more frequent bombings, and each time the bomb alarm sounded we would go down to the bomb shelter or bunker. It seemed safe now for Sabina's husband to come down with us. The Russians were coming nearer. We spent most of our time in the bunker, and it was while we were there that the house was bombed and we were buried under the rubble. Russian soldiers dug out an opening to find us sitting there huddled together. Our Nazi informer neighbor was taken away immediately. How distinct the scene is and how bizarre. A Russian soldier walked up to Sabina and pointed a gun at her head. She grabbed me and showed me off. Here was a Jewish child she had kept during the war. How could she be a Nazi sympathizer?

Sabina and her husband took me back to Zbarazh hoping to find some relatives to whom they could return the saved child, now six years old. They were told that the only survivors of this large family were the Gassenbauers, Gusta and Welo. I was taken to their address, but as the Gassenbauers were not at home, they left me to await their return with a woman who was stitching at a sewing machine in their room. Gusta recounts that they came home to find a little girl playing on the floor with bits of material and presumably recognized me as her cousin's child. There was a period of time, then, when I was nobody's child. One grownup had put me down, but another had not as yet picked me up. I have no memory of how I felt at the time, but the picture of this little girl, alone in the world, still arouses strong feelings in me.

Gusta and my father, Schulem, were first cousins, my paternal grandmother and Gusta's mother being sisters. Gusta was the youngest of six children. Every one of her siblings, along with their spouses and children, had been killed. Welo's two older sisters, Susia and Erna, had survived the war. Initially Gusta and Welo intended to send me to an orphanage that had been set up for Jewish children to build them up with good farm food, but I apparently clung to them and cried bitterly, so I was not sent away. I called them "ciocia" and "wujek," Polish for "auntie" and "uncle."

During the initial period with the Gassenbauers, my body was telling its own story of the years of privation and malnutrition. Even now I have low resistance to infections. I suffered from one childhood disease after another. Every part of my body was covered with sores and scabs. I had my head totally shaved three times to get rid of lice. While still in Soviet-occupied Galicia, now Western Ukraine, Welo developed kidney problems and had to go to another town for treatment. I was given into the care of his sisters, Aunties Susia and Erna. They made a living baking bread rolls to be sold on the black market and lived in a house by a river. I loved it there.

I started school, where we spoke Russian and would decorate a large portrait of our *batko* (father) Stalin with flowers. Like a good little Russian girl, I would join the First of May parade, wearing a navy skirt and white blouse and proudly carrying a little red flag. At the same time I knew that things (like the baking of bread rolls by Susia and Erna) had to be kept secret from the NKVD, the security police, and I would cross the street on the way to school so as not to pass close to their building.

Sometime in 1946, in an exchange of populations, there was a mass exodus, via overcrowded goods trains, of Polish people from Western Ukraine for Poland. The Gassenbauers were going first and came to take me away from the aunties, who did not want to give me up. I was literally being pulled by each of them and finished staying on with Susia and Erna for the time being. They soon followed the Gassenbauers to Bytom in Upper Silesia, previously part of Germany. On arrival there, I went to live with Gusta and Welo, who presented me with a new red and white checked dress—a great thrill. I seemed to be ready to attach myself to whoever was good to me. They, along with another family, had moved into an apartment, which was being vacated by a westward-moving German family. Welo became a most loving, affectionate and protective father, and I soon attached to him strongly. He was a man of integrity and compassion, with a very fine analytical mind. He had a law degree from the University of Krakow.

Welo obtained an excellent job in Bytom, Poland, as head of the legal division for the mining department of Silesia, an important coal-producing region. However, a good job like this would not be given to a Jew even in postwar Poland, so he went under the name of Gajewski. I was now Dasia Gajewski and again needed to keep quiet about my real name. My most vivid memory of my time in Bytom is of playing with the little girl of the family who shared our apartment. Her name was Mucha, and, like me, she had been orphaned and was in the care of relatives. I remember that I felt myself to be lucky as my ciocia and wujek were kinder than hers.

Bad things were happening again. In July 1946 there was a pogrom in Kielce, where forty-two Jews were attacked after a Polish eight-year-old boy manufactured a story that he had been kidnapped by the Jews and kept in a cellar, with a subsequent resurgence of anti-Semitic sentiment. Gusta, standing in a bread queue, heard a woman say to those around her, "Isn't it good that they are killing Jews at Kielce? A pity Hitler did not finish them off." She came home crying and frightened The decision was made to flee the graveyard of Poland and get out to the West—to freedom.

We crossed the border illegally to Czechoslovakia and stayed for a while in a refugee camp, Hlubatin, outside Prague. A vivid picture of a group of Zionist youth on the way to what was then Palestine, visiting the camp and everybody standing and singing the rousing Hebrew song "Tchezakna" (Strengthen our hands) to the accompaniment of a clarinet played by one of the musicians in the group. It inspired my Zionism.

Welo and Gusta were taken across the border into the American zone of occupied Germany by a group of young Jews calling themselves the Bricha, the Escape. They crossed the river at night, with their few belongings bundled into a number of bags. I was taken across the bridge at the official border crossing by a Czech woman as her little niece and brought to a refugee camp, where they joined me a few hours later. Our first meal in the West was prepared for us by Americans, who had set up a reception place for refugees on the German side of the border. Condensed milk on white bread! We were not impressed.

We eventually found our way to Stuttgart, a town in the American zone of southwest Germany, known for its famous opera house. A new life started. It was 1947. In September of that year Welo and Gusta formally adopted me. Reluctantly and with much urging as well as reinforcement in the form of monetary rewards, I came to call them Mummy and Daddy and as my mother and father I will now refer to them. My name was no longer Hadassa Ester Braun Kahane. It was now Hadassa Gassenbauer. I was pleased to have parents just like other children. One thing was made clear to me by my new parents. I was not to let anybody know that they were not my real parents. Others may talk. Sometime during that period I received a photograph from a relative in Israel of my natural parents, young and beautiful Schulem and Chana.

A number of Jewish communal institutions had been set up along a street in a rather nice quarter of the city, which had been reserved for the Jewish community. These included a Jewish day school, called Sefer Beit Bialik, which I attended. Most Jews lived in the Jewish quarter, insulated from the newly de-Nazified German environment. My parents, however, were able to sublet two rooms with shared bathroom and kitchen from a German couple in a villa in a very beautiful lilac-lined street outside the Jewish area. Those two rooms were to be home for the next five years. Our landlord had been a member of the Nazi party and proud of it, and his wife was a minister's daughter. In spite of the occasional spats my mother and our landlady had in the kitchen, we somehow got along and they became rather fond of me.

My American relatives, the recipients of my father Schulem's letter, managed to contact the Gassenbauers to find out about me and were assured that I was in good hands. Through them and through CARE, organized by a Jewish welfare organization, we received parcels of food and clothes at regular periods. My favorite was a lovely red coat that I wore with pride, probably donated by a family somewhere in the States. I also loved the dark Cadbury chocolate that was often included in the food parcels. I became a rather chubby child but full of energy.

At Beit Bialik we learned to read and write in Yiddish and Ivrit. I was introduced to the richness of Shalom Aleichem and other Yiddish writers. I was an excellent student, and my parents expected only the best from me. Even losing one mark and getting a 9/10 instead of 10/10 was an occasion for disappointment and detailed analysis of how and where I lost that mark. Being first in class was an assured way of obtaining approval and recognition as being a worthy person and making my new parents proud of me. I was set to be a high achiever.

The day Israel declared its independence, on May 15, 1948, all the Jews in Stuttgart solemnly stood in the street and sang the Hatikvah. They laughed and cried. The joy of Israel. Those scenes of communal solidarity by Holocaust survivors given hope by the birth of their state, of their own homeland, were repeated on each occasion when a group of young people, including some of my older classmates aged sixteen to eighteen years, would leave to enlist to fight in the Israeli War of Independence. Some died there.

At some point my parents decided that we would go on Aliya to Israel. Having had a love of Zion ingrained into every cell of my body, I was overjoyed. A refrigerator was bought to take with us. The day it was delivered my parents were not in, and I spent hours polishing it. Here was proof that we were really going there. But it was not to be. My father had kidney stones and had one kidney removed. It was felt that my father was not healthy or robust enough to take on the challenge of a life in Israel. Ironically, he died in Australia at the age of fifty-three. I had been so close to fulfilling my father Schulem's "desire that she build her life in Israel." At the same time, the U.S. visa remained elusive.

By the end of 1949, in the wake of the great emigration of European Jews to the New World, there weren't enough Jewish school-age children in Stuttgart to sustain a Jewish school, and Sefer Beit Bialik was closed. I was the only Jewish child in my age group remaining in town. At this point, my father made an important decision. The next year, 1950, I was to attend the first year of a prestigious German girls' high school, Morike Oberschule. Among the thousand students there was only one Jew—me. Though the principal of the school was a man of liberal ideals and integrity who promised that I would be made to feel welcome, it was thought advisable for me to be known by a German name. So Hadassa became Hedwig and in the French class, Hedwigée. I gained further experience of adapting to living in an alien environment and learning to act as "one of them."

I was now exposed to German literature, learned French and English, and improved my German. Though I made friends with some of my German classmates, I never invited them home nor they me. I was Jewish, and they were German. I could talk to them about school things, but I knew instinctively that anything to do with my family, my Jewishness, my story, had to remain hidden. There was mutual cordiality most of the time except for two occasions where the chasm was starkly revealed. On arrival in class one day, I found a few girls huddled together whispering. When the ever-apologetic-in-manner teacher arrived, one of the girls announced that this was the anniversary of Hitler's birthday and we should celebrate. The teacher blushed and said that this was not the time to talk about it and just went on with the planned lesson. Her timidity enraged me. Now I teach my students, with conviction, that a weak stance by authority figures toward any form of racism is taken as condoning it. The other incident arose when I brought some Israeli stamps to swap and one of my classmates made a derogatory comment about Israel. I do not remember what the comment was, but I do remember us getting into a physical fight, wrestling on the floor, beating each other with our fists, and pulling each other's hair. I was and still am petite, and she was a big girl, so I obviously came home badly beaten. My father went to see the principal, who called a whole school assembly and apologized to me formally. That whole year at Morike Oberschule was one of the loneliest in my life. At a time when children lose interest in their parents and look to their peers for mutual confidences and support, I had nobody. After school I would play for a while with the younger children in the street and then go back home and read and read and read. I was a very serious child.

With the outbreak of the Korean War, my parents, along with the diminishing remnant of Jews in Germany, panicked. There was talk of a third world war and fear that Germany might rise again. We had to get out. We applied for a visa to Canada and Australia and were prepared to go to either country. The Australian visa arrived first. It was a country few knew about, at the bottom of the globe. Scary. A tutor was engaged to improve my English, which I learned quite well but with a Polish-German accent. It has stayed with me all my life and even after forty-six years immediately identifies me as foreign.

The great journey took us by train to the Italian port of Genoa, by a Greek ship through the Suez Canal and the Indian ocean to Melbourne, and then by train to Sydney, where we arrived in April 1951. Once again I faced the challenge of adapting to a new life in this distant land.

The Lessons of My Childhood

Friends of my parents who welcomed us to Sydney remember me as an attractive, academically bright girl with a lively personality, in the secure care of my devoted and caring adoptive parents. Ahead of me lay a supposedly open-ended and promising future. Yet it is only now, with the relative detachment of a child psychologist looking from a third person perspective at Hadassa's growing into adulthood in peaceful Australia, that I understand and deeply regret the fears that I brought with me from my childhood and their constraining impact on my development. I have also come to respect the resilience and the strength of the underlying adaptive mechanisms, which saved this child from death and destruction. I have tried to understand what sense I, a little girl aged three to six, made of the world in the ghetto and of my time with Sabina, where I learned that there were no parents to protect and take care of me. How did the experiences of different schools, different names, different countries affect me? What did I learn about the ways and means of survival?

Above all, I learned that the world was dangerous. I learned fear of death and fear of people who were in a position of power doing bad things to me and my dear ones. This has been the basis for the guiding theme in my early life, which I see recurring well into my adulthood. It was the imperative of hiding. Hiding my identity, hiding my difference.

Calling yourself by your "real" name, asserting who you are, your religion, your beliefs, and your ideas, is fraught with danger. Survival entails keeping quiet to fit in with the demands of threatening environments, be it hiding in the forest the night the Germans were going through Mikolince or in the Zbarazh ghetto cellar during Aktions (raids) while Gestapo were searching for us above; being Stasia, an Aryan child, who must never admit that she is Jewish and later becoming Dasia, an adopted child, who must never talk about her natural parents. In writing the next section, "Growing up in Australia," I have also become aware of how often during my childhood and young adulthood I chose, in both my personal and professional life, to cling to the safety of the margin, with all its constraints, rather than risk center-stage involvement where one's difference might be seen clearly. On the positive side, I have had a great deal of practice in viewing the world from multiple perspectives, a basis for my work with marginalized groups.

A little girl in a dangerous world could not survive without protection from grownups. So as a result I developed a talent for and an interest in relationships and the ability to evoke people's protectiveness toward me. I developed a heightened sensitivity to cues from others, what it was that pleased them, what made them like me. I also learned that being a good girl who was also smart, who did well in school, who won prizes was effective for winning approval. The emotional legacy of my personal Holocaust has been a hunger for connection and a fear of abandonment by the important people in my life.

Growing up in Australia

My father approached the selection of a school for me with the naive misunderstanding of a new immigrant. There was never any doubt in his mind that I would go to university. However, with his experience of living in communist countries, he thought that, in a workers' country such as Australia, claiming proletarian aspirations would gain one a place in the best institution. So, when asked by the Department of Education what he wanted me to be, my father said, "a seamstress." As a result, I was allocated a place in a home science high school rather than the academically selective girls' high school to which my high score in the entrance exam entitled me. There were Jewish girls in my vocational high school whose company I enjoyed and some of whom have remained my lifelong friends. I was, however, in many ways the odd one out in this nonacademic school and incurred the envy of some of my

Australian classmates who teased me about being a "brain," a fairly nasty putdown in this school.

My friends still recall what a strange sight I made on my first day at my new Australian school. I had long braids piled up high in the German Gretchen style. I wore long white socks, at a time when everyone wore them short, and I carried an umbrella! What is more, my name was Hadassa Gassenbauer. This was not a name, it was a short story, I was told. It must be anglicized. My parents conceded, and not only was I now to be called Hedda (first part of Hadassa), but they changed their surname to Gasson. I was now Hedda Gasson, though at home I was still called Dasia, the diminutive form of Hadassa. In further efforts to remake me into an Australian girl, my long braids were considered unsuitable, so off they went. At no stage did I even conceive of protesting, and I continue to be impressed by contemporaries with similar backgrounds who, along with their parents, insisted on retaining their awkward names and ways of being foreign.

Due to the good grounding I had received in my German high school in academic subjects such as history, and my parents' insistence on excellence, I was soon achieving high marks. But I still had not developed the confidence to come out of hiding, nor was I encouraged to do so. In preparation for special occasions, such as Anzac Day (a memorial day for Australians), we would be asked to write an essay to be read aloud at the school assembly. Mine was frequently chosen as the best, but I was not allowed to read it. The teachers would arrange for a student without an accent to deliver it in front of the whole assembly. I never questioned their right to do so.

I was socially uncomfortable. My mother dressed me in the "good taste" conservative clothes of a European girl, totally out of kilter with the trendy clothes of my friends. I started going to parties and teenage dances but lacked confidence and was extremely self-conscious about my accent, the way I dressed, my pimples. I just was not one of them.

As a teenager, I joined a Zionist youth group who read, danced, sang, and talked and talked about anything to do with Israel. My fellow idealists became the core of my social life. I was looking forward to spending a year in Israel with some of them.

University

I gained a scholarship to go to the University of Sydney. My heart was set on studying medicine. But here again I was a good and obedient girl and followed the advice of my father, whose overriding concern was a secure future for me, not necessarily one that would be personally fulfilling. Medicine was not, he declared, an appropriate profession for a woman. Who was I, not yet turned seventeen and with little practice in self-assertion, to argue with my wise father, who decided that pharmacy was practical and suitable for a girl? "Dull!" I cried, hating the idea. But that is what I would do. I had also set my heart on a year in Israel before starting my studies. But no, my parents would not hear of it. We had survived the Holocaust, and now I intended to leave them for a year and expose myself to possible dangers? Out of the question.

Fortunately I could not get a position that year as an apprentice in a pharmacy, a prerequisite at the time, so I started on a bachelor of arts degree. I loved my first year at university. I majored in history and psychology—history because I loved it and psychology because it was vocationally useful. Strangely, it was only recently that I learned from my cousin in Israel that my father Schulem had majored in history at the Institute of Jewish Studies in Warsaw. I made friends with fellow students, many of similar background. We talked of ideas and shared our dreams. My confidence grew.

However, my discomfort and timidity in what I thought of as center-stage situations were evident. One incident stands out. I was studying ancient history under an eccentric professor, an Egyptologist. On one occasion a group of us stood around him after a lecture asking questions. He invited us back to his room for further discussions and a cup of coffee. What an invitation to an intellectual circle! I could only dream of it. But it was not for me. I immediately shrank inside, overcome by my unworthiness to be included in such a group. What would I say? What if what I said was not good or clever enough? I declined and walked away—to the safety of the margin.

After my full year at university, I took up my position as an apprentice at a small, quiet pharmacy. I now made my first step toward fulfilling my own aspirations and interests. I would study pharmacy during the day to satisfy my parents and study arts as an evening student for me. I wanted to get out of the protective but highly constraining parental home. Marriage was the answer. "He" had to satisfy certain minimum requirements, drummed into me by my parents and their social milieu. He must be Jewish, of course, have a profession, demonstrate good character, and, above all, be a protector. I was ready to fall in love with any "qualified" man who would show interest in me. Within a year I found what I thought was such a man, gave up pharmacy, and married.

Marriage, Children, Study

I blossomed as a young married woman. I loved the security of a man loving me, the social status of a married woman, the freedom to build my own life, and above all, children. I threw myself into having children, running a house, entertaining friends, emotionally supporting my husband and very soon a widowed mother, and continuing my studies. I set very high standards for myself. I rarely said "No" to any demands. My husband was a good man, sensitive, and very devoted to me, and he encouraged my continual studying. As it turned out, however, though twelve years older than me, he was not the father figure, the protector, I thought I had married. I became the organizer, the initiator, the mover, perceived by our friends as the strong one. There was little time for frivolity, for leisure, for lightness. We stayed married for twenty years, during which I would have described myself as happy, had I stopped to ask myself the question.

Within nine and a half months of our marriage, my first son was born, and we named him Selwyn after my father Schulem (his Hebrew name). He was a most beautiful baby, and I fell madly in love with him. My father Welo adored him but died six months later of complications of a weak heart and kidney. I was devastated. He had been my rock, my source of nurturance and strength, my wonderful second father. His death left a big hole in my life.

But there was also much joy. My younger son, Ian, named Zeev in Hebrew after my father Welo, was born two and a half years after Selwyn. He was a most energetic, very bright, and joyful little boy who brought much laughter into my life. My sons were the center of my life. They have now grown into fine young men whom I respect enormously, have married, and have produced between them a crop of five magnificent children, my grandchildren. They are still at the center of my life.

Whatever else I was going to do, I was determined to go on with my university studies. Through pregnancies and child rearing, through time of grieving for my father and supporting my husband after his father's death, I studied. This area of my life, just like my devotion to the children, was not negotiable. After graduation, with my sons starting secondary education, I found a rather satisfying part-time job teaching modern history to senior students at a nearby Catholic girls' high school, while also obtaining a professional teaching qualification.

No More Hiding

During my period of teaching at the Catholic girls' high school, an incident occurred that put my growing assertiveness and determination to no longer hide my identity to the test. The cardinal was visiting the school. All teachers were lined up on the central balcony on the first floor of a U-shaped building with a thousand girls standing in orderly lines in the quadrangle below, facing us. We were told that the cardinal would walk along the balcony and greet each of us. At that moment we should kneel and kiss the ring on his proffered hand. On his arrival the whole body of students knelt down. So did the teachers, each dutifully kissing his ring. With all my being I knew that I was not going to kneel to anybody or kiss his ring. I no longer had to. I could feel my heart beating fast; I broke into a sweat; I went red in the face. He was coming closer. Standing very upright, I shook hands with him. One thousand girls and thirteen teachers were kneeling. I was the only one standing, visible to all. I had chosen not to hide my difference. A significant moment in my development but a hard one. At the end of the day, I went home, got into bed, covered myself with a blanket, and stayed curled up for hours.

Three years later my ambition and need for intellectual stimulation propelled me toward enrolling in a master's in education honors degree. For logistic reasons I did not pursue my first love—history. For my thesis, I combined my background of teaching history and study of cognitive psychology and chose to research the impact of questioning in the history classroom on students' higher-level cognitive processes. I took a year off work to give me time to work on it. I had collected the data, when, suddenly, I lost all interest in the topic. Quite inexplicable at the time. Here was I, so conscientious, priding myself in always finishing what I started, having already spent six precious months on my thesis and now deciding that I would not go on with it. I very quickly found what I really wanted to do. I was going to research the development of concepts of justice in children, in particular how they judged people distant in place or time, an area in which I had become interested in a master's course on child development. I threw myself into the new research topic with great vigor and completed the thesis in record time. Something had shifted in me, though at the time I did not understand how and why. I was beginning to ask myself questions about what mattered to me, what I wanted rather than what was sensible, approved of, and expected by others. On reflection, I see this period as the beginning of the process of thawing of one major legacy of my Holocaust experience—the deeply embedded and oppressive fears of what might happen were I to come out of hiding and openly express my thoughts and beliefs. I was taking the first steps toward my own liberation. Having spent all the years of her life up to now dancing to the tune of others, as Stasia, Hedwig, or Hedda, Hadassa/Dasia was reemerging with her full life force.

At the end of my studies I was offered a position as a lecturer in education at a Catholic university, which I accepted, as it fit in well with my family responsibilities at the time. I was again a minority, one of two Jews among a staff of 120, though they included quite a number of non-Catholics. At the same time, it gave me the opportunity of working closely and forming friendships with colleagues from quite different religious, ethnic, and cultural backgrounds.

The shift in my academic approach carried over into my personal life. Twenty years into my marriage, with my sons at the threshold of adulthood and my master's degree behind me, I rebelled. My impulse was to break the shackles of responsibility, discipline, and continual search for security that I had imposed upon myself. I learned to sail on Sydney's beautiful harbor, to ski; I dreamt of passion and lightness of life. Who was going to be my partner in such a life? My husband, increasingly tending toward melancholy and passivity, was an unlikely candidate. We separated and subsequently divorced. The experience of actually being alone, unprotected by the status of the marriage institution, if not the actual strength of a partner, was devastating. It revived my childhood fears and exposed my vulnerability. At the same time, there was also a growing sense of my competence in making a life for myself.

I put my energy into providing a home for my sons, now university students, researching for my Ph.D., and exploring new relationships. My destiny was waiting for me. Within two and a half years I met the man who fulfilled my dreams for joy, laughter, and great love. Gerry. An original, brilliant mind, witty, highly respected, and much loved by his numerous friends and colleagues, a strong man with a delicious streak of irreverence. In a highly responsible job as an economist, he found time for frivolity, for adventure. In the language of the voice dialogue therapy model, he was my disowned self. He was a protective father but also my playmate. We eventually married. I changed my name formally from Hedda to Dasia. Regretfully I did not go one step further and formally call myself by the name my father Schulem gave me—Hadassa. Gerry introduced me to a whole world of people who were center-stage in politics and academia. And I, with much initial timidity and trepidation, made a discovery. They accepted me with all my differences. No more hiding my self. Four years after our marriage, Gerry died suddenly of a stroke. A deep, dark hole opened before me. Such a struggle not to let myself fall into it, to learn to live alone, again.

Research Themes

My professional life has been that of a university teacher and researcher and, more recently, a child psychologist. Much of my teaching has been with minority groups, including Asian Australians and Aboriginal people in their communities. We understand each other well. My research effort over the last three decades has included investigation of concepts of justice in children, focusing on reciprocity in human relationships; communication of empathy in the teacher-pupil relationship; and the development of ethnic and racial attitudes in children. Each set of studies appeared to be connected to specific demands of my work situation or social and demographic changes occurring in the Australian community at the time. I certainly was not aware, till recently, that each was an aspect of the underlying motive of my life, nor was I aware of the motive itself.

A clue came from an encounter with my interstate colleague and friend Anne, who was from Adelaide. Over lunch on a sunny Sydney spring day, three years ago, we were discussing our mutual areas of research and teaching. Our conversation turned to our thoughts and feelings about difference, racial, ethnic, religious, cultural. Anne said that she was attracted to the different. I, in contrast, looked for commonality between people. Anne found commonality boring. One's common humanity could, after all, be taken for granted. "But, Anne," I cried out, "what you take as a given was a matter of life and death for me." The vehemence of my reply surprised us both. I then proceeded to tell her a little of my experience during the war as a Jewish child in Nazi-occupied Poland. The jump in our conversation from research to my childhood was unexpected.

What I now understand is that each of my research themes—reciprocity for those distant in time and place, empathy between people of different status, development of racial tolerance—has focused on reducing barriers in the relationship between self and the different other, on crossing the borders of difference, on connecting with one another as equal human beings. At the core is the belief that the recognition of each other's human dignity, our commonality, is a basic condition that allows us to make connections.

Jean Piaget's theory of the development of moral reasoning in children provided the theoretical orientation for my first research project, investigating how adolescents judged historical figures in unfamiliar contexts in terms of right and wrong. Central to a developed sense of justice was reciprocity, defined as the ability to see others as equal to oneself in their human dignity. Reciprocity underpinned social relations based on mutual respect and the equal rights of individuals in a just society. Research had shown that, by adolescence, most children were considering the equal rights of others when judging members of their own group. But, I wondered, how would adolescents judge the actions of people distant in time and place? The study confirmed that even the cognitively mature adolescents were judging historical characters much more harshly than they would familiar people, focusing on their actions rather than internal states and conditions and advocating punishment rather than rehabilitation. The study had implications for history teachers. They could contribute to the development of moral maturity of their students by providing them with opportunities to meet and extend reciprocity to people who lived in distant places and under varying circumstances, by focusing on their intentions and motives rather than their actions.

At the time when I was searching for a topic for a doctoral dissertation, I was teaching developmental and educational psychology to student teachers. I became convinced of the need for specific human relations training programs for teachers to improve their interpersonal communication skills, noting the complaints of young people I had interviewed in a number of schools that they were not seen by their teachers as individuals but "were treated like a herd of cattle." I was attracted to Carl Rogers's notion of empathy as the most important condition in effective interpersonal communication.

The fundamental question of my doctoral thesis was that of how one could promote relationships based on empathy in educational contexts. The research involved refining the concept of empathy-in-action (in professional relationships) and the development and evaluation of an empathy-training program for student teachers. Empathy-in-action involved three phases, including establishing an empathic set, where one attends to the other; looking at the world from the other's perspective and resonating with his or her experience; and appropriate communication of one's understanding to the person with whom one is empathizing.

It was the first phase, concerned with our readiness to empathize with another person, that engaged and puzzled me most. In everyday life we often feel empathy toward those who are close to us, and we are usually able to communicate our empathy to them. But what about people outside our social group? It appeared that the type of social relationship we have with another person influences our preparedness to empathize with that individual. A number of studies had shown that children were more likely to extend empathy to others of the same age, same gender, or same race, as compared with children perceived as dissimilar. Judging another to be "like me" or "like us" was a crucial condition for establishing an empathic set and attending to his or her experiences and feelings. It appeared to me that this was the very process involved in the Piagetian concept of reciprocity, the focus of my earlier research. Establishing an empathic set toward unfamiliar others involved broadening the range of people with whom one related on the basis of mutual respect for each other's human dignity. My contribution to the largely uncharted area of empathy-in-action was a comprehensive analysis of the process and a focus on the empathic set as well as on empathic ability and effective communication, which had been the focus of earlier studies.

Soon after the completion of this research project, I met Gerry and took time to be with him and for us to adventure together. My teaching was leading me in what appeared, at the time, a new direction. In the 1980s, Australian governments and institutions were putting in place multicultural policies with an emphasis on the maintenance of a mosaic of cultures within Australian society and intercultural understanding. Understanding of other cultures was believed to lead to mutual appreciation and interaction. Both my personal experience and knowledge of history, as well as emerging research, indicated quite clearly that mere knowledge of other cultures is not likely to prevent intercultural hostility and conflict. I was eager to lift the mantle of multiculturalism and find out whether, beneath it, the entrenched societal racisms and prejudices were still to be found.

My first study on ethnic attitudes in children measured the extent of ethnocentrism, and the related phenomena of discrimination and ethnic prejudice, among Australian elementary children in culturally and ethnically diverse schools. It found that for all the children, be they majority or minority, ethnicity was a significant social marker and that perception of difference was related to rejection and social distance in closer, out-of-school situations. I suggested that since children were having difficulty in grasping the complex proposition of different but equal, there was a case for teachers to focus on the commonalities and similarities, rather than differences, in children's experiences and backgrounds, especially in the early grades of schooling. I was aware of the emotional fervor, even pas-sion, with which I wrote up the findings of the study.

It was at about this time that I became involved in teaching child development to Aboriginal students in a number of outlying rural com-munities as part of their study for a teaching degree. I was acutely aware of the racism toward Aboriginal people that was inherent in the Aus-tralian white culture. At the same time, it appeared that intolerance within the Australian community toward people from the old established immigrant groups of European descent was being replaced by intoler-ance toward people from different racial backgrounds, characteristic of more recent immigrants, such as Asian Australians. The idea of being a multiracial society was a relatively new phenomenon on the Australian contemporary scene, as the White Australia policy, which had kept non-Europeans out, only came to an end in the late 1960s. What was hap-pening in schools? I wanted to discover the attitudes of Euro-Australian children toward Aboriginal people and those of Asian background. I was looking for a suitable research methodology when I read the Canadian Frances Aboud's *Children and Prejudice.* She and her collaborators at McGill University in Montreal had developed a free-choice measure of racial attitudes that appeared more satisfactory than the widely used forced-choice measures or social distance scales. I thus made plans to spend three months of my sabbatical with her to learn about her methodology.

Four weeks before my departure Gerry died, suddenly. Against the advice of family and friends I decided to proceed with my visit and went onto McGill. Aboud related her findings of a decline of racial prejudice in the early years of schooling to children's growing ability to perceive similarity between outwardly different looking people and their ability to reconcile different viewpoints. I was attracted to the possibility of schools developing specific strategies to promote the development of these mature cognitions, thereby decreasing children's global thinking about others along the us-good/they-bad dimension. When I came back to Aus-tralia, I was ready to adapt and apply Aboud's research methodology to the Australian context in collaboration with my colleague Fay Hickson.

We carried out a number of large-scale studies on racial attitudes of Euro-Australian school children toward their own group and toward Asian and Aboriginal Australians. We measured age-related changes in negative and in positive attitudes in different social contexts. While our studies supported the role of cognition in the development of prejudice in younger children, it was also clear that the social context in which these attitudes developed played a significant role, particularly with older children. The primary emphasis on cognition and rationality as the basis of combating prejudice, we concluded, was limited in its effectiveness. The battle to ensure that each child, irrespective of racial, ethnic, cultural background, is treated with respect and acceptance of his or her difference needs to go beyond the content of curricula, beyond the school gates, to the immediate community, to the social relations that educators and children are engaged in, to the media, to the wider society, to the political sphere.

Connecting the Personal and the Professional Stories

In writing, reading, and rereading the account of my research effort, I am struck by the strength and persistence of the underlying motive. It is the issue of crossing the borders of difference—how we come to judge other people as equal, to empathize and show tolerance toward the other. What does this process, which enables us to see each other as individuals and not as a category, as subjects and not as objects, a "they," involve? There is also an interest in the reverse process, whereby an individual becomes a they—a category.

In my teaching, the theme of the outsider, the marginalized, is also apparent. I have always been attracted to working with minority students. My work with them has focused on them asserting their right to be seen and heard as individuals. I appreciate the courage it takes to speak out from the margin and in a foreign accent. In my adolescence and even young adulthood, I felt my own marginality very keenly, and I looked at the apparent confidence of those in the center with envy. Now I can share the experience of my own journey to and from the margin.

It is only now, on nearing the end of this chapter, that an incident has come to mind that vividly reveals the profound impact that my experience as a Jewish child under Nazi occupation has had on the direction of my personal and academic lives. It is at the root of my two narratives. I am aware that I am writing this part with some trepidation. Ten years ago I attended a two-week Gestalt psychology workshop, which was being held in a tiny village in Austria. It was my first visit to a German-speaking country since I had left Europe. In our group of thirteen psychologists, eight were German, three Polish, one British, and I, the Australian, was the only Jew. They had all come with friends or were in daily contact with their spouses. Because of difference in time zones and prohibitive cost, it was difficult to contact Gerry regularly. I felt isolated and was able to relate closely only to my British colleague. The theme that emerged very quickly in the group was racial and national difference. In one of the evening sessions during which I was the protagonist, I suddenly saw enemies all around me. The facilitator mishandled the hostile reaction that my feelings aroused in the group and allowed the session to end without a resolution. I retreated into my room. I wanted to hide from everyone.

It was then that I had an experience the recollection of which even now, years later, chills me. I felt myself falling, falling into a deep, dark hole. There was no ledge, nothing to hold onto. There were no people to reach out to. Nobody knew. Totally alone. I felt sheer terror. What could I do? I looked at photos of my children, of Gerry, I tried to write a letter, but nothing helped. This was my reality. I could not bear it. I stayed in that state for some time.

Eventually I went downstairs to make some tea in the communal kitchen. Someone spotted me and dragged me into the room where they were all talking and drinking. They embraced me; they hugged me; they told me how angry they were at what had happened in the session. I had survived. I now believe that it was a reexperience of my terror when at the age of six I was told that there were no parents for me any more. Out of the abyss of my aloneness, I have been trying to reach out to people all my life, personally and professionally, across the border of our differences.

The Quest for Continuity

A Personal Account of the Dubious Wisdom of Hindsight

Shlomo Breznitz

Biographical Note

Shlomo Breznitz emigrated from Czechoslovakia to Israel after the war. After living on a kibbutz and in Jerusalem and serving in the Israeli Defense Forces, he received his degree in psychology from the Hebrew University in 1965 and taught at the same institution until 1974. He became rector and president of the University of Haifa, where he is currently Lady Davis Professor of psychology and director of the R. D. Wolfe Centre for the Study of Psychological Stress (which he established). He also holds an appointment as professor of psychology in the graduate faculty of the New School for Social Research in New York City. He has published six books and many articles on the subject of stress and coping, as well as his memoirs, Memory Fields *(Knopf, 1993).*

⟫•◦•⟪

Introduction

Following the Hegelian tradition, this chapter consists of three parts. In line with the primary focus of this volume, it begins with the thesis that early life events determined much of what followed, including my research interests. In the second part, the antithesis questions the validity of such claims, offering a host of alternative explanations, as well as contrary evidence. Finally, in the third part I try to offer a synthesis that delineates the limits of retroactive claims for causality.

Anyone faced with this type of task must find it quite tempting, since it holds the promise of providing potential insights into both one's professional career and one's life trajectory in general. At the outset, it calls for a brief autobiographical sketch and a summary of the main themes representing my intellectual interests.

Early Experiences

What are the appropriate criteria for selecting the experiences that will be thought of as relevant and proper to report? Considering the danger of a posteriori bias, one is left almost exclusively with the single criterion of drama. In other words, only events that took place many years ago, and appear today to be of some dramatic intensity, pass the inclusion criterion. There are probably several reasons for this, the foremost being the belief that *in order for events to have lifelong impact they ought to be intense.* Another possibility is, of course, that early dramatic events have a better chance to survive the harsh test of forgetting. While such a bias for the outstanding may well turn out to be invalid, there is hardly any alternative.

When describing a child's experiences during the Holocaust, there is no shortage of extreme drama. That darkest of all ages provided plenty of traumatic material, which is particularly well suited for psychological theorizing about long-term impact.

I told the story of my first nine years, between 1936 and 1945, in *Memory Fields* (Breznitz 1993). What follows is a brief summary of that period of my life.

In 1936, when I was born, Bratislava still belonged to Czechoslovakia, but what my parents referred to as "the good times" were quickly coming to an end. Hitler's Germany was already heavily breathing down the neck of the small democracy, and local Nazi sympathizers were quickly gaining strength. Being Jewish meant being singled out for persecution that became systematically more pronounced and aggressive.

And yet, in spite of the gathering storm, I recall the first five years of my life as comfortable and quite secure. True, the adults, my parents included, appeared to be worried and scared, but for the most part they managed to hide their fears from the children. Ours was a nuclear family of four. My father was one of the chief engineers in the Slovak electric company, a position that gave us some protection in the years ahead. He was entirely assimilated into the culture of central Europe, with minimal ties to his Jewish Orthodox background. Mother was more in touch with her own family, who lived in Trencin, a two hour drive from Bratislava. My sister, Judith, was four years older than I, and she was father's darling. We were a typical middle-class family and, although far from wealthy, could afford a small car. In those days Mother never had to work, and we had sufficient household help.

My mother liked to tell the story of my struggle with double pneumonia at the age of one. This was before antibiotics, and when on top of this I contracted measles, the hospital staff urged her to take me home, where I could die more comfortably. There was nothing they could do, and they didn't believe that I would pull through. Mother, however, insisted on my staying and kept her vigil until my "miraculous" recovery. Over the years, this story became for me the prototype of her unqualified dedication, as well as the prototype of personal survival. The fact that both share a common ancestry might yet, at some later stage, lend itself to speculation about a possible causal link between the two.

First memory. Hundreds of picnickers dotting the bank of the Danube in Bratislava. I am four years old and suddenly get lost among the multitude of similar-looking blankets and people and can't find my parents. The dread builds up, and I start crying. Somehow I get to the huge bridge and start crossing to the other side. I stop occasionally to survey the bank from the height, which adds to my anxiety. . . . And then, in the middle of the bridge there is my father; he picks me up, hugs me close, and carries me to safety. Lost and found.

Then, suddenly, we had to leave our home and move to another town. Jews were no longer acceptable in the "respectable" neighborhoods. A few months later we moved again, this time to a small village. It used to have a big Jewish community, but most of it was by now gone. Gone also were my grandparents from Mother's side, my aunts and uncles, and all the cousins. Disappeared. Taken by the Slovak Guards. Presumably to labor camps, but since they were never heard from again, the possibility of systematic killings grew daily. Words like *Auschwitz* were whispered in dread. *Transport* was another bad word. Later there were many others.

There was no running water, and my sister and I took turns pumping the well on the street. In the winter the well froze. The place couldn't be properly heated, and we experienced the first instances of privation. Father continued to work in Bratislava, and we saw him on weekends only.

One Monday, shortly before leaving for the city, he took me aside and, looking deep into my eyes, said, "Don't forget who you are, and always remember that you must be the best in the class!" Then he was gone, leaving me with the heaviest of burdens. It was my first day of school.

It was in this tiny village, Vrbove, that we all studied to be Christians, hoping that it might save us. We deluded ourselves into thinking that nobody knew that we were Jewish. But not for long. Early one morning, while Father was away, we were told to quickly pack our essential belongings and were put on a train to a camp in Žilina, a transition camp en route to Auschwitz. At the camp we experienced frequent selections. People whose names were read had to board the "transport." Each selection was a nightmare. They often took place during the night, and I learned to sleep with my clothes on, ready for the journey.

One night, Mother woke me gently, whispering that we were leaving the camp by the front gate. I couldn't believe our luck, but it was true. At the gate there was Father, waiting to take us to safety. The letter from President Tiso, intimating that because he was necessary to the country's economy neither he nor his family should be sent away, worked. At least for now.

We stayed in Žilina. By the end of summer 1944, while some parts of Europe had already been liberated, the situation in Slovakia was desperate. The brief uprising by the partisans had been cruelly put down by invading German armies. They were now in charge, and for the few remaining Jews that meant the end of the road. Father received a tip that we would be picked up by the Gestapo within twenty-four hours. There was an offer for a hiding shelter, but he declined. "The war is still far from over," he said. Besides, because he was a diabetic, his chance of surviving was minimal. But the children might still make it, provided a custody could be found.

They tried the Benedictine sisters first but were turned down. They were shown the Jewish children that had already been accepted. There was no room for more. The only remaining option was the orphanage of the sisters of Saint Vincent. Here they met with success, and my sister and I were quickly taken there. The parting from our parents was heartbreaking. I was now eight years old and understood that even if the two of us somehow survived the war, our chances of seeing our parents again were minimal. My father asked for someone who could play chess. As a child I was a chess prodigy, and he hoped that involvement in a game would make the parting less painful. Cognitive preoccupation as an anesthetic. It didn't work.

At night Father and Mother were taken by the Germans, and for me began a year unlike any other. I was among the youngest in the group of orphans and certainly the weakest physically. At first I was better clothed and looked "rich." My suitcase was searched and vandalized on the first evening. More important, however, was the constant need to guard against discovery of my Jewishness. Since all the boys shared the same room, the danger of being observed naked was always present.

Boys were groomed for priesthood and girls for sisterhood and were thus kept totally separated. It was only on rare occasions that I could briefly talk to my sister, Judith. But I could see her from a distance every morning during mass, and that was wonderful. One of the older boys was in love with her, and I exchanged brief written notes between them. I got some protection in return.

In the orphanage, almost everything was settled by brute force. Certainly food, which was very scarce, had to be fought for constantly. Sometimes we ate from the same bowl, and it was then that I developed the bad habit of eating extremely fast. It is something that has stayed with me throughout my life. There was a lot of aggression for aggression's sake, and one could never anticipate where the next blow would come from. I learned to sit in a corner, protected from behind.

Our days started around five with the summons to the early mass. We dressed quickly and, half asleep, frozen by what turned out to be one of the coldest winters in Europe, marched to the chapel. It was a beautiful chapel, and later I often volunteered to assist the priest during mass. I liked the way the sounds resonated in the huge but closed space. Most of all, I liked the smell of incense.

The mass over, we would get our breakfast, which consisted of caraway soup and a piece of bread. It was warm, and it filled our bellies for a while. Next we cleaned our room and went to school. The walk to school in the snow and sleet was always tricky since many boys liked to attack the weaker ones, particularly if they heard rumors that they were Jewish. Throwing snowballs containing rocks was a traditional method. Another favorite consisted of forcing a lump of ice between the back and the shirt. After school we had assignments, such as peeling potatoes, scrubbing the closets, or shoveling snow. Then homework and finally the late afternoon mass. By the time we went to sleep we were physically exhausted.

But it wasn't a bad life, certainly not in comparison to what other Jewish children had to go through at that time. We were always hungry, but we were not starving. We were always cold, but we didn't freeze to death.

We were undernourished, and lonely, and scared, but we survived. And there was always the distant hope that the war would end, that the Germans would lose, and that our parents might yet come back.

Following Christmas Eve we were never far from death, and it was by our own doing. It was a festive dinner, and the boys and girls shared the same room. The food was plentiful, and we were happily singing Christmas carols. Suddenly the door opened, and a German general entered with the mother superior. He had brought a cake for us. Being a devout Catholic, he wanted to spend the evening in the orphanage. After a while he asked whether someone could sing "Holy Night" for him in German. It was then that Judith made the mistake of volunteering. Seizing the opportunity to be next to her, I joined her and we started to sing it the way we were taught by our mother.

Halfway through the song Judith realized the terrible blunder she had made, for in that region of Slovakia only Jews knew German. Struck by terror she couldn't go on, and our song remained unfinished. Finally we were found out and by no other than the chief commander of the German army in town. The general asked us to approach and then, gently stroking Judith's hair, he said, "Don't be afraid; the parents will come back." Just like that. But it was clear now that he knew, and things might look different to him on the next morning or the morning after that. In short, the threat was now permanent.

It was not long after Christmas that my situation changed dramatically. As a child I was fortunate to have an outstanding memory, both visual and auditory. While the first helped me to read early and fast and may have contributed to my chess playing, the second may well have saved my life. I don't know who it was that discovered that I could recall the long Latin prayers by heart, but one day I was summoned to the office of Mother Superior, and there she tested me. Apparently I passed with flying colors, because since that day the attitude of Sister C., who was in charge of the boys, changed significantly for the better.

Several weeks later, I was ushered to the home of the prelate himself, where he too tested my memory of the various litanies. Since I could have heard them only once or twice by listening to the sisters, and since neither they nor I could understand any of the Latin, they viewed it as a special "sign." It was only after the war that I learned that the prelate invoked an old fable, stipulating that a Jewish orphan would one day become the pope, to account for my mysterious gift. He urged the sisters to protect me by any means available.

The Germans came to the orphanage several times looking for Jewish children, but on all occasions we were quickly hidden. Unlike the Benedictine sisters, who gave up their Jewish protégés at the first opportune moment, our mother superior, while endangering herself and the rest of the orphanage, protected us against all odds. The prelate too was a good man, and that must have been the reason why he was beaten to death by Hitler Youth hooligans brandishing sticks and shouting, "Jesus war ein Judenkind!" (Jesus was a Jewish child). I was there; I saw it happening.

Žilina was liberated by the Red Army on May Day, long after Berlin itself fell. The outpouring of happiness was matched only by the sadness of the long lines of displaced persons that followed in the wake of the liberating forces. Thus started the long period of waiting. I would stay next to one of the main entrances to the town and closely observe the people dragging themselves on foot or occasionally sitting atop a cart pulled by emaciated horses. They looked haggard, lifeless, even the women closely shaved, barely having strength to move. For hours I would search those faces for signs of familiarity. A mixture of hope and fear.

It was only many weeks later that a neighbor came to summon Judith and me to her house. There, in the semidarkness that she asked for in order to hide her appearance, was our mother. She told us about seeing the children from the Benedictine orphanage in Auschwitz shortly after arrival. The chances that we were alive were slim. No word from our father yet, nor later. He died somewhere in the killing fields of Europe. My mother, though, waited for him for many long years.

Although I was only nine when the war ended, I choose to stop my story at this point. This decision is not based on any theoretical claim that the main components of one's character have by then long been established. Neither can I argue that my life since was uneventful; quite the contrary. Logically, however, the exercise requires that one has to take stock at some point in time. In order to keep the analysis as precise and as uncontaminated as possible, the sooner that is done, the better.

Main Research Themes

In my own case, given the events described above, the thesis about early determination of later intellectual pursuits is relatively easy to argue. Starting with my doctoral dissertation (Breznitz 1967), and throughout most of my professional life, I have been working primarily on issues of fear and threat (Breznitz 1984) in situations of objective helplessness

(Breznitz 1983a). This was followed by attempts to explicate the various facets of denial (Breznitz 1983b) as a way of coping with adversity. More recently, I have become interested in studying the effects of *hope* (Breznitz 1986, 1997) on negotiating extreme distress.

With a few exceptions, all of this work was experimental, utilizing, whenever possible, autonomic, biochemical, and immunological indicators of stress (Breznitz and Zinder 1988), as well as the more traditional behavioral and self-report measures. The independent variables that I used most frequently consisted of different kinds of information about some threatening event in the future, with particular emphasis on issues of time.

Many of my volunteer subjects had to spend long minutes in helpless anticipation of some frightening event. Was this some kind of distant echo of my own fears and anxieties? In the orphanage there was one boy younger than myself, the only one that I could treat as the others treated me. In *Memory Fields* I describe how I tried my hand at some petty cruelty: "There is little actual physical harm inflicted—only an occasional twisting of the arm or pinching of the flesh. The threat rather than its execution is the technique, and fear rather than pain is the goal" (Breznitz 1993, 52).

First there was the anticipation of being rounded up and sent to Auschwitz. It loomed like something inevitable, like the fate that had already struck all our relatives. There were many cues suggesting that the point in time when this threat would materialize was constantly approaching. The warnings were all around us. And yet, we had been rounded up once before and managed to come out unscathed. Was it just a false alarm?

Oddly enough, I have been systematically studying the effects of false alarms for several years (Breznitz 1984). To this day I am fascinated by the complex impact of a threatening event that in spite of all the expectations to the contrary ultimately did not happen. Such an experience dramatically reduces the credibility of subsequent similar threats. Moreover, the greater the initial fear of the impending danger, the more pronounced the drop in fear following such a false alarm episode. At some point, if they are repetitive, one almost stops heeding the signs of danger altogether.

Once this takes place, although conceptually and etiologically very different, such neglect of obvious threats is phenotypically synonymous to denial. Human capacity for carrying on with life even under the most distressful circumstances has virtually no limits. The various kinds of denial may temporarily cushion the impact of external hardships. Not seeing, not hearing, and not thinking about the "thousand natural shocks that flesh is heir to" are not only prevalent but can also be extremely beneficial.

In an important chapter on the costs and benefits of denial, Lazarus (1983) explicated the two conditions in which denial can be particularly useful. The first relates to objective helplessness; that is, the situation must be entirely uncontrollable. This makes both psychological and logical sense, since in such circumstances denial does not preclude any useful action from taking place. The second condition refers to the peak of the stress incurred by the person. It is then that even a temporary relief could play a critical role in one's overall capacity to cope with the situation. The studies by Hackett, Cassem, and Wishnie (1968) of denial in intensive care units convincingly demonstrate both conditions.

For years I kept thinking about the choices made by my father during that dark period. There were several years during which he could see the writing on the wall and could have taken his family into safety. After the war Mother mentioned that he was planning to relocate to Bolivia but kept postponing it until it was too late. Even much later, the special presidential letter must have given him a false sense of security. This is something I later labeled as *denial of personal relevance*. It is the most prevalent type of denial, comforting its user with the thought that irrespective of whatever is happening all around, it will not happen to him or her.

But it is the second type of denial in my list of seven (Breznitz 1983b) that is frequently the most devastating one. I refer to *denial of urgency*. Precious time is wasted because people believe that although there is an obvious threat, it is not imminent. Typically, by the time the falseness of that belief is realized, the opportunity for escape is gone. In fact, it is often only after the closing of borders that people realize the need to cross them as soon as possible. Were it not for this kind of denial, millions in Europe could have been saved.

I view denial and hope as remotely related, since both are attempts to boost one's morale even under the least favorable circumstances. They are, in fact, indicators of putting up a fight even in situations when one is essentially helpless. In this respect, such palliative efforts could almost be viewed as some psychological vital signs. But there are crucial differences between the two. Whereas denial produces distancing of one form or another in order to be effective, hope requires almost the opposite. It calls for a major investment of effort and cognitive resources. In fact, I prefer to think of it as work.

It was the *work of hoping* that kept me good company during those lonely months in the orphanage. Hoping was also what sustained my mother in Auschwitz. Hoping against the odds but not entirely unrealistic hope; not necessarily a mere illusion.

On the day we were put into the orphanage, why did my father decline the offer of a hiding shelter for the entire family? Later, Mother explained that he didn't think there was any chance to survive until the end of the war. But then, of course, nobody could know when the war would be over. In the absence of such information, it was very difficult to sustain a realistic measure of hope.

In my research, hope is manipulated by information about the termination of a stressful ordeal. As in the "tour of duty" phenomenon discovered in the context of U.S. pilots during World War II (Janis 1949), my subjects are either given or not given information about the light at the end of the tunnel. Sometimes that information is deliberately too encouraging or too discouraging, only to be altered later. This basic paradigm allowed me to study the impact of hope-generating information on performance in a variety of situations (Breznitz 1990, 1999; Breznitz and Ben-Zur 1994; Breznitz, Ben-Zur, and Vardi 1992). In addition, information change provided vital clues about the impact of sudden encouragement or sudden discouragement.

If my father knew that the war in Europe would be over in eight months, would he have acted differently? Would he have taken the risks and saved himself? The futility of these questions does not preclude their insistence; nor does it reduce the fascination with the psychological variables that have since occupied so much of my interest.

What are the antecedent conditions that enhance one's capacity for hoping? Why are some people more disposed toward an overtly optimistic outlook on the future than others? While this is probably based on a variety of factors, including some genetic ones, it is not entirely unrelated to false alarms and near misses. The experience of major threats that do not materialize might, in some measure, enhance the capacity for hoping under duress. Being in a concentration camp, and subsequently being taken out, is clearly a case in point.

Thus, the central research questions that I have been struggling with clearly resonate with themes from the past. The question remains, however, To what extent were these themes set down as a personal agenda, a kind of unfinished business, pregnant with motivational force? Some obvious connection exists, but can a causal link be established? And if yes, in which direction does the causal stream flow?

Methodological Difficulties

First, a word of caution. The argument about early determination of one's life path is much more general than the particular focus of the present chapter. It could be argued that the domain of research interests is in many ways one of the worst contexts for such an inquiry. One's intellectual activity is probably several steps removed from the more immediate context of emotions. Consequently, from the viewpoint of dynamic psychology, such a sterile domain cannot be considered a fair test case. With this in mind, we can now approach the primary difficulty of the task at hand.

Since the central thesis rests almost exclusively on hermeneutic reasoning, no amount of face validity can be taken as a scientific proof. No matter how appealing and plausible the interpretations, a stringent empirical test is called for. As in any empirical testing, what are needed are appropriate controls. But there's the rub, for one cannot expect to live one's life over again to check whether the same early history would inevitably lead to similar outcomes. Consequently, the only other remaining option is to test whether entirely different outcomes could be effectively accounted for by the same starting conditions.

There are several ways to carry out such an exercise systematically. Thus, for instance, I could pick up a psychological journal at random and ask whether the topics of interest represented in that journal could have been my own. Unfortunately, most journals are too specific, and the range of different themes would be very limited.

I chose an alternative approach. Since I am a member of two very different psychology departments, one in Haifa and one in New York, I decided to go over the areas of research of all my colleagues in both places and check those. Here are the results of that brief intellectual exercise. While for obvious logical reasons I had to check the areas of all my colleagues, in the interest of brevity I mention only a few, to illustrate the point.

Colleague 1: Early and late attachment. The strong bonding with my mother and the subsequent abandonment by both parents could easily make the above my primary research interest.

Colleague 2: Decision making in emergencies. Father's decision to stay. Later, the decision not to hide. The decision to put us into the orphanage. All in emergencies, all critical to my life.

Colleague 3: Facial recognition. The attempt to remember my parents in the absence of a photograph. Later, the long days watching the dispersed people passing through the town, searching for a distinguishing feature in their faces.

Colleague 4: Memory without awareness. The litanies. The long Latin prayers that I recalled without knowing how and that probably saved my life.

Colleagues 5 and 6: Evolutionary psychology. Basic issues of survival. Competitive advantage of certain social and intellectual skills. My father's unfortunate statement on my first day of school. Learning and memory as a survival tool.

Colleague 7: Perception. Attentional blindness. My father's attempt to involve me in a game of chess in order to create attentional blindness during our parting. Moreover, this is so close to issues of denial that any involvement in this type of research could be easily traced to the same origins.

Colleague 8: Psychology of religion. A Jew turned Catholic, saved by the nuns, and becoming Jewish again after the war; there is surely enough here to account for a lifelong interest in issues of religion.

And so on, and so forth. Even a superficial analysis suggests that with my particular background, I could have become involved in a variety of research issues other than the ones that I actually study. The reason is quite obvious, namely, there are simply too many degrees of freedom, and the number of meaningful connections that can be made is virtually unlimited. While not all of them are necessarily equally plausible, some certainly are. Consequently, in spite of the temptation to argue the contrary, early experiences cannot explain the actual path that I have followed.

The Model

Any attempt to force the complexity of the issue into a schematic model is, almost by definition, bound to be superficial. Indeed, what follows should not be taken necessarily as a valid description of the processes involved but rather as a tangible focus for the inquiry itself. The simplicity of the paradigm will, hopefully, be outweighed by potentially greater conceptual precision.

Let us assume an initial starting condition A leading to a choice point

B, where our hypothetical person preferred the route b2 over b1. This brought him to point C, at which c2 was once again preferred over c1. The person now faces dilemma D. Even such a primitive tree that has only two branches at each choice point is expanding very quickly, and after n choices produces 2^n possible paths. Thus, with each additional choice point, and there must be millions of those in a lifetime, the original starting condition becomes more remote.

But the number of intervening steps, though obviously very important, is not the only determining factor in this process. Rather, the question is, What is it that happens at each single choice? The forces that determine the outcome of any decisional process consist of two kinds; those that are carried over from the past and those active primarily at present. These latter factors are sometimes called *random shocks*. While not necessarily random in nature, from the perspective of one's past they are.

It is through the impact of random shocks that motivational determinants based on past experience cannot fully determine the next choice. Their contribution is necessarily a partial and a probabilistic one. Once it becomes clear that the determination of stage $n + 1$ is only partially determined by the factors represented at stage n, the number of discrete choice points becomes particularly important. Even a very high correlation between adjacent branches would be dramatically reduced after just a few steps (e.g., if a correspondence between any two sequential branches is 0.8, those two steps removed correlate only 0.64, with the next steps being 0.51, 0.41, 0.33, etc.). It is precisely this feature that guarantees that if there are enough intermediate steps between the point of origin (the presumed cause) and the outcome, any branch of the tree can be reached from almost any starting point. Stated differently, after the event, anything could be interpreted.

Our model, which is basically similar to "path analysis," must allow, in principle, the possibility that at any given choice point there are direct effects of early events, unmediated by what followed. Stated differently, this would assume that forces active at point A or B would have some impact on the decision at point D, irrespective of the route chosen so far (i.e., b2, c2 in our example).

Even such partial "independence of path" is, however, very unlikely. Conceptually, it can happen only if distal factors are more powerful than proximal ones, undoubtedly a highly questionable psychological requirement. Since random shocks are cumulative over time, proximal predictions will typically be much more accurate than distal ones. The classical psychoanalytic argument needs to assume, among other things, that most events, and certainly the later ones, do not leave any significant memory traces. However, this is in direct contradiction with yet another basic tenet of psychoanalysis, namely, that of psychic determinism.

A Few Notes on Random Shocks

What are these so-called random shocks, and what is their modus operandi? An element most often neglected in psychological discussions is, of course, the role of luck in human affairs. Not only is there nothing profound that psychological theory can say about it, but its very existence threatens the validity of much theorizing about causality. In a rare attempt to face the challenges that luck presents, Bandura (1982) tried to explicate some of the parameters involved, such as personal factors and milieu properties.

In pondering the imponderable, there is no need to evoke such concepts as luck, chance, or even fate. We all have firsthand experience with the impact of external constraints on our ability to carry out even the simplest of intentions. Those are the hundreds of unplanned, and unwished for, aspects of a situation that pose obstacles to our actions, often derailing them from their original path. Thus, some of these random shocks are expressions of the complexity of the world in which we live. No action, even if planned to the smallest detail, can be expected to happen exactly as anticipated. We do not operate in a vacuum, and where our life paths cross those of others, there is no way of knowing what will happen.

The central argument of this volume does not refer to the impact of early experience on the type of research that we hoped to do, or wished to do, but on that research that we actually carried out. This makes reality considerations particularly salient. How often did we give up an idea because of absence of funding? How often did we take up a study because a student came up with an exciting idea? These are typical random shocks with major impact on our choices.

My choice of psychology as an area of study was probably determined almost exclusively by fortuitous timing. At that time the Hebrew University was the only Israeli institution teaching humanities and social sciences, and psychology was not one of them. A bad teacher in high school (another random shock) made me give up my earlier ambition to study mathematics, and after my army service, I was inclined to take up philosophy and political science. Just then it was announced that the university would try to open a small psychology department after all. Were this to have happened a few months later, my path would have been entirely different.

When planning a course of action, we often play down objective constraints in order to be able to sustain some measure of optimism about the value of the effort (Weinstein 1982). The more realistic appraisal of the depressed person often leads to total passivity. Attribution research suggests that even after the event, particularly if the outcomes are favorable, we have a clear tendency to play down the role of random shocks (Weiner 1986).

Objective constraints are a major issue even when we plan to carry out a simple, conscious plan. Consider how much more serious the obstacles are when the goal is unconscious, probably unrealistic, ambiguous, and at cross-purposes, that is, conflictual, with other wishes! However, those are precisely the attributes of motivational forces as envisaged by psychoanalytically oriented approaches to the problem.

Moreover, unconscious determination is assumed to operate according to primary processes. Consequently, as in dream work or in the more general Von Domarus principle (Von Domarus 1944), similarity can stand for identity. When interpreting backward, such a loose criterion of correspondence inevitably increases the hermeneutic degrees of freedom even further, almost to the point of absurdity.

Retroactive Reconstruction

We abhor random shocks, because they demonstrate the limits of our ability to control our destiny. It would be logical to resist any strong determinism for the same reason. Some form of weak determinism, one that leaves room for choice at all stages of life, is probably psychologically more acceptable. While it provides a framework for a meaningful organization of one's life experiences, it does so without evoking a sense of coercion.

The need to insert meaning into our life stories may, however, introduce a great deal of post hoc interpretation even in places where it is unwarranted. Such a quest for meaning, combined with our extraordinary capacity to provide it, can smooth, and even filter out, many unexplainable sudden twitches and jerks in our life stories. Thus, convergences between early experience and later choices that appear to make sense could be the product of retroactive reconstruction rather than actual proactive causality.

This process is further facilitated by our inability to recall or even notice the full context of any particular action. The small details, as well as the numerous objective constraints that played a critical role in a decisional dilemma, are among the first casualties of memory. The stage is then left for post hoc appraisals, thus making more sense of our actions than they deserve.

The quest for meaning is, however, easily matched by yet another powerful motivational force, the *quest for continuity*. This is directly relevant to the central issue of this chapter, since by its very nature, continuity implies strong ties to the past. We like to think of ourselves as being essentially the same persons that we were at prior stages of our lives, including childhood. Attempts to preserve such a sense of continuity are often challenged by dramatic transitions. By the same token, probably nowhere is the force of this tendency more pronounced than when small changes are spread over relatively long periods of time. We are often the last to take notice and admit gradual, hard to detect changes in ourselves.

These types of retroactive reconstruction of causality could, of course, operate on the unconscious level, making them more resistant, practically invulnerable, to corrective measures. People with some knowledge of the principles of psychodynamic interpretation are, perhaps, particularly susceptible to such unconscious efforts to introduce theoretical sense into their life trajectories.

Last, but not least, our perception of the past is itself significantly determined by present interests and involvements. This might act as a filtering device, leading to selective memory of the past. Thus, past events that have better hermeneutic correspondence to our current situation could have some competitive advantage over those that don't. Such a late determination of what constitutes our most relevant past can be viewed as retroactive reconstruction at its most extreme.

Synthesis

The above arguments on both sides do not lend themselves to a conceptual synthesis. Consequently, the only remaining possibility for accommodating the two opposing views is a matter of degree, a compromise.

Let us briefly go back to the model presented earlier. A strict determination by the past argues for a continuously reduced number of options. Not only are early events of critical importance, but in every following stage the amount of free space is progressively reduced. The argument is one of a narrowing path, an inverted tree. By contrast, our model views this in an exactly opposite manner, namely, a tree that is branching out and expanding all the time. Our choices become a part of our history and thus partake in determining future choices.

As we move from one choice point to the next, the direct impact of our past is progressively weakened. Instead, it is now represented indirectly, by the proximal forces. However, since the latter are themselves a compromise formation between earlier determinants and a sequence of several stages of random shocks, that representation is only partial. Furthermore, as we move on in life, these partial representations of past determinants become progressively more removed from their original.

And yet, in spite of all this dilution of power, the past can and often does find a way to circumvent these limitations. In fact, the random shocks themselves can sometimes provide the stimulus for the reassertion of the past. I have already described the fortuitous opening of a psychology department just when I was about to choose an entirely different route. The announcement also mentioned that of all the potential applicants only a very small number of students would be accepted. I recall taking this as a personal challenge, perhaps a residue effect of my father's ill-chosen words on my first day of school: "Don't forget who you are, and always remember that you must be the best in the class!" This event, going back very far indeed, could have played some role in my choice. But, then again, the announced selection itself was just another random shock.

During the Holocaust, survival itself was primarily a matter of luck. This was true even within the most terrible of all contexts, that is, the daily selections in Auschwitz. One's chances depended to a large extent on such factors as position in the line, the number of those who already had failed the selection, a chance eye contact with one of the SS guardsmen, and a whole host of personal whims of the selectors. As with many personal tragedies, it was basically an issue of being in the wrong place at the wrong time. The effects of early psychological determinants were, at best, marginal.

Finally, this analysis cannot be completed without mentioning the potential importance of the thematic material itself. Although some content variables might also be important in the sense that they subsequently might be evoked more frequently than others, I wish to emphasize a different aspect of the material, namely, its richness.

A rich and varied past can be correlated to a wide variety of life trajectories much more easily than a more impoverished one. Stated differently, if a lot happened, the task of subsequent interpretation of presumably causal links would be a relatively simple one. This is once more due primarily to the availability of many degrees of freedom. At the same time, for exactly the same reason, there are potentially more different possible life trajectories. In other words, the tree has many more branches already close to its base, providing a greater variety of options.

It is an interesting paradox that an extremely uneventful past also provides opportunities to branch in many directions. By virtue of the mild character of early events, such a past leaves more room for subsequent events to play a key role.

In sum, it is the impact of experiences that are neither too rich and varied, nor too shallow and unimportant, that can have a more lasting effect on a person's life. I have tried to argue that even then, the richness and variety of subsequent life would inevitably blunt their edge.

REFERENCES

Bandura, A. 1982. The psychology of chance encounters and life paths. *American Psychologist* 37:747–55.

Breznitz, S. 1967. Incubation of threat: Duration of anticipation and false alarm as determinants of fear reaction to an unavoidable frightening event. *Journal of Experimental Research in Personality* 2:173–80.

———.1983a. *Denial of stress.* New York: International Universities Press.

———.1983b. The seven kinds of denial. In *Denial of stress,* edited by S. Breznitz. New York: International Universities Press.

———.1984. *Cry wolf: The psychology of false alarms.* Englewood Hills, NJ: Lawrence Erlbaum Associates.

———.1986. The effect of hope on coping with stress. In *The dynamics of stress,* edited by M. Appley and R. Trumbull. Plenum. New York.

———.1990. Enhancing performance under stress by information about its expected duration. Final Technical Report to the U.S. Army Research Institute.

———.1993. *Memory fields.* New York: Alfred A. Knopf.

———. 1999. The effect of hope on pain tolerance. *Social Research* 66: 629–52.

Breznitz, S., and H. Ben-Zur. 1994. Enhancing effective decision making by information management techniques. Final Technical Report to the U.S. Army Research Institute.

Breznitz, S., H. Ben-Zur, and N. Vardi. 1992. Enhancing cognitive performance by information management techniques. Final Technical Report to the U.S. Army Research Institute.

Breznitz, S., and O. Zinder, eds. 1988. *Molecular biology of stress.* New York: Alan R. Liss.

Hackett, T. P., N. H. Cassem, and H. A. Wishnie. 1968. The coronary-care unit: An appraisal of its psychologic hazards. *New England Journal of Medicine* 279:1365–70.

Janis, I. 1949. In *The American soldier: Combat and its aftermath*, edited by S. A. Stouffer et al., vol. 2. Manhattan, KS: MA-AH Publications.

Lazarus, R. S. 1983. The costs and benefits of denial. In *Denial of stress*, edited by S. Breznitz.. New York: International Universities Press.

Von Domarus, E. 1944. The specific laws of logic in schizophrenia. In *Language and thought in schizophrenia*, edited by J. Kasanin, 104–14. Berkeley: University of California Press.

Weiner, B. 1986. *An attributional theory of achievement and motivation*. New York: Springer-Verlag.

Weinstein, N. D. 1982. Unrealistic optimism about susceptibility to health problems. *Journal of Behavioral Medicine* 5:441–60.

Languages of War

Mary Engel

Biographical Note

A member of Phi Beta Kappa, Mary Engel received her Ph.D. from George Peabody College of Vanderbilt University. After a postgraduate fellowship with Gardner Murphy and Helen Sargent at the Menninger Foundation, she became supervisor in the postdoctoral clinical psychology program at the Michael Reese Hospital in Chicago. She then moved to Harvard University to become director of the school psychology training program. During this time, she served as one of the chairmen of the Joint Commission for Mental Health of Children and coauthored its report to Congress, summarizing its findings and recommendations concerning the health and mental  health of children in the United States. Subsequently, she moved to City College of the City University of New York where she served as one of the directors of the Ph.D. program in clinical psychology.

Her research focused on mental health problems of children and adolescents, the lives of street children in the greater Boston area, and infancy and minority status. Most recently she had done research with newcomers in New York City, especially culture change in relationship to English language learning. In her spare time, she was an avid equestrian.

Dr. Engel died on March 10, 2001, as this book was going to press.

My father was Philip Engel, born in New York City in 1886. His parents were Hungarians who later returned to Budapest. There, he eventually became one of the owners of the Corvin Film Company and later was executive officer of Fanamet, an American firm. Writings of the times credit him with opening up much of the European market to American movies. His first wife died, leaving him with a teenage son, Gyuri. In 1929, he married my mother, Lily, a Hungarian girl of great beauty who had just completed her education as an ornamental wife in a Viennese finishing school. In those days, a large difference in ages was not unusual. My father was a contemporary of the composer Kodály, who, at age seventy-seven, proposed to a young music student: "Madam, how would you like to be the widow of Kodály?" She accepted.

Lily was nineteen, his son was eighteen years old, and, as my father explained, "The children did not get along." Gyuri left Budapest for the Sorbonne, where he joined a group known as "1930 Communists," composed of young Jewish intellectuals. There he met László Rajk, whose trial for treason took place in 1949. Theirs became a friendship that had a decisive influence on his fate.

My father was in New York when I was born. Family lore maintained that my interest in languages dated from his transatlantic call to us; my first act in life was "talking" on the telephone. Lily's present for her travails was a Daimler, a kind of Mercedes; upon me he bestowed a fluffy white Pomeranian and Nana, a nurse for babies. My firm belief that I was Catholic grew out of my love for Nana, the source of all my early knowledge of the world. It pleased her that my father named me Mary, which she knew to be the English version of Mária. She put this together with my family name, Engel, which means angel in German, and explained that the blue, winged angels, frescoes on the ceiling of my room, were a true representation of my relationship to Christ.

This then was my immediate family: mother, father, half-brother who resided in France, nurse Nana. And there were Lily's mother, Grandmother Hermione, and her second husband, Marcel Varga. Later, Nana was assigned the duties of housekeeper. German-speaking governesses came and were replaced by those who spoke French, so that by the time I entered grammar school, in addition to being able to recite Nana's Latin prayers, I was fluent in Hungarian, German, and French.

While small, I did not spend much time with my father and spent even less time with my mother. Thus, I had little chance to learn details about my family from my parents. As I write this in the autumn of my life, and try to construct a narrative as true to facts as possible, I attempt to untangle cause from coincidence by relying on a few letters and objects, information from return trips to Budapest, history books, and diverse sources that include the reference library of the West Point Military Academy. By the time Hitler entered Hungary and Eichmann came to Budapest to round up the Jews, I was completely alone. But let me reassure the reader that the fact that my father was born in New York gave me, in the end, all the rights and privileges of a citizen of the United States.

Between world wars, Hungary became the first European country to enact anti-Jewish legislation. In spite of restrictive laws, my early years would have been happily uneventful, had it not been for certain isolated incidents that were replete with foreboding. When I was four years old, Lily, governess, and I traveled to a mountain resort in Goezing, Austria. I was to have lessons in reading. Fräulein was excited about searching for an elusive flower, edelweiss. No sooner had we unpacked and settled in the dining room when the doors swung open and a large group of officers entered. Amid loud heel clicking and surrounded by bowing waiters, they sat down at the table next to us. Fräulein was in rapture. She whispered that I should take a look at the one at the head of the table for he would soon become a very famous man. I was looking at Adolf Hitler. The following morning, we returned to Budapest.

In the mid-1930s, Father had to relinquish his U.S. citizenship in order to remain in Hungary. His work permit bears a red "Zs," which stands for the Hungarian word, *Zsidó,* for "Jew." At that time, he began to import French films. Each movie had to be seen by censors before it could be shown. There were films that were so badly cut by these censors that their mutilated remains were useless. Censorship was forever a topic in our home. Once Hungary entered the war, everyone was prohibited from listening to radio stations from the Allied side. The BBC broadcast news in many languages, including Esperanto. Father listened to them all. Someone turned in a complaint. Soldiers burst into our house, tore everything out of closets and drawers, read a severe warning about Father's transgressions, and put a lock on the radio that kept the dial from being turned to London. As soon as they left, Father removed the lock, put a down comforter over the radio, and resumed his listening, in a tireless expression of resistance. Eventually, the BBC must have learned about these restrictions. In the 1940s reports of the war were relayed via song titles. My father's spirits truly flagged when he heard a song from London: "Spring will be a little late this year."

Resistance may run in our family. We found out that Gyuri and his wife had joined the French underground. At first, news about their whereabouts was rare; later there was no news at all, causing my father inexpressible anguish. Yet outwardly we continued life as usual. Lily was busy with furriers and dressmakers. I was passionately involved in ballet school and figure skating, and at home, I was lost in books. Everybody "knew" that I read under my napkin during endless conversations at the dinner table. *Emile und die Detektieven* was followed by *Les aventures de Sophie,* then Shakespeare, Heine, Goethe, and long epic poems about the history of my country. Father interrupted my reading only occasionally with one of his gentle criticisms. When I slurped the soup: "Fräulein, I think the radio is on." When the food displeased him: "Lily, is the cook in love?"

The cook was not in love, but Lily was. It soon became known, and grave troubles ensued that culminated in her death by her own hand, at the age of thirty-two. By this time we lived on Donati Street, a part of town Jews were not allowed to inhabit. Our home was under someone else's name. It was near the Fishermen's Bastion, built to commemorate Hungary's liberation from Turkish rule. From one set of windows one could see the Parliament on the Pest side; from my room, the spire of Saint Mátyás Church, built in the thirteenth century. It was a beautiful place, in the Castle district, but it was an unhappy place that I visit only when I can bear the sadness, heavy as lead.

At Lily's funeral, a well-dressed, elderly gentleman introduced himself, and it was revealed to me that Lily's parents had divorced, that Grandfather Varga was not really my grandfather. The "new" one was married for the second time, and soon an invitation for tea came from him and his wife. She was a lovely, intelligent woman, sister of Dr. Jenö Bársony, a surgeon known in many parts of Europe. He was celebrated not only because of his skill as a surgeon but also because he was an accomplished cellist and an art collector, owner of a considerable collection of French and Hungarian impressionists. Among his medical students were several who later emigrated to the United States, including the psychoanalysts Dr. Teresa Benedek and Dr. Robert Bak, President of the New York Psychoanalytic Society. Jenö Bársony, Uncle Bársony to me, played a central role in organizing medical services in the Budapest ghetto (Braham 1981).

After Lily's death, my father began to spend more time with me. Long talks began of which I recall several. He believed that each language one spoke gave one a totally new way of thinking. I would ask him, "How do you say this in (whatever language)?" only to have him reply, "You can't." More than once he advised that people who do not know what to do next, whose backs are to the wall or who cannot see a way out, should learn a new language.

My new grandparents, Leopold and Serena, lived near the Basilica, across the street from the office and apartment of Jenö Bársony. Now this part of the city, on the Pest side, began to play a decisive role in my life. As an only child, a Jew, first in a Catholic elementary school, then in an anti-Semitic Lutheran gymnasium ("Will that Jewish girl in the back resume the recitation . . ."), I really had no close friends. Now I met young people, children of friends of Serena. Among these was Kati, a girl a few years my senior, about whom much will be written in what follows.

Kati was raised in a family of more modest means and had no governess. She was independent and outspoken. I thought she was beautiful. Her talents as an artist were especially awe inspiring: she could draw anything she wanted to represent. A tall brunette with a slender face, she had a characteristic walk that was swaying and womanly. She was at ease with boys, which I was not. That such a girl wanted to be friends with me made me feel especially fortunate. She became my first real friend.

Elsewhere (Engel 1984), I analyzed how adolescents cope with the disasters of war. I suggested that in extreme situations, adolescents are capable of "rerooting"; that is, in a very short period of time, they may involve themselves in intense personal relationships with each other. These are exaggerations of age-appropriate attachments and serve survival.

It is written that air raids over Budapest began on April 3, 1944. This is not my recollection. I discovered that this may have been the date of the first American bombings but that Russian Mig planes might have attacked earlier. Americans "shuttle bombed" Hungary, loading in Sicily, dropping on Budapest, loading again in Russia, and bombing on the way back. This was referred to as "Operation Frantic." Mig planes often came singly, swooped down from great heights, and rose incredibly fast after unloading their bombs (personal communication, Sergeant Battapaglia, Reference Library, West Point Military Academy Library). I recall an air-raid warning on the evening of March 1, during which Father and I remained upstairs to watch the converging searchlights in the night. Father suffered severe chest pains, and I, in animal panic, tried frantically to telephone his doctor. Once reached, he refused to come and leave his family on such a dangerous night. By morning, Father died in my arms.

Languages of War

On the morning of March 19, 1944, German troops and the Eichmann *Sonderkommando* entered Budapest. In the Castle district people awoke to the rumbling of tanks and the shouts of soldiers. This was a new German sound. This was a new vocabulary. *Achtung! Abtreten! Verboten!* The language of war.

The 20th of March, I was registered as residing with Grandmother Hermione and her husband, at 39 Paulay Ede utca (Paulay Ede Street), in the maid's room, without my dog, who was sent to stay with my grandfather. In a few days, the compulsory wearing of the yellow star was in effect. Jews were allowed out of their buildings only for a few hours of the day. Deportations in the countryside began. Jews fled to the city in great numbers, bringing news of atrocities. I kept to myself. I did not feel Jewish. I tried Nana's prayers: "Agnus Dei qui tollis peccata mundi, miserere nobis" (Lamb of God who takes away the sins of the world, have mercy on us).

As Allied bombings increased in frequency, residents had to take turns staying awake at night by a radio, ready to alert everyone once enemy planes were announced to have crossed the border. Awakened, sleepy, frightened residents made their way down the steps to the shelter. Once its heavy door clanged shut, it could not be opened until the all clear sounded. Therefore the pushing and shoving to get into the basement could grow to brutal proportions, as courtesy gave way to rudeness, then to utter disregard for the safety of anyone but oneself.

Between air raids, my grandmother Hermione performed her obsessional routine: this day to wash, that day to iron, another day to polish her silver. Should a bomb hit the house, should the walls of her apartment crumble and reveal the intimate interior for all to see, no neighbor should ever be able to say that she did not keep a spotless house, that she did not keep her silver polished to a perfect shine! Denial was a daily presence everywhere I turned. Going to visit my dog in my grandfather's apartment, I sometimes was caught there during an air raid. Rushing to get to the shelter, I saw him grab silver candelabra that once belonged to his mother ("May she rest in peace!"). Leaving more necessary items behind, he explained that the candlesticks would protect us by reminding his mother, now in Heaven, to intercede on our behalf. None of us would die during a bombing; none of us would be deported.

Kati's evaluation of the situation was pessimistic. Her father had already been inducted into one of the labor camps whose reputation was infamous. To me, she began to serve in loco parentis. Without the customary respect youngsters were supposed to show adults, she unceremoniously pronounced my grandparents to be fools. By October, anti-Jewish atrocities in the city reached a new level, no doubt due to the coup against Regent Horthy and the ensuing terror by members of the Arrow

Cross (Nyilas) Party, the Hungarian counterparts of the Nazis. If caught, Jewish males who tried to avoid labor camps were executed instantly, with cruelty not known before. Often three were tied together, the middle one was shot, and the entire group tossed into the Danube, there to drown. It is now estimated that fifty to sixty such executions took place every night (Braham 1981). By November, plans to move all Jews into a ghetto were complete. I left my grandmother's apartment, met Kati under the arches of the Royal Hungarian Opera House, removed the yellow star from my coat, and went into hiding.

Memory denies a sense of continuity to the events that ensued. There are an unpleasantness, an incompleteness in this recollection, something wrong in a *recherche du temps perdu,* an endless search for answers that will never come. The mind asks over and over again, "Did this happen first?" or "Did this happen after that?" To write about it, one must put aside the anguish over what gaps there are and tell what can be recalled that is still in memory. Perhaps this is because of the utter disorder, the hour-to-hour existence that took place that fall and winter. Time lacked direction, and space changed with every bomb that dropped, turning a familiar city into debris. In one instant, a bridge with a graceful span over the Danube changed to a heap of stones and cables. Like a swan injured beyond hope, its neck shattered, its back broken, it collapsed into the water. Or a person with whom one had talked the day before could not be found the following morning; fortuity led a bomb to find him, and a friend became a corpse, tossed frozen, stiff, onto a heap of other bodies. On warmer days the entire city reeked with the sour stench of rotting dead. Once the war ended, three thousand corpses awaited burial in the ghetto alone (Braham 1981).

As food supplies dwindled to none that could be bought or traded, scavenging and looting began. Finders were keepers of whatever edible there was. Between air raids, shabbily dressed people crawled into the bowels of destroyed buildings, looking for food supplies, beans, lentils that might be spilling out of bags, cans of food that might be rolling around among torn-up furniture.

Hunger whimpers in the morning, but by nighttime it screams and demands and does not leave one's brain. Hunger takes one's thoughts by the scruff of the neck and swings them around and permits no other thoughts to exist but those that have to do with something to eat. Hunger is like a black vulture of death, following, watching, waiting. Hunger destroys form, control, and shame. He who is hungry no longer minds who knows it. Hunger is when at the sound of an all clear, weary residents climb out of their shelter and, knives in hand, find a horse smitten by shrapnel, its neck and head and bulging eyes in a pool of blood in the snow, an animal still warm to the touch, and they tear at it and chop and pull its flesh, like sharks in a feeding frenzy.

Kati's instructions were to find a place to stay until she could procure false papers for us and send for me. My parents had known the owner of a textile shop, and she told me to go there and ask to stay there for the night. The shopkeeper was far from glad to see me. It could cost him his life, he reminded me, harboring a Jew. Nevertheless, he allowed me to stay for the night and showed me into a room in his basement, equipped with bed and washstand. The room was below street level, but two narrow windows opened onto the sidewalk. Through the grillwork one could see the shoes of passersby. The street was noisy most of the night, as arriving Germans explored the city. Their boots passed by my face as I stood peering out at them, holding my breath.

Morning finally came, and the shopkeeper announced that a man was there to see me. He was sent by Kati. His name was Johnny, an English name like mine. His mother, an American-born Jew, was already in a Swiss House. His father, bearing the name of an ancient and noble Hungarian family, was away. After fetching some things for me from my grandmother, he planned to take me to the Swiss House, to stay with his mother.

Johnny was tall, freckle faced, blond, and blue eyed. About ten years my senior, he spoke with confidence and calm. I felt secure in his presence. Returning with one of Lily's valises, he guided me to a restaurant on Erzsébet Square, in a kiosk that no longer exists. Inside, in another world of white napery and fresh flowers, Johnny explained that bombings could be expected to escalate, that the occupying German forces would soon be surrounded by the Allies. The Arrow Cross (Nyilas) Party's atrocities had not subsided; it was dangerous to be on the street or in public places. The Swiss House would offer temporary protection until Kati procured false papers for us. Then we would join her and some others in the Gröbel Pension, 4 Kossuth Lajos Square, next to the Danube and the Parliament.

On November 21, 1944, I was registered in the Swiss House for "protected Jews," as a relative of Johnny and his mother. The registry pass, still in my possession, bears the stamp of the Portuguese Legation.[1]

In the Swiss House, cots were so close that one could hardly walk between them. The stench of unwashed bodies pervaded the air, and no one talked. My papers show that we exited on December 3, 1944. On that day, Johnny and I were registered under an assumed name, as brother and sister, children of an actual Hungarian general, in the Gröbel Pension.

Here Kati's talents as an artist were put to use manufacturing false identification papers. I carry an image of her, leaning over her forgeries, a petty frown on her forehead, wrinkling up her nose, turning an innocent, open face to anyone who interrupted her. Where did she get the blanks for her forged documents? No one knew, and no one asked. After drawing stamps with blue ink, she folded the ID's, stepped on them, and made them look like they had been in someone's pocket for years. People came and went and took the papers she made and left us food and other things we needed. Once ceaseless bombings forced us to live in the shelter, she continued her work, using Lily's luggage as her table. There she worked on top of the pigskin suitcase with its labels from Abasia and Bled.

When those who needed false identification papers were stuck outside the city, escapees from trains headed to concentration camps, they sometimes were able to send word for help. Kati would promise. But who would deliver? One of us, a boy, was arrested and shot. It was dangerous for men to be on the street. Why are they not in the army? Why are they not in a labor camp? I was the obvious choice to carry papers to those who awaited them. Small for my age, able to talk fluently when stopped by a German: "Ignorant soldier, do you not know whom you are talking to? Show courtesy to the daughter of a Hungarian noble family." It worked in the city. It worked on every street corner. I could do this.

And so it was around Christmas 1944 when we heard by relay that four Jews had hopped off the train and were hiding in a bombed-out lightbulb factory, Tungsram, on the outskirts of the city. Kati went to work on papers. There were three men and one woman. I stuffed the papers into my boots. Kati said it was far, not to try to come back the same day. I headed out Váci út, a wide road leading from a railway station to Tungsram. The snow was deep but not as deep as my boots were tall. Soon, I heard gunfire. It became ever louder and was then followed by German soldiers, running in pairs toward the city. I made a *Heil* sign, and they motioned for me to follow them. I did but lagged behind; then, mercifully, they forgot me. I arrived at the gates of Tungsram.

A few of the timeworn buildings stood in defiance of the bombs, others had wounds ripped into their sides. I could hear voices, talk and laughter. I found the Jews in a large, empty hall. One was flat out in the corner, snoring, another was dancing with a woman, the third waved a bottle at me. I was speechless. I had risked my life for a group of drunks! I took the bottle, smashed it to the wall, threw their IDs at them, and left.

Marching in fury, I stopped only to eat snow and salt I carried with me. I felt betrayed, used, and ridiculed. At the first train stop, I sat down to rethink what had happened. I left them to save my skin. I left them helpless in their alcoholic stupor. Who knows what they had been through? They found some liquor, and they drank it . . . to blot out the terror . . . to blot out the grief. I had failed to help them.

Continuing my journey, close enough to the city to sense it, I heard rustling in the snow. There was a ditch with something dark in it. I heard hoarse, crumpled words: "Tovaaarich!" Then I saw the Russian soldier. Now I understood the fast-running Germans of a few hours ago. A hand reached toward me; I took it. "Voda! Voo-dd-aa!" I scooped up snow and spread it over his face. He licked his lips like an animal. He let go of his hold on me. Slowly, with great effort, he turned over his hulk. His coat fell open; his arms spread out. His bleeding intestines spilled out onto the snow in a red, violent pile.[2]

In the shelter of the Gröbel Pension, Kati asked, "How did it go?" I told her, "I have been to Russia." Then I passed out.

Another time, following an air raid and driven by hunger, Kati and I went foraging in the ruins of a bombed-out building. It was badly hit; the dust had not yet settled among its ruins. The building was sliced down the middle, one half still standing. The gash allowed a view of the inside of an apartment and the life that had been led there. Between the stones, the leg of a grand piano extended into the air, a comic dancer leaving the stage. The piano leg provided a hanger for a woman's pink nightgown, fluttering in the breeze.

We made our way up an incline of the ruins and found ourselves in a stairwell. After one floor, then another, we stood before an apartment door half ajar. Entering, we were in a hallway, complete with mirror, coatrack, and hatstand. We looked for a pantry, usually off the entrance halls of such apartments. Suddenly, we heard voices. Men were talking. The language was unmistakable. By the time I whispered to her to let us leave, it was too late. A German soldier stood in the doorway, and another soon appeared, motioning for us to join them. "Schöne ungarische Mädchen, kommen sie herein" (Pretty Hungarian girls, come in).

As was usual in such a situation, I had to do the talking. They were eating! We were offered sausage and wine. Polite conversation ensued about how they found the food. There were four boys, hardly older than ourselves. Three talked; one sat in the corner, food in hand, head hanging onto his chest in a pose of immobile despair. I inquired if he was ill, and the others explained that he was not sick: "Er hat Heimweh" (He is homesick). Kati wanted me to talk to the homesick one, and I went to sit next to him on the floor. Out of a worn-out wallet came the picture of a girl in a dirndl, a kind of peasant dress, smiling into the lens. Tearfully he described the girl, her sweetness, beauty, fidelity, and grace, and he began to sob, his shoulders shaking. When he reached the apex of his grief, he doubled up and let his head rest on my lap. I patted his back as one would console a child, "There, there, there," until his sobbing abated and I could disengage myself. After more polite conversation, we thanked them, descended the stairs, and ran as fast as we could into the shelter of the Gröbel Pension.

Gargantuan explosions left the dead strewn over the streets, where their bodies lay uncollected, for us to step over. Some were covered with newspapers held down by stones, lending the dead some measure of privacy. Others were thrown into a heap inside the cavernous spaces of bombed-out storefronts. We made our way through this grotesque cemetery with the firm conviction that this was "them" and could never be "us."

Shortly after New Year's, an older man came to see us in the shelter. He told us that he and his crippled wife had escaped from a train, a cattle car filled with older Jews. They managed to squeeze through a crevice in the door, threw themselves off the train, spent the night in a ditch, and sneaked back into the city. His wife was injured. She needed a doctor, but without false IDs he dared not take her anywhere. He found food in his old apartment, miraculously unharmed by bombs. He wanted false papers for himself and his wife and offered us the food in return. No, he would not need anyone to take the papers to him; he would be back the next day. Kati made promises, and brimming with gratitude, he left.

The following morning there was an unusually long all clear. Kati went out for some air and left the papers for the old man and his wife with Johnny and me. We were sitting on our mattresses talking, when the old man appeared. He took the papers from us, thanked us, and gave us a packet. But, suddenly he was back. This time, not alone. He was accompanied by two Arrow Cross (Nyilas) Party guards. He pointed at us and said, "These are the ones."

A short street leads from the Parliament to the wide avenue named after Hungary's first Christian king, Saint Steven. This avenue, Szt. István körút, begins on the Pest side of a bridge that connects both sides of the city to St. Margaret Island. At the beginning of the avenue, facing the island, on the shores of the Danube, stands a building that served as one of the headquarters of the Nyilas Party. Along with a small group of Jews who were standing, flanked by guards, outside the Gröbel Pension. This was the building into which the guards led Johnny and me. Pushed and shoved through the snow, too terrified to look at each other, we obeyed orders and ended sitting on a long bench, inside the courtyard of the building. Guards rushed past us, talking, laughing, heel clicking to superiors, slapping each other on the back. One or two at a time, the Jews in our group were called or dragged or pulled off the bench and disappeared behind doors. Finally, it was our turn, and obediently we followed one guard, shiny black boots, black pants, into a large room with nothing but an antique desk in it. Here we were to be interrogated.

We had talked often about what we would do if we were arrested. Long ago, we had decided that we must stick to our story, that we were not Jews; that we were, as our false papers indicated, the children of a Hungarian general, fighting now on the German side, and that we had come into the city to flee the incoming Russian forces. To our interrogator we also maintained that we did not know Kati but that some woman had left an envelope with us to give to a man who would come for it. In short, we maintained that arresting us was a mistake. According to Kati, the name our papers bore was indeed that of a real Hungarian general. It ended with the traditional "y" as in Andrássy or Eszterházy. Such names often indicate where the bearer comes from and show that the family is gentile and that its members are, if not of the aristocracy, then certainly of the landowner class. Our false name was Kennedy, which, however, was not meant to indicate any connection at all with the future president of the United States.

I do not recall many details about this interrogation except that it was conducted in a reasonably civil way, including none of the atrocities or torments we heard about. Johnny's blond, freckled, and blue-eyed appearance lent the story some credibility, and perhaps my appearance of those days did not contradict it either. But, at some point additional proof was required. Unceremoniously, they requested that Johnny drop his pants. Complying without fuss, he showed them his penis as one who thinks it only reasonable that he should be asked to do this. His uncircumcised state was duly noted. In the end, one Nyilas guard informed us that our story, our relationship to the general, would have to be verified and that this might take some days. In the meantime, we must remain in the headquarters. And so, they escorted us into the basement of the building, and a jail door clanged shut behind us.

Inside it was dark, and it took a while to see that we were not alone. There were five or six others, sitting on the floor or on a narrow bench underneath a window that, however, did not open onto anything more than the opposite wall of a light well. Almost as soon as we were settled on the bench, the door sprang open, and several people were dragged out. We never saw them again. We remained with an older couple and a young man. The older gentleman had sustained a head wound, his wife was cradling his head in her lap, stroking his hair, whispering to him, while he uttered an occasional moan. Later that evening they were also taken away, never to return.

As usual, the night was terribly cold, and time dragged on while air raids came in waves of thunder. Explosions shook the building more than once. The young man told us that he was a violinist, that he was arrested fleeing a labor camp, and that he did not expect that any of us would be left alive by the Nyilas guards. Hands sunk into his raincoat, he paced slowly, up and down the narrow cell, softly whistling the same tune, over and over again. The ruling melody of the Mendelssohn Violin Concerto in E-minor!

By dawn, they came for him.[3]

That night, left alone in our jail, Johnny and I began to say farewell to each other. I had fallen asleep when another explosion sent a load of shrapnel though the light well, into the cell. Johnny gently removed a small one that lodged in the skin, on my forehead, and put it into my pocket. When the door creaked open at daybreak, we hugged each other and kissed, but only I was led out. I was taken to a room filled with washtubs and soiled shirts and was made to soap the linens and rinse them. Once in a while a woman entered, wearing the same uniform as the Nyilas guards, and directed my efforts. Some hours later, she appeared with a plate of food. It was cooked food that I had not eaten for some time. I ate ravenously. In the evening, I was led back to our cell, where we survived another night. We reasoned that they must be checking on the whereabouts of the general, our "father." We also thought that they kept us alive out of sufficient uncertainty about our story, due largely to Johnny's appearance. How long this uncertainty would last, we could not tell. We were, in fact, quite prepared to be found out. While we did not know of the method that might be used, or the place of our impending demise, our spirits flagged as each hour passed. By the second morning, our hope of surviving was at a very low ebb. So, when we heard footsteps approaching, we again hugged and kissed and said farewell.

The door swung open. And there he stood. An officer of the Russian Army. It must have been January 17, 1945.

Johnny, Kati, and I were three of the small number of Hungarian

Jews who survived the Holocaust. According to Braham (1981), over half a million of an original Jewish population of 762,007 perished in labor camps and crematoria.

Soon after we recovered from our arrest, it became apparent that we had been living with a fantasy. We believed that once the city was liberated, life would quickly return to normal. Collapsed bridges would rise from the water, the walls of buildings would stand again, restaurants would reopen, water mains would be instantly repaired. Right away, we would have heat and hot water. Above all, our lives would no longer be in danger. Not so.

Occupying Russian troops regarded all Hungarians as enemies. While some of the officers understood the situations of Jews who had been in hiding, common soldiers did not make any distinction between Jews and others. Also, they had been in the worst kind of combat during the long siege of the city and were themselves war weary, tired, and hungry. Their wounded had scant care, and their dead were many. Most of them were illiterate and were unfamiliar with indoor plumbing and other accoutrements of life in a cosmopolitan city. For all these reasons, danger to life, looting, raping, robbing continued, and we had to learn fast how to protect ourselves anew.

The item that served as the chief source of fascination for Russian soldiers was any kind of watch, be that a wristwatch, an alarm clock, a grandfather clock, or a cuckoo clock, it did not matter. It was not unusual to see a Russian soldier, man or woman, whose machine gun was threaded to the hilt with clocks and watches of all sizes. As one of these timepieces would go off and sound a loud alarm, the soldier would stop, remove it from the others, and hold it to an ear, smiling with delight, as a child might upon hearing the sound of the sea inside a shell. Residents risked their lives if a soldier commanded that a watch be handed over and discovered any kind of hesitation. Those foolish enough to hide a wristwatch by carrying it on their ankle soon found themselves in one of the many mass graves that had to be dug by other residents. Thus it was that in 1945 I began to learn yet another language. At the point of a machine gun: "Davay chassy!" (Give me your watch!). Another war was just beginning.

The mothers of both Johnny and Kati survived the siege, but her father had died. My grandparents and Uncle Bársony survived in the ghetto, even my griffon dog made it through the bombings. But, while Kati wanted to return to her grieving mother, neither Johnny nor I was ready to take up residence in yet another air-raid shelter. Even in buildings that were reasonably unharmed, windows were broken. Because of the bitter cold, life had to continue in one bomb shelter or another. When requiring work with rubble clearing, Russian soldiers would enter a shelter, point their machine guns at the residents, and recruit forced labor. Their women soldiers were as brutal as the men; often one could not tell the difference anyhow, for Russian women soldiers were large, loud, and overbearing. Men and women huddling in shelters were equally afraid of them.

And so it happened that we heard that certain buildings, more intact than others, had been declared public shelters. One of these was the Tungsram lightbulb factory, the same place where my disastrous encounter with the Jews had taken place. A pass still in my possession admits me to live in the Tungsram buildings in February 1945.

I was unwilling to return to the gymnasium, where I had finished only the first two of eight years. Instead, I reentered the ballet school, which later expanded to a film and theater school, and danced as much as I could to make up for lost time. I was also unwilling to resume life in the household of Grandmother Hermione and her husband. While I spent a good bit of time there, I lived with Grandfather Leopold and his wife, Serena, next to the Basilica, across the street from the apartment and consulting rooms of Uncle Bársony. He began to act as my guardian and periodically wished to hear how I was spending my time. Dr. Bársony's art collection, consisting of canvasses by Rippl-Rónai and Renoir, was declared a property of the state, and numbers were affixed to each painting. Their existence was recorded so he could not sell them. But the paintings were left in their place (where else to put them?), and so one could enjoy them even though they were no longer his.

During the first few months after the war, the Hungarian currency, the Pengö, lost value by the day. At first, what had cost one Pengö cost ten, then a hundred, then a thousand, and before the life of the Pengö ended, we carried it in large paper bags and did not even bother to count it, just paid fistfuls for whatever could be bought. Then, one morning the entire country awoke to the news that the Pengö no longer existed. No matter how much of it one had, or had saved or earned, it mattered not. It simply did not exist anymore. The announcements also stated that there would be a short time before new currency, the Forint, would be available. In spite of all threats of punishment by the communist government, black-marketeering proliferated.

There followed a time of bartering that took up most of one's waking hours. A person would ring one's doorbell and say he or she had two chickens to trade for a pair of boots of a certain size. One wanted to have the chickens but did not have such boots. Then one thought hard, and if one knew someone who did have boots like the ones requested, one went along with the chicken person to find the third party with the boots. In this way, food procuring became a highly personal business and took up immense amounts of time. The same procedure was followed for almost anything one wished to get. Thus, it was no surprise that black-marketeering grew to such proportion. All this added fuel to a malaise about the future that had never abated since the war ended, it only changed focus.

For the two years I remained in Budapest, life failed to return to normal. German soldiers, fleeing westward, found sacks of flour in mills. Not having time to set fires, they turned rat poison into the flour. My grandmother bought flour on the black market and baked bread. The flour contained arsenic. Her husband died instantly. She remained paralyzed for the rest of her life. I too suffered a temporary paralysis.

Russian rule did not result in a lessening of anti-Semitism. My brother Gyuri was back in Budapest, a central member of the Rajk circle. Mistrusted by old-guard members of the party for their "Western influence," the entire cabinet was soon to be arrested.[4] Problems of growing up were laced with those of survival because "a child is nothing by himself." I had become a youngster who has to "bring himself up without a father . . . learn . . . to grow alone, in fortitude, in strength . . . to be born . . . in relation to others . . . without roots and without faith" (Camus 1995, 195).

As the year turned to 1947, I presented myself at the American Legation and introduced myself as the daughter of Philip Engel. I was received with great kindness and courtesy. It was explained that I had two citizenships. In the ordinary course of events, minors were not asked to choose between them. However, the Iron Curtain was coming down. The State Department could not long be responsible for my safety. Should I elect to retain my U.S. citizenship, I would be taken to the United States under a State Department program for repatriation, to be, in fact, "repatriated" into a country in which I had never been and whose language I did not speak. I would soon leave Hungary and, with State Department guidance extended to such minors, be helped to make a new life in the United States.

It did not take long to make up my mind. Grandfather Leopold's wife moaned, "Go so far without a chaperone!" Her husband was always prone to attribute opinions to the dead: "Your poor parents are turning

over in their graves." Two weeks after my first visit to the American Legation, I was provided with a U.S. passport, several hundred dollars in cash,
tickets, reservations, and a date to board the Arlberg Express to Paris and
another train to LeHavre, there to board the *Marine Falcon,* a converted
Liberty ship, which would take me to New York.

The Lamp by the Golden Door

Life in the United States began in Nashville, Tennessee, under the supervision of distantly related relatives. In spite of not having completed high
school, I was admitted to Peabody College of Vanderbilt University.

The English language and local customs turned out to be a minefield
of difficulties. Lexical problems were numerous. I struggled with
"weather," "wether," "whither," "whether," and "wither." In history class,
instead of "slavery" one had to say, "involuntary servitude." In place of
"Civil War," it was "the War between the States." It was implied that this
regrettable incident would have seen speedy resolution had it not been
for a few minor episodes that put Southern armies at a disadvantage. I
made fruitless searches in my dictionary when addressed as "honey
child." Changes in language, climate, food, customs all came at once. My
mistakes became the source of amusement. I insisted on taking my passport when "crossing the border" into the neighboring state of North
Carolina. Erroneously generalizing from this gaffe, I failed to take it with
me to Canada. Not being able to give proof of citizenship, I was detained
at reentry into the United States. Friends arranged a blind date, then
found me reading a book on how to conduct oneself with the blind: is
one allowed to pet his seeing-eye dog? I found refuge from the problems
of culture change in departments of French, German, Italian, and Russian literature.

In the pre–Martin Luther King South, a white person did not attend
movie showings at Fisk University, an African American college. Nor was
one expected to treat African American people with courtesy and sit
next to them in the back of the bus. Resistance reared its head at these
injustices, and I was more than once reprimanded by teachers, bus drivers, and people whom, up to then, I had considered friends. In view of
my brother's position in Hungary, my opinion about the ongoing
McCarthy hearings had to remain private.

As an undergraduate, I was designated to represent Vanderbilt University in the Collegiate Delegation to the United Nations. I took my
work in New York deeply seriously and returned having decided to

become a translator. I imagined that in that profession I would help prevent another war. "I dreamed of a world / without the sick and the fat, / without dollars, / francs, / pesetas, / where there are no frontiers / no governments, / rockets and stinking newspapers. / I dreamed of a world where everything is freshly created" (Yevtushenko 1966). I applied to graduate school to perfect my knowledge of languages.

My Phi Beta Kappa key did not open the door to graduate school; I was denied admission. Vanderbilt University had a quota of one for a Jewish woman in the humanities. That place had already been taken. The decision was relayed to me by Dean Meredith Crawford, who later became one of the officers of the American Psychological Association. Becoming a graduate student in psychology was a joint consequence of the numerus clausus and the availability of an assistantship to the late Nicholas Hobbs. One of my publications was determined by early interest in censorship and not-so-unconscious anger at the university. It chronicled the discharge of a Vanderbilt professor for refusing to recant his evolutionary views (Engel 1956). Other choices were also conflict dominated.

I had been troubled by my tendency to hoard food. For a long time, I could not resist buying items that had been scarce during the war, tea, soap, and cigarettes. My first experiment was the investigation of the effect of early food deprivation on hoarding behavior in rats.

In the last year of graduate school, ten years after the war, I was still not able to deal with any person in uniform. I harbored deep ambivalence about the Allies' destruction of Budapest. I accepted a part-time job at Sewart Air Force Base. I was compelled to take another look at those who destroyed my city. The mission of this base was to keep up pilots' flying time. It did not matter where they flew. Bermuda. Need any perfume? South America. Need any coffee? Flying in and out of exotic places was the order of the days and weeks, with no end in sight.

A peacetime base, it brought out the worst in many pilots, because between flights there was little to do except sit in the Officers' Club and drink. I was often called upon to "talk to" one pilot or another and try to persuade him to mend his ways. I obtained a view of life from the other side. Complaints about marital problems, worries over the behavior of children, debts, uncertainty about the future, they were all there, on that other side that I never knew. I had thought American bombardiers to be beyond human concerns, a kind of superhuman species who could not be destroyed or even hurt by troubles that beset the rest of humanity. The experience at Sewart Air Force Base neutralized all anger and conflict about soldiers, uniforms, and bombardiers.

My early publications bear the imprint of profound concern with developmental discontinuities and normal and pathological development in adolescents (Engel 1955, 1958a, 1958b, 1960c, 1963). But before I could go on with confidence, I felt the need for additional training and became a postdoctoral fellow at the Menninger Foundation, Topeka, Kansas. Here I was fortunate to join Gardner Murphy's research team.

The reader will note an absence of reference to my personal life, friendship, attachment, and marriage. A conventional early childhood was precipitously changed to an unconventional one. It is largely because of this that I found society's restraints and the ready-made narrative of the "marriage plot" unworkable and chose the "quest plot" instead. My college years provided a much needed moratorium from casting about among identities, with a "profound sense of vocation, with no idea of what that vocation is" (Heilbrun 1988, 50–53).

Conflict and Conviviality

Aspects of the past take up residence in the self and await an occasion for expression. The contents of these events may even reside in consciousness, their peremptoriness does not. They cannot be let go because they lack resolution. Tension is experienced because these events once fit a self that no longer exists, they belong to a world left behind in time and place. Ideally, resolution would be gradual, but the adolescent personality changes and grows rapidly. The stream of new life is swift. Intrapsychic or external acts have to put tensions at rest, lest they hobble attainment in the new world.

Contexts of adolescence and young adulthood may provide opportunities to create syntheses between the still active past that no longer fits the self and features of ongoing developmental issues. To the extent that contexts offer the opportunity of creating congruence, the past, while it is never really over, may be brought into resolution with the present and allowed to fade into the background of preoccupations.

When features of present contexts offer the possibility of balance between aspects of the past and the givens of the new, the occasion is seized and celebrated by emotional involvement of considerable magnitude. There is, in Kubie's terms (1958), a "swift condensation" of communicable ideas from the past with those generated by the present. Such are the "passionate aspects of intellectual commitment . . . [These enter into] . . . every act of knowing . . . the contribution of the person is . . . no mere imperfection, but a necessary component of all knowledge . . .

[Here we have] . . . the complete participation of the person, . . . self-abandonment" (Polányi 1958, 88–93).

It is possible to arrange acts of attainment along a conflict-to-context-dominated continuum, which in the narrative that follows corresponds to developmental time. Conflict-dominated for a long time, in Topeka, my professional life began to admit the role of context, in the form of conviviality. In many ways, the Menninger Foundation was a little Europe in the middle of Kansas. In classes with Rudolf Ekstein, research meetings with Gardner Murphy, lectures with David Rapaport, the cultural distance dwindled to none. I was able to focus on professional problems suggested in these meetings and to concentrate on issues in psychotherapy with disturbed adolescents (Engel 1960b), as well as on those in experimental psychology (Engel 1960a), on problems outside of my own concerns. Research supervision by Helen Sargent turned out to be an unforgettable experience, her influence followed me for many years in the form of internalized values and points of view (Engel 1958, 1961a, 1961b, 1963, 1966b, 1966c). These associations continued as I left for my first position, at the Psychiatric and Psychosomatic Institute of the Michael Reese Hospital, in Chicago, Illinois, as supervisor in the postdoctoral clinical psychology training program. But the full meaning and importance of conviviality did not become clear until my assistant professorship at Harvard University. Here, I became passionately involved with research and public service, an absorption not experienced until then.

Why is one problem chosen over another? For Polányi, there is an ineffability to the wellsprings of knowledge. Research problems are not chosen on rational bases. Added to personal interests of the researcher, the interpersonal context, "diffuse emotional conviviality," is of determining importance. Much knowledge is tacit, composed of understandings one knows to be correct yet that one cannot specify. The knowledge of violin makers, teachers, researchers, and wine tasters is of this kind. Large gaps exist between what one knows and that which one can articulate. These gaps create tensions. Which of these one attempts to resolve is determined by the context provided by others whose store of inarticulate knowledge is sufficiently similar to one's own to permit the use of imprecise terms, who "under similar circumstances . . . have derived from these experiences the same relation between . . . symbols and the recurrent features which they represent" (Polányi 1958, 204). In Kubie's terms, each of us possesses a "central core of meaning," the implications of which, their nuances of thought and feeling, are represented by "an intermediate form of mentation," not rational but "figurative and alle-

gorical . . . it is called preconscious . . . [Whence arise] . . . special competence and knowledge to express . . . [what is] . . . conflict laden"
(Kubie 1958, 30–31).

And so it happened that, while on vacation from Harvard, I was traveling in North Africa. In Fez, Meknes, and Marakesh, my group was
accosted by small children. They were offering to change currencies, be
tour guides, show landmarks, introduce male members to their sisters,
rent a taxi, find a better hotel. The children spoke in French, Arabic, or
English, depending on what language might work. They were persistent,
yet polite. We saw them in restaurants, lobbies, and markets and in
leather tanneries, where their job was to stand in tubs of paint and keep
animal skins from coming to the surface. There were blue, green, yellow,
red children. Buoyant, busy, accommodating, swift, they were surviving
in a multilingual adult world. They seemed to belong to no one.

Not long after meeting the street children of Morocco, I found
myself in San Miguel de Allende, near Mexico City, at the Escuela
Equestre, a school for riders, run by members of the Mexican cavalry.
There they were again. The children were sitting patiently next to their
shoeshine boxes, waiting for riders to dismount, so they could offer to
shine their boots. Once I was back in Cambridge, there they were again,
on Harvard Square. The street children, working. Not having noticed
them before, I was drawn to them daily and finally passed out parent permission slips ("Lady, she'll sign anything"). The "job" for which I
recruited them was talking to a tape recorder.

Indeed, I *was* one of these children. I was the child who sat by a
shoeshine box, one eye peeled for police. I was the one who walked into
a grocery store and found the manager: "Mister, can I bring in the shopping carts?" I was the child helping construction workers or filling station
attendants, or I was the other one helping a special-delivery letter carrier
distribute mail. I was one of these children, throwing newspapers onto
driveways while others were still asleep, pressing my nose against the windowpane of normal life inside. I too had been a stranger, looking in.

The research project, "Saturday's Children," was developed under
the aegis of the Center for Research in Careers, created by Anne Roe. In
the beginning, her immediate comprehension of half-formed ideas was
invaluable in validating my enthusiasm. She understood why it might be
important to understand these children. Why did they work? How did
they spend their time? I wanted to describe their self-invented games,
played on the subway system, with messages hidden under bricks; their
relationships to their families; and how they achieved in school. The sup-

port of Frank Keppel, Anne Roe, Israel Scheffler, and Beatrice Whiting was responsible for the fact that the idea of this project did not go the way of many unrealized ones. The support was sustaining at times of doubt, and thanks to this, the project eventually encompassed the greater Boston area, including children from all social classes.

We developed a conceptualization of work styles in children whose interviews showed that earning money was not the only motivation for children to work. The inner need to move away from the world of mothers and women teachers, to have the freedom to try one's ability to survive, and to identify with men who worked, motivated the sons of the rich as well as poor boys to seek work (Engel 1967a, 1967b, 1968, 1971, 1972).

During a semester's leave from Harvard University, I settled into the Library of Congress, turned my attention to how one might transmit the excitement of research to students (Engel 1966a, 1966b), and began work on a book (Engel 1970). Later, I shuttled back and forth between Cambridge and Washington as consultant to the United States Department of Labor concerning child labor. I was invited to become a member of the Joint Commission for Health and Mental Health of Children and later became chairperson of Task Force II, conducting studies of school-age youngsters.

The commission was created in the wake of the assassination of President Kennedy, as a reaction to the disastrous mental health history of the assassin, Lee Harvey Oswald, described in the *Warren Report*. How many such disturbed children are there, what might the country do about them, how much would it cost? I worked closely with colleagues on our report to Congress (Engel 1970a, 1973, 1975).

Upon the departure of Frank Keppel to Washington as U.S. commissioner of education, President Nathan M. Pusey began to act in his place. I was still learning from Anne Roe how to stay viable in a chauvinistic university. We succeeded in lifting the ban on women using the main entrance to the Faculty Club, but we sat numb in a faculty meeting when the president remarked that should the war in Vietnam last much longer, all we will have on the campus will be "the blind, the lame, and the female." I was still not allowed into one of Harvard's libraries, the bequest of which forbade the presence of women in it. At that time, attainment notwithstanding, women were not given tenure. But the years in Cambridge remain deeply meaningful in the experience of conviviality and its meaning for accomplishment.

As time went on, I continued work concerning ever younger children: a longitudinal study of firstborn African American babies (Engel

1975a), research into the effect of war on children (Engel 1984), an investigation of the effect of drug addiction in pregnant women on their newborns at forty-eight hours of life (Engel et al. 1990).

All the while, the identity of students at the City College of the City University of New York was changing. I had taught white, American-born students most of my life, but now my classes slowly began to be filled with newcomers to the United States. By the early 1990s, the college accommodated students from over eighty countries. They constituted more than half the incoming class. I found personal contacts with these young people moving but teaching them difficult, due largely to their pervasive problem with the English language. Formalizing this interest, I left work with children and began yearly interviews with a small group of students from Africa, Asia, Europe, and South America concerning problematic aspects of culture change and learning the English language (Engel 1996a, 1996b).

I found that research in language learning has stayed mainly on the level of the problems of beginners, to the neglect of advanced fluency and the use of figurative language. Conviviality became more important as I wandered into an area new to me and resulted in work on the understanding of American idioms (Engel and Glucksberg 2000). Some of our results point to the special culture change and language learning difficulties of young people from China.

At the time of this writing I am spending time with immigrants and refugees from China and Hong Kong and analyzing interview and language data. Individual differences are large and are mostly hidden under New Yorkers' perception of the Chinese inhabitants, which accords them no more individuality than sparrows in Central Park. Is their cultural isolation partly a result of the language barrier, or is it the other way around?

I read about Confucius: "Not to know speech is not to know a person" (Schwarcz 1998, 52). What is the history of those who have achieved fluency in English? What will happen to others who cannot use the telephone, whose speech is difficult to understand? I am in my office with a young man from Beijing. His parents, professionals, were banished by the Cultural Revolution and sent to work on a farm. He was returned to the city and raised by others. Many years later he was reunited with his mother and father in a South American country. From there, family reunification provisions allowed them to rejoin relatives in New York. Now he is struggling with his new language. It is difficult for him to read words like *ruin* and expressions like *thick and thin*. Compliantly answering personal questions is part of his efforts at culture change. A bond is developing between us. I read that the student from Beijing and I have much in common. We are both trying "to piece together fragments of broken time . . . [and share] . . . the nightmares that are the common inheritance of Chinese and Jews in the twentieth century" (Schwarcz 1998, 11, 29). I finish the interview and thank the student from Beijing in halting Chinese.

NOTES

1. The heroic Swede Raoul Wallenberg claimed protected status for Jews who, he maintained, had foreign relatives who were preparing to sponsor them to resettle elsewhere. For a brief while, these Jews were housed in "protected houses," which became the nucleus of an "international ghetto," containing 15,000 Jews, under the protection of Portugal, Spain, Sweden, Switzerland, and the Vatican. (Thus the Portuguese stamp on my pass.) In one month's time, the protected houses were no longer in existence, their residents deported or killed. But while the protection still lasted, 7,800 Jews were crowded into 72 buildings, often 50–60 persons in a two-room apartment (Braham 1981).

2. We now know that by November 1944 Soviet armored columns stood eight miles south of Budapest and that the German and Hungarian armies began to withdraw in panic. Soon the city was almost completely surrounded by Russians. Allied bombings escalated to the point where there was almost nothing left to bomb. House-to-house and hand-to-hand combat ensued into which the Russian command sent its most expendable soldiers. They liberated the Pest side of Budapest on January 17th and 18th, but the liberation of Hungary was several months away and was not accomplished until April 4, 1945, a month before the end of World War II in Europe, on May 9, 1945.

3. To the right of this building a short path leads to the shore of the Danube. A ceramic plaque, sunk into the sidewalk, commemorates the place where executions took place.

4. No account of the events between January 1945 and my departure to the United States, in April 1947, would be complete without a description of my brother, Gyuri, who returned to Hungary with his wife, Panni, and two infant sons, Balázs and Ádám. During the war, Gyuri and his wife left Paris and the dangerous northern part of France, which was loyal to the fascist Petain. They settled in the south of France under an assumed name, as a gentile family. When their sons were born, they had them baptized. Around Grenoble, both Gyuri and his wife became members of Franc Tireurs et Partisans, a left-wing resistance group, loyal to de Gaulle. A paper signed by Charles Tillon shows that Gyuri's rank was lieutenant and that Panni was a contact agent in the French Resistance. Once, when I asked her about her wartime activities, she recalled a time when she was to deliver explosives to a certain spot. The explosives were to blow up a bridge. She put them into a baby carriage and put one baby on top of them. She rea-

soned that someone might be suspicious about the contents of a baby carriage but not if an infant was also in it. In this way, she delivered the explosives to where they were expected.

Gyuri's return to Budapest brought several surprises. He had changed his name to Angyal, the Hungarian equivalent of Engel. He was a high-ranking member of the Communist Party, a member of the inner circle around László Rajk, the ill-fated minister of the interior. It was my impression that this first communist government of Hungary consisted mainly of "1930 communists," like my brother. Gyuri was put in charge of all of Hungary's film industry, and, according to his wife's report, his conflict with the then premier Mátyás Rákosi began almost right away. Gyuri had a sharp sense of humor. (As a young man, he had a rowboat on the Danube in which, I am told, he did much of his courting. The name of the rowboat was *Polygamy*.) He was given to making loud and more than slightly insulting remarks about Rákosi. This was a short, fat man, totally bald. Gyuri had remarked about him, "How can he expect to revitalize Hungary's agriculture when he cannot even grow hair on his head?"

I do not know how my brother died. What I do know was found out in small bits. Sometimes, years intervened between gaining items of new information. Facts emerged from a former member of the Hungarian secret police; then a book was published about the unforgettably evil chapter in Hungary's history in which communist testified against communist, during the course of which torture of the most inhumane kind was used by comrade against comrade to extract and finally obtain confession upon confession of treasonous activities against the state. These led to death by execution or suicide of the defendants. The people whose names fill these darkest times in postwar history, those who perished at the hands of their comrades, were ousted from their party; their families were dishonored, shunned, and driven into poverty. But in 1956, these same people's names were reinstated into the Communist Party; their remains were reburied in a ceremony in which their caskets were carried out of disgrace into places of honor by the very people who once testified against them.

After I left Budapest, I never saw my brother again. In 1949, at the age of thirty-eight, he was arrested by a member of the secret police and was not heard from again. At the same time, arrested were Lászlo Rajk, András Szalai, Tibor Szönyi, Otto Horváth, Dezsö Németh, András Villányi, György Pálffy, and many others, most of whom were executed in the fall of that year, others of whom committed suicide, still others of whom survived several years of incarceration. At least one wrote a book about the infamous Rajk trial, under the title *Volunteers for the Gallows*. It first appeared in Brussels in 1963 and later in several other languages and countries. Béla Szász, the author of the book, served as press secretary to the newly formed communist government after the war. He was one of the defendants in the Rajk trial and later lived in England, where I found him after reading his book. Much of what I know comes from correspondence with Mr. Szász.

More recently, I found a book in a Budapest bookstore, by István Soltész, with the title *Rajk Dosszié* (The Rajk files), published in 1989 by Lang Publishers in Hungary. The latter volume gives verbatim transcripts of the interrogations and of the trial, as well as the confessions signed by Rajk and his men. Gyuri's name appears in the latter volume but not in the former, and it was this lack that caused me to seek out Béla Szász. His letter to me in 1981 states that he knew Gyuri in Paris and later as one of the directors of the Hungarian film industry. He was not included in *Volunteers for the Gallows* for the simple reason that he was not tried. He died in a cell before he could be brought to trial: "I am sorry I can't tell you more about Gyuri and I doubt if anyone could—unless he had been in the same cell with him during the interrogation by the secret police" (Béla Szász, personal communication, November 11).

The Rajk trial actually consisted of several "side trials," but the main one took place in September 1949. According to Szász's book, it had three major objectives. It was, in part, a crusade against Yugoslav (Titoist) "heretics." Also, there was strong motivation to embarrass the so-called Western communists, those who returned to Hungary after the war and whose views differed from those of the "old guard" party members. Last, the surrounding countries as well as the West had to be shown that Russian supremacy would prevail in Hungary. Béla Szász himself fell into the "Western" communists' group, having spent ten years in Paris and having, as he was told by one of his interrogators, brought into Hungary foreign, dangerous, and destructive ideas and values.

Such party members were seen as saboteurs: the party had to destroy them, lest they spread an epidemic. Szász was told by his jailers that people like him and Rajk and all the others arrested were just as harmful to the party as if they had been blowing up bridges. Szász never confessed to any treasonous activity. He was tortured for five months, and six years passed before he was released. Rajk confessed to everything they accused him of and thus took with him several of his associates. It is indeed one of the bitterest legacies of this war, not knowing, not being able to find out facts that have a burning importance, that would be central to one's understanding of the fate of one's family.

REFERENCES

Battapaglia, Sergeant. Personal communication, Reference Library, West Point Military Academy Library.
Braham, R. L. 1981. *The politics of genocide: The Holocaust in Hungary.* New York: Columbia University Press.
Camus, A. 1995. *The first man.* New York: Vintage Press.
Engel, M. 1955. The development of a scale to be used in play therapy research. *Transactions of the Kansas Academic Society* 58:561–65.
———. 1956. A chapter in the history of academic freedom. *History of Education Journal* 7:157–64.
———. 1958a. The development and applications of the Children's Insight Test. *Journal of Projective Techniques* 22:13–25.
———. 1958b. The stability of the self-concept in adolescence. *Journal of Abnormal and Social Psychology* 58:211–15. Reprinted in J. Seidman, ed., *The Adolescent* (New York: Holt, Reinhart, and Winston, 1960); M. Gold and E. Douvan, eds., *Adolescent Development* (1969); J. P. Hill and J. Sheldon, eds., *Readings in*

adolescent development and behavior (Englewood Cliffs, NJ: Prentice Hall, 1971).

———. 1960a. Shifting levels of communication in the treatment of adolescent character disorder. *American Medical Association Archives of General Psychiatry* 2:94–99.

———. 1960b. Some parameters of the psychological evaluation of children. *American Medical Association Archives of General Psychiatry* 2:593–605.

———. 1960c. With Charles M. Solley. Perceptual autism in children: The effects of reward, punishment, and neutral conditions upon perceptual learning. *Journal of Genetic Psychology* 97:77–91.

———. 1961a. With Sidney J. Blatt and Lee Mirmow. When inquiry fails. *Journal of Projective Techniques* 25:32–37.

———. 1961b. With William Rechenberg. Studies in the reliability of the Children's Insight Test. *Journal of Projective Techniques* 25:158–63.

———. 1963. On the psychological testing of borderline children. *American Medical Association Archives of General Psychiatry* 8:426–34.

———. 1966a. The style of the quest—Observations on the education of researchers. In *Educational Therapy,* edited by J. Hellmuth. Seattle, WA: Special Child Publications.

———. 1966b. Thesis-antithesis—Reflections on the education of researchers. *American Psychologist* 21:781–87.

———. 1967a. Children who work. *American Medical Association Archives of General Psychiatry* 17:291–97.

———. 1967b. With Gerald Marsden and Sylvia Woodaman. Children who work and the concept of work style. *Psychiatry* 30:392–404.

———. 1968. With Gerald Marsden and Sylvia Woodaman. Orientation to work in children. *American Journal of Orthopsychiatry* 38:137–43. Reprinted in S. Chess and A. Thomas, eds., *Annual progress in child psychiatry and child development* (New York: Brunnel-Mazel, 1972).

———. 1970a. With members of the Joint Commission on Mental Health of Children. *Crisis in child mental health.* New York: Harper.

———. 1970b. *Psychopathology in childhood—Social, diagnostic, therapeutic aspects.* New York: Harcourt.

———. 1971. With Gerald Marsden and Sylvia Woodaman Pollack. Child work and social class. *Psychiatry* 34:140–55.

———. 1972. With Gerald Marsden and Sylvia Woodaman Pollack. Hostile impulse expression and work style in boys. *Journal of Consulting and Clinical Psychology* 38:274–80.

———. 1973. With members of Task Force II of the Joint Commission on Mental Health of Children. *Mental Health: From infancy through adolescence.* New York: Harper.

———. 1975a. With Herbert Nechin and Arthur Arkin. Aspects of mothering: Correlates of cognitive development in the second year of life in black male infants. In *Child personality and psychopathology,* edited by A. Davids, 15–61. New York: Wiley Interscience.

———. 1975b. With Dane Prugh and William Morse. The classification of emotionally disturbed children. In *Issues in the classification of children,* Behavioral

Science Series, edited by N. Hobbs, vol. 1, 261–300. San Francisco: Jossey-Bass.

———. 1982. The children's cadre. *Croton Review* 5:1–15.

———. 1984. Children and war. *Peabody Journal of Education* 61:52–71. Special issue, The Legacy of Nicholas Hobbs: Research on education and human development in the public interest, edited by J. R. Newbrough and P. R. Dokecki.

———. 1993. Personal attributes and acculturation of international students. Symposium on issues in multicultural education. Columbia University, Teachers College Symposium on Diversity in Education.

———. 1996a. Loose cannons, the horse's mouth, and the bottom line: Idioms and culture change. Twenty-sixth International Congress of Psychology, Montreal, Canada.

———. 1996b. Passionate attachments and culture change. Twenty-sixth International Congress of Psychology, Montreal, Canada.

———. 2000. With Sam Glucksberg. Idioms and ethnicity. Manuscript.

———. 1990. M. Engel, K. Kaltenbach, and L. P. Finnegan. Sonographic characteristics of the neonatal cry of infants exposed to drugs *in utero. Early Child Development and Care* 65:13–21.

Heilbrun, C. G. 1988. *Writing a woman's life.* New York: Norton.

Kubie, L. S. 1958. *Neurotic distortions of the creative process.* Lawrence: University of Kansas Press.

Polányi, M. 1958. *Personal knowledge.* Chicago: University of Chicago Press.

Schwarcz, V. 1998. *Bridge across broken time: Chinese and Jewish cultural memory.* New Haven: Yale University Press.

Szász, B. 1971. *Volunteers for the gallows: Anatomy of a show trial.* New York: Norton.

———. 1981. Personal communication, 11 November.

Soltész, I. 1989. *Rajk Dosszié.* Budapest, Hungary: Lang.

Yevtushenko, Y. 1966. I journeyed through Russia. *Bratsk Station and other new poems.* New York: Anchor.

From Shoah to Sinology
A Roundabout Road

René Goldman

Biographical Note

Switching from his initial choice of an academic field, contemporary Chinese history, Professor Goldman earned his M.A. and the Certificate of the East Asian Institute from Columbia University, where he studied on a Ford Foundation Fellowship. He has spent his academic career at the University of British Columbia, except for a 1980 term as visiting scholar at the Truman Institute of the Hebrew University of Jerusalem.

His publications include L'antre aux fantomes des collines de l'Ouest *(with Andre Levy), a collection of Chinese short stories translated into French, as well as a number of papers on current developments in China and on the moral and ethical philosophies of Chinese and Jewish sages.*

Introduction: Arrival in China

The year was 1953, a year highlighted in my memory by three great events, one of which marked a turning point in the history of the world and two a turning point in my personal life. On March 5th of that year

Stalin died: the death of the "immortal supreme genius" and "father of peoples" so completely filled Poland's newspaper columns and radio waves that the death on that same day of the great composer Sergei Prokofiev warranted only the briefest of obituaries.

At the time I was a grade eleven student soon to successfully pass the challenging series of examinations that in Poland crown an adolescent's completion of secondary school with the awarding of the Certificate of Maturity, or *Matura*. As a prize for having obtained a full grade in Polish, which I had undertaken to learn only three years before, the head-mistress of my school recommended me for an elite summer vacation camp for boys born in France of Polish immigrant families. Those luxurious summer camps were one of the propaganda means by which the communist regime of the time sought to influence the "Polonia," that is, Polish populations living outside of Poland.

The most surprising and joyful event, however, was that my application to the Polish ministry of higher education for a scholarship to study in China was approved. The surprise was all the greater because I had scant hope of being accepted: a close friend whose background was similar to mine (a child survivor of the Holocaust, brought up in the same children's home near Paris), who was very active in the communist youth league of her school and whose father was well connected, saw her application to study in the Soviet Union turned down on the grounds that, having lived in Poland only five years, she was not yet sufficiently assimilated. I had only lived in Poland three years, and my participation in the activities of the youth league was so lukewarm that the crude little Bolshevik who was the *Gruppenführer* of my class called me a "Western European liberal." Little could he have guessed that what his mouth uttered in derision rang to my ears like flattery!

And so it happened that one balmy, sunny early December afternoon (the severe winter of North China was long in coming that year), one of those rickety little "Dakotas," which were known as "flying coffins," disgorged the small group of Polish students to which I had been attached on the Nanyuan airfield south of Peking. Had I landed on the moon, I would not have felt more thrilled; stepping on the soil of China closed in my youthful imagination the opening act in a Marco Polo–like voyage of adventure that held the promise of untold marvels waiting to be discovered.

We journeyed from Warsaw in a succession of five-to-six-hour flights separated by intervals of only a couple of hours: first to Moscow, then to Sverdlovsk (Ekaterinburg), Krasnoyarsk, Novosibirsk, and Irkutsk, where we were allowed to rest at last, two nights and a day. Along the way we descended by stages into winter: from rainy late autumn weather in Warsaw to freezing level in Moscow, minus sixteen degrees in Sverdlovsk, and minus thirty-two degrees in Irkutsk the morning of our takeoff from that city's airport. Until then we had flown aboard small "Ilyushin" planes, but from Irkutsk on we flew aboard the already mentioned "Dakota," which was not only smaller but also evidenced rather scary signs of age, such as metal plates of different colors welded together.

This last leg of our trip featured two brief landings in Mongolia: one in Ulan Bator, the capital, the other in Sayin-Shand in the Gobi Desert. That whole trip had been stressful: during landings I felt at times as if my head was about to explode. But in the end it was so exciting. . . . Years later I still vividly remember the gasp of wonderment that seized me when from the airplane window I beheld the Great Wall of China snaking and twisting its majestic silhouette punctuated with turrets at regular intervals up and down barren mountains, from infinite horizon to infinite horizon. And then came the descent over Peking, in those days still girded with rings of monumental walls and gates, resplendent with thousands of tiled roofs gleaming in the sun: it was too fabulous for words.

I consider myself fortunate to have known Peking when it still was a lovely ancient city, as unique in character and culture as Paris, Jerusalem, or Kyoto. Travelers who visit today's "Beijing" behold a monstrous metropolis, hideously defaced by the communist bureaucrats' version of "progress." Rows of gray, soulless concrete barracks have obliterated the quaint winding lanes of yesteryear. These lanes were lined with low-rise houses, which presented to the outside little more than walls and ornate gates, while their windows sensually faced inner courtyards sheltered from evil spirits, and the gazes of passersby, by a spirit wall that stood on the inside of the gate and upon which sometimes carved were dragons or other auspicious creations of the imagination.

But enough of these parenthetical ramblings. On the day of our arrival our group was met at the airport by a welcoming party from Peking University. We were driven to that revered institution, which in the next five years would become my alma mater, across the Outer City. Then, as soon as we passed Da Qianmen, the "Great Front Gate" of the Inner City, I beheld Tiananmen, the imposing Gate of Heavenly Peace, which is the southern entrance to the Forbidden City of the emperors of the Ming and Qing dynasties. Fronting Tiananmen in those days was not the vast concrete desert of today, which is framed by the National People's Congress, the mausoleum of Mao Zedong, and other such Chinese versions of Stalinesque architecture, but a much smaller square lined with trees and red walls: it almost reminded me of the Tuileries gardens in Paris. How many times had I seen pictures of Tiananmen in books and illustrated magazines and dreamt that perhaps some wonderful distant day I would behold it before my very eyes! That oft imagined and dreamt of moment had now, almost unexpectedly, arrived.

Thoughts of the unknown but promising future that seemed to lie ahead of me at this blessed moment of my first day in China mingled in my mind with images of my past life. I was nineteen years old: standing on the threshold of adulthood, I naturally looked to the future. But I was also a child of the Holocaust: that supreme catastrophe of Jewish history carried away my parents and gave my life an entirely different direction than would have been the case had my parents lived. It also carried away, with no trace other than a few photographs found in a tattered old handbag of my mother, the innumerable aunts, uncles, and cousins in Poland, whom I never got to know, except for one paternal uncle who survived Auschwitz, emigrated to Canada, and founded a new family in Toronto. Thus, notwithstanding my youth, I already evidenced a propensity to tarry in thought in the past and dwell on images of the happiness that might have been mine, had my parents not perished.

Childhood and Adolescence

I was born in Luxembourg, capital of the Grand Duchy of Luxembourg. Among the earliest childhood images stored in my memory is one of a Sunday morning of 1940, when my father and I, out for our customary weekly stroll about town, happened upon the railway station at the very moment when German soldiers marched out of it to occupy the small country. Soon after that day, my parents made the mistake of moving to Brussels, instead of following Rabbi Serebrennik, who led most of the Jews then living in Luxembourg across France, Spain, and Portugal to safety in the Dominican Republic, whose maverick dictator, Leonidas Trujillo, welcomed Jewish refugees from Europe.

In Brussels I began my primary education in a Flemish school. It was also in Brussels that I first became aware of what fate held in store for us for no reason other than that we were Jews. We lived on Boulevard Poincaré, a short walking distance from the cavernous Gare du Midi from which left the grim trains bound for the death camps. As I grew to be seven, and then eight, I also grew aware of life becoming ever more unpleasant and even dangerous. Once, during a cinema projection for children, I found myself caught in a cross fire of boos and catcalls when, upon taking off my coat, I revealed the regulation yellow star with the inscription "Juif" sewn on my jacket. Mortified, I announced to my parents that no matter what, I would never wear that star again. My parents, surprisingly enough, concurred. Thereafter none of us wore the star.

Eventually, signs went up at entrances of cinemas, theaters, and public parks, warning that Jews and dogs were not admitted. German patrols prowled the streets in search of Jews who were in violation of the regulations. My mother once ordered me to cross the boulevard and walk on the other side after she espied not far ahead two uniformed Germans checking out the odd passerby. One night, on our way home, as I stepped out of a streetcar a passing car hit me, and my mother fell on top of me. Who should have been driving that car but three German soldiers! Luckily, I was only slightly hurt: the Germans drove us home, bandaged my head, and returned the next morning to check on me. They did not inquire as to our identity or otherwise ask questions.

And so it came to pass that my parents and a number of their friends decided to finally make an attempt to flee Europe. We left Brussels in August 1942, hoping to reach Marseilles and from there to sail to Montevideo. We traveled by train and on foot through northern France and found in a small village south of Besançon a passeur, who led us across the demarcation line separating the occupied zone from the "free zone." After a night's march through fields and woods we managed to cross that line, only to be caught on the other side by the French police, who interned us in a small hotel at Lons-le-Saunier.

Two weeks after our arrival in that town, my father was momentarily out one morning, when the police came to arrest most of the refugees from Holland and Belgium interned in the hotel. My mother and I were marched in a humiliating procession through the town by policemen, who shoved us and hurled anti-Semitic insults. Just as we reached the railway station, where a train was waiting to transport us to the internment camp of Rivesaltes in French Catalonia, my maternal aunt, who was a French citizen and therefore under the "protection" of the French government, happened to come off a train just arrived from Limoges. She managed to get me released from the clutches of the brutal commissar, who was about to throw me into the train, while my mother was being dragged, screaming, across the station floor.

Stunned by the traumatic experience I had suffered at the railway station of Lons-le-Saunier, I was hospitalized soon after my aunt brought me to Limoges. A few weeks later I was parted from her and my uncle and led by unknown protecting hands from pillar to post, that is, from one hiding place to another. The place where I was sheltered longest was a convent school for boys, where I spent a year and three months. The nuns there made me pretend that I was a good little Catholic French boy named René Garnier born in Châteauroux, a city I had never seen. Fortunately I loved theater and was endowed with a fertile imagination. But I had to take care never to bare my circumcised penis. In the summer of 1944 my father hid me with a farming family in a rural village between Lyon and Grenoble. One day I happened to walk past some young yokels who, suspecting that I was Jewish, decided to pull down my trousers; luckily I was a fast runner and eluded their chase.

My father, who fought in the Jewish underground resistance movement, was caught by the French police one month before the liberation of Lyon and handed over to the Gestapo; he left France on the very last train bound for the death camps and never returned. A description of that nine-day train ride can be read, in all its horror, in Ted Morgan's *An Uncertain Hour* (New York: Arbor House, William Morrow, 1990), a book on the city of Lyon under the thumb of Gestapo chief Klaus Barbie, the notorious "Butcher of Lyon," who for forty years after the war enjoyed asylum in Bolivia before being extradited for trial to France in 1987. My mother perished in Auschwitz, along with other internees of Rivesaltes who had been transported there.

My aunt and uncle of Lyon, who had material difficulties raising their own three children, entrusted me at the beginning of 1945 to the care of the Zionist organization Dror, which ran a children's home at Bourg-d'Oisans in the Alps, but I was unhappy there. They then placed me, half a year later, in the care of the Commission Centrale de l'Enfance (CCE), founded by veterans of the UJRE, the Jewish underground organization to which my father had belonged. This CCE ran a network of homes (orphanages) for children whose parents had perished in the Shoah. In these homes we were brought up along progressive lines and, unfortunately, in the communist ideology. Deep down I wished that our educators were somewhat less progressive, and rather more conservative, for what my soul truly craved was to unabashedly be a child, instead of being reared on the milk of "political consciousness" and exhorted to be politically active. I was an energetic child capable of great happiness but also prone to protracted bouts of depression, especially when, after two or three years of vain expectations, I had to come to grips with the awful evidence that neither of my parents would ever return.

I was (and to this day remain) grateful to the organization that adopted me: my peers and I were fortunate in that we were schooled and wanted for nothing. In addition we led a life rich in cultural, artistic, and sportive activities. We ran a variety of manual workshops, a library, and a press of our own: the press comprised a handwritten and illustrated "wall journal" (*journal mural*) and a review, which we printed in our own shop. Our prizewinning four-voice choir performed on various occasions in Paris, and we went to theaters and cinemas. On Saturday evenings we entertained ourselves with "vigils" (*veillées*): these featured impromptu theatricals, storytelling, games. . . . I should have felt happy, but, instead, as I entered adolescence I grew sad and alienated and fantasized about living somewhere else, far away, in Russia (misled as I was by our communist upbringing) or in the east, a life that would somehow suit my temperament better. At school I strove to excel, not merely for the sake of excellence but also to prove to my classmates, from whom I felt inescapably "different" (at the *école communale* of Andrésy we often got into fistfights with village boys who shouted anti-Semitic insults at us), that I could master the arcane intricacies of the French language and the classics of French literature as well as, if not better than, they did. It was a matter of great pride for me to receive top grades in the French compositions that we had to write on weekly assigned topics. Also, I wrote a great deal of poetry. But even in the children's home, among my peers, I felt "different," lonely. If only I could have opened myself to a caring and professionally competent person, my life would not have taken the course I mistakenly chose, when at age sixteen I decided that I wanted to live in Poland, where my parents had come from, but whither they would not likely have returned, even if my father had remained a communist.

I used to spend the Christmas and Easter vacations with my maternal uncle's family in Lyon; though everyone was welcoming and kind, I sensed deep down that I was neither a brother to my three cousins nor a son to my aunt and uncle, only an orphaned nephew. This feeling of not fully belonging anywhere sustained escapist moods fed by a fertile and fanciful imagination. For three years in a row I spent one month every summer in England at the invitation of a wonderful young couple, under whose wings I participated in the activities of Brady's, the oldest Jewish boys' club in London. They took me to the club's country house in Kent and summer camp on the Isle of Wight. I loved England: English manners, English ways, the English language, all these appealed to me. During the school year I counted the months, then the weeks, and finally the days that separated me from the next vacation in England. And I always felt sad when the moment to leave England approached. On the last morning of my last vacation there, as we rode a bus to London's Victoria Station, my kind and caring hostess suddenly asked me whether I would like to go to school in England. The question made my heart leap with excited anticipation: I was burning to say yes, but, to my chagrin, she dropped the matter.

The Road to China

Alienation and escapist promptings were, I believe, fed by the hurt and constant uprooting that I endured as a child, not only during the war but perhaps even more in the years that followed it. These laid the tracks along which I eventually wandered into sinology. When people first learn that I am a professor, they usually assume that I teach French; great is their astonishment when they hear that I teach Chinese history. Some even wonder what led a "Jewish boy like me" into Chinese studies. I never quite know how to answer such a question. And yet I sense that my childhood experience of anti-Semitism, the murderous kind of the years of the Shoah, besides the "ordinary" kind, led me in some way to China and the career that I elected.

But where did it all begin? I inherited from my father, who was a dreamer, a passion for geography and a fascination with strange and far-away lands: indeed, the further from Europe, the more enticing the land. During the few weeks that I spent in hiding with my family in Lyon in the spring of 1944 the questions that I most persistently put to my father, whenever he was home to tuck me in at night, were: When will the Allies at long last land? Will Mother come back? and Where will we live after the war? He reassured me that the Allies would land soon, that Mother would come back, and that after the war we would emigrate to England, to Norway, or to some beautiful faraway land.

I remember that at least as early as 1945, when I was only eleven, the mere mention of China pricked my attention. I knew the name of Chiang Kai-shek, since he was included in the group portraits of the Allied leaders alongside Roosevelt, Churchill, Stalin, and de Gaulle, but I had not heard yet of Mao Zedong. That was to come three years later, when in the final stages of the Chinese civil war, newspaper stands displayed maps on which the advancing front of the victorious red tide was drawn. I was unaccountably curious about that faraway country, where people lived whose looks, whose food, whose ways were said to be so wonderfully different from those of Europe and who, moreover, had during the war been the gallant allies of our liberators. Also, the mother of my closest friend occasionally spoke of her sister, who fled Germany and lived in Shanghai. Decades later I learned that about twenty thousand European Jews found refuge in that great city during the Holocaust. The fact that China was a land unsullied by anti-Semitism made it uniquely attractive.

But there is little likelihood that I would have leaped from fascination with China to resolving to actually live and study there had it not been for the Shoah and the loss of my parents. Born and raised in western Europe, I would not have experienced anti-Semitism to such a violent degree as did the Jews in Poland and might therefore not have had cause for bad feelings about Europe. We might have gone on living in Luxembourg, if not in Belgium or France, and if we had emigrated somewhere far from Europe, it would likely have been to a country of the Americas, not to China.

Neither does it seem likely to me that my parents would have returned to Poland. That country would not have been saddled with a communist regime if the war had not provided the Soviet army with an opportunity to march into it. In any case I have grounds to suspect that my father would have outgrown his communist convictions in the face of mounting evidence of the evil nature of the Soviet system. Also, as a hardworking and skilled tailor, he could eventually have prospered. A distant relative told me that in 1944 he had confided to her his yearning to become his own boss after the war and to vacation on the French Riviera. Like him, I might have settled for dreaming of faraway places, while pursuing more "mainstream" studies, had I been fortunate enough to avail myself of a university education.

Much as I was fascinated with China, my real passion in the postwar years was, in consequence of the indoctrination that I had received, Russia. I even fantasized about going to live there one day and to later become the Soviet ambassador to China! At fourteen I purchased Nina Potapova's Russian textbook for speakers of French and proceeded to assiduously study that language on my own in my free time, while at school I studied English and German. One day my maternal cousin, Simon Domb, who is a generation older than me and was at the time a high-ranking official in the French government, remarked that I had a real aptitude for learning languages. He then suggested that when I become old enough to enter university I should study Asian languages, such as Chinese. That piece of advice, congenial to my taste for the exotic, remained engraved on my mind. Years later, when I returned from living in China and Poland and found myself in Paris at loose ends, unsure of my future, my cousin denied ever having thought up such an idea! He furthermore argued that there were only two countries in the world in which I could find employment in the field, unusual to him, that I had elected: the United States and the Soviet Union!

In the meantime, roughly a year after my cousin suggested the enticing idea that I should consider Orientalism for an academic career after graduating from secondary school, circumstances and the ideological conditioning that I had received led me to a fateful decision. In 1949 I was included in a delegation of children from the homes of the CCE that was sent to Poland for the summer vacation, at the invitation of the official Jewish organization of that country. It was a wonderful summer of sightseeing, of visits to Jewish and non-Jewish cultural and other institutions, of warm camaraderie with the boys and girls of the model children's homes and summer colonies, where we sojourned. These peers of ours were brought up in more conventional ways: they were genuine children, not aspiring adults as we were conditioned to be. My deep, secret yearning to still be a child strangely blended in with my escapism and my political convictions. These three factors combined into a resolve to return to live in Poland. Nothing and no one managed to dissuade me from embarking on that foolish form of juvenile rebellion. I persuaded myself that, had my parents lived, they would have returned to Poland, like so many other Jewish communists from France. And so, in the fall of 1950 I emigrated to Poland. This time reality held me in its grip: bitter as my disenchantment was, I felt that I could not withdraw and had to make the best of a bad situation. With difficulty I did adapt and even mastered Polish, the most difficult language I ever learned. The memories of my adolescent years in Poland are by no means all bad. As fate would have it, Poland turned out to be for me the way station to China, for when I graduated from secondary school in Warsaw, my application for a scholarship to study in China was, to my astonishment, accepted.

While Simon Domb may have planted the idea in my mind, the fortuitous encounter with a man named Jean Rosenbaum, who actually studied Chinese at Warsaw University, placed sinology in the center of my thoughts about the choice of a career. Still a secondary school student, I looked up to Jean with envy and amazement as he read Chinese texts with a pair of scissors in his right hand, coursing down vertical lines of intriguing-looking characters. Once, when I dropped in on him at the university's *Katedra Sinologii* (Chair of Sinology), I was ushered into the awesome presence of Professor Witold Jablonski, Poland's premier sinologist. He was a ruddy-faced, heavyset old gentleman, known for his copious daily imbibing. I met Jablonski again at the time of his visit in Peking in 1957; there, at the end of a day of scampering about ancient temples in the Western Hills, he peacefully died in his sleep. Like a Taoist sage he seemed to have lightheartedly accepted the world as it was, rather than pit himself against its cruel stupidity, and he died abiding in the Tao: the mysterious and wonderful cosmic Way of the great ancient sage Lao-Zi (Lao-tzu).

Although at the rational level I look upon the teachings of Confucianism, which are as ethically unequivocal as the Ten Commandments, as a foundation for an orderly and civilized society, at a deeper level my soul echoes the Taoist spirit of "live and let live." Confucianism and Taoism are opposites but, like the cosmic forces yin and yang, they are complementary rather than antagonistic philosophies of life. The wise among the Chinese tend to combine the social values taught by Confucianism with the contemplative attitude of the Taoists. Unfortunately, the Taoist spirit of freedom never overcame that curse of China's political history: tyranny. The Buddhist teaching of universal compassion amplified the Taoist call for tolerance. Buddhism is a voluminously literate and wonderfully sophisticated religion. Surging out of India it conquered Southeast, Central, and Eastern Asia without shooting a single arrow or uttering a single word of damnation of "infidels." Its message was one of compassion for all sentient beings: not only humankind but all that breathes and feels pain. I have often reflected that, were I not already committed to Judaism, I would have embraced Buddhism as my faith.

But, to return to my beginnings in China, I shall admit that I shared the excitement of finding myself in China, of living in China and attending school there, with other *liu xuesheng* (foreign students)—at least those capable of appreciating the new world into which we had come. For me, however, there was the additional cause for happiness of living in a country that had no tradition of anti-Semitism, that curse of Christendom and Islam. In Europe, even when schoolmates, teachers, and others were good to me, I remained aware of the Jewish heritage that set me apart from them. Even though I did not "look Jewish," I assumed that, from merely knowing my surname, Gentiles would deduce that I was Jewish and talk about it when I was out of their sight.

Not long after our arrival one girl from the Polish group, who had been all smiles and sweetness to me, confided to a compatriot who was a graduate student her unhappiness that "even here" (i.e., in China) a Jew should sneak in among Poles. Little did she know that her confidante, who was blond like herself and whose maiden name was concealed by her marriage to a Pole, was Jewish also. The confidante reported that utterance to the ambassador's wife, who was Jewish as well! That lady acted as a mother to the Polish students: she invited them once a month to the embassy for a meeting followed by a delicious lunch. At the first such meeting attended by our newly arrived group, she lashed out against unnamed individuals who dared to engage in anti-Semitic gossip, all the while staring at the culprit who, burning with shame, looked as though at any moment she might slide under the table.

I readily made friends among the Chinese students. Indeed, in no time so many would drop by the foreign student dormitory to see me that my Polish roommates took to asking me in a mocking tone how many new Chinese friends I had made that day. The childlike simplicity and friendliness of so many Chinese appealed to me. I felt at ease among them and sometimes sensed an ineffable bond with them. Most Chinese did not even know what a Jew was, and those who did held notions that were rather flattering. I found that the only Jews most Chinese could name were Einstein and Marx! Nowadays many would name Kissinger as well . . . alas.

Liang Pengfei, who at times acted like a mentor or even an older brother to me, was a student in the French department. A native of Harbin in northern Manchuria, he not surprisingly spoke fluent Russian and knew something about the Jews, since Harbin housed in the first half of this century a large and prosperous Russian-Jewish community, with a magnificent synagogue (the building houses nowadays a high school of the local Korean minority). One summer day we went into the center of Peking and rambled around Beihai Park, famed for its lake and hill crowned with an imposing white Buddhist dagoba. Moments after we had come out of the park a massive rainstorm hit the street, and we ran for shelter under the porch of the Peking Public Library. The storm lasted long enough for us to chat at leisure, and Pengfei suddenly looked at me, smiling, and said, "I suspect that you are not a real Pole. . . ." As I turned to him in surprise, he added, "I think that you belong to a certain national minority known to be the most intelligent people in the world!"

Even though with the passing of time I suffered many a cruel disenchantment, I yearned to immerse myself in the land. Had it been my fortune to be born and to come to China in earlier times, I would no doubt have settled there forever and become one of those eccentric westerners who lived in China, spoke the language, and became acculturated so completely that they acquired Chinese manners and were seen with amused indulgence by other foreigners as *enchinoisés,* just like those eccentric Englishmen of the nineteenth century who chose to live in Italy and were characterized as *Italianati*. Unfortunately, it was the "New China" of Chairman Mao that I was fated to live in: there was no escaping the predicament of being a foreigner bound to leave the country after the completion of my studies, besides being pigeonholed as a member of the Polish student contingent.

When in the summer of 1955 I completed Peking University's two-year Chinese-language course for foreign students, I pleaded with the authorities who had charge of us to allow me to begin my undergraduate studies at a provincial university: in Nanking, Kunming, Chengdu, or wherever there were no European students. When those bureaucrats objected, saying that outside of Peking they could not offer me the living standards to which as a westerner I was accustomed, I retorted that I had not come to China to live like a European but to live with Chinese students, even if that meant meager diet and crowded dormitories. But to no avail. The policy of the time was to keep European students concentrated and pigeonholed by nationality in Peking. Marriages to Chinese students were actively discouraged.

In later years officially imposed segregation became ever more stringent, and by the time I left China in October 1958, Chinese students had grown afraid of befriending foreign students. Such was the atmosphere of fear and mistrust engendered by the brutish stupidity of a regime whose totalitarian intolerance squandered the stores of goodwill with which Chinese citizens of all classes had welcomed "liberation" in 1949. Forced into unwilling isolation from Chinese people, I envied foreign students in Taiwan who could live where they pleased: in rented flats, with Chinese families, or in university dormitories.

Still, in September 1955 I looked forward to becoming a first year student at Peking University. Although I had to stay in the capital, at least I could attend classes in the company of Chinese students. The future looked bright, notwithstanding the campaign against "counterrevolutionaries," which had swept the campuses of China during the summer recess. I pictured myself marrying some lovely Chinese woman to found a family in Peking, Tianjin (Tientsin), or Shanghai. But I had yet to decide what to study: Chinese history or other Asian languages—Japanese and Korean. After some hesitation I became a first year student in the history department and never looked back. As I grew older and eventually joined the faculty of the University of British Columbia, history became a veritable passion with me. I realized that history held the key to understanding the past and, through the past, the present as well. In addition, by making one understand a particular country, it also helps one understand the world and humankind in general.

The three years that I was a history undergraduate student at Peking University enlarged my circle of friends and acquaintances considerably. European students tended, with few exceptions, to be distant and, in some cases, even arrogant toward the Chinese, which embarrassed me. When therefore Chinese students told me that I was not like other foreign students, that my ways were more like theirs, this to me was a compliment. I even had the good fortune of being invited by classmates to their parental homes, at a time when such hospitality was frowned upon by the authorities. Such marks of affection touched me.

As I already hinted, being a Jewish youth marked by the tragedy of the Holocaust motivated me, in a semiconscious sort of way, to reach out to the Chinese because they were untainted by the anti-Semitism endemic to Europe and, also, because their nation had suffered so much humiliation at the hands of European imperialists. Yet, I was driven by contradictory feelings: I was obviously a European, and felt like one, yet somehow I wanted the Chinese to understand that I was not really one of "them." In addition, I wonder whether as a Jew there was also something else that nourished in me a sense of affinity with the Chinese, even after the initial enchantment with the country was dispelled. For I must admit that the longer I lived in China, and the more I got to know the Chinese people, the more critical I became of them. But at the same time some string in my heart continued to vibrate with them. Lu Xun (Lu Hsün), who is universally regarded as the greatest Chinese writer of the twentieth century, subjected the failings of his compatriots to blistering criticism and also ridicule, yet he loved them deeply. And they forever love him.

Judaism and China

That something else I alluded to previously, and of which I was perhaps only faintly conscious in my youth, are the apparent similarities, or at least parallels, that I discern in the cultures of the Chinese and the Jews. I am not here laying claim to original findings: similarities, such as strong family values, respect for learning, entrepreneurship, and business acumen, have long been remarked upon by Jews and Chinese alike. But beyond such impressionistic observations, there are in my opinion tangible parallels. I surveyed some of these in a recent study[1] and continue to research them.

I know of no other peoples on the face of this earth who share so overarching a sense of history as do the Chinese and the Jews, no other peoples whose hearts so vibrate with historical memory that they readily draw parallels between present and past situations. Jewish history, as far back as our knowledge reaches, is almost as long as Chinese history. The century of the Exodus from Egypt is also the century in which the Zhou (Chou) people, leading a coalition of "barbarian" tribes, invaded from the west the domain of the Shang civilization, which, under a debauched and cruel tyrant, had reached the ultimate stage of decadence. The Zhou conquerors created a new state and laid the foundation of that complex of ideas, rites, values, symbols, and other cultural traits peculiar to China throughout the ages. On that foundation was erected "traditional" or "historical" China, in which dwell, along with the saintly Confucius and those who elaborated his doctrines throughout the ages, the bemused Taoist mystics Lao Zi and Zhuang Zi and those brutally cynical ideologues of Realpolitik and of the totalitarian state: Shen Buhai, Shang Yang, and Han Fei. This formative process began in the centuries of turmoil during which the Zhou feudal kingdom disintegrated into a collection of warring states. Eventually, the fragments of a vastly expanded Chinese world coalesced into a centralized bureaucratic empire under the first imperial dynasties of Qin (Ch'in) and Han, while rival philosophies meshed by a characteristically Chinese propensity for syncretism. Those were the centuries across which Israel and Judea came under the domination of a succession of mighty empires: Assyria, Babylon, Persia, Egypt, Macedonia and its Hellenistic successors, Rome.

The ethical principles taught by Confucius, which became the foundation of public morality in China, convey essentially the same instructions as the Ten Commandments. The "Supreme Sage of Mankind," as Confucius was officially consecrated during the Han dynasty, told his disciples that a "single thread" bound all the subjects that he taught: "reciprocity" (*shu*), which he spelled out as meaning "that which you do not wish others to do unto you, do not unto others." Confucius thus taught the Golden Rule nearly five hundred years before Rabbi Hillel put it in identical terms in his reformulation of the Deuteronomic maxim: "Thou shalt love thy neighbor as thyself."

Judaism, like Confucianism, is a holistic philosophy that proclaims the unity of thought and action and teaches individual responsibility and ultimate allegiance to absolute and eternally valid moral principles. Confucianism, in a spirit akin to the Judaic *tikkun olam* (mending of the world broken by men's deeds), calls upon man to study in order to achieve wisdom and, in the process, improve the world. It was with real enthusiasm that I was led by my comparative studies of Confucianism and Judaism to such findings. That Confucianism and Judaism, independently of each other, taught essentially similar moral principles is testimony enough to the universal validity of these principles.

I had long been aware that Jews had lived in our century in cities such as Shanghai; Tianjin (Tientsin); and Harbin, whose magnificent synagogue building I saw in 1954. Most of those Jews left China after the communist takeover and emigrated to Australia and Canada. I did however meet a few who, for various reasons, chose to stay: some, like Israel Epstein in Peking, had committed themselves to the Chinese revolution; others, whom I met in Shanghai and Tianjin, because they could retain their property as long as they lived there or had no place else in the world to go. I also met Jews who had married Chinese citizens, and I also came into contact with children of mixed marriages like the architect Leon Hua in Peking, whose wife, Irene, like his mother, was a Polish Jew from France! But what surprised me most was to learn that Jews had dwelt in China long before modern times.

In February 1957 the history department of Peking University organized for its international students an excursion to noted historical sites in Henan (Honan) and Shaanxi (Shensi) Provinces. The second of these sites was Kaifeng in Henan, a slumbering backwater of a city on the shore of the Yellow River. The sight of our Caucasian faces drew such a press of wildly curious mobs onto the streets of that city that one might have thought Martians had landed. Yet, under the Northern Sung dynasty (960–1127 C.E.), Kaifeng had been the capital of the empire and a prosperous commercial metropolis that drew traders from all over Asia.

Our group of twenty-odd foreign students included Dr. Timoteus Pokora, a Jewish postgraduate from Czechoslovakia. On the long train ride from Peking to Zhengzhou he briefed me on the exciting story of that small Judeo-Persian–speaking community, which settled in Kaifeng in the twelfth century, prospered there, and became assimilated to the point of virtually melting into the Chinese milieu. That story, quite unique in the annals of the wanderings of the Jewish people, was romanticized by Pearl Buck in her novel *Peony*. The small size of the Jewish community of Kaifeng, which at its peak numbered two thousand people at the most, has been the subject matter of innumerable academic and journalistic articles, in addition to several books.

Jewish travelers wandered into China even long before the Kaifeng community was established. From Babylonia they followed the trail of

Arabs and Persians along the "Silk Route," which linked the heartland of China to the shores of the Mediterranean. Visions of their teams of camels and mules loaded with precious merchandise from both ends of the Asian continent, slowly making their way across the formidable mountain ranges and deserts of Central Asia, stirred my imagination no end. Jews also manned stalls in the West Market of Changan during the glorious Tang dynasty (618–907 C.E.)! Jewish documents dating back to that period were unearthed early this century: these include commercial correspondence in Judeo-Persian found in Chinese Turkestan (Xinjiang, or Sinkiang), and a Hebrew *selichah* prayer found in Dunhuang, Gansu (Kansu) province. Limited historical evidence suggests Jewish presence in other cities of China in the Tang and subsequent dynasties as well, notably in Yangzhou, Hangzhou, Ning-po, Nanking, and Canton.

The night of our arrival in Kaifeng an official of the city committee of the Chinese Communist Party visited us at our hostel; in his speech of introduction to the city, its history, and the current situation, he made no mention of the Jews. When during the question and answer period Dr. Pokora and I asked whether there were still Jews living in Kaifeng and whether we could visit any, the official pleaded ignorance and told us that he would inquire with his superiors. The next day another official came, who informed us that there were several hundred people in Kaifeng who identified themselves as Jews, even though they were completely assimilated, and over a thousand who no longer acknowledged their Jewish ancestry. How those figures were arrived at was a mystery that we did not attempt to elucidate; in any case statistics reported by westerners who visited Kaifeng in more recent years are at variance not only with those offered to us in 1957 but with each other.

That same day in the afternoon a truck came to pick up Pokora and myself to take us to meet Chinese Jews. Needless to say, the two of us were elated; however, no sooner were we seated in the truck than eight East German students climbed aboard as well. Next, as if that had not dampened our joy enough, an official from the local party committee arrived to chaperon the lot of us. Pokora and I were at pains to suppress the anger that burned in us at the prospect that the eagerly anticipated encounter with our Chinese brethren would now be shorn of the privacy that the occasion demanded.

We were thus driven to the historical "Lane of the Religion That Plucks the Sinew" (an allusion to the kosher method of preparing meat), along which people thronged to stare at us, while urchins seated on top of walls shouted and waved hands. Soon we were ushered into the home of an elderly couple surnamed Li (I later learned that the original surname of the Jewish Li clan was Levi). Curiously enough, this was the only house in China in which I ever saw an ancestral tablet; above it, however, hung a portrait of Mao Zedong. We sat in a circle around the hosts: considering the circumstances, old Mr. Li could only make the kind of ritualistic statements one heard everywhere and in every place in China in those days: namely, that the Jews, like everybody else, were supposedly oppressed under "the reactionary regime of the Kuomintang" and that the Communist Party "liberated" them. A few minutes later we all filed out; Pokora and I arranged to be the last ones in the line: this enabled us to whisper to the hosts that we were Jews. The old man's eyes lit up and, holding our hands as if he did not want to let go of them, turned to his wife and softly said, "We are one people, one people!" (Zanmen shi yi ge zu de, yi ge zu de).

During our stay in Kaifeng we also saw the lengthy Chinese inscriptions that the Jews had engraved on stone stelae in 1489, 1512, 1663, and 1679. Broadly historical and doctrinal in nature, these inscriptions, which the Jesuit Jerome Tobard translated into French in 1912, strove to establish the antiquity of the Jewish presence in China, as well as the identity of the ethical principles taught by Moses and Confucius. These stelae once stood in the courtyard of the synagogue, which has long since disappeared, and were moved around 1919 by the bishop Charles White of Toronto to the grounds of the Canadian Anglican Mission, which he founded. It is rumored that local authorities plan to rebuild the synagogue as a tourist attraction, for it is not likely to ever become a place of worship again. No matter how hard the descendants of the once genuine *kehila* (Jewish community) strive to win from the Chinese government recognition as a "national minority," instead of being counted as part of the majority Han Chinese population, Judaism, alas, remains little more than a memory in Kaifeng.

As in Nanking, Yangzhou, and other cities that it once graced with its presence, Judaism might not even have remained a memory in Kaifeng had the *kehila* not been discovered in the seventeenth century by the first Jesuit missionaries who came to China. The amazing story of the accidental encounter, which took place in 1605, between Matteo Ricci, founder of the Jesuit mission in Peking, and the Kaifeng Jew Ai Tian is known to all interested in the subject.[2] Ricci subsequently met Ai's three nephews, who, like their uncle, had come to the capital to compete in the metropolitan examinations for admission into the mandarinate. Thereafter, Jesuits repeatedly visited Kaifeng: they reported on the decline of knowledge of Hebrew and Torah and left drawings and descriptions of the synagogue on the basis of which was built the miniature model now on view at the Museum of the Diaspora in Tel Aviv. The Jews at first welcomed the Jesuits, but it was not long before the latter aroused well-grounded suspicions of their intentions: these brought contacts to a stormy end.[3]

Subsequent to my visit to Kaifeng I read Bishop White's three-volume compendium of studies and articles *Chinese Jews* (Toronto: University of Toronto Press, 1942) and Ricci's memoirs, as well as sundry other materials. Having plowed through this voluminous literature, I became erroneously convinced that nothing more could be said about Judaism in China, since it was obviously dead. Indeed, I found it surprising that so much had been written already about so tiny a community. As a graduate student at Columbia University I wrote a paper in 1962 that purported to be a summary analysis of the subject and thought no more of it.

When I entered upon my studies in New York I elected modern Chinese history as my specialty, a decision that I grew to bitterly regret, for it led me into a research dead end after years of wasted time. Too late did I come to realize that my heart rested in the old China, particularly in the magnificent, sophisticated Sung period, during which the Jews settled in Kaifeng, not the increasingly ugly China of the present century (and of the twenty-first century). Had I understood this in my student years, my career would have been more productive, even if I had not returned to the subject of Judaism in China. The mere fact that I had translated popular short stories relating to the Sung period into French during my stay in Paris in 1960 should have initiated me into a Sung-focused research career.[4]

As it turned out, the best of the research on the Kaifeng Jewish community was produced in the half century that followed the publication of Bishop White's compendium. Several major works have seen the light of day since the mid-1960s, notably *The Survival of the Chinese Jews* by Australian scholar Donald D. Leslie (Leiden: E. J. Brill, 1972), who authored several other in-depth studies on the subject; and *Mandarins, Jews, and Missionaries,* a masterful exposition on the historical experience of the Jews in China, by Michael Pollack (Philadelphia: Jewish Publication Society of America, 1980). Significant contributions were also made by other scholars, notably Raphael Israeli, Irene Eber, and Dan Ross.[5]

The field of Chinese-Jewish studies is further enriched now by the contributions of Chinese scholars, notably the stunningly dynamic Nanking University professor Xu Xin, who in 1989 founded the China

Judaic Studies Association. Xu studied Hebrew at Ulpan Akiva in Netanya, Israel, and Yiddish at the YIVO Institute in New York. His prolific writings include a one-volume Chinese-language volume entitled *Encyclopedia Judaica* (Shanghai: Shanghai People's Publishing House, 1997) and a three-hundred-page book, *Anti-Semitism: How and Why* (Shanghai: Sanlian Publishing House, 1995) that is a history of anti-Semitism from biblical times to the present.

Xu's activities and publications highlight the amazing surge of interest in Judaism and Israel among the Chinese. Since the late 1980s at least eight centers of Judaic and Israeli studies have been established in China, while Hebrew is taught in at least two Chinese universities. A long-range program of translation and publication of masterpieces of Jewish literature, entitled Milestones in Jewish Literature, has already produced several volumes, notably novels by Shalom Aleichem and Isaac B. Singer. At the same time cultural, economic, and other exchanges between China and Israel are thriving. The Israel Academy of Science and Humanities opened a liaison office in Peking in 1990, and the world's first Chinese-Hebrew dictionary has been published in Israel. In October 1996 the city of Nanking hosted the International Conference of Judaic Studies. At about the same time, permission was granted to build a Jewish history museum in Kaifeng.

The opening of China to the world and the establishment of full diplomatic relations between China and Israel in 1992 was followed by official visits of President Chaim Herzog and the late prime minister Izhak Rabin to China. The Chinese government has, at least for now, abandoned the virulent anti-Israel stance that once characterized communist regimes. There is hope that newspaper cartoons depicting Israel in the form of a hooknosed figure, such as the one that shocked me during the Suez crisis of 1956, will never be seen again. The Soviet inspiration behind such cartoons was obvious: indeed, ever since the work *The Protocols of the Elders of Zion,* that infamous fabrication of the tsar's secret police, was translated into Japanese at the beginning of this century, Russia has been the chief disseminator of anti-Semitism in East Asia.

Anti-Semitic activities by Russian and German agents, and perhaps by Christian missionaries, as well as Chinese reactions to these, need to be researched further. This is one project I would like to undertake in the future. We know that in 1923 Dr. Sun Yat-sen, father of China's first republic, identified in a letter addressed to N. E. B. Ezra, editor of Shanghai's *Israel's Messenger,* his revolutionary movement for China's national renaissance with the Zionist cause. About a decade later his widow,

Soong Ching-ling, led a delegation that comprised the outstanding educator T'sai Yüan-pei and Chinese-American writer Lin Yü-t'ang to the German consulate in Shanghai to lodge a protest against Nazi anti-Jewish outrages. Decades later, Chinese intellectuals who survived the persecutions, tortures, and murders of the infernal years of Mao's "Cultural Revolution" (1966–76) readily drew comparisons between their sufferings and those endured by the Jews during the Holocaust.

When in the spring of 1958 I visited Shanghai for the second time, I wandered in search of vestiges of the exuberantly rich Jewish life that had graced that great metropolis for more than a century. Though unable to find the Shanghai Jewish Circle, whose shield my eye had caught from the window of a speeding bus, I was introduced to a Czech Jewish couple who were old-time "Shanghailanders." Several months later I wandered about Tianjin (Tientsin) in search of vestiges of Jewish life there as well. A Chinese pedicab driver led me to a synagogue, which had been converted into a Christian church. Nearby, I encountered several Russian Jews, remnants of a once vibrant community; they informed me that they met for prayers at the home of a Dr. Preobrazhensky.

China has thus over the centuries, and even millennia, been home to more than one Jewish Diaspora. The age of the "treaty ports," which began in the wake of the Anglo-Chinese conflict of 1840–42 known as the "Opium War," witnessed the settlement in Shanghai of Baghdadi Jews, who laid the foundation for a prosperous Asian-Sephardic community, which by the turn of this century numbered over eight hundred persons. In addition to two synagogues, they built schools and a broad spectrum of community organizations. Then, at the beginning of this century, Russia's cruel persecution of the Jews and the Bolshevik revolution brought into existence the four-thousand-person-strong Russian-Jewish community of Shanghai, which had its own synagogues, schools, community organizations, and newspapers. But the largest Russian Jewish community was the one established in Harbin.

The approach of the Shoah brought to Shanghai some twenty thousand Jewish refugees from Germany, Poland, and Lithuania. The story of how Shanghai became a major asylum from the Holocaust has long intrigued me and deserves to be better known. Shanghai was at the time occupied by the Japanese, who could not comprehend the anti-Semitic fury of their German allies. Many of the refugees were transported to Shanghai from Kobe, where they had first found asylum thanks to the lifesaving visas issued in Kaunas (Kowno), the prewar capital of Lithuania, by Japanese consul Chune Sugihara and his Dutch homologue Jan

Zwartendijk. The inauguration in 1994 of a Holocaust memorial in the rundown old Hongkew area, where the Japanese occupation authorities had, under German pressure, set up a "ghetto" for the European refugees, enshrines remembrance of these edifying events.

It is commonly assumed that the Jews of Kaifeng became assimilated and lost their Jewish identity because of the following factors: (1) living in isolation from the Jewish world, they were in effect an "orphan colony," as the philo-semitic British diplomat James Finn called them in the title of his book *The Orphan Colony of Jews in China,* published in 1873; (2) China was a land free of anti-Semitism; (3) Chinese society readily assimilated foreigners who settled in its midst. Though true enough, those considerations need, however, to be qualified. The Chinese empire was a unitarian, centralized, bureaucratic state, and Chinese culture tended to uniformize all who lived under its sway; yet, at the same time Chinese society was also fragmented into semiautonomous units: clans, lineages, guilds, religious sects. The Jews of Kaifeng retained their identity longer than did those of other Chinese cities, probably because their community was larger, and also, as Dan Ross argues in *Acts of Faith,* because they had in effect evolved into a Chinese-style religious sect, known as *Tiao Jin Jiao:* "the sect that plucks the sinews." But religious sects at times caused the authorities to harbor well-founded suspicions of subversive activities, a fact that accounts for the apologetic tone that can be detected in the affirmation of identity between the teachings of Judaism and Confucianism that we read in the Jewish stone inscriptions of Kaifeng. Another fact that may have accelerated assimilation was the conversion of Chinese women destined to marry Jewish men.

But the most decisive factor of assimilation was the Chinese official examination system, which acted like a magnet upon the social elites of the empire. In the course of their careers, Jewish mandarins were called by their duties to live away from their native province of Henan. Immersed in the Chinese milieu, isolated from fellow Jews, they could not observe the *kashruth* (Jewish dietary laws). The scrolls inscribed for the synagogue by the brothers Zhao Yingchen and Zhao Yingdou, who were the most honored of Kaifeng's Jewish mandarins, attest to loyalty to their roots. But in a general kind of way, the long years of arduous preparation for three successive levels of fiercely competitive examinations left Jewish candidates little, if any, time to study the Torah. The Jew Ai Tian and his nephews confessed to the Jesuit Matteo Ricci that, anxious to succeed in the examinations, they had indeed neglected study of the Torah.

A final factor in loss of Jewish identity was the presence of much larger Moslem communities in every city where Jews settled before modern times. Evidence suggests that in Nanking, Yangzhou, and other places, the Jews, few in numbers, ultimately converted to Islam. In Kaifeng the Jews adopted the terminology of Islam: they called their rabbis *manla* (mullahs) and were known in the Chinese population as "blue-capped Moslems," in distinction from the Huis, or Chinese Moslems, who wore white skullcaps. Isolation from the wider Jewish world, besides similarities in rituals, terminology, and diet, facilitated assimilation into the Moslem community. By the mid–nineteenth century, there was no one left in Kaifeng who could read Hebrew; the synagogue lay in ruins; and the Jewish community, now poverty stricken, sold many of its artifacts to westerners, notably Bishop White's Canadian Anglican Mission.

My curiosity about premodern Jewish settlers in China, how they lived and what they experienced there, will likely never be satisfied, for the reasons that the Kaifeng community alone bequeathed written documents and even these are meager. Not one Chinese Jew has written the history of his or her people in China, which is sadly paradoxical when one considers that the Jews and the Chinese are the two most history-conscious nations on the face of the earth! Cross-cultural studies, however, particularly the comparative study of Judaism and Confucianism, constitute for me a fruitful endeavor, as the philosophy of life taught by the Confucian school so remarkably bears juxtaposition to that of Judaism. That both teach the Golden Rule is only one of several coincidences. Confucianism, like Judaism, exhorts fathers, and men who are called to lead in general, to vow loyalty not merely to masters or sovereigns but, beyond them, to universalistic and timeless ethical principles. Confucianism, like Judaism, affirms life and values learning. It also binds learning to the achievement of sagehood: whosoever enters the gate of learning must strive to become a self-reliant sage who sets an example of moral conduct for the people to follow. The Confucian man of noble character (*junzi*), like the Jewish man of rectitude (*zaddik*), proclaims the unity of thought and action by binding his moral self-cultivation to interaction with others and thereby to the betterment of society and of the world.

Having fortuitously discovered that Maimonides (Moses ben Maimon) (1135–1204), the great renovator of Judaism, and Zhu Xi (or Chu Hsi, 1130–1200), who reinterpreted the entire legacy of Confucianism, were contemporaries, I set out to investigate their respective epistemologies and am presently in the process of completing a comparative study of these. In that study I note with some enthusiasm that, although Maimonides makes knowledge of man and of the physical world a pathway to knowledge of God, while Zhu Xi draws on knowledge of the physical world to illustrate human affairs, matters of human conduct constitute nevertheless an epistemological ground on which Confucianism and Judaism meet.

Maimonides and Zhu Xi similarly married reason to metaphysics and set for learning the ultimate objective of acquiring in one and the same process knowledge, moral excellence, perfect conduct, and an all-encompassing wisdom. Both sages prescribed a curriculum and a methodology to arrive at wisdom by sustained personal effort under the firm guidance of a teacher. Both dictate that in conduct humankind avoid extremes of any kind and not be deflected by spiritual yearning from recognizing tangible reality. To Maimonides, God almighty, immanent and transcendent, is the fount of knowledge, wisdom, and goodness, while Zhu Xi derives goodness from a mysterious, virtually undefinable Heaven, whose spiritual Pattern or Principle (*li*) informs, organizes, and apportions all things and phenomena. Zhu challenges those who set upon the path of learning to investigate in all things, phenomena, or affairs the manifestations of that Principle.[6]

Another avenue of research, the feasibility of which I have yet to investigate, is to determine the extent to which Chinese intellectuals of the late nineteenth and early twentieth centuries, who were conscious of world affairs, saw parallels between the destiny of the Jews and what fate held in store for China. Some of these intellectuals feared that China was doomed to be subjugated, because of the incapacity of its rulers to carry out the thoroughgoing reforms needed to resist the onslaught of Western civilization; some even ventured the thought that, just like the Jews of ancient times, the Chinese stood in danger of losing their country. Chen Duxiu, one of the originators of the New Culture movement of the second decade of the twentieth century and founding father of the Chinese Communist Party, warned in 1905 that China could meet the fate of ancient Judea.

Now, sixty years after the "dirty thirties" and fifty years after the Holocaust, this most terrible century of recorded history ends as the world drifts into a new dark age: one of irrationality beyond what even Kafka or Orwell imagined. The new age is one of electronic obscurantism, of universal unculture and amorality, and also of murderous depravity reminiscent of Nazism. To reach, under such circumstances, for community and abide in the universalistic values embedded in age-old cultures, which everywhere face the onslaught of ideologues of the "bottom line" and "deconstructionists" of all stripes, is to light a beacon in the creeping darkness. To light a beacon, be it ever so small, is indeed my modest aspiration.

NOTES

1. René Goldman, "Moral Leadership in Society: Some Parallels between the Confucian 'Noble Man' and the Jewish 'Zaddik,' " *Philosophy East and West* 45, no. 3 (July 1995).

2. See Matthew Ricci, *China in the Sixteenth Century: The Journals of Matthew Ricci, 1583–1610,* trans. Louis Gallagher (New York: Random House, 1953). Several books on Ricci have been published subsequently.

3. Accounts of the efforts expended by the Jesuits to procure some of the Kaifeng Torah scrolls can be found in the compendium of eighteenth-century Jesuit correspondence entitled *Lettres Edifiantes et Curieuses* and in Michael Pollack's excellent *Mandarins, Jews, and Missionaries: The Jewish Experience in the Chinese Empire* (Philadelphia: Jewish Publication Society of America, 1980).

4. André Levy and René Goldman, *L'antre aux fantomes des collines de l'Ouest* (Paris: Gallimard, 1972).

5. Mention should be made here of Michael Pollack's other work, *The Torah Scrolls of the Chinese Jews* (Dallas: Bridwell Library, Southern Methodist University, 1975); Donald D. Leslie's sundry studies, notably his *The Survival of the Chinese Jews: The Jewish Community of Kaifeng* (Leiden: E. J. Brill, 1972); Sidney Shapiro's *Jews in Ancient China: Studies by Chinese Scholars* (New York: Paragon, 1984); Raphael Israeli's studies of Islam in China; Irene Eber's "Kaifeng Jews Revisited: Sinification as Affirmation of Identity," Monumenta Serica 41 (1993): 231–47; Dan Ross. *Acts of Faith: A Journey to the Fringes of Jewish Identity* (New York: St. Martin's Press, 1982). Much ongoing research is reported in *Points East,* the highly informative bulletin of the Sino-Judaic Institute, Menlo Park, California.

6. A synopsis of my study entitled "From the Two Extremities of the World: Knowledge and Moral Self-Cultivation in Zhu Xi and Maimonides," appears as a chapter in A. Harrap, *Contacts between Cultures,* vol. 1 (Lewiston, New York: E. Mellen Press, 1992).

The Uses and Limitations of Perspective

Martin O. Heisler

Biographical Note

Martin Heisler was born in Hungary and schooled in Budapest, Paris, and Los Angeles, receiving his degrees in political science from the University of California, Los Angeles (Ph.D., 1969). He taught at the University of Illinois and is now professor of government and politics at the University of Maryland and a member of the faculty of its Harrison Program for the Future Global Agenda. He has been a Fulbright professor in Denmark, a senior research fellow at the Centre National de la Recherche Scientifique in France, a visiting fellow at the University of Warwick in Britain, and, most recently, visiting professor at the Institut  *d'Études Politiques in Paris. He is the author of many articles and coauthor or editor of several books. Much of his current work, on the shifting bases and functions of identity and citizenship from the eighteenth through the twentieth centuries, is being done in conjunction with a small, informal team of scholars from several disciplines and countries.*

Professor Heisler is an active member of national and international professional organizations. He is a fellow of the Society for Comparative Research and has held major offices in the International Studies Association. His public service has included consulting with the National Science Foundation, National Endowment for the Humanities, United States Institute of Peace, Council for the Inter-

national Exchange of Scholars, Economic and Social Research Council of the United Kingdom, and U.S. State Department.

⟶•◦•⟵

N'avons nous pas tous un même père? Un seul Dieu ne nous a-t-il pas créés?

—Malachi

Introduction

Only recently have I begun to realize how much and in what ways the Holocaust influenced my choice of career, as well as my life. Writing this chapter has been the main catalyst for letting me see that it strongly affected who I became, how I relate to people, what I work on, how I think, and what I believe. My growing awareness of those influences created puzzles, even confusion, about the connections between the Holocaust in general, as an epochal event, and the fate of my family and my experiences—"my Holocaust." Slowly, and with difficulty, it came to be apparent that my experiences and the fate of my family before, during, and after World War II reverberate through my beliefs, worldviews, and day-to-day behavior and moods, even half a century after those events. But these are not coherent, consistent, or harmonious beliefs and views. They embody an unresolved tension between the cosmopolitan values and hopes expressed in the epigraph at the head of this chapter, on the one hand, and the pursuit of the warmth of communitarian ties, on the other.

The first drafts of this chapter reflected my own approach to dealing with the Holocaust over half a century: to abstract, conceptualize, and analyze it through theories in the social sciences. I relegated my memories and emotional responses to footnotes and parenthetical asides. Later drafts tilted either toward self-analysis or, at the other extreme, hyperintellectualization. It has taken an inordinate amount of time and effort to accept that for most of us vacillation is an inescapable part of the Holocaust's legacy. Working through these thoughts and recollections has sometimes been painful and immobilizing; but the exercise has been literally therapeutic.

My Holocaust

Until a few years ago, the connections between the Holocaust and my life and work were opaque and fragmented, outside my consciousness. It is still difficult to see them as discrete influences. A part of the reason may be that for me the Holocaust was preceded and followed by other traumas, so that it began before the rounding up and extermination of most of the Jewish population of my native Hungary; and it has not yet ended. Finding the beginning and end has presented intellectual and political puzzles, as well as personal ones. I begin with the personal.

Three aspects of my childhood disposed me to observe my surroundings from more detached, perhaps unusual, and eventually useful vantage points. First, between 1943 and 1949 I was first entirely and then partially immobilized physically. Doctors in two large hospitals in Budapest sought to score a coup in the effective treatment for what was said to be tuberculosis of the bone, a disease manifested near joints but difficult to localize.[1] Unknown to my parents, some of the doctors were active members of the Nyilas Kereszt (Arrow Cross) Party, the Hungarian mimickers of Germany's National Socialists. Although I did not have the disease, they added me to a small control group of uninfected children (as far as I know, all either Jews or Gypsies) for an experiment to treat the ailment by completely immobilizing the hip joint. I was in a cast from waist to ankles for six months, then in orthopedic braces for nearly three years.

Physical immobility made me more observant and analytical than the average five to eight year old. My memories of such events as the departure of my father for a labor camp in Austria in mid-1943; the German occupation of Hungary in March 1944; the roundup and deportation of those wearing the yellow star, including my mother;[2] and the long and ferocious battle of Budapest between Russian and German forces in the bitterly cold winter of 1944–45 are vivid. My great-uncle carried me outside and held me in his arms when those of us in the Swedish protected houses on Pozsonyi út were taken outside and lined up to be machine-gunned into snow-covered embankments near the Danube. I (vaguely) recall Raoul Wallenberg's efforts to save as many Hungarian Jews as possible, including me and the other survivors in my family.[3]

My father returned from Austria shortly after the Russian liberation of Budapest. My mother did not, and I waited for her, expecting her to return as well. I recall sitting by a window for the first few months, watching the street for her arrival. But just as the conditions in Pozsonyi út and the battle of Budapest had preoccupied me in the months after her disappearance, so too conditions of life and learning to walk again after the liberation often distracted me from her absence. For more than a year, my father and I lived with my uncle, aunt, and cousin in their one-bedroom apartment. (I slept across the foot of my aunt and uncle's bed.)

After several years of immobility, I had difficulty walking. I had a severe limp and for two years wore an elevated shoe.

Since I was already seven and had never attended school, my father enrolled me in the first school that opened in the spring of 1945. It was a Hebrew-language school, and the six months or so I spent there provided previews of difficulties I would encounter later in Paris and Los Angeles. First, while I could read and write Hungarian and German, I did not know a word of either Hebrew or Yiddish, the two languages students and teachers used. Second, my limp, brace, orthopedic shoe, and difficulty in walking set me apart. Teachers ("He is as illiterate as a Goy") and peers ("Hey, look at the gimp") made feeling normal difficult.

Adjusting to life without my mother, surrounded by a grandmother, aunt, uncle, and cousin, with my father away much of the time, trying to find ways to support us, added to a focus on daily life, rather than on reflections on the past. Although my memories of this period are vivid and—comparisons with the recollections of adults who were there and recent visits to the sites suggest—fairly complete and accurate, I did not link my physical condition, my father's long absence, the loss of my mother, and our unsettled home with the Holocaust until much later.

The loss of my mother was a second source of my detached and analytic disposition. Growing up without a full-time "primary caregiver"—a role filled intermittently by my father's cousin, my paternal grandmother, and subsequently an aunt—made me introverted. My mother's absence was not discussed, so I had no cues from adults for coping with it. Only my maternal grandmother and later my great-uncle József[4] talked with me about my mother, and, doubtless to cauterize their pain, they did so less with the passage of time. My mother had not been warmly embraced during her life by my father's side of the family, which consisted essentially of his long-widowed mother, a sister, and a niece. My father's family considered themselves as near aristocrats as assimilated Jews could in Hungary, while my mother came from a family of small shopkeepers who were Orthodox. Her family was said to be "from the East," while those on my father's side prided themselves as "European." She was seldom talked about after her death, and there was little responsiveness to my questions about her.[5]

My father's silence could only partly be explained by his enormous responsibilities. He was the rock on which the surviving members of the extended family leaned, both in Hungary and in Los Angeles, after he arrived there in 1950. He doubtless suffered a deep sense of guilt for what he believed to have been a cataclysmic decision in the days after I was born. One of his sisters, who had emigrated to the United States in the late 1920s, urged him in the early spring of 1938 to join her in the United States. In a letter he wrote a few days after I was born, he responded that things were not as bad as some said. As an established, assimilated family that had given several of its sons to the defense of Hungary in World War I (his own father, posthumously decorated for bravery, was killed in battle on the Eastern Front in 1917, when my father was eight), we were not going to be bothered. In any case, there would be plenty of time to act if things deteriorated. He informed her later that he planned to hire a German governess for me by the time I was two or three, so that I would be fluent "and without accent" in what was the second language in our milieu. (This he did; and I learned German as a toddler, only to lose much of it shortly thereafter.) He never spoke about that letter or the choice he made in 1938. More important, he never spoke with me about my mother and for the rest of his life explicitly and persistently refused to respond to my questions about her.

Four years after the war my father and I fled the communist regime in Hungary and for a short period became stateless refugees.[6] After we spent three months together in the Rothschild Hospital in Vienna, which served as a refugee reception center, he managed to send me to a boarding school in Paris while he waited for an entry visa to the United States.[7] He joined his sister and his mother (the latter had left Hungary legally in 1948) in early 1950. I followed in August 1950.

Initially I felt lost in strange surroundings in Vienna, Paris, and Los Angeles. These serial dislocations before my thirteenth birthday doubtless made it difficult to isolate the impacts of the Holocaust from what followed. Coping with my changing surroundings kept me focused on the present and did not permit, or protected me from, contemplating the past. This was the third factor.

There is a danger of imputing too much influence, not to speak of causality, in approaching these questions more than fifty years later. The Holocaust clearly influenced my choice of career and how and on what I work, just as it has been a crucial, if unmeasurable, factor in shaping me as a person. But I had and made work-related choices, and, on the personal plane, I do not see my life as that of a victim.

My career as a migrating refugee and the need both to adjust and to explain myself to those around me, teachers as well as peers, kept issues of identity and the need to have an analytic grasp of my social surroundings at the front of my consciousness. This also served, I think, as a strong stimulus for detached observation and perspective. My household in Los

Angeles was peopled by an asymmetrical, stress-laden extended family.[8] It provided structure without coherent content, independence without appreciable autonomy, and subsistence without much consistent nurture. But incomplete integration is also partial detachment. I became an observer and often an inwardly directed analyst of what I saw and experienced.

The Choice of Career

The dislocations in my childhood made me a quintessentially marginal person. I was an outsider in school in Budapest after the war, then in France, and finally in Los Angeles. Many comparativists in the modern social sciences could also be characterized as marginal—suspended between societies or subcultures, fitting well into more than one but fully into none. These traits were shared by many of the early and creative scholars in such fields as social anthropology, sociology, and social psychology and in my own discipline of political science, especially in the fields of comparative politics and international relations. As refugees or voluntary migrants, they had the advantage of knowing several societies (and languages) firsthand and of comprehending alternative ways of life and thinking. This is how I gained the more detached perspectives on cultures, social relationships, and ideas on which much of my professional life is built. That was the upside of my circumstances. The downside was on the plane of emotions. I very much wanted to fit in, to belong, in the successive settings in which I found myself. This need has played an increasingly important part in my research and theoretical positions in recent years, and I shall return to it shortly.

I had not initially sought the ability to detach myself analytically from my surroundings or to be adept at shifting cultural and societal perspectives. It took time for me to grasp that these qualities could be consciously cultivated and harnessed for work. That occurred in my junior year at UCLA, as I contemplated changing majors from astrophysics to something at which I was better. Mathematics beyond calculus, required for the interdisciplinary program in which I began undergraduate studies, proved increasingly difficult. In contrast, the few courses I had taken in the social sciences, to meet distribution requirements for graduation, were fun. I had read more history and was much more comfortable with geography than most others and enjoyed being near the top rather than near the bottom of my classes. In my senior year I changed my major to political science. The change in undergraduate majors was probably not directly related to the Holocaust. But the decision to do graduate work and prepare for a career in higher education, the topics on which I focused, and, more speculatively perhaps, my evolving theoretical perspectives and substantive research, were.

I leaned toward an academic career several years before I settled into the social sciences. It was probably the first major life-affecting decision I made consciously. It reflected a strong desire for respite from the sense of instability and incompleteness that had pervaded my childhood and, given my unsettled family life, my teen years. The academy seemed orderly, sheltered from the nastier aspects of life, and, at the same time, stimulating.[9] Compared with my father's world of small business or the medical and legal professions he wanted me to enter (and that many of my high school friends chose), universities appeared peaceful and rational places. There, one seemed to be judged on merit, knowledge was valued, and work proceeded through individual effort and skill. The defining qualities of universities were for me, in my almost complete ignorance of them, calm and reasoned discussions with high-minded colleagues, all driven by curiosity and the quest for knowledge, if not for truth. Above all, I presumed them to be islands of civility in a world in which civility was eroding. Only slowly, resentfully, and seldom gracefully did I come to accept the rather different reality.

Given the sense of competence I felt in my last undergraduate semesters, I would probably have chosen to do graduate work in political science even without an emotionally important intervention by a professor with whom I had taken several courses. In my senior year he asked if I wanted him to nominate me for a fellowship designated for undergraduates who wanted to prepare for a career in higher education. This sign of confidence in my abilities and potential, coming from someone I respected and admired, provided an emotional boost that sealed my decision.

Growing up with multifarious, often acute, stresses and striving to fit into changing surroundings made me particularly averse to instability and conflict in most forms. I sought to cope by identifying and learning the rules appropriate for a given setting and to relate to those around me through reason or logical discourse. It is not necessary to have psychoanalytic credentials to connect these dispositions to the choice of the academy as a place to work or to the focus on identity, community, integration, migration, and the peaceful management of conflict as the substantive foci of that work. For that matter, my more recent interests in cognitive and constructivist approaches and a growing preoccupation with relationships between social and formally organized institutions can also be traced to these orientations.

Seeking Shelter

A tension between the utilities of detached perspective and cultural adaptability, on the one hand, and the desire to belong to some sort of "community" on the other has been a hallmark of my work and my life. This personal tension has also been an intellectual, political, and scholarly enigma. The field of political sociology, perhaps because it brings the social scientific, political, and policy dimensions of problems together with normative concerns, has been my most comfortable intellectual home. Most of my work is located within the admittedly loose and ill-defined confines of that field—perhaps because its boundaries are blurry and readily penetrated. However, like many who have lived in the same house for a long time, I have added more rooms. Increasingly, since the mid-1980s, I have sought to link political sociology with international relations.

In the past few years I have found like-minded scholars in several disciplines and on both sides of the Atlantic who are engaged in similar endeavors. We have in common a concern with cutting across disciplinary and intellectual conventions in order to better understand the larger changes in the governance of societies, the interpenetration of states, the transformations of international systems, and the place of individuals and collectivities in this world of flux. We have created informal working groups, exchange ideas frequently, and occasionally undertake joint research and publication. Such collegial reinforcement is one of the most satisfying aspects of my work now. One source of satisfaction is the promise it holds for progress in what I deem to be the most important theoretical and "real world" ideas. But for me it is no less important that it provides the reassurance of an intellectual and professional community with which I identify and in which I am a valued contributing member.

I see my career as a chosen, lifelong studentship of some of the larger philosophical and social scientific issues of our time. If it once held the promise of escape from the harsher aspects of the larger world, I soon found that escape route illusory. And eventually I concluded that I neither needed nor wanted to escape.

Between Gesellschaft and Gemeinschaft

The centrifugal tug of a secular "middle European" life and the centripetal force of a strong Jewish communal identity would no doubt have pulled me in opposite directions, even if the Holocaust had not occurred. These tensions were evident in my parentage, and they entered some of my earliest memories.

The secular tendency was embedded in my father's side of my family. For several generations, they had been as thoroughly assimilated as Jews could be in central Europe. The Heislers had moved to the Turkish-occupied part of Hungary from Moravia in the sixteenth century.[10] My paternal grandmother's ancestors, the Bleiers, had migrated somewhat later, also from what is now the Czech Republic.[11] Although my father passed through the rite of bar mitzvah, only one of his two sisters was (somewhat) observant. In the sharpest possible contrast, my mother's family was rigorously Orthodox. They had migrated to Hungary in the mid–nineteenth century from what is now Moldova. Some settled in Szabadszállás (literally, free settlement), others in Transylvania. My maternal grandparents and my mother and her younger brother were meticulous in their observance. My father's second language was German, my mother's Yiddish. It was a point of pride in my father's family that no one knew Yiddish.

Our house in Szabadszállás had two kitchens, a kosher one in which my mother cooked and another, not kosher, for my father's long-widowed mother, who lived with us. One of my earliest memories is of a quarrel between my parents, when I was not yet three, about whether I should eat bacon (more precisely, salt pork). My father, who had no compunctions about eating pork, believed it would make me stronger (he thought I was anemic); my mother thought it would "ruin me for life." I do not remember the outcome but clearly recall the loud exchange and my mother crying.

Venturing a parallel between these differences in my family and the Gesellschaft-Gemeinschaft dichotomy developed by social theorists in the late nineteenth and early twentieth centuries risks gross oversimplification. But I have experienced the pull between those two poles in my intellectual as well as emotional life, and it reverberates through much of my work. The assimilationist stance of Hungarian Jews assumed a practical distinction between secular society and its public institutions, on the one hand, and a private domain in which subcultural differences could find expression. This stance coincided with notions of modern, enlightened, and secular society—Gesellschaft, as sketched by such social theorists as Tönnies, Durkheim, and Weber. Orthodox Jews, in Hungary and elsewhere, opted for the warmth and shelter of communal life, relatively closed, in the manner of what such writers termed Gemeinschaft.

The epigraph at the head of this chapter is taken from the facade of the principal Reformed synagogue in Brussels, built in 1934. For me, it embodies the self-effacing, assimilation-oriented posture many European Jews sought to hold between the world wars. It also resembles the attitude of my father and paternal grandmother toward religion and society. In direct contrast, my maternal grandmother and my great-uncle József often spoke about categorical distinctions between "us" and "them." "Us" referred more to Jews in Hungary than to Hungarian Jews. These differences have occupied my thinking and much of my research since I began field research for my dissertation in the 1960s. They elude "solutions" but must nonetheless concern us with increasing urgency and for the foreseeable future.

Personal Questions Are Professional Questions Are Personal Questions . . .

The tensions between citizenship in a secular society and the embrace of subsocietal or transsocietal collectivities are, thus, personal issues for me, but they also relate directly to my work in ethnic relations, migration, and the management of conflict. They are connected with the Holocaust as an epoch-defining event and with the Holocaust's legacy for me and my children and grandchildren. Ethnic cleansing in Bosnia and Kosovo is related to the Holocaust, which, in turn, is related to other genocides in this and previous ages, as well as to the ethnic cleansing of indigenous populations by conquerors and colonists.

Throughout all history, until the camps in and around Germany were opened and filmed in 1945, the predominant modes of dealing with diversity were persecution, subjugation, ethnic cleansing, and extermination. The perception of the desirability of finding harmonious ways for dominant cultural majorities and ethnic, religious, and other ascriptively based minorities to live at least side by side, if not together, has become more urgent since the Holocaust because knowledge of the Holocaust makes some "solutions" unacceptable. The general problematic takes many forms and can be encountered on many levels. In some instances—current examples are the ethnic genocide in the Great Lakes region of Africa, the conflicts in the former Yugoslavia, and the ongoing wars of Kurdistan—it takes the form of life-and-death conflict. In other cases it revolves around the distribution of resources or according of respect to one identity group or another.

I came on this set of issues by happenstance. While doing field research in Belgium for my dissertation, "Benelux in the European Community," in the 1960s, I encountered nascent Flemish and Walloon ethnic movements and saw the creation of a political party in Brussels by the city's French-speaking majority. The latter feared being "minoritized," as the more radical politicians in the country's Flemish majority demanded a redistribution of power in the capital's institutions. The residents of Brussels had been among the most thoroughly "secularized," cosmopolitan Belgians. The city was and is surrounded by communities of Dutch-speaking Flemings.

Although I had gone to study economic cooperation and legal and regulatory coordination on the international level, I found myself drawn more and more to Belgium's "communal" substate politics. After much agonizing and rewriting, and aided by the fact that faculty departures from UCLA necessitated the reconstitution of my committee, I somehow managed to integrate my original and newly stumbled-upon topics into a coherent dissertation.[12]

I was able to focus on ethnic politics in Belgium per se in the 1970s. In the course of several extended stays I looked at legal and public policy approaches to managing relations among the "linguistic communities" (the Belgian euphemism for ethnic and culturally distinguished segments of the population). But while the form my work took was the case study, in fact Belgium was my laboratory for more general problems confronting deeply divided societies. Between the mid-1970s and 1990 I focused increasingly on the normative elements of this process. In the earliest pieces I emphasized the peaceful, orderly aspects and contrasted these with developments in Northern Ireland, the Basque country of Spain, and numerous non-Western cases of conflict-ridden relations among ethnic or subsocietal cultural groups.[13] Indeed, writ large, the record of Western democratic regimes in dealing with ethnocultural cleavages has been relatively enlightened in the post-Holocaust era.[14] The lessons of the Holocaust and the normative changes occasioned by it are clearly more instrumental in such regimes than elsewhere.

Belgians managed their newly politicized cultural differences peacefully, through constitutional engineering. In the course of twenty-five years and several revisions of the constitution, the state's unitary architecture was rebuilt into a federal one. Belgium became a country of three regions, one Flemish, one Walloon, and one "mixed" Brussels. But if the process was democratic in that it was underwritten by large majorities, it violated other vital democratic norms. The civil liberties and individual and familial choices of minorities in the two larger regions and of the vast majority of French speakers in the Brussels region were essentially bargained away in the process. This bartering away of the rights and prerogatives of minorities in the interest of majorities concerned me more than it did most other observers of Belgium's solution to ethnic differences, and it continues to concern me.[15] The successes of Western societies in managing cultural differences and the nagging problems of protecting minority rights while accommodating majorities reflect both the learned and the undigestible lessons of the Holocaust.

The publics of Western democracies have internalized the values and norms in those lessons, and they seem to expect that their governments will export them to "less enlightened" places. Such efforts at the transnational propagation of one's own values are not new, of course. But their recent manifestations are noteworthy for their potential to reshape international relations as well as such justifications for war as humanitarian intervention. This trend is less indicative in my view of what Samuel Huntington has termed a "clash of civilizations"[16] than of the emergence of new normatively based hierarchies among countries and world regions.[17]

There is, of course, a way to resolve the tension between Gesellschaft and Gemeinschaft: nationalism. The reduction of the population in the state's territory to one all-encompassing Gemeinschaft coextensive with the German state was the National Socialist ideal, and cleansing the continent of "inferior" or "undesirable" population groups was the Nazi approach to rendering Europe into a civilization to the liking of their leaders. Ethnic cleansing in any guise is generically related to such radical nationalism. If we are to avoid such extreme and usually violent "solutions," we must content ourselves with managing such differences and moving them from the more virulent toward the more negotiable.

My strong preference for cosmopolitan, Gesellschaft-like frameworks for public life makes me dislike nationalism. At the same time, however, I appreciate nationalism's functions in integrating states and societies. It would be difficult to build modern, secular societies without such integration. The tension between my two "inherited" tendencies is evident here. I am particularly troubled by the question of how such societies can be created today without recourse to the sorts of nationalism (and, for that matter, also ethnic cleansing) crucial in the not-too-remote past in the formative processes of what are now secular Western democracies. These concerns began to shift my research focus from ethnic relations per se to a consideration of how new minorities fared in Western democracies. By "new minorities" I mean migrants or immigrants.[18]

My earlier tendency toward ambivalence when confronted by choices between assimilation and communal distinctiveness has been an undercurrent in my work on migration and the treatment and circumstances of migrants in the host societies. I am sensitive to the tensions between inclusion in public life through secular roles and institutions, on the one hand, and the potential that enclaves and other forms of self-segregation have for mitigating the harsh, less than welcoming realities migrants often face, on the other. While I certainly have no answers for these and related problems, with the passage of time I have become fairly firmly attached to the secular, integrative orientation to which I alluded earlier.

A Bias in Favor of Inclusion

Most of my work shows strong biases toward liberal democratic political and constitutional arrangements, inclusion and integration.[19] At one level this may be simply a reflection of coming of political age in the late 1950s and early 1960s, during the integrative phase of the U.S. civil rights movement of which Dr. Martin Luther King Jr.'s "I Have a Dream" speech was emblematic. And, while I cannot identify specific words or actions through which he might have transmitted it to me, my stance seems an extension of my father's, as an assimilated, middle-class, central European Jew who grew up in the 1920s and early 1930s.[20] But it also follows from my interpretations of the Holocaust. At first emotionally and unconsciously and later based on more careful thought, it occurred to me that the first outrage lay in the distinctions drawn in populations—of Germany, then the rest of Europe, and, in the large, the world.

The liberal democratic inclination favors the rights of individuals over those of collectivities. It often interposes the state—civil, civic, and secular authority—between social groups (such as the family or the church or the ethnic group) and the individual, in order to protect the latter. It tilts toward Gesellschaft and seeks opportunities for moving away from the more claustrophobic, tyranny-of-the-group aspects of Gemeinschaft. It stresses citizenship over identity. Ideally, if all individuals are protected, then the members of all groups are protected—as long as their practices as members of the group do not impinge on the liberties of others.

This view is clearly losing favor. My steadfast adherence to it reflects some combination of my "background," young adult socialization, and deeply held commitment to cosmopolitan values and Weltanschauung. In sum, I believe that to reify group boundaries through formalizing and institutionalizing cultural, ethnic, religious, or other such traits is to legitimize the sorts of claims or "hold" that the group can have on people. These were the chains of stifling social control against which Rousseau agitated. In such cases, it is the subsocietal group, rather than the larger society or the state, that is the source of threat to individual liberty. Allowing social institutions to exercise such power permits the sorts of distinctions that are the precursors of discrimination, persecution, and ultimately even genocide. Such normative, and eventually institutional or legal, bounding of ascriptive identities tends to undermine the effectiveness and legitimacy of formal institutions—schools, government, laws, and so forth. It makes majorities impossible and consensual bargains among particularistic groups much more difficult. This is a reason to oppose, as I do, strongly, the cultural particularism or self-segregation that is increasingly observable in many otherwise democratic societies.

Nonpracticing, essentially assimilated Jews in central Europe, like my father's family had been for generations, gained personal freedom by balancing the Jewish dimensions of their identity with the secular, civic elements. Like Protestants, the largest religious minority in Hungary, they associated those elements with security and opportunity, and, given the extent of freedom of religious practice in the country, embracing them did not appear to entail undue sacrifice. And, viewed with or without irony, ultimately it made no difference. My point is not that the fates of assimilated and nonassimilated Jews should have differed. Rather, it is that what I have termed *ethnic nominalism* deprived them of influence over their own identities. This was not the case for nonassimilated Jews.

Reading Different Lessons into the Holocaust

In *Politics in Europe* (1974), I treated issues in style and method in the field of comparative politics in a way that was at once critical and constructive; and the work also marked the orientation to theory building I still follow: expanding the scope of a theory's coverage by modest moves up the ladder of generalization. I sought to provide a single set of internally consistent, testable propositions that shed light on the political structures and processes of a larger number of what had been, for earlier writers, two or more distinct classes of smaller European democracies—in particular, the Low Countries, the Nordic states, Switzerland, and Austria and, in more qualified ways, such larger countries as Germany and France.

The substantive thrust of that work was a threefold emphasis on inclusion that is still my central occupation, both normatively and theoretically. First, as just noted, it aimed at theoretical cumulation and the progressive inclusion of more cases and types within the purview of a coherent theoretical framework. Second, the political style and substance by which it characterized European democracies hinged on the "co-optation" or inclusion of most segments of populations and political groups.[21] Finally, I began to articulate, twenty-five years ago, a normative disposition toward inclusion, integration, and institutional approaches to the management of differences.

These views now permeate my work on ethnic relations, identity, and transnational migration (and, to a lesser extent, in a realm I cannot explore here, in international relations).[22] They have led me to disagree with the analytic, theoretical, and prescriptive positions of scholars whose work I hold in the highest possible regard, whose social and political values fully accord with mine, and several of whom are my friends. The disagreement is most notably reflected in my resistance to their tendencies, at once analytic and prescriptive, to treat ascriptive group boundaries as fixed or "right" and appropriately preserved through the legal and institutional agency of the state.

There are such tendencies in the work of such writers as Arend Lijphart, Donald Horowitz, and Ted Robert Gurr.[23] In different ways, each of them tends to reify and fix or freeze the identitive boundaries of ascriptive groups. Their aim may be to provide recognition for minorities, in order to protect them from oppression or violence (Gurr); or to limit contacts (and, thus, potential conflict) among ordinary people with fundamentally different and perhaps hostile values and goals, so as to permit the presumably more enlightened or farsighted leaders of factions to negotiate intergroup differences (Lijphart); or to devise electoral schemes and party systems that will help to prevent a sense of isolation and threat among minorities (Horowitz). While the protection of minorities, and perhaps even the assertion of group (as distinct from individual) rights, was greatly energized and largely legitimated by the lessons of the Holocaust, I drew a different lesson.

I term the reification of the boundaries of ethnic, religious, or other sorts of ascriptive groups *ethnic nominalism*.[24] Unlike with some of my other theoretical and normative positions, I recognized its antecedents even as I was formulating it: they reside in what I see as the first phase of the Holocaust—the conditions, processes, and norms that preceded the event itself. When the National Socialists fomented anti-Semitism, they also challenged the autonomy of individuals, families, and communities to define themselves and to determine the hierarchies of their identities and loyalties. Assimilated Jews in Germany became particular targets in the early stages of the Third Reich, and assimilation was, in a perverted fashion, cited as evidence of the great threat of "insinuation" into German society. Subsequently, they became targets in many of the occupied countries of central Europe as well.

My bias against demarcating segments of populations, including ethnic or religious minorities, in a formal, institutionalized fashion on the basis of shared nominal characteristics stems from this interpretation of the Holocaust. Persecution is wrong, by definition. Using ascriptive traits as the basis for persecution was and remains absolutely wrong, by any moral standard we can adduce. It is perhaps a lesser wrong, but wrong nonetheless, to deny people the opportunity to be masters of their own identity. In central Europe, in particular, fully assimilated people were redefined, even while others were defined, by the state, by fiat. This lesser wrong was a precondition to genocide, both logically and operationally. It facilitated, perhaps even permitted, the perversion of the norms and machinery of the legal systems of the states that committed those acts. It provided the perpetrators with a very thin veneer of justification that helped to sell inherently illegitimate policies to populations more or less disposed to accept en masse nominal characterization where case-by-case prosecution and adjudication by conventional laws would clearly not have worked. (In other parts of Europe, particularly in the former Soviet Union, identities have long been externally imposed, and changing them has been problematic.)

These perspectives and biases reflect my strong commitment to secular society. A few commentators find my work on migration and citizenship conservative or hostile to immigrants because I express concern for the dominant cultural majorities in receiving countries as well as for the newcomers.[25] But, for me, such concerns reflect not so much conservatism (although I do not shy from the label as regards societal institutions and culture) as a radical commitment to secularism and the equitable, evenhanded, and impersonal rule of laws common to all. The Holocaust represents the grossest possible violation of such secularism and societally universal laws. To abandon hope that secular regimes based on the republican ideals of the Enlightenment are possible would accord the Holocaust's perpetrators a posthumous victory long after their demise. At least in the democratic West and where its values may gain sway, the hope seems worth keeping. Holding on to it is one way of combating the tendencies the Holocaust embodied.

To be sure, much of the world is not at all like western and central Europe, and perhaps western and central Europe no longer resemble the mental images or models by which I characterize them. For several reasons, my differences in approaches to the complexities and dangers inherent in divided societies with the scholars to whose work I alluded above may already be losing relevance. They are, for the most part, concerned with different parts of the world; or they may see threatening tendencies on the horizon that are less apparent to me; or I may come to realize that my values derive from skewed images of the past—a sign of the pathology of the survivor. But I think not. My values reflect continuity from a particular cultural, social, and political past in early-twentieth-century central Europe (my paternal grandfather's and father's world) to my coming of age during the struggle for civil rights in the United States. These optics may limit, rather than sharpen, my sight, but they do not reflect such pathology.

For me, the Holocaust is more a bridge than a chasm. It leads me to see British policy in Northern Ireland as clumsy and ineffective, but, at the same time, I am offended and distressed by the methods, from murder and "kneecapping" to ostracism, used by Protestants and Catholics in the province to enforce group solidarity. The appropriate response, in my terms, is to develop more inclusive norms and effective integrative institutions—culturally sensitive, to be sure, but secular—at a higher (i.e., larger societal or state or even multistate regional or, eventually, universal) level. I would like to believe that, except for the Holocaust, that is what my nuclear family would have become.

How Should We Read the Normative Lessons of the Holocaust?

But what of others, Jewish or not, who place less emphasis on the freedom of individual choice in the liberal democratic ethos than I do? Should liberal democratic norms regarding the individual's autonomy in determining her or his identity, or the according of primacy to secular public institutions over the ascription-based solidarity of subsocietal groups, be imposed on them? Who decides, using what sorts of criteria? What—whose—norms should prevail? And is the security of a group sometimes a precondition for the security of its individual members, in a fashion that militates in favor of a sharp and public identification of group boundaries, the more inclusive the better?[26] Or, from the perspective of minorities, must the group be exclusive, orthodox, or "pure"? Are intermarriage and assimilation threats to identity, culture, and the political influence of a larger minority, even perhaps giving rise to the metaphor of "cultural genocide"?

The literatures on "multiculturalism"[27] and "pluriculturalism"[28] point to dangers as well as possibilities. I am not confused or intimidated by the complexity or dissensus in those literatures and the discussions that revolve around them, but I am troubled by some of the real world manifestations of the issues. The absence of symbiotic relationships or evident constructive connections between social and formal institutions and the progressive, by now quite serious, erosion of the capacities of the latter (in almost all domains, in many countries) is a source of significant concern.[29] But some of the possible forms of such connections would be no less troubling.[30]

Two sets of problems accompany the group-focused, pluricultural thrust of many scholarly as well as political ideas in vogue today. I have already noted my main concern at the micro level: the individual's (and, for that matter, the family's or small group's) prerogatives in actions, associations, lifestyles, and self-identification may be sacrificed for a collective good that may well be imaginary. The larger society, acting through the state, will not be able to balance the social and psychological instruments of suasion at the disposal of the group with legal and civil protection. What may appear as solidarity or community at the level of the group, whether evoked for defensive (i.e., the protection of minority rights) or other purposes, is exclusivist and potentially conflict fostering at the levels of the society, the multicountry region, and the world. The rules and institutions for harmonious, constructive interaction across group boundaries are more, rather than less, difficult to envision and construct, in my judgment, than are rules and institutions for harmonious, constructive interaction within larger social units. There is no compelling reason to think that it is easier to avoid or regulate conflict between people delineated into ethnic or religious or national identity groups than to achieve peaceful civil relations within integrative frameworks.

Finally, in this normative vein, is there an attainable, felicitous balance between the protection of minority rights *cum* group rights and social, cultural, economic, and political change over time? If we heed those lessons of the Holocaust that militate in favor of protecting minority groups' rights as collective rather than individual rights, and if we institutionalize the boundaries of ascriptive groups through transnational norms and international agents, do we end up with ethnocultural zoos? Will the political and social (and perhaps even economic) structuration of minority groups, abetted by normatively sanctioned international protection, foster less intergroup conflict? Will it promote the well-being of the members of protected groups? Is such circumscription of culturally (and, at least at the boundaries, essentially only nominally) identified populations the best we can do to protect the vulnerable from persecution or extermination? The sad history of the intracommunity dynamics of Catholic-Protestant relations in Northern Ireland is, regrettably, only one of myriad illustrations of the answer.

One function of writing this chapter has been to explore this ground. From here, I can perhaps proceed to a more comprehensive reconstruction of my life and of the early experiences that shaped the seemingly rational social scientist and person I have projected, both outwardly and to myself. That exercise will be both an imaginary explanation to my mother of my life's course and that of the world after her death in Bergen-Belsen and an introduction for my grandchildren of an important part of their foundations. And in it I will take great pains to imbed the personal in the public—self in the family, the family in the society, and the society in the world. To borrow the line that Philip Roth gave a psychiatrist, to end one of his novels, "Now perhaps we can begin."[31]

NOTES

I am deeply grateful to Peter Suedfeld for the invitation to participate in this enterprise and for many helpful, constructive editorial suggestions; to David Rapoport, who, though retired, continues to be my teacher through his sensitive reading of an earlier draft; and to my grandsons, Raoul Joseph Heisler and Seth Navon Goldstein, for the inspiration to undertake and stay with this somewhat painful exercise in applied memory.

1. Mickey Rooney, then a teenage movie star, was said to suffer from the ailment, and its visibility on the research landscape seems to have been high in the late 1930s and early 1940s. I was taken to see the reputedly best orthopedic specialists in Budapest when my recovery from a bruised bone, caused by a fall from a tree while picking berries, was slow to heal.

2. My mother was taken from a streetcar in one of those roundups, on

November 15, 1944, while she was desperately looking for a place for us in one of the "Swedish protected [apartment] houses" created by Raoul Wallenberg, on the last day designated for finding such *relatively* safe haven. Unknown to her, others in the family had found such an apartment hours before. She died in Bergen-Belsen in March 1945. The dictate requiring all Jews over the age of six to wear the yellow star took effect on April 5, 1944. That was my sixth birthday; perhaps that, and the fact that my mother's maiden name was Stern—German for star—is why I have always taken the wearing of the star personally.

3. Except my father, who was in a labor camp in Austria from early 1943 until the end of the war. Of course, I did not know who Wallenberg was. What stayed in my mind were the dark car; the tall man in a long, dark coat; his heated discussions with the soldiers; and the end of the shooting and our return inside.

4. He was both my great-uncle, my maternal grandmother's younger brother, and my uncle by marriage, married to one of my father's two sisters. It is his widow, Elizabeth, now in her nineties, who has helped me to place many of my memories from the 1940s.

5. From about the time I was ten until József, Elizabeth, and their daughter and her family arrived in the United States after the Hungarian uprising of 1956, I do not recall any mention of her at all. It was József who brought her memory back to me in the last years of his life.

6. My father had been active in the last pre-communist coalition government and had resisted the takeover. Fearing arrest in early 1949, he—with me in tow—sought to escape the country. After being caught once at the Czechoslovak border and once near the Austrian, we succeeded crossing the latter with the aid of a guide who had a mixed reputation for knowing his way through the minefield and barbed wire. (That his reputation was mixed could be deduced from the hand and part of one foot he had lost in earlier crossings.) In addition to the clothes we wore (I virtually lived in my one suit for more than a year), we had some diamonds my father had sewn into seams in his trousers.

7. There were about three hundred refugees, mostly Hungarians and Czechs, in one ward, separated into one hundred "rooms" with blankets suspended from strings serving as walls. I do not know how my father made the arrangements for my placement, but the resources for my trip and tuition came from some of the diamonds sewn into his clothes.

8. The stressful atmosphere is readily explained by my father's predicament and the effort of the other adults in the house (his mother and widowed sister) to treat him with consideration. He had to find a way to support us (and, after remarrying, a wife and stepchild), initially knowing no English and having no relevant trade or profession, capital, or contacts. He succeeded to a remarkable extent but at a high cost to himself and those around him.

9. For better or for worse, my ideas of academic life came from the earliest of C. P. Snow's Strangers and Brothers novels.

10. The Turkish administration had opened three small towns to Jews in 1526 and used the right to own land as incentive for them to settle. The name Heisler may derive from a German term for a landless peasant.

11. The information about the Heisler side comes from the landholding records of Apostag, one of the three towns in question. Those records were pre-

served through World War II. My father traced his ancestry on his mother's side, the Bleiers, through similar, though more fragmentary, records in Szabadszállás, another of those towns. The family business, lumber and building materials, was established in Szabadszállás in the mid–nineteenth century on land owned by Heislers and Bleiers. Szabadszállás was our home, as well as that of my maternal grandparents and my father's mother before 1944.

12. *Political Community and Its Formation in the Low Countries* (Ann Arbor: University Microfilms, 1970).

13. See, for instance, "Institutionalizing Societal Cleavages in a Co-optive Polity: The Growing Importance of the Output Side in Belgium," *Politics in Europe: Structures and Processes in Some Postindustrial Democracies,* edited by Martin O. Heisler (New York: David McKay, 1974), chap. 5; "Managing Ethnic Conflict in Belgium," *Annals of the American Academy of Political and Social Science* 433 (September 1977): 32–46; "Ethnic Division in Belgium," in *Self Rule/Shared Rule,* edited by D. J. Elazar (Ramat Gan, Israel: Turtledove Publishing, 1979); "Scarcity and the Management of Political Conflict in Multicultural Polities" (with B. G. Peters), *International Political Science Review* 4, no. 3 (1983): 327–44.

14. Martin O. Heisler, "Ethnicity and Ethnic Relations in the Modern West," in *Conflict and Peacemaking in Multiethnic Societies,* edited by J. V. Montville (Lexington, MA: Lexington/D. C. Heath, 1990), chap.2.

15. Martin O. Heisler, "Hyphenating Belgium: Changing State and Regime to Cope with Cultural Division," in *Conflict and Peacemaking in Multiethnic Societies,* edited by J. V. Montville (Lexington, MA: Lexington/D. C. Heath, 1990), chap. 12; Martin O. Heisler, "Belgium," in *Global Studies: Western Europe,* 6th ed., edited by H. J. Warmenhoven (Guilfold, CT: Dushkin/McGraw-Hill, 1999).

16. Samuel P. Huntington, *The Clash of Civilizations and the Remaking of World Order* (New York: Simon and Schuster, 1996).

17. I have broached some of these ideas in a few places and am currently developing them in longer studies. See, for instance, "Migration, International Relations, and the New Europe: Theoretical Perspectives from Institutional Political Sociology," *International Migration Review* 26, no. 2 (summer 1992): 596–622; "Some Normative Caveats in the Pursuit of the Rights of Ethnic Minorities," *Journal of Ethno-Development* 4, no. 1 (July 1994): 79–82; "Contextualizing Global Migration: Sketching the Socio-Political Landscape in Europe," *UCLA Journal of International Law and Foreign Affairs* 3, no. 2 (fall/winter 1998–99): 557–93; "Now and Then, Here and There: Migration and the New Normative and Political Divides in International Relations," in *Identities, Borders, Orders,* edited by M. Albert, D. Jacobson, and Y. Lapid (Minneapolis: University of Minnesota Press, forthcoming); and in several other works currently in press.

18. See, for instance, Martin O. Heisler and Barbara Schmitter Heisler, eds., *From Foreign Workers to Settlers? Transnational Migration and the Emergence of New Minorities, Annals of the American Academy of Political and Social Science* 485 (May 1986); Martin O. Heisler and Barbara Schmitter Heisler, "Citizenship—Old, New, and Changing: Inclusion, Exclusion, and Limbo for Ethnic Groups and Migrants in the Modern Democratic State," in *Dominant National Cultures and Ethnic Identities,* edited by J. Fijalkowski et al. (Berlin: Free University of Berlin, 1991), pt. 1, 91–128; Heisler, "Contextualizing Global Migration"; Heisler, "Now

and Then, Here and There"; and a book in progress, tentatively entitled "Migrants, Refugees and the Future of World Politics."

19. It is "liberal democratic" in the classic nineteenth-century sense elaborated by such political philosophers as John Stuart Mill, but it has often also been liberal democratic in the contemporary U.S. political sense. Classical liberal democracy offers protection to the individual from oppressive social institutions (civic rights—consider the opening passages of Rousseau's *Social Contract*) as well as from the state (civil liberties—which are based on the individual's standing). In general, I find Daniel Bell's self-characterization congenial: pluralist in politics, socialist in economics, and culturally conservative. (See Daniel Bell, *The Winding Passage* [New York: Free Press, 1980].)

20. Some of Peter Gay's essays, as well as his recent book, *My German Question: Growing up in Nazi Berlin* (New Haven: Yale University Press, 1998), provide eloquent testimony to that frame of mind, as does Reinhard Bendix's *From Berlin to Berkeley: German-Jewish Identities* (New Brunswick, NJ: Transaction Books, 1986), at once a biography of his father and an autobiography.

21. A recent illustration of theoretical use of my formulation can be found in Bart Caimans, "Do Institutions Make a Difference? Non-Institutionalism, Neo-Institutionalism, and the Logic of Common Decision-Making in the European Union," *Governance* 9, no. 2 (April 1996): 217–40.

22. More complete and sophisticated theoretical statements on the inclusion of minorities and the sometimes associated exclusion of immigrants appear in "Ethnicity and Ethnic Relations in the Modern West"; Heisler and Heisler, "Citizenship—Old, New and Changing"; "Migration, International Relations and the New Europe"; and in my chapter, with Zig Layton-Henry, in *Identity, Migration, and the New Security Agenda in Europe,* edited by Ole Wæver et al. (London: Pinter, 1993).

23. No single work by these three very prolific as well as very important scholars captures the concerns I have in mind here. Most of Lijphart's work deriving from the assumptions of his well-known "consociational democracy" model and his book on South Africa are relevant; Horowitz has several theoretical and prescriptive or institution-design articles that apply, as does his monograph on a democratic design for South Africa. Among Gurr's writings, perhaps his 1993 book, *Minorities at Risk,* is the most obvious here.

24. Heisler, "Ethnicity and Ethnic Relations in the Modern West"; and "Some Normative Caveats."

25. See, for instance, Robin Cohen's introduction in the anthology *Politics of Migration,* edited by Robin Cohen and Zig Layton-Henry (London: Edward Elgar, 1997), in which an earlier article of mine is the opening selection.

26. This is my interpretation of the position underlying much of Ted Robert Gurr's recent work.

27. See, for instance, Amy Guttmann, ed., *Multiculturalism,* 2d ed. (Princeton: Princeton University Press, 1994).

28. On the instability of the multicultural ideal and its tendency to degenerate into pluriculturalism, see, especially, Jean Bethke Elshtain's *Democracy on Trial* (New York: Basic Books, 1995).

29. This is the thrust of many of the recent expressions of concern over "the

loss of social capital." See, for example, Robert Putnam, "Tuning in, Tuning out: The Strange Disappearance of Social Capital in America," *Political Science and Politics* 28, no. 4 (December 1995): 664–83.

30. I sketched some of the argument in "Some Limits on and Utilities of Notions of Social Capital in Analyzing Transnational Economic Activities of Ethnic and Immigrant Groups," a paper for a workshop entitled "Social Capital, International Trade, and Investment" convened at the National Bureau of Economic Research West, Stanford University, March 1996, to explore some of the issues raised by Putnam's seminal argument.

31. More precisely, "So [said the doctor], Now vee may perhaps to begin. Yes?" Philip Roth, *Portnoy's Complaint* (New York: Random House, 1967), 274.

Studying and Promoting Altruism and Studying and Working to Prevent Genocide

The Guiding Role of Early Survival

Ervin Staub

Biographical Note

Ervin Staub is professor of psychology at the University of Massachusetts, Amherst. His primary areas of work have been in altruism and helping behavior and in harm doing, especially genocide and other collective violence as well as torture and youth violence. In addition to having writ-ten many articles and book chapters, he is the author of Positive Social Behavior and Morality *(two volumes) and* The Roots of Evil *and editor of several other books, including* Patriotism in the Lives of Individuals and Groups.

Professor Staub has received the Otto Klineberg Intercultural and International Prize of the Society for the Psychological Study of Social Issues and other awards. He has recently served as president of the Peace Psychology Division of the American Psychological Association and presi-dent of the International Society of Political Psychology. He has applied the results of his research to many public concerns and issues, including positive child rear-ing, racism, school bullying, motivating bystanders to intervene when violence occurs, teacher and police training programs, and, most recently, a project in Rwanda on healing, reconciliation, and forgiveness.

<hr/>

Introduction

The connection between much of my work and my Holocaust experience is quite obvious. My work was probably also affected by my post-Holocaust experience of living under a communist system in Hungary, escaping from Hungary without my family, living in Vienna, then coming to the United States alone.

I did some early work on fear, control and lack of control, and the use of information and control to reduce fear. At the time, in no way did I connect this work to my own life experiences. I have spent most of my career studying what leads people to help others, what leads them to remain passive in the face of others' need, what leads them to harm others. The latter included the study of the origins of genocide and other collective violence. Underlying all my work has been an interest in change: How can we develop caring in children? How can people become more helpful? How can we reduce youth violence? How can we eliminate violence by groups against innocent people? A thread through all my work has been the study of the passivity and the potential power of bystanders, of individuals and groups who witness suffering or harm inflicted on others.

While the connection of this work to my Holocaust experience is quite clear, for many years I ignored and disregarded this connection, almost denied it. I survived the Holocaust and I was involved with my work, and I emotionally separated these two domains.

The connection broke through at some points. I started this kind of research in the late 1960s. I remember reading Leon Uris's book *Mila Seventeen* sometime in the early to mid-1970s, a book about a German doctor in the post–World War II world, a seeming humanitarian and altruist, who was a Nazi doctor at a concentration camp during the war. He conducted some of the horrible, cruel, Nazi "medical experiments." I cried at one point and felt a renewed determination to do my work on helping and altruism. I felt deeply that I wanted to do what I could to help create a world in which human beings won't do horrible things to others.

Why did I need to disconnect my early experience and my work? Did I want to think that I was doing science, studying what was "objectively valuable," rather than indulging in something related to myself? Did my training in psychology lead me to believe that studying something that arose out of my life experience would make my work less valuable? Did I think that it would make my work less credible? Did I feel it would make me into a victim, treated condescendingly? Or was I defending myself from more directly engaging with the Holocaust, with my experiences and their impact on me? Perhaps all of these were true, to varying degrees.

From Survival to Becoming a Psychologist

I was six years old, living in Budapest, when in the summer of 1944 bad times were replaced by the worst of times. That summer all the Jews in Hungary who lived outside Budapest were driven or taken from their homes, packed into cattle cars, and transported to Auschwitz. Most of them were immediately killed. After the summer more were taken from Budapest. Out of a total of about 600,000 Jews in Hungary, about 450,000 were killed.

The bad times started for us way before that. Hungary was a voluntary ally of Germany, and it tried to match Hitler's anti-Semitic policies. In some ways it preceded them. For example, in 1920 a law was passed, the so-called numerus clausus, that limited Jewish entry into universities.

Our family and my mother's sister's family lived together in a large apartment in Budapest. The two families owned a small business together. They made trousseaus for women about to marry—bed linen, nightgowns, tablecloths, and so on. My earliest clear memory is of lying in bed at night as my uncle said good-bye to me and next morning waking up to sounds of crying as my family gathered to tearfully say good-bye to him as he left for a forced labor camp. All Hungarian Jewish men were called up for forced labor. I do not remember when my father left.

There were many "memorable" events in the years 1944 and early 1945, until the Soviet army liberated Budapest. In the spring of 1944 the ruler of Hungary, Admiral Horthy, realized that the war would be lost. He approached the Allies for a separate peace. The Germans discovered this and occupied Hungary. I was on the main street of Budapest, a street that encircled the city, with our maid Maria (nicknamed Macs, who joined our family before I was born and remained until she was the last surviving member in Budapest) when the German tanks rolled down the street. It was after this that a small group of Germans, helped by Hungarians, transported all Jews from the countryside to Auschwitz.

Things were bad in the city as well. Some people behaved in an intensely anti-Semitic manner. A coal merchant from across the street used to come into our apartment house around dawn, stand in the courtyard, and scream threats and degrading epithets at the Jewish residents of the building. In the fall the Hungarian Nazi Party, the Arrow Cross, took over the government. They gathered many Jews, took them down to the Danube, and shot them. Sometimes they tied several people together, shot some but not all of them, and pushed them all into the river.

My mother and aunt were courageous women and, like many survivors, did all that was in their power to save us. There were a number of incidents in which they showed courage and determination. For example, once we were told that all young men of a certain age were to gather in the courtyard, to be taken to work. My aunt prohibited my fifteen-year-old cousin from going. When he insisted, too scared to stay away, she slapped him, an infrequent occurrence in our household. He stayed. Those who went did not return.

In an incident that vividly stands out in my memory my aunt also saved her thirteen-year-old daughter. There was a bakery right next to the entrance of the apartment house where we lived. One late afternoon my cousin Eva went outside, a perilous enterprise, to stand in line for bread. She did not wear a yellow star, perhaps because of a curfew on Jews. Someone recognized her and proclaimed that she was Jewish. She ran into the house, with three young Nazis chasing her. They wanted to take her away. My aunt encountered them just inside the entrance to the house. She shouted at them. She was so forceful that she intimidated them. They said they would come back with the police, but they never did. I watched this scene from the top of the stairs leading up from the entrance of the house to the mezzanine.

At some point my mother and aunt managed to get us protective passes. These passes were the creation of Raoul Wallenberg, a Swedish diplomat. Wallenberg was a member of an extremely wealthy and distinguished family, but he came from an impoverished branch of that family. He was the partner of a Hungarian Jew living in Sweden, with whom he operated an export-import firm. In this connection he had visited Hungary and met his partner's relatives who were still living there. After the terrible summer of 1944, he was asked to go to Hungary to try to save the lives of some of the remaining Hungarian Jews.

Wallenberg agreed. He threw himself into his mission with great intensity, determination, and courage. On his arrival in Budapest he immediately created a document that said that the bearer would move to

Sweden after the war and would be under the protection of Sweden for the duration of the war. He cajoled the Hungarian authorities into respecting a certain number of these, constantly negotiating, threatening, persuading government officials. He as well as the underground created many more of these documents. He repeatedly endangered his life. He helped people in many ways: for example, pulling Jews off trains, handing them protective passes, and then claiming that they were under Swedish protection.

He bought apartment houses in Budapest, and people with protective passes moved into them. We were among these people. I remember the night when we left our apartment, pushing a cart with some belongings on the way to the protected house. We were very scared that someone, whether police, Arrow Cross, or hostile civilians, would stop us. At that time and place Jews were fair game for anyone.

On our arrival we first slept on mattresses in the basement with many other people. Later we graduated to the one-room apartment of an old woman who was ill. The old woman was in bed most of the time. I don't remember how we did this, but I believe eight of us stayed there.

I think that my lifelong concern with those who don't remain passive but instead help others, my interest in "active bystanders," was to an important extent inspired by Macs, even more than by Raoul Wallenberg. I regard her as my second mother, a woman who loved me, my sister, and my cousins dearly. In these terrible times she did all she could to help us. Sometime before we received the protective passes she took me and my sister into hiding with a Christian family. I remember walking with her on the street, holding on to her hand; arriving at the house and then standing in front of the door of the apartment where the family lived; entering the apartment and seeing a woman sitting on a stool peeling potatoes. That is just about all I remember from the week or two we spent there. When some people in the house where this family lived seemed suspicious of the "child relatives visiting from the countryside," Macs moved us to another family. After we received the protective passes, she brought us back home.

During our stay at the protected house, she prepared bread, which she took in a baby carriage to be baked at a bakery. The bread and other food she acquired fed many people in the house. Once she was stopped by Arrow Cross men and accused of helping Jews. She had to stand for hours with her hands held up, facing a wall. She firmly denied helping Jews. They let her go, and she continued helping us.

She went to the separate labor camps where my father and uncle were doing forced labor and brought them copies of the protective passes. These were useless in their situation. But perhaps possession of a pass gave my father courage. Whatever enabled him to do it, when his group was taken to Germany, during an overnight stopover at some army barracks in Budapest he escaped. He was the only one of the group to survive. He came to our protected house and hid there until the Soviet army arrived.

During a number of raids on our house, miraculously, he was not found. The protected houses were constantly raided, and many people were taken away. Once during a raid my father was hiding under an armchair that was pushed into the corner, with a blanket casually thrown over it. The Arrow Cross raiders searched every closet, every drawer, but did not find him. I was the one who saw them march down the street toward the house, called out to inform the rest of my family, and ran to the apartment door to check that they were actually entering the house. I don't know whether hiding my father under the armchair was a plan my mother had designed earlier or a strategy that she thought up in that terribly dangerous moment.

Finally, late January 1945 our part of the city was liberated by the Soviet army. A number of my relatives did not survive. My uncle froze to death in the forced labor camp. My father's sister and her two children were killed in Auschwitz. But we were "luckier" than most people. The fathers of most of the Jewish boys who survived died in forced labor camps or in German death camps.

From Communist Hungary to the United States

Life after the Nazi period was complicated and difficult but not life threatening to us. We moved back to our apartment. My parents restarted their business but on a very small scale, selling men's, women's, and children's underclothing at their small store. They had to start from scratch, since most of the people to whom they gave goods from their business for safekeeping did not return them. They claimed that the merchandise was taken by the Germans or the Russians. My mother later repeatedly saw tablecloths in the apartment of the superintendent of our apartment house, one of our trusted keepers of goods, that were supposedly taken by the Russians or Germans.

In 1948 the communists took power. After a wave of nationalization, they finally reached the bottom of the barrel and in 1953 nationalized very small businesses. My parents' business was closed, the goods in it taken away with nominal compensation. My parents were religious; my father did not want to work on Saturdays, so he went to work in a newly created Jewish toy making cooperative. At age fifty-seven, after a lifetime of working with textiles in some way or another, he started to work on a machine, making toys. My mother took orders for sweaters from individuals and had the sweaters made for them. This was illegal, since one was only allowed to sell sweaters that one had made oneself. We had an old weaving machine at home, a machine that did not actually work, in case the police came.

Our family had disintegrated. In 1949 my cousins escaped from Hungary. They had to escape, since the communist government did not allow people to leave. They went to Israel. In 1953 their mother was allowed to follow them.

In 1956 I finished high school, a technical high school. Not being of worker or peasant origin, and therefore considered politically unreliable, I was afraid of not getting into a university and of having few options after high school. Even though the engineering studies in my school did not appeal to me, I followed the only university possibility that seemed available. I succeeded in enrolling at a technical university in Miskolc, another Hungarian city, to study engineering.

Soon after this, in October 1956, the Hungarian revolution began. I had a variety of adventures during this time, of which I will mention one that says something both about me and about the persistent anti-Semitism in Hungary that probably reinforced some of the psychological effects of the Holocaust. One day the police barracks in Miskolc were raided and the police in them arrested. I was in front of the police building when this happened. A revolutionary council, or something like that, took over the city. My somewhat adventurous nature landed me, the day after, inside City Hall. Outside people were milling around, demanding that the now jailed police be handed over to them. A number of people, communists, secret police, whatever, had already been tied to cars and pulled around the city in revenge. There were discussions inside the building that I participated in. It was decided that a few students who were in the building would put on armbands to indicate they were from the university, go outside, and try to calm people.

Outside, people converged in small groups. Jews were one of the central points of their heated discussions. They believed that the new prime minister, who turned out to be quite temporary, before Imre Nagy took over, was Jewish. He was not, and I tried to assure them of that, acting as an informed, neutral person. I could have been in serious trouble had they found out I was Jewish.

When Miskolc calmed down, students with guns on their shoulders began to direct traffic, and I decided it was time to go home. I made my way to Budapest by train, by hitching rides on trucks and other vehicles, and by walking. Life there was very exciting, with hope for a better future. Then the Russian troops returned and after intense fighting put the revolution down. Even before this, an exodus to the West began. Mines and barbed wire that used to protect the border had been removed in the course of the easing of communist repression that was a precursor to revolt. Once the revolt started, the border was relatively unguarded. While some people were caught and some were shot, almost two hundred thousand people got through the borders surrounding Hungary.

I was one of them, leaving with two friends. I immediately wanted to go to the United States, but I did not get a visa. I lived in Vienna for two and a half years. I first did nothing, then enrolled at the technical university, then changed to the University of Vienna. Because I went to a technical high school in Hungary, in order to transfer I was required to take the final high school exams again. After one year at the university, in July 1959 I came to the United States.

I went directly to Minnesota, arranged to study at the university, and supported myself with varied jobs while doing so. I received my B.A. in psychology in 1962 and went to graduate school at Stanford, where I received a Ph.D. in 1965. I specialized in personality psychology my first year, then also took clinical courses and did clinical practica. In the fall of 1965 I started my first job as assistant professor of clinical psychology in the Department of Social Relations at Harvard University.

There were a couple of important influences on me during the graduate school years. One of them was the rigorous research orientation at Stanford, as represented at that time by my adviser, Walter Mischel; Al Bandura; Eleanor Maccoby; and others. Another was the cognitive-behavioral orientation of Arnold Lazarus, who during a one-year visiting professorship had a strong influence on a number of students. A third was the friendship I developed with Perry London, who at that time was involved in the first study of rescuers of Jews in Nazi Europe, a study he and his associates could not complete because they could not receive funding. This says something about the mood of the times. In psychology an attempt to understand behavior that took place two decades earlier was not regarded as credible. The public's and academics' attitude toward the Holocaust at the time was primarily to ignore it.

Research

Control, Information, and Fear

At Harvard I began a series of studies of the effects of lack of control on fear and physiological responses and of the impact of control and information in reducing fear. Enabling people to exercise control, whether over a snake (Staub 1968) or in setting and administering shock levels to themselves (Staub, Tursky, and Schwartz 1971), reduced fear and physiological responding. Providing people with information about snakes or about the properties of shocks (Staub and Kellett 1972) also reduced fear and physiological responding.

One may surmise that my interest in fear and control had to do in part with the tremendous threat, powerlessness, and lack of control over our lives that existed during my childhood. But perhaps my interest in control also had to do with the fact that in spite of this, within the narrow limits of still existing possibilities, my family did all it could to exercise control. We managed to survive because of those efforts. My mother and aunt standing in line with many people and somehow managing to get those letters of protection, my father escaping, our hiding him, and many other acts of control saved our lives.

I also had a strong interest in need for control. I developed a questionnaire to study it, but subsequent work crowded it out, and I never actually did the research. I was aware, by that time, that an overly strong need to exercise control, that is, difficulty in letting go, is counterproductive, in myself as well as others. Accepting circumstances one cannot control is, I believe, difficult for most survivors.

I wonder whether even my interest in information had some roots in my experience. I only have a foggy memory of this, but at one time I was in the basement of some building—probably the protected house. There was a raid, with uniformed men milling around. I believe I was sick and very scared that my parents would be taken away. I remember crying. My mother brought one of the uniformed man over, and this "kind" man assured (informed) me that my parents would not be taken (or, if this was the protected house, perhaps it was only my mother, since my father was in hiding during such raids). Obviously, such a connection between my work and a specific event is highly conjectural, but this and other life threatening events at the time had to have a great impact.

I did not continue with this line of research, which preceded most of the later interest in control in the field (although not Julian Rotter's early work on internal-external locus of control, which appeared around the time I began this work). It was supplanted by my increasing involvement with research on helping; generosity; altruism and the corollary of it, bystander passivity in the face of other people's need.

Sharing and Helping

My research in this domain was clearly stimulated by my Holocaust experience, while also at first greatly removed from it. It was in the course of conversations with Perry London at Stanford about his study of rescuers of Jews in Europe that I began to think of studying sharing. As the researcher I was trained to be at Stanford, I wondered how one might measure generosity. I arrived at Harvard with the thought that weighing the amount of candy children shared would be a good measure. This certainly does not seem a revolutionary idea, but with this idea my lifelong career in studying helpful and violent behavior began.

Our first study was one of reciprocity in sharing, an undergraduate honors project I supervised (Staub and Sherk 1970). Then, stimulated by the research of Latané and Darley (1970) on bystander behavior in emergencies, I did an extensive series of studies on children and adults responding to a crash and sounds of distress coming from the adjoining room. Among the many findings, a few were quite striking. We found that helping behavior increased from kindergarten to first and then to second grade, remained at the same level in fourth grade, and then declined in sixth grade to about the same level as helping by kindergarten children. This was true both when children heard the distress sounds alone and when they heard the noises in pairs (Staub 1970).

In this study, contrary to the findings of Latané and Darley that the presence of other bystanders decreases helping, when another bystander was present, that is, when kindergarten and first grade children were in pairs, helping increased. This seemed to be because young children did not hide their reactions from each other. There was no pluralistic ignorance, everyone looking unconcerned and thereby leading others to interpret what was happening as not an emergency. When young children heard the distress sounds, they reacted openly, talked to each other about them, and moved together to help.

I hypothesized that the decrease in helping in sixth grade was the result of children overlearning social rules that prohibited them from interrupting work on their task or entering a strange room in a strange place. In exploring this I found that when children received permission to enter the adjoining room, for an irrelevant reason, they were much more likely to help in response to the sounds of distress than children in a no information (control) group, who helped as little as children who were prohibited from entering the adjoining room (Staub 1971).

Many other studies with children and adults followed. I want to mention two series of studies, in my mind the most important of my work in this area. Unfortunately, I was running out of steam; my interest was turning to the study of the Holocaust, other genocides, and violence by groups against other groups. As a result, while I described these studies in several of my books and in chapters of edited volumes, I never formally published them.

The first series of studies demonstrated that a particular personal characteristic, which I called prosocial value orientation, was strongly associated with a variety of different kinds of helping. My students and I first measured this using already existing measures (Staub 1974, 1978; Feinberg 1978; Grodman 1979). These were factor analyzed and provided a strong factor, with scores on these factors representing individuals' prosocial value orientation. Males who scored high on this measure were more likely to enter another room in response to distress sounds. Whether they entered or not, confronted with a person in distress they were more likely to engage in varied efforts to provide help (Staub 1974). Females who scored high on this test were more likely to respond to another person's psychological distress, primarily by suspending work on a task and attending to the person in need (Feinberg 1978; Grodman 1979; Staub 1978).

At one point, I developed my own measure of prosocial value orientation. This measure was published as part of a larger questionnaire developed for *Psychology Today* (Staub 1989b). An analysis of over seven thousand responses indicated strong relationship of prosocial value orientation to various forms of self-reported helping. It also showed, together with other information gathered in the questionnaire, that people have different helping styles and domains of helping. Prosocially oriented persons helped in many different ways. A politically liberal orientation led people to work on positive social changes. Religiously oriented helpers tended to be volunteers and made donations. Materialistically oriented people (interested in wealth and financial security) tended to be unhelpful (Staub 1992, 1995a).

The second series of studies demonstrated learning by doing. It showed that children learn to become helpful when they are guided to engage in helping others. While the studies had complex results, overall they showed that children who participated in making toys for poor, hospitalized children or taught something to younger children were later more likely to be helpful (for a review of these studies, see Staub 1979, chap. 6; 1995a; 1995b). Providing children with information about the beneficial consequences of their initial helping tended to enhance the effects of participation. So did more positive interaction between teacher and helper in the teaching studies.

While doing all this research I was also working on a book on helping behavior, which turned out to be two books (Staub 1978, 1979). I edited a third book around the same time (Staub 1980). With all this done I collapsed for a while, fortunately during a sabbatical.

The Holocaust and Other Group Violence

Around the end of this sabbatical, I began to read about the Holocaust, for the first time in a serious way. Most likely, the interest in doing so evolved jointly from my own life experience and my work. As I studied helping, again and again the implicit question for me (and others) had been why people so often remain passive bystanders in the face of others' need. This was an essential question with regard to the Holocaust. As I began reading about the Holocaust, I felt that the concepts I had been using provided me with tools to make the incomprehensible at least understandable, to explain how the motivation for genocide could evolve and the inhibitions against killing could diminish.

I began to develop a conception of the origins of the Holocaust, progressively extending this conception to other genocides as well as to lesser forms of group violence (Staub 1989a). It was clear to me from the outset that to understand such horrible behavior by groups of people an interdisciplinary approach is necessary. The conception I developed started with difficult social conditions, which are the usual starting point for the evolution toward genocide. These conditions frustrate and thereby intensify intense human needs for security, positive identity, effectiveness, positive connection to others, and some meaningful comprehension of the world and one's place in it.

Frequently, groups of people impacted by difficult life conditions attempt to fulfill these needs by scapegoating some group for life problems and creating ideologies, visions of a better life, while also identifying enemies who stand in the way of fulfilling these visions. As they turn against the scapegoats and ideological enemies, an evolution begins. As individuals and groups harm others they change. Learning by doing occurs. Discrimination and violence become easier and more likely. A society can move, with "steps along a continuum of destruction," toward genocide.

Certain characteristics of the culture make all this more likely. These include a history of devaluation of a group of people, very strong respect for authorities, lack of pluralism, a past history of the use of violence to resolve conflict, and some others. Recently I have come to realize the importance of unhealed wounds in a group, due to past violence against them, as a cultural characteristic that can make genocide more likely (Staub 1996b, 1997, 1998).

Bystanders, tragically, are often passive, which has crucial impact. Passivity by internal bystanders—members of a perpetrator group who themselves are not perpetrators—and by external bystanders—outside individuals, groups, and nations—encourages perpetrators. As perpetrators move along the continuum of destruction, they frequently develop intense commitment to their ideology and to the destruction of their victims. Only actions by bystanders can halt their further evolution toward genocide. Bystanders have great potential power. But frequently they are not only passive but, by continuing with business as usual in their relationship to perpetrators or by actively supporting the perpetrators, they encourage genocide.

I described this conception and applied it to four instances of group violence in *The Roots of Evil: The Origins of Genocide and Other Group Violence* (1989a; see also Staub 1993, 1996a). These instances were the Holocaust; the genocide against the Armenians; the "autogenocide" in Cambodia; and a much smaller scale violence, the disappearances in Argentina. There are starting points or instigators of the process leading to genocide, that I mentioned in *The Roots of Evil* and also described in other places, in addition to the difficult life conditions noted previously in this chapter. They include conflict between groups, especially when these conflicts involve vital interests, such as territory needed for living, and especially when there has been a history of mutual antagonism between the groups. They involve conflict within a society between a superordinate group and a subordinate group with limited rights and privileges. Occasionally, the evolution starts with the pursuit of material self-interest by perpetrators (Staub 1989a, 1996a, 1997, 1999).

In *The Roots of Evil* I also began to write about the prevention of group violence. This is now one of my two major professional (and personal) concerns (see Staub 1996b, 1997, 1998, 1999, 2000). Prevention has to involve bystanders, individuals, nongovernmental organizations, international organizations, and nations. It requires motivation to act. For nations to act requires that their citizens expect them to act.

My other current major professional concern, related to prevention but also independent, is raising caring and nonviolent children. In addition to my work on the origins of altruism, and rescuers of Jews in Nazi Europe as exemplars of altruism (Staub 1989a, 1993), I have also done work on the origins of youth violence (Staub 1996a). In general, I have done a great deal of research, writing, parent training, and teacher training with a focus on raising caring, effective, nonviolent children. A major avenue for raising such children is through the schools. "Caring schools" (1995b) can be so structured that they provide children with experiences that promote connection, concern about others' welfare, and helpful action.

The Impact of the Holocaust on Me

Even while I was studying the origins of the Holocaust, I ignored, neglected, the emotional impact that the Holocaust had on me. I simply avoided looking at it. I did not understand that one can be a professionally highly functioning person and still be deeply emotionally affected by traumatic experience.

I was pushed and pulled by a friend, Paul Valent, an Australian psychiatrist who is also a child survivor of the Holocaust from Budapest, and my wife, Sylvia (from whom I am now divorced), to go to the first meeting in New York of children hidden during the Holocaust. It was a powerful experience. I saw people who were all different but in some significant way all like me. Talking to them about experiences during the Holocaust and their impact on me was easy and natural. I realized that, like many of them, I have often experienced a film between myself and other people, a small divider. I am glad to say that since then, this film has more or less dissolved.

I believe that engagement with my personal past has affected my work. For the first time, I seriously began to think about victims. I became concerned about the importance of healing from genocidal violence in order to make it less likely that victims, in their intense need to defend themselves in a dangerous world, become perpetrators. My work has more firmly focused on prevention and, as part of prevention, on the need for groups of people with historical antagonism to reconcile (Staub 1998, 1999, 2000).

Some "Real World" Efforts

Increasingly over the years, I have wanted to do things that actually make a difference. One of my efforts in this direction was developing a training program for the state of California, following the Rodney King incident, to reduce police violence by training police officers to be active, constructive bystanders to each other who step in when confrontations move toward violence. Another has been engagement with Facing History and Ourselves, a national and now international organization. Central to its many activities has been to train teachers to use a curriculum that the organization has developed. Using the history of the Holocaust as its primary avenue, this curriculum teaches about human cruelty and about the possibilities of caring, of people becoming conscious of decisions they make and becoming concerned, active bystanders. I have done workshops for Facing History, especially as part of their teacher training institutes.

Also independently of Facing History I have done teacher training and have worked on the creation of caring schools. My vision is that in such schools a milieu is created in which all children feel part of a community, where children are participants in ways that affirm them, where they are guided to act in others' behalf and learn by doing. These are schools that help children develop inclusive caring and the moral courage not to be passive bystanders. As part of my concern with the development of caring I have been writing a book with the tentative title *A Brighter Future: Raising Caring and Nonviolent Children*, that is both scholarly and hopefully accessible to parents, teachers, and everyone else who is concerned about children.

Another of my real world efforts was organizing and leading a conference on activating bystanders that took place in Stockholm in June 1997 (Beyond Lamentation: Options for Preventing Genocidal Violence). A number of active efforts have emerged from this conference. One of them is the creation of a human rights organization led by young people (Staub and Schultz 1998). I have also engaged over the years with the media, in the hope that they can influence public attitudes about caring and violence.

Another effort has been an intervention research project that I and Dr. Laurie Anne Pearlman have been conducting since 1998. The purpose of this project, on healing, forgiveness, and reconciliation (supported by the John Templeton Foundation), is to make renewed violence between Hutus and Tutsis less likely, and to improve the lives of people deeply affected by the horrors of the genocide in Rwanda in 1994. The project is an intervention, with both psychoeducational and experiential elements. We have worked with the staff of local nongovernmental organizations, talking to them and discussing with them how genocide originates, what the effects of such trauma are on survivors, and what might be avenues to healing. They have also talked to each other, in small groups, about what happened to them during the genocide, supporting each other as they talk about very difficult experiences and feelings (Staub 2000).

The people we trained then worked with groups in the community. We set up an elaborate and formal research project, with varied control groups, to evaluate the effects of our training as it was transmitted to people in the community. Early results indicate that our training reduced trauma symptoms over a period of time, made people aware of the complex origins of violence, and led them to be more open to work with members of the "other" group for positive goals, such as the welfare of children and a better future. It also resulted in agreement with statements that they would forgive the other group if the other group acknowledged what they did and apologized. While healing, forgiveness, and reconciliation seem daunting tasks after a horrible genocide, they are of crucial importance.

Where Am I, at This Time in My Life?

I have had a very strong need to make a difference in the world, to improve the world. But the world is not visibly improving. In the last few years I have been less intensely upset as I read about, hear about, or see on television violence in the world. I seem to have developed some emotional distance, while still continuing to work hard on these issues. Perhaps I have also experienced some vicarious traumatization (Pearlman and Saakvitne 1995), through so much exposure in the course of my work to violence, brutality, killings. And after a period of distress about being less distressed, I am beginning to think that perhaps there is some good in a degree of emotional numbing, in being less impacted when I read about horrible things being done to people.

I have always worked extremely hard, not quite understanding the source of my intense motivation. And the number of things I am involved with seems to grow. What is my motivation in all this? What needs drive me? How much of this hard work is a compulsion that somehow derives from my Holocaust experience? In what part may it be the desire to create a better world; in what part a need to feel worthwhile and important that is dependent on doing; on what part a difficulty with just being? While working hard is satisfying, I also feel it is too encompassing. I will certainly continue but very much hope that I can learn to balance doing with being. I have long thought and talked about this desire for balance. Perhaps, it will come, any day now.

REFERENCES

Feinberg, J. K. 1978. Anatomy of a helping situation: Some personality and situational determinants of helping in a conflict situation involving another's psychological distress. Ph.D. diss., University of Massachusetts, Amherst.

Grodman, S. M. 1979. The role of personality and situational variables in responding to and helping an individual in psychological distress. Ph.D. diss., University of Massachusetts, Amherst.

Latané, B., and J. M. Darley. 1970. *The unresponsive bystanders: Why doesn't he help?* New York: Appleton-Crofts.

Pearlman, L. A., and K. Saakvitne. 1995. *Trauma and the therapist.* New York: Norton.

Staub, E. 1968. The reduction of a specific fear by information combined with exposure to the feared stimulus. *Proceedings, seventy-sixth annual convention of the American Psychological Association,* 3:535–37.

———. 1970. A child in distress: The influence of age and number of witnesses on children's attempts to help. *Journal of Personality and Social Psychology* 14:130–40.

———. 1971. Helping a person in distress: The influence of implicit and explicit "rules" of conduct on children and adults. *Journal of Personality and Social Psychology* 17:137–45.

———. 1974. Helping a distressed person: Social, personality, and stimulus determinants. In *Advances in experimental social psychology,* vol. 7, edited by L. Berkowitz, 203–342. New York: Academic Press.

———. 1978. *Positive social behavior and morality.* Vol. 1, *Social and personal influence.* New York: Academic Press.

———. 1979. *Positive social behavior and morality.* Vol. 2, *Socialization and development.* New York: Academic Press.

———. 1980. Social and prosocial behavior: Personal and situational influences and their interactions. In *Personality: Basic aspects and current research,* edited by E. Staub. Englewood Cliffs, NJ: Prentice-Hall.

———. 1989a. *The roots of evil: The origins of genocide and other group violence.* New York: Cambridge University Press.

———. 1989b. What are your values and goals? *Psychology Today,* 46–49.

———. 1992. Values and helping. Manuscript, Department of Psychology, University of Massachusetts, Amherst.

———. 1993. The psychology of bystanders, perpetrators, and heroic helpers. *International Journal of Intercultural Relations* 17:315–41.

———. 1995a. How people learn to care. In *Care and community in modern society: Passing on the tradition of service to future generations,* edited by P. G. Schervish, V. A. Hodgkinson, M. Gates, and associates. San Francisco: Jossey-Bass Publishers.

———. 1995b. The caring schools project: A program to develop caring, helping, positive self-esteem and nonviolence. Manuscript, Department of Psychology, University of Massachusetts, Amherst.

———. 1996a. Cultural-societal roots of violence: The examples of genocidal violence and of contemporary youth violence in the United States. *American Psychologist* 51:117–32.

———. 1996b. Preventing genocide: Activating bystanders, helping victims, and the creation of caring. *Peace and Conflict: Journal of Peace Psychology* 2:189–201.

———. 1997. Halting and preventing collective violence: The role of bystanders. Background paper presented at symposium, Beyond Lamentation: Options to Preventing Genocidal Violence, Stockholm, Sweden, 13–16 June 1997.

———. 1998. Breaking the cycle of genocidal violence: Healing and reconciliation. In *Perspectives on loss,* edited by J. Harvey. Washington, DC: Taylor and Francis.

———. 1999. Genocide, mass killing, and other group violence: Origins and prevention. *Peace and Conflict: Journal of Peace Psychology* 5:303–36.

———. 2000. Genocide and mass killing: Origins, prevention, healing and reconciliation. *Political Psychology* 21:367–83.

Staub, E., and D. S. Kellett. 1972. Increasing pain tolerance by information about aversive stimuli. *Journal of Personality and Social Psychology* 21:198–203.

Staub, E., and T. Schultz. 1998. Youth movement targets violence prevention. *Psychology International* 9, no. 3:1–2.

Staub, E., and L. Sherk. 1970. Need for approval, children's sharing behavior, and reciprocity in sharing. *Child Development* 41:243–53.

Staub, E., B. Tursky, and G. Schwartz. 1971. Self-control and predictability: Their effects on reactions to aversive stimulation. *Journal of Personality and Social Psychology* 18:157–63.

A Generalist in Search of a Specialty

Peter Suedfeld

Biographical Note

Arriving in the United States in 1948, Peter Suedfeld attended public schools and then Queens College, with a break of three years for service in the army. He received his Ph.D. in psychology from Princeton University and taught at Princeton, the University of Illinois (Champaign-Urbana), and Rutgers before moving to the University of British Columbia (UBC) in 1972. There, he has served as head of the Department of Psychology and later as dean of the Faculty of Graduate Studies. Currently, he is professor of psychology and Distinguished Scholar in Residence at the Peter Wall Institute of Advanced Studies at UBC. He is a fellow of the Royal Society of Canada and many other scientific and professional societies, including six divisions of the American Psychological Association.

Professor Suedfeld's research focuses on adaptation to and coping with extreme and unusual environments. It has included laboratory studies of stimulus reduction, fieldwork in polar stations, and content analyses of high-level decision-making processes and narratives of the Holocaust. The results have been reported in several books and over two hundred journal articles and book chapters. Professor Suedfeld has received the U.S. Antarctica Service Medal, the Canadian Psychological Association's Donald O. Hebb Award, and the ISPP's Lasswell Award for distinguished scientific contributions. He was president of the Canadian Psycho-

153

logical Association in 1998–99 and has held many other offices in various scientific organizations.

——————➤•◄——————

Introduction

Riding off in Many Directions at Once

During much of my career as a professor and research psychologist, I had trouble answering the question, "What area of psychology are you in?" Semifacetiously, I labeled myself a cognitive experimental, social, environmental, political, health, personality psychologist—an answer that made me feel silly and the questioner feel rebuffed. But I really could not come up with a shorter or more sensible answer, because I am in fact a generalist whose long-term interests span all those areas (and who has dabbled in a few others as well).

When I got down to specifics, the list was long. I had started out as a graduate student doing experiments on the cognitive effects of what was then called sensory deprivation (lying on a bed in a dark, silent chamber for twenty-four hours or more). At the time I began, in 1961, the general view of sensory deprivation was that it was very stressful. Subjects experienced negative moods, hallucinations, anxiety, thinking disturbances, "temporary psychoses," and an overwhelming desire to get out. My first experience with this condition was as a naive subject; I was stressed enough that I quit after about three hours, giving up $20 (a lot of money for a poor graduate student) and risking the disapproval of my mentor, Jack Vernon, who ran these studies. I guess my reaction to this foreshadowed much of my future orientation in psychology: what other researchers accept as axiomatic is often what I find most intriguing.

Struck by how uncomfortable I had been in the chamber—after all, a few hours lying on a bed in the dark is no unusual experience for most people, and I certainly could have used the sleep—I decided to investigate this surprising phenomenon. After some pondering, I hypothesized that my reaction might have been not so much to the chamber itself but to the procedures I had undergone before the experiment actually started.

First, I had been told to sign a release form promising not to sue the university if I sustained any physical or mental damage during the experiment. Then I was blindfolded before being taken into the chamber, so I was quite disoriented. My hand had been guided to the food, chemical toilet, door, and so on, and to a large "panic button" that would sound an alarm heard all over the building and bring a monitor running to let me out. These steps, standard in sensory deprivation studies, could have induced in subjects (including me) an expectation that unpleasant things were about to happen.

I decided to try a different approach. In my own research, I let subjects look and walk around the chamber before the lights went out, showed them how to walk out by themselves or by calling the monitor calmly over the intercom (eliminating the panic button and *never* mentioning the word *panic*), and dumped the release form. The revised orientation material emphasized that the environment was basically just a dark, quiet, comfortable room. The results were dramatic: almost nobody quit the study before the scheduled end of the session, and absolutely no one panicked, had hallucinations or minipsychoses, or experienced any other overwhelming aversive emotions. In fact, most people reported that the experience was indeed relaxing, and they showed improvements in memory and some kinds of reasoning. Quite rapidly, nonfrightening orientation procedures became the norm in the area. Panic buttons, legal forms, and anxiety attacks disappeared. In a book published in 1980, I renamed the technique to eliminate the scary connotations of "sensory deprivation": most people now call it, as I did, the restricted environmental stimulation technique, or REST.

Exploring the positive effects of REST, I discovered that a few earlier researchers had used the technique successfully as an adjunct to therapy. Their explanations of its efficacy tended to center on its stressful or bizarre aspects—for example, that it was a womblike environment and thus induced a regressive, infantile state of mind that enabled the therapist to establish faster transference. Being trained in experimental psychology, I was not inclined toward such explanations. I thought that a situation in which external stimuli were minimized would lead to greater sensitivity to internal stimuli, including memory, personal problems, emotions, and so on. This would lead people to concentrate on why they had been unable to deal with various personal issues and to be creative in finding new solutions. The low level of stimulation should also lead them to be more attentive and open minded to suggestions made by a therapist.

I, of course, was no therapist. I looked for a real-life problem that was analogous to experimental conditions in attitude change research, but with behavioral consequences, and found the ideal area in smoking cessation. It seemed to me then, and still does, that a day of darkness and silence would have no serious impact on a habit (some say, an addiction) that has proven so recalcitrant to all kinds of therapy, drugs, hypnosis, propaganda, financial cost, and health scares. It took some dozen studies, in my lab and others, to convince me that I was too cautious. In fact, REST does have an impressive effect: not only is it as powerful as the best of other psychological cessation methods, but when combined with other techniques it reduces the relapse rate—the major problem in all substance abuse treatments—by as much as 50 percent. It has similar levels of success with weight loss and alcohol abuse interventions.

Later, I expanded my REST research to include the flotation tank version REST, using the chamber and the tank in studies on the reduction of blood pressure and chronic pain, the treatment of autism and insomnia, and the enhancement of memory and athletic performance as well as scientific, musical, and artistic creativity. The findings from our laboratory were central in changing the professional and public image of sensory restriction, from a frightening and intolerable situation that could result in temporary psychosis to a technique that brought about pleasant relaxation and was useful in a wide variety of beneficial interventions. Perhaps most importantly, REST offers a chance to establish or regain control over processes that have become, or that always were, autonomous.

My interest in REST eventually led to field research on prisoners in solitary confinement and on workers in Arctic and Antarctic stations and also to theoretical and review papers on solitude, loneliness, extreme and unusual environments, space travel, and altered states of consciousness. Again, my findings have emphasized the incorrectness, or at least incompleteness, of catastrophic assumptions popular both among the general public and among psychologists. In fact, I have found that most individuals deal quite well with such environments and are able not only to overcome but to enjoy and benefit from their encounters with a variety of challenging situations. Even convicts in solitary confinement for the most part do not find restriction and social isolation to be intolerable, although other aspects of the situation—for example, reduced opportunity for hobbies and work, cold food—make the experience unpleasant. Nevertheless, many prisoners use the period for introspection and to engage in both physical and mental exercise. My review papers, based on literature produced by other people as well as myself, have shown many instances and high proportions of successful coping and self-assessed personal growth among former prisoners of war, torture victims, hostages, and the like.

In studying how people cope with adversity, I also became interested in why some people can do so better than others. I had from the beginning of my REST research included personality measures to see whether they mediated environmental effects. One of the personality factors was conceptual complexity, a dimension based on the extent to which people use information in flexible, combinatorial, contextualized ways. I used this cognitive trait as an intervening variable in experiments on attitude change, the effects of information input and clarity, creativity, and problem solving.

I started thinking about how complexity could play a role, and be studied, in real-life contexts. Originally, complexity was viewed as an essentially unchanging personality trait that determined how people use information. It was measured by a specially administered test. I developed a technique for scoring complexity from almost any connected verbal material and reconceptualized it as a "state" variable responsive to environmental and endogenous factors. Basically, I studied complexity as a characteristic of speeches, writings, interview responses—the end products of thinking—from which the nature of thought could be inferred, rather than as an underlying aspect of the individual's personality. With the help of students and colleagues, I have for the past twenty years been conducting archival studies on cognitive complexity related to major political and military decisions, as well as to how people have coped with personal stressors.

This research led me to formulate the "cognitive manager" hypothesis, that people generally process information quite effectively, at a level of complexity determined by the availability of psychological and other resources on one hand and an estimate of the complexity needed for a good solution on the other. This model argues that people can actually decide how to make decisions and can do it well. As I reflect on this, I see the analogy with my REST and isolation research. Many current theories in cognitive psychology emphasize the universality of unconscious cognitive shortcuts that contravene the rules of strict logic or probability. Such shortcuts (biases or heuristics) are widely assumed to increase the probability of poor, sometimes disastrous, decisions. My own view, that shortcuts tend to be used when they are in fact appropriate, is much more optimistic about the adaptiveness of human behavior.

Combining the scoring technique for complexity with those developed for archival materials by other researchers, my team eventually undertook a project analyzing videotaped autobiographies and autobiographical questionnaires provided by Holocaust survivors. Again, we have found that our respondents recall using appropriate, problem-oriented strategies for dealing with the horrendous events of the Holocaust and have generally gone on to lead happy and successful lives—contrary to the conclusion of scholars who view survivors as permanent and hopeless psychiatric casualties.

All of this research went on more or less concurrently; I find it difficult to drop an ongoing series of studies when a new one begins. And always, when anyone asked—or I spontaneously pondered—the common feature of this diverse set of investigations, the only answer I could come up with was that these topics happened to arouse my interest. This answer probably made me seem like something of a dilettante, but it was the best I could provide; and I never questioned why it was that these particular issues attracted me.

Enlightenment dawned only after twenty-five years of not knowing (and not really caring about) the reasons for my research path. During a conversation with Robert Krell, then a professor of psychiatry at my university, we discovered that we had both been Jewish children, hidden among Christians and "passing" as Christian, during the war—he in Holland, I in Hungary. Rob invited me to contribute a videotape to his Holocaust documentation project, but I demurred; in my worldview, "Holocaust survivor" meant concentration camp survivor, and I did not qualify. After many conversations, I was persuaded that, regardless of labels, I had something worth recording. In the course of that 1983 interview, Rob asked me the common theme of my research. I couldn't answer then, but that question, in that context, started me thinking.

Flashback

I was born in Budapest, in 1935, to a thoroughly assimilated Hungarian Jewish family whose paternal forebears had been exiled from Spain in 1492, wandered through western and central Europe, and wound up in the Austro-Hungarian Empire in the eighteenth century. The family had produced a number of writers, scholars, and musicians, some of them quite well known in their time. I know less about my mother's family, which had engaged primarily in business; but they, too, had been in Hungary for many generations.

During my early childhood, I was the only child of my generation in the family. Predictably, I was the apple of everyone's eye, and I remember many excursions and vacations, not only with my parents but also with uncles, aunts, and older cousins. Visits to both sets of grandparents and other relatives were frequent; everyone seemed to live fairly close together in Budapest. My father was often away, either playing in a large dance band traveling around Europe (he played the clarinet and saxophone, although his real love was classical cello) or called up for his summer military duty as a reservist; my mother worked as a legal secretary. I was mostly cared for by a woman I called Csita, a maid of all work such as those found in most middle-class Hungarian families.

Being assimilated, I always knew I was Jewish, but my identity as a Hungarian was paramount. We did go to a synagogue instead of to a church, and we celebrated some holidays that were different from those of most of my friends, but we spoke the same language at home as other Hungarians; wore the same clothes; ate the same foods; went to the same public school; and shared the same games, friends, attitudes, and loyalties. As I tell people now, I never heard of Yiddish nor saw a bagel until I got to New York some years after the war.

It was not until I was about seven years old that the distinction between Jewish and gentile Hungarians became a real difference. As Hungary allied itself with the Axis and as the war went on, the formerly genteel aspects of anti-Semitism grew more crass: our country was telling us more and more emphatically that it didn't want us any longer. I was bewildered; like most little boys of the time, I had been brought up on Hungarian patriotism, hoped that Hungary would be a winner in the war, and was proud of the fact that at least four generations of my male ancestors had spent significant time serving their country as soldiers, in the Napoleonic Wars, the Hungarian Revolution of 1848, World War I (in which my grandfather reached the rank of captain and collected an impressive set of decorations for valor), and various Balkan squabbles.

Now, suddenly, I had to wear a yellow star; live in a specially marked house; stay away from my accustomed school, cub scout troop, playgrounds, and playmates; remain indoors except during a very few hours every day; and think of myself as a Jew, not as a Hungarian. My father, not an enthusiastic soldier but a competent one, had spent his reserve training as the first sergeant of a machine-gun company; now he, like my uncles and like all Jewish soldiers, was disarmed; his uniform was replaced by a cap and an armband; and he was transferred to a forced labor battalion. It was bewildering and humiliating, and—foreshadowing my adult reaction to slights—I reacted with anger. I cheered the ever-increasing Allied air raids that attacked Budapest around the clock, made rude gestures at uniformed Arrow Cross (Hungarian Nazi) militiamen (fortunately, they didn't see me do it), and stubbornly refused a last-minute conversion to Catholicism that my family mistakenly thought might save us from worse persecution.

My relatives' fates during the Holocaust varied—a microcosmic illustration of the important fact that "the Holocaust" consisted of many diverse experiences. Many members of my extended family just disappeared from my awareness and never came back; most likely, they died in camps or the ghetto. My father's labor unit was assigned to the Western Front, from which he was sent to Mauthausen and eventually liberated by the U.S. Army. My father's three brothers survived forced labor service: one escaped and joined the Yugoslav partisans, one went to Mauthausen with my father, and one escaped and returned to the Budapest ghetto to look after my grandmother. My mother's brother was killed, probably on the Russian front. One of my mother's sisters escaped with her husband and traveled through Turkey to India, where they were interned by the British as enemy aliens. The other, who played a major role in my survival, helped her parents survive the ghetto (although not for long) and left Hungary during the 1956 revolution. Both of these aunts now live in Australia, one just past her ninety-second birthday and the other her ninetieth.

A few weeks after the German army entered Budapest in March 1944, my mother called a policeman to protect her employer from two thugs who were assaulting him and ransacking his office. The thugs turned out to be a German and a Hungarian secret police officer, who a week later came to our apartment with two German soldiers and arrested her. She said good-bye to me with tears in her eyes, which I thought strange; it never occurred to me, as turned out to be the case, that I would never see her again. She was sent to a holding camp in central Hungary and eventually shipped to Auschwitz; her exact fate is unknown, but this was where large groups of Hungarian Jews died. Most of the rest died in other camps and in ghettos, where toward the end of the war the Arrow Cross roamed and murdered at will; although Hungarian Jews were chronologically the last to feel the full impact of the Holocaust (because of Hungary's alliance with Germany), in less than one year about two-thirds of the estimated 825,000 Jews in Hungary and Hungarian-controlled Rumania were killed.

After my mother's arrest, I was taken in by her sister, with whom I lived for several months. The war had intensified for us; Budapest was subject to almost constant aerial bombardment, and we spent much of our time in the cellar of our apartment building. By this time, Jews were not allowed in public air-raid shelters, nor to ride on public transportation, use public facilities such as parks, hold a large variety of jobs, own businesses, attend school, go to hospitals, participate in social organizations (even exclusively Jewish ones; I especially missed my scout troop), or have any close contact with Christians. When the Jewish population of Budapest was ordered to prepare for evacuation, my aunt found a Christian former employee who was willing to smuggle me to safety.

Safety—well, relative safety—in this case was an orphanage run by the International Red Cross. Among the thirty or so genuine war orphans and quasi orphans (e.g., children whose fathers were in the army) there were a small number of hidden Jews. A few members of the all-female staff (not all of whom were aware of what was going on) equipped us with false Christian papers, aliases, and backgrounds and trained us to avoid detection. I was drilled in my new identity, taught how to behave at a Roman Catholic mass, and shown how to use the washroom without revealing the fact that I was circumcised. None of us ever knew which, or how many, of our fellow "orphans" were in fact Jewish.

A few months after my arrival at the orphanage, the Soviet army began the siege of Budapest, recently described in an article in the *Quarterly Journal of Military History* as "one of the most frightful urban battles of World War II." During the six weeks of the siege, we moved repeatedly and surreptitiously from the cellar of one bombed-out building to another. We grubbed for food in the snow-covered frozen ground of backyard vegetable gardens, searched for it in the ruins of destroyed houses, and tried to steal it from packages parachuted to the defending German and Hungarian troops, hoping to find it before they did. When not engaged in the hunt for food, we were "cellar children" living in the unheated, unlighted basements, formerly used for now unavailable coal and firewood, that served as shelters from bombs and shells. We never once took our clothes off or washed; we had no running water, soap, combs, or toothbrushes. The sick and injured were taken away, we never knew to where or to what fate; new children arrived with equally little information. We passed the time playing games or listening to staff members tell stories; at night, we huddled close for warmth and tried to sleep through the noises of the war.

When I try to remember my emotions during this time, I recall relatively few except for worrying about my family; for myself, I took things as they came and made the best of them. A few moments of happiness stand out: finding a pot of beans in a ruined house; and receiving a piece of chocolate from a German soldier who praised me for being a "handsome Aryan boy" because of my blond hair and blue eyes (I still remember how the irony of this gift made it taste even better). So do a few episodes of anger: being taunted for having lice by a boy whose mother, a staff member at the orphanage, enabled him to be probably the only one among us who did not have them; and anti-Semitic Arrow Cross slogans mouthed by another staff member to which I, of course, could not respond as I wanted to. I also underwent one major change in philosophy, foreshadowing my later adherence to the scientific method as a source of knowledge and a basis for action: having decided that an "experimental" week during which I didn't say my accustomed prayers was no more unpleasant than a prayerful "control" week, I became an atheist.

We were liberated late in the winter of 1945, when a Russian infantryman threw open the door to our cellar. Our staff members avoided Russian invitations to "peel potatoes" (much later, I discovered that this was usually a prelude to rape), but we children learned the few words of Russian needed to beg food from the field kitchens. A major in the Red Army, upon being told that some of us were Jewish orphans, secretively showed us his Mogen David pin, shot a horse passing by our shelter, and gave it to our staff. The resulting soup was the first solid meal we had had during the winter.

In the next couple of months, our material condition improved gradually, but my emotional state worsened as more and more children were retrieved by relatives and no one had come for me. I realized that all of my family might well be dead; and even if any survived, they might never find me under my false name, Sugár Péter (the family name comes first in Hungarian), and in a location far from the original orphanage building. I had almost given up hope by the time that, sitting on a garden wall in the spring sunshine, I saw my aunt walking up the street. She and my returned partisan uncle (who that day was detained for forced labor by a passing Russian patrol) had been methodically following a list of all places where the Red Cross maintained groups of children. The sight of her, to say nothing of the large basket of food she was carrying on her arm, was, and remains, the most joyous moment of my life.

In the absence of my parents, I was taken to live with my paternal grandmother, whose husband had died in 1943 and who was the iron-willed matriarch of the clan. We waited through the year as relatives trickled back to Budapest, my father returning in early fall with a surprise. After recovering his health and strength, he had made contacts and obtained a job offer with a band playing in an American NCO Club in Vienna. My mother's last letter, smuggled from the holding camp before she was sent to Auschwitz, begged him that if he and I survived he should take me out of Hungary; and he had for a long time wanted to live in the United States. Before the war, while touring the Vatican, he and one other man were alone in declining a group audience with the pope. When asked why, my father had said, "I am a Jew; I will not kneel to the pope." The other man said, "I am an American; I will not kneel to anybody." My father right then decided that this was the place for him, and the attitude permeates my own values, in which freedom is the dominant force.

Late in 1945, my father and I sneaked into Austria by climbing in and out of various train windows and took up residence in Vienna while we waited for a U.S. visa.

As an employee of the U.S. military, my father was paid in dollars, whose value in Europe is now difficult to imagine. We were almost rich; we could afford black-market veal cutlets and tailor-made clothes. Unfortunately, I was also undisciplined and used to fending for myself; I soon joined a gang of street urchins from whom I learned—among other things—a version of German that was unusable in polite company. Our favorite sport was rock- and fistfights with other gangs; as the son of a former high-ranking amateur boxer, I was pretty good at the latter. These diversions, coupled with an incurable penchant for reading with a flashlight under the covers when I was supposed to be asleep, persuaded my father to enter me in an expensive boarding school in Grinzing, a pleasant suburban district of Vienna.

What he didn't think of is that the families of the other boys there were well off without working for the United States. This meant that they had been affluent during, and therefore in favor with, the Nazi regime. I guess I must have become less careful once the war was over, and it wasn't too long before someone noticed that I was circumcised. For the next six months or so, my life as the one Jew among dozens of Nazi-indoctrinated teenage boys consisted of school (where I learned good German), taunts, and fistfights. I never told my father just how much I hated the place—he thought he was doing what was best for me, and I saw no reason to trouble him.

Eventually, finally, we got our long-awaited visa. After an adventurous cattle-car trip to Bremen, and a seasick voyage across the Atlantic, we landed in New York. My father stepped aside on the gangplank so that I could be first to touch our new homeland. For the next four years, we lived in Harlem with a widowed great-aunt and her unmarried daughter. Neither of them had any idea of how to deal with an adolescent male, especially one like me. My father was away for months at a time, playing at resorts in New England and Florida. I was again a member of a minority—this time white, as well as foreign and Jewish—and learned to fit in by roaming around with undesirable friends as I learned street English to replace my street German. Eventually, my father gave up hoping that my mother would reappear, and he married again. His new wife was appalled by me and refused to move from her (now their) one-bedroom apartment so that I could live with them. They boarded me out with an older couple whose own two children were grown up, married, and living elsewhere.

This couple, Morris and Sarah Nagin, took a great interest in me. They were both well educated, Morris a civil engineer who had immigrated from Russia before World War I and Sarah a schoolteacher from an old U.S. Jewish family. They encouraged my interest in reading and schoolwork, at which I had always been good. My opportunities for mischief vanished when I passed the test for Stuyvesant High School, a science-oriented public school that required me to study intensely and to commute by subway for about three hours daily. After graduation, I entered Queens College, a tuition-free institution; again, what with study, commuting, and after-school jobs, I had little time or energy for trouble or even for socializing. My pervasive shyness made the latter lack easy to accept.

My ambition during most of this time was to become a career military officer. This plan had many roots. Among them were my forefathers' military service and a remote kinship to Sir John Monash, an eminent Australian general of World War I; my gratitude to the United States and the Allied armed forces for defeating the Nazis; a determination never again to be a defenseless victim; anger at oppression, which also turned me into a zealot for the freedoms guaranteed by the Bill of Rights, an activist for civil rights, and an enemy of all dictatorships; and, perhaps, the wish for an orderly, structured life within a powerful and respected organization. My revulsion against being defenseless had another result as well: I felt it important to know how to use weapons, and even before entering the service I competed in high school and college rifle matches with some success. Poor eyesight excluded me from the military academies, but I did well as an ROTC cadet in college. Nevertheless, I dropped out in the middle of my second year to enlist and gain experience in the ranks, serving three years as an infantryman in various places in the United States and then in the Philippines.

After returning to college in 1958, I became cadet commander of my unit and readied myself for active service. In my very last term, however,

I took a required course in experimental psychology—and caught fire from the excitement of doing research that could discover things no one had ever known before. Frantically writing off for admission to graduate schools and for release from further military obligation, and receiving both, I entered the graduate program at Princeton in 1960, a step that was made possible by the G.I. Bill and generous fellowship and assistantship support from the university. I got married in 1961, a marriage that ended in divorce some fifteen years later. I received my Ph.D. in 1963.

At that point, I began a professional career that in thirty-five years has taken me to faculty positions in New Jersey and British Columbia; to visiting appointments at the University of Illinois, the University of New South Wales, Yale, and Ohio State; and to research and other activities in many places around the world. Along with teaching and doing research, I have filled many administrative roles, both in my own institutions and in professional organizations, ranging from department head and dean in the university to president of my national (Canadian) psychological association. I think this reflects a desire to control my environment, a need that in turn may be an outgrowth of how little control I had during much of my early life. Fortunately, I am a good administrator: I'm quite efficient and willing to make decisions, although I have a tendency to be insufficiently tactful at times.

Back to the Future

Rob Krell's question in 1983 for the first time juxtaposed the memories of my early experiences with the consideration of what my research was all about. When I later pondered the question I could not answer during the interview, the answer struck me suddenly. Three aspects of my scientific career seem to me related to the period of the war. One is my tendency to grasp at opportunities for new research areas, new experiences, and new challenges. I chronically overload myself with deadlines; I accept almost all invitations to write papers or give talks. I think this is a combination of proving myself over and over again and of cramming everything in while I have time.

The second is that most of my research has been based on a rejection of what was then the accepted, axiomatic truth in the area when I started to work in it. Stimulus restriction was known to be aversive and deleterious; extreme and unusual environments were known to be dangerous and at the very extremes to lead inescapably to breakdowns and stress disorders; people making decisions, especially under stress, were known to make bad ones. Generally rebellious, I refused to take these conclusions for granted, and my findings have justified that reaction.

Last, and most pervasive, is that all of my research deals with people who are facing (or have survived) adversity, novel and strange situations, and in some cases danger. In retrospect, it does not surprise me that such events—various versions of which had characterized my life from middle childhood until the end of adolescence—attracted my professional interest. It is also no surprise that my emphasis has been on the people who were successful in coping with and exerting control over the difficult and hazardous situations they encountered: trying to understand their personalities, problem-solving strategies, perceptions, memories, and thoughts.

Restricted sensory input, polar and space stations, prison cells, the pressures of command and leadership, and of course the Holocaust are all daunting experiences; yet most people manage to meet their challenges and emerge not only victorious but often strengthened in unexpected ways. This is not to deny or gloss over the fact that many people encounter situations that damage or destroy them, nor to imply that such victims are less worthy or less able than those who surmount their obstacles. As everyone who went through a natural or man-made disaster knows, luck has a lot to do with one's survival regardless of intelligence, talent, strength, or any other personal attribute. But the focus of my field has been so overwhelmingly on negative outcomes that I have no misgivings about trying to counterbalance that lopsided view. One thing that has always astounded me is the extent to which some colleagues remain fixated on their negative biases, maintaining even against their own data that the effects of stressful environments are necessarily destructive.

Some of my characteristics as a scientist also appear in other aspects of my life. I try, not necessarily consciously, to fill every day with as much stimulation as I can. I don't sleep much, and I like to try lots of new things. I'm fairly adventurous, enjoying traveling to many places and engaging in such sports as scuba diving and skiing. I have also loved doing field research in the Arctic and Antarctic.

My skepticism toward authority affects my political views, my contacts with customs agents and similar officials, and my actions as an administrator (sometimes I wonder how I would have fared as a career soldier). My modal negative affect is anger; it is close to the surface and emerges easily in response to slights to myself and injustice toward anyone. I have noticed that many other child survivors think of themselves as more easily irritated than most people, but I am not sure to what extent these

observations are accurate nor whether these characteristics are consequences of our early experiences.

Many other lessons emerging from my early life are permanently
engraved. I have mellowed (not all of my friends and colleagues would
agree) under the influence of my gentle and loving second wife, Phyllis
Johnson, and of my beloved children and grandchildren. But I still like
to engage (albeit not physically) in good fights for good causes; I still
strive to exert control, or at least significant influence, over the events
and circumstances that affect me and those I care about; and I still
defend the principles I learned early to value: individualism, freedom,
objectivity, and science.

In spite of my recognition of the flaws in my very first experiment, I
am still an atheist, but my Jewish identity is increasingly important to me.
I am pleased that my grandchildren are being brought up with an appreciation of our shared traditions and background, and I have realized
with some surprise that almost every year I have added another holy day
to celebrate or another component of the ways of celebrating it that I
had forgotten or ignored for half a century. Since my first encounter
with Rob Krell, I have added to my other spare-time activities attendance
at both local and international gatherings of child survivors of the Holocaust and participation in Holocaust education programs at colleges in
the Vancouver area.

Although my career has moved along a path very different from the
military life I had desired, my gratitude to and respect for the Western
democracies, their cultures, and their armed forces persist. I have also
developed an avocational interest in military history and a vocational
one in studying military leadership—a nonpareil example of life-or-
death decisions having to be made under stress.

I have also been active in organizations that oppose all forms of discrimination and defend civil rights and civil liberties. My political
positions tend to be individualistic, or even libertarian, and my classical
liberal beliefs are mostly incompatible with what is considered "liberal"
in North America today. This has led to some interesting controversies
with academic colleagues, so many of whom have embraced "identity"
(i.e., group-based) politics and other principles that I find distasteful
and self-defeating. Having experienced a system in which people were
judged, and their treatment was decided, by their ethnicity, I find it out-
rageous that similar policies have proliferated with the enthusiastic support of so many academics (and so many North American Jews, who
should certainly know better).

Several of my political-philosophical positions also put me at odds with many of my fellow child survivors. For example, I oppose attempts to silence or punish people who deny the reality of the Holocaust; I believe in very limited government; I am against all forms of preference based on sex, race, or other nonmerit criteria; and I strongly favor a strong national defense. I also think, and am not ashamed to say, that the democratic, capitalistic, individualistic system developed in western Europe and its colonized offshoots is, in spite of its imperfections, the best kind of society ever invented. Perhaps most important, I am highly respectful of the ability of human beings to deal effectively with both ordinary and extraordinary problems.

The title and theme of a paper that I published in 1998 (*Canadian Psychology* 38:164–73) sum up much of my research and theorizing, as well as my personal beliefs. They are taken from the poem "Invictus" (unconquered, or unconquerable), by the Victorian poet William E. Henley. The title of my article is "Homo Invictus: The Indomitable Species"; I relate each of my major research areas to one of the stanzas of the poem. There is no point in summarizing the paper here, but the first stanza of "Invictus" sums up what my research and my life have taught me about human nature.

Out of the night that covers me,
    Black as the Pit from pole to pole,
I thank whatever gods may be
    For my unconquerable soul.

Part 2

The Refugees
Persecution and Escape

Reflections of an Internationalist

Henry P. David

Biographical Note

Henry P. David (Ph.D. in clinical psychology, Columbia University) is the founder and director since 1972 of the Transnational Family Research Institute in Bethesda, Maryland, a nongovernmental and nonprofit research organization in the behavioral sciences with a focus on reproductive behavior (with offices in Aptos, California; Prague; Moscow; and Mexico City) and cofounder and director of Population and Development International (offices in Bethesda, Bangkok, and Hanoi). During the past thirty years, he has participated in cooperative research projects on reproductive  *behavior with colleagues on five continents and has served as a board member or consultant to many international organizations concerned with family planning and other population issues. He is the author, editor, or coeditor of seventeen books and over three hundred papers.*

Dr. David's awards include the 1991 Medal of Charles University (Prague), the 1993 American Psychological Association Award for Distinguished Contributions to the International Advancement of Psychology, and the 2001 American Psychological Foundation Gold Medal for Lifetime Achievement in Psychology in the Public Interest. He is past president of the International Council of Psychologists and several American Psychological Association (APA) divisions. In 1997 the Autonomous University of Santo Domingo, the oldest university in the Americas, invested him as Honorary Professor in the Humanities.

Introduction

In the summer of 1927, when I was four years old, my family posed for a formal portrait photograph, sitting on wrought iron garden furniture in a shady niche of my paternal grandparents' garden in Hagen, a small city in the western industrial section of Germany. The garden, dominated by a majestic linden tree with walking paths encircling it, extended from the four-story family home with high stone walls on the remaining three sides. My grandparents are on a bench in the middle, flanked on one side by their son, my lawyer father, with my beautiful young mother and, on the other side, by my father's older sister with her banker husband and daughter. Stretched on the ground in front of my grandparents are their two grandsons, both dressed in starched white sailor suits—my cousin Herbert, born in 1921, and I, born in 1923.

Taken nearly a decade after the end of World War I and before the crash of 1929 and the rise of Hitler, the portrait, with everyone dressed in their finest clothes, conveys a sense of prosperity and well-being as well as pride in being thoroughly assimilated German Jews. Anti-Semitism was believed to be waning. In 2001, more than seventy-four years later, my cousin, now in Israel, and I are each others' only living relatives.

In this autobiography I will reflect on my family history, on growing up Jewish in Nazi Germany, on coming to the United States alone as a fourteen-year-old adolescent in 1937, on returning to Hagen as an American soldier and again in later years, and on how my life experiences influenced my career as a clinical psychologist, working internationally in the field of reproductive behavior.

Roots

The David family can trace its history in Germany through several generations. My great-grandfather, Isaac David, born in January 1807 in Unkel am Rhein, moved to Hagen as a young man, opened an optical business, and was among the first importers of steel springs from England. Widely traveled, he died in Hagen in 1868. My great-grandmother, Lina David, was born in 1819 in Lünen (in Westphalia) and died in Hagen in January 1888.

My grandfather, Louis David, was born in Hagen in June 1854. In 1880 he established a wholesale business, specializing in semifinished iron and steel goods. He died in Hagen in June 1929, just a week short of his seventy-fifth birthday. My grandmother, Alwine Harff David, was born in September 1857 in Wesel. She was unusually well educated for the time, passed the state examination as a *Lyzeum* (secondary school) teacher, and was among the first German women to serve as a private tutor and governess in England. She was the second elected president of the Hagen Jewish Women's Association, serving in that capacity for twenty-five years until appointed honorary president. She passed away in February 1935 at age seventy-eight.

My father, Ferdinand David, was the eldest son, born in Hagen on April 8, 1885. After studying law at the universities of Bonn, Munich, and Münster, he graduated in 1910 with a Dr. jur. degree and obtained additional training as an assessor before opening an office for the practice of law in Hagen in 1912. From 1914 to 1918 he served with distinction on the Western Front, attaining high noncommissioned officer rank and an Iron Cross, Second Class.

On return to Hagen, he reestablished his law practice and was appointed a notary public in 1921. In that year he married my mother, Ilse Gerson, the daughter of a Magdeburg banker. They had been introduced by my father's only sister, Grete David, who had married the banker Moritz Rothschild from Magdeburg.

For the next twelve years my father participated extensively in Hagen civic, cultural, and political life. He served as legal counsel to the Social Democratic Party (SPD); was elected to the Hagen city council (1929–33); was appointed a labor relations court judge; held numerous honorary positions as a trustee or board member of social, cultural, and welfare organizations and public institutions; chaired the Hagen and regional chapter of the Central Verein Deutscher Staatsbürger Jüdischen Glaubens (Central Association of German Citizens of Jewish Faith); and was an active council member (from 1922) and later board member (from 1937) of the Hagen Jewish Community. He was also a member of the Reichsbund Jüdischer Frontsoldaten (Association of Jewish War Veterans). His younger brother, Philipp, was emotionally devastated by his prisoner of war experiences in World War I and died shortly after his return home. The public esteem in which my father was held in Hagen was apparent from his reelection to city council in the last open German election in April 1933, three months after Hitler's coming to power. He was not permitted to take his seat.

Growing up Jewish in Nazi Germany

From the time of my birth on May 28, 1923 until late 1933 we lived in a comfortable apartment adjoining my father's law offices, located within a short walk of City Hall. As the only child of socially active parents, I was reared largely by maids and a succession of nannies. On the floor above us resided the family of a physician prominent in the local Nazi party. His son, Werner, and I were the same age, became friends, and played together but never in his parents' apartment. It was through my friendship with Werner that I grew increasingly aware of the negative implications of being Jewish. For me it meant being different, not being allowed to join the Hitler Youth, not wearing a uniform, and not marching behind a drum and bugle corps. For a ten year old, reading about Jewish history and tradition could not compensate for the pageantry of the Hitler Youth. I remember standing behind the curtained window of our apartment on the night after Hitler's assumption of power on January 30, 1933 and looking for Werner marching in his brown uniform behind the red banners emblazoned with black swastikas on white circles in a torchlight parade. Why did I have to be Jewish? Why could I not be there too?

In April 1933 my father was suddenly stripped of his civic offices and, after twenty-one years, was no longer permitted to practice law on the grounds that he had defended known communists (although he was never accused of having been a communist). Despite vigorous appeals and affidavits from prominent persons, my father lost to the newly empowered Nazi officials whom he had defeated in previous political battles. We gave up our apartment and moved into the house purchased by my grandfather in 1891, where my father was born and in which my grandmother still resided.

Within an increasingly hostile environment, our economic situation steadily deteriorated. Through a good friend my father obtained a job as a sales representative, while my mother gave bridge lessons in our home and became a discreet matchmaker for Jewish men and women. Despite the Nazi boycott of Jewish stores, the suppression of opposing political parties, and the Nuremberg Laws, my father continued to view himself as a German citizen of Jewish faith, whose primary loyalty was to the Fatherland. He firmly believed that the Hitler regime was a temporary aberration that would end as the "good" German people came to their senses. His faith in German culture and liberal traditions remained steadfast, reinforced by old SPD comrades and by the decency of a former schoolmate, now a high-ranking Gestapo official, who usually called him to suggest taking a vacation out of town a day or so before a concentration camp roundup was to begin.

Meanwhile I had completed the four grades of the Jewish Volks-schule (elementary school). Werner and I were both admitted to the 1933–34 freshman class of the Fichte Gymnasium, the oldest boys' school in Hagen, founded in 1799. Jewish boys were excluded with the exception of sons of World War I front-line soldiers. While older teachers seldom showed bigotry and were "correct" in their classroom behavior toward me, younger teachers, often with swastikas in their lapels, became increasingly hostile and cynical in their remarks about Jews. Amid the growing anti-Semitic taunts and shunning by fellow students, Werner continued to walk part of the way home with me—until his father expressly forbade it. By 1936, I was the only Jewish boy remaining in my class, the only nonmember of the Hitler youth, and the only one specifically excluded from extracurricular school activities and patriotic events. When informed that the special privileges granted to children of Jewish war veterans had been rescinded and that I would be excluded from the gymnasium as of the 1937–38 school year, I realized that there was no hope for completing my higher education in Nazi Germany. Classes in the Jewish community school were still held in one room, conducted by one teacher (who lived above the school and also served as rabbi in the synagogue next door).

In the spring of 1937 fate appeared in the guise of a U.S. social worker representing the German-Jewish Children's Aid Committee of New York. Apparently my father had learned of this organization, which offered to place children under the age of fourteen in suitable U.S. Jewish homes able to sponsor their education. The committee provided a corporate affidavit guaranteeing that the children would not become public charges, would attend school at least until age sixteen, and would not be gainfully employed until then. The committee did not propose to bring over children for adoption but rather to leave the way open for an eventual reunion with their parents if that proved possible (Davie 1947).

When asked whether I would like to come to the United States, I agreed immediately. For me the United States was the land of cowboys and Indians, where dollars grew on trees and where I could continue my education. Six weeks later I sailed from Hamburg on the USS *Roosevelt* (named for Theodore Roosevelt). It was just three days before my fourteenth birthday. To mark that occasion I changed my name from Heinz Philipp David to Henry Philip David, determined to reject the Nazi past and become an American from my day of arrival in New York City. We arrived on June 6, 1937. The early morning view of the Statue of Liberty, beckoning me with an irresistible force, will always remain a vivid memory. As I learned some years later, I was one of only ninety-two children who came to the United States in 1937 unaccompanied by their parents (Davie 1947).

Shortly before my departure from Hagen my parents gave a party in our garden. Nearly a year after my bar mitzvah, it was a bittersweet event. Standing around the linden tree, some of us wondered where and when we would meet in the future. Most of us never saw each other again. My parents were severely criticized by some of their friends for permitting their only child to leave Germany alone. They had agreed to do so in the belief that it offered the best opportunity to continue my education and that our separation would not last longer than two or three years. Their assumptions were correct but not in the way they had expected.

On the morning of my departure we sat down to a very solemn breakfast. I was dressed in my best knickers, looking ahead to the future while saddened by the separation confronting us. My father presented me with a Hebrew-English Hagadah, originally published in New York in 1863 and purchased by my great-grandfather. He had inscribed it with the names of those David family members who had used it, ending with the comment that it was now returning to the land of its origin with the great-grandson. "May it always be part of a happy and joyous Passover." I have told the Hagadah's history over the years as we celebrated Passover with our children and grandchildren.

As I boarded the USS *Roosevelt* my mother wept while my father stoically tried to reassure her. This American ship was somehow an omen that the United States had come to Germany and would deliver me safely to a new land, planting fresh roots for a sturdy family tree. And indeed, that was the message of the letter my father handed me at the last moment with instructions to open it on my birthday. He detailed the David family history in Germany and expressed his faith in his only child to continue the tradition in a new land. It was a view of the future that differed from his previously expressed expectations of an early return to Germany.

In America

Adolescence

My American sponsors were a prominent Jewish pediatrician and his wife, a past president of the Council of Jewish Women, residing in Cincinnati, Ohio. They had expressed a willingness to take into their home a fourteen-year-old German-Jewish boy, reared in a physician's or lawyer's household, where the father was a stamp collector (as my sponsor was). I matched those criteria and was expected to be a companion to their fifteen-year-old son, Frankie, who had cerebral palsy. A second older son was in college.

My sponsor met me in New York, introduced himself as "Uncle Victor," and took me on the overnight Pullman train to Cincinnati. We communicated by my bits of English, his bits of German, and both of us pointing to words in an English-German dictionary. The next morning in the dining car, when asked what I wanted for breakfast, I blurted out the name of the first American food that came to mind—"steak." Uncle Victor laughed, ordered Wheaties with fruit and milk, and never tired of telling the story for the rest of his life.

In Cincinnati, I was greeted by "Aunt Fanny" and her mother, "Granny." They immediately assured me in German that I was welcome in their home and that I would be part of their family but that they did not intend to replace my parents. On my second day in Cincinnati, Aunt Fanny took me shopping, replacing all my German clothes with American clothes to make me look more like an American boy. I was introduced to the children of my sponsors' friends and to the country club, where I was perceived as the "German boy" who had to be accepted.

In my second week, I was placed in the seventh grade of summer school, slightly below my proper academic level. It was thought this would give me more of a chance to improve my English rapidly without special aid. At the end of the summer I was promoted to the ninth grade and admitted to high school. Strongly motivated to please my sponsors, I studied hard, attained excellent grades, completed high school in three years, and won a scholarship to the University of Cincinnati. This achievement motivation was in strong contrast to my low grades in Germany. The drive to succeed, to be accepted and respected for what I could accomplish intellectually, stayed with me over the years and into "retirement."

My social and emotional adjustment was more difficult. I rejected the friendship offered by German boys my age who had come to Cincinnati with their parents. I wanted to be American, to have American friends. Companionship with Frankie was difficult. He was mentally far younger than his chronological age. When he died within a year of my arrival, I was saddened but also felt relief—the burden of being his companion had been lifted. I was freer to make friends and did so with boys whose families did not belong to the country club and were willing to accept me as an equal.

Religion was a problem. Despite expressing atheist sentiments, I was obliged by my sponsors to go to Sunday school in a Reform temple where they were prominent members. I must have annoyed my teachers by writing essays with titles such as "Why I Don't Believe in God" and wanting to debate everything they said. I had been forced to acknowledge being Jewish and being different in the eyes of society, but I did not wish to participate in formal religion. Today, I am more of an agnostic, accepting my Jewish heritage but still questioning the existence of a God.

Throughout my stay with them, Uncle Victor and Aunt Fanny wrote lengthy reports to my parents. They embellished my adjustment, skipped over problems my sometimes aggressive behavior had created, and emphasized the opportunities the United States offered me. Meanwhile, living conditions in Germany steadily worsened for Jews. My father finally recognized the deadly seriousness of events after the *Kristallnacht* on November 9–10, 1938, when our house was among those ransacked by out-of-town Nazi storm troopers. This time there had been no advance warning. Much of our furniture and many of our antiques and books were wantonly destroyed. My father was thrown out of the first-floor window and reinjured his back, which had been severely wounded in World War I. He was operated on at the local Catholic hospital and kept in closely supervised care for fifty-six days to protect him from arrest and possible dispatch to a concentration camp. As my father wrote later, "They have beaten my body, but not my thoughts." Everyone had underestimated the Nazi threat. The Night of the Broken Glass was inconceivable until it happened. Uncle Victor and Aunt Fanny immediately responded by providing an affidavit, placing my parents on the then ever-lengthening waiting list for a U.S. visa.

Soon after my father's release from hospital, my parents were forced to sell our house at a steeply depressed price. My father was deprived of any means of earning a living. He and my mother moved into a tiny apartment while awaiting permission to travel to England and wait there for the issuance of a U.S. visa. They reached London in the summer of 1939, shortly before the outbreak of World War II. Soon thereafter my father was interned by the British as an enemy alien because of his World War I service in the German army. By personal appeal and a bit of bribery with jewels they had smuggled out of Germany, my mother obtained my father's release after three months. My father never complained about what he deemed justifiable action by the English government. In September 1940 my parents received their visa. Braving submarines, they crossed the ocean and arrived in Cincinnati in October 1940.

To prepare for my parents' arrival, Uncle Victor and Aunt Fanny obtained a small apartment, furnished it with all essentials contributed by family and friends, and paid the rent for more than a year in advance. My parents were accepted as family members and participated fully in the Friday night gatherings. Their English had improved during their year's residence in Britain and was further enhanced by their decision to speak only English with each other. One month after his arrival, my father accepted a job as a night watchman in a coal yard. The descent from a highly respected professional life in Germany to his present circumstances never depressed him; he was determined to begin a new career in a new land at age fifty-five. My mother worked as a practical nurse.

My readjustment to living with my parents was difficult. I moved in with them and completed my freshman year at the University of Cincinnati while working some afternoons and every Saturday to contribute to the family income. The sudden change had its effects. I missed the good life I had enjoyed and resented having to delay my educational goals to help support my parents. This situation was exacerbated when I took a full-time job as a stock clerk in a department store during the 1941–42 academic year, continuing my university studies at night. Meanwhile my father found a daytime clerical job in a printing plant.

With the support of U.S. friends who recognized his legal training and administrative abilities, my father applied for and obtained the position of superintendent of the Home for Jewish Aged in Cincinnati. He was appointed in 1942, joined by my mother as matron. Within two years of his arrival in the United States, my father had once again attained a position of some prominence, gained the respect of the Board of Trustees, and achieved leadership in the community of German-Jewish newcomers. I returned to the university full-time but chose to live outside the Jewish Home in a room of my own, dividing visits between my parents and Uncle Victor and Aunt Fanny. In the summer of 1942, at age nineteen and after completing my sophomore year, I was inducted into the U.S. Army.

World War II

After induction, I was sent to Miami Beach for basic training in the Army Air Corps. Military service qualified me to become a naturalized citizen on October 8, 1943 in a ceremony at the Miami Federal Court

Building. It was the fulfillment of a dream cherished since my arrival six years earlier.

On completion of basic training I was assigned to the Air Corps Medical and Psychological Examining Unit. Its function was to select candidates for training as pilots, copilots, navigators, and bombardiers. Most had never seen the inside of an airplane. As one of the youngest and least educated privates, I became a psychological assistant, administering psychomotor tests. It was my introduction to psychology.

Following short stints as a classification specialist at air force bases in Kearney, Nebraska, and Boise, Idaho, I was assigned to Ninth Air Force Headquarters in Colorado Springs. Then, suddenly, a telegram came instructing me to report to an unnamed unit in Greensboro, North Carolina, an embarkation port for Europe. It was quite a shock to find myself among a group of German-speaking men, the vast majority of whom were Jewish immigrants, the very people I had tried to escape. Beset by conflict, I denied my German birth and insisted that I had been reared in Cincinnati.

The game was up a few days later when somebody checked my record. My rejection of my German-Jewish background was apparent, but it was not held against me very long. The prospect of joining the fight against Nazi Germany elated us. However, as we marched through the Greensboro embarkation port, singing old German songs, some of us speculated whether we would be trained as spies and parachuted into Germany, whether we should throw away our dog tags to avoid religious identification if captured, or whether we were to become counterintelligence agents and be part of military government.

After arrival in London in early 1945, we were told that our unit was the U.S. Strategic Bombing Survey (USSBS), established in November 1944 pursuant to a directive from President Roosevelt to assess the physical, economic, and psychological effects of the air war. I was assigned to the Morale Division, which had as its objective to determine the direct and indirect effects of bombing upon the attitudes, behavior, and health of the civilian population. My initial responsibility was to read samples of captured German civilian mail and analyze comments on the psychological effects of the air war. A few months later I was assigned to a small forward field unit entering German towns behind the front-line troops and searching for morale reports compiled by local agents for the German Propaganda Ministry.

Higher-level USSBS civilian staff, stationed in London, made periodic field visits. Perhaps most meaningful for me was my assignment near the end of the war to work with Otto Klineberg (professor of social psychology at Columbia University). I became his jeep driver, body-guard, and notetaker for interviews he conducted with senior Nazi officials at a prisoner of war camp aptly named "Ashcan." The long evening talks with Otto Klineberg, a Montreal-born physician/psychologist who spoke nine languages, strongly influenced my career path but in a way rather different from what we imagined at that time.

On two occasions I escaped potential death or serious injury. Once in London, when I remained in my bunk during an air raid, a heavy metal part of a gear from a V-2 rocket crashed through the roof, landed on the floor, and bounced, spent, onto my chest. It is the one war souvenir I brought back with me. The other occasion occurred in Munich when a colleague and I followed our advance troops into Nazi headquarters in a search of documents. Suddenly, we heard footsteps. Coming around the corner were two armed German soldiers. My partner shot them both before I could get my pistol out of my holster. Again fate had intervened on my side.

Soon after the end of the war in Europe, while still stationed in Germany, I filled a jeep with canned rations and drove to Hagen, then in the British Zone of Occupation. Much of the city had been destroyed, and people were living amid rubble. On checking with British headquarters and explaining that I wished to deliver the rations to the Catholic physician who had saved my father's life in November 1938, I was told that many persons had asked when my father would return as lord mayor. After delivering the rations, I looked for our house but drove past it at first. Only the outer walls still stood. But, the garden with the majestic linden tree was untouched. Miraculously, the nearby grocery store was open. The grocer, an old Social Democrat, recognized me and began to sing my father's praises. He recalled the *Kristallnacht* of 1938 and how for several days he had brought groceries to my mother under the cover of darkness.

At the Fichte Gymnasium, much of which was still standing, I found the old *Hausmeister* (housemaster). He told me that my friend Werner had died at Stalingrad and that most of my classmates had either "fallen" or were prisoners of war. I will never forget the thought that flashed through my mind—how fortunate I had been to have been born Jewish, to have escaped Germany, and to have a future in the United States. It was a long way from that day in 1933 when I envied the boys marching past so proudly in their Hitler Youth torchlight parade.

Shortly before leaving Germany, I arranged a reunion with my cousin

Herbert. He had changed his name to Yehuda and served in the Jewish Brigade of the British Army, then stationed in the Netherlands. It was our first meeting in nine years. As we reflected on our experiences, we were proud to have served, to have helped defeat Hitler, to have stopped the killing of Jews. The immensity of the Holocaust was still unclear. We had escaped, but, strangely, we did not experience feelings of revenge or hatred for all Germans. The suffering so apparent all around us served perhaps to repress those feelings. While realizing that what had happened must never be forgotten, first priority now had to be given to assisting the masses of displaced Jewish refugees and establishing a Jewish homeland. My cousin, long committed to the creation of a state of Israel, returned to fight in the War of Independence. How I felt about Nazi Germany was expressed a few days later when my closest USSBS friend and I urinated against the remaining wall of the destroyed Berghof, Hitler's favorite retreat in the Bavarian Alps near Berchtesgaden.

From Clinical Psychology to Public Health

After I was discharged from military service in April 1946 and returned to Cincinnati, my goal was to complete my studies as rapidly as possible. I had decided to become a psychologist, to try to understand human behavior and myself. Moreover, I wanted to earn a Ph.D., to be called "doctor," matching the achievements of my father and my sponsor. My wartime experience and the G.I. Bill of Rights provided the opportunity.

Living in a room above my parents' apartment in the Home for Jewish Aged, I immersed myself in university studies. In 1948, I received a B.A. with high honors in psychology and was invited to join Phi Beta Kappa. I also qualified as a research patient in the Cincinnati section of the Chicago Institute for Psychoanalysis, being seen for fifty minutes five mornings a week for one year. This intense experience helped me to resolve many of my conflicts about my parents and Uncle Victor and Aunt Fanny, the insecurities that had influenced so much of my aggressive behavior, and the ambivalences about Nazi Germany. But I could not find an answer to the eternal question of the unique circumstances that had assured my survival.

In 1949, after obtaining an M.A. degree in clinical psychology from the University of Cincinnati, I was admitted to the clinical psychology training program at Teachers' College, Columbia University. I graduated with a Ph.D. degree in June 1951, having completed my doctoral studies in three years. Otto Klineberg served on my doctoral committee.

I lived at International House on a frugal budget, supplemented by a part-time position at Teachers' College. Without the G.I. Bill, I would never have had the opportunity to achieve a doctorate.

My mother attended my graduation. My father had died in 1950, ten years after his arrival in the United States. In 1946 he had been invited to give the main address at the annual Cincinnati "I am an American" day. In 1947 he received an official letter of apology from the city of Hagen for his mistreatment in Germany. It was signed by the first elected post-war lord mayor, who later became state governor, an old SPD buddy long imprisoned for his political beliefs. In the letter he recalled my father's many contributions to the city and reassured him that he had been as much a German as any other Hagen citizen.

Shortly after graduation I left New York, driving to Kansas, where I had obtained a postdoctoral position at Topeka State Hospital. At the time, Topeka was the U.S. mecca for postgraduate education in the mental health professions. A year later I accepted the position of instructor in the Department of Psychiatry at the Western Psychiatric Institute of the University of Pittsburgh Medical School. It was in Pittsburgh that I met and married my wife, Tema Seidman, in 1953. She was the American-born granddaughter of Russian-Jewish immigrants. We had a son, Jonathan, born in May 1955. We lost him in May 1980, the saddest day of our lives. Our daughter, Gail, born in 1957, is married to Steven Heydemann, the son of a German-Jewish immigrant who also married an American woman of Russian-Jewish descent. They have two daughters, Sarah and Julia, who have made us happy grandparents.

In subsequent years I held positions as assistant professor and director of psychology at the Lafayette Clinic in the Department of Psychiatry of Wayne State University in Detroit (1955–56) and as chief psychologist for the New Jersey State Department of Institutions and Agencies in Trenton with administrative responsibility for more than one hundred psychologists and students working in state hospitals, community clinics, schools for developmentally disabled persons, and correctional facilities. During my tenure from 1956 to 1963, I recruited a number of European colleagues, whose training, professional experience, and intellectual contributions greatly strengthened the state program. When I was criticized for accepting several German-born colleagues, I rejected the concept of collective guilt and focused on qualifications. My own background helped to overcome the bias of Jewish colleagues. During this time I was elected chair of the Association of State Chief Psychologists and president of APA Division Eighteen (Public Service). My interests had moved from primarily clinical practice to a public health policy orientation.

International Interests and Population Issues

In June 1954 I participated in the International Congress of Psychology in Montreal, Canada, where I met Helmut von Bracken, a German physician-psychologist. He was an old Social Democrat, and his congeniality, liberal political ideology, and shared international ideals facilitated a productive partnership. Based on presentations in Montreal, we developed an edited volume, *Perspectives in Personality Theory*, with contributions by twenty-two colleagues from nine countries. Published in 1957 in the United States and in Britain, and subsequently in Switzerland and in Argentina, it was the first volume to be issued under the auspices of the International Union of Psychological Science, with all royalties allocated to the union (David and von Bracken 1957). In 1957 I organized and led the first APA charter flight to the International Congress of Psychology, held in Brussels, Belgium. With J. C. Brengelmann, another German-born M.D./Ph.D., who was gravely wounded in Stalingrad and lived in London, I planned an edited volume, *Perspectives in Personality Research*, with contributions by twenty-seven psychologists from eleven countries. This work was published in the United States in 1960 and in Switzerland in 1961, and all royalties were again donated to the International Union (David and Brengelmann 1960). Otto Klineberg, then secretary-general of the International Union, contributed a foreword to both volumes. As a member of the Organizing Committee for the 1963 International Congress in Washington, I suggested a young psychologists program that would raise funds to support travel and hospitality for young colleagues from abroad. The tradition established in Washington has continued at every subsequent international congress.

My international interests grew into a full-time career in 1963 when I was invited to become associate director of the World Federation for Mental Health (WFMH), then headquartered in Geneva, Switzerland. During the next two years I traveled widely, worked closely with colleagues in the World Health Organization, and gradually realized that population growth, reproductive health, and women's rights were closely associated with mental health.

Among the several books I edited under WFMH auspices (David 1964a, 1964b, 1966, 1972) was *Population and Mental Health*. As noted in the Editor's Preface, the Executive Board of the World Federation for

Mental Health had declared in January 1962 that among "the most important international problems of the 20th century is the very considerable acceleration of population growth." The board cited the anxieties and tensions generated by rising expectations and the mental health problems associated with both advocacy and condemnation of means of fertility regulation. It concluded that "the ways in which these questions are answered in the various societies of the world are of the greatest importance, both directly and indirectly, to the mental health of people all over the world." As I was to discover, however, population specialists were more interested in demographic trends than in the psychology of reproductive behavior. At the same time, colleagues profoundly interested in the psychosocial development of children were giving scant attention to the procreative aspects of sexuality and the possible etiological and epidemiological significance of chance versus planned births. Nearly twenty years later (in 1984), I was invited to establish the WFMH Committee on Responsible Parenthood and served as chair for thirteen years. During this time I was elected to the WFMH Board for two terms.

It was the desire of my wife for a more stable and settled family life that stimulated our decision to return to the United States in 1965. I had hoped to find a position that would combine my experience in mental health with my new international interests in reproductive behavior. Alas, there were no psychologists in the population field, and psychology departments were not interested in population issues. It was Edwin Fleishman, then director of the Washington office of the American Institutes for Research (AIR), who invited me to join AIR as associate director of the AIR International Research Institute and develop the field through grants and contracts. We returned to Washington, bought a house in Bethesda, and have lived there for more than thirty-three years. In a grand family compromise, we settled in one place, but I could continue my international activities.

NIH Center for Population Research and TFRI

By 1967 restrictions on legal abortion were increasingly challenged in the U.S. courts. When the Center for Population Research (CPR) was established in the National Institute of Child Health and Human Development (NICHD) in August 1968 and expressed interest in a better understanding of the abortion experience in other developed countries, I suggested a closer look at the health systems in some of the socialist countries of Central and Eastern Europe where abortion had been legal for some years. Award of one of the first CPR contracts allowed me to travel and interview colleagues abroad. The result was a monograph summarizing available information about procedures and trends related to legal abortion. It also presented demographic data and developed a psychosocial perspective on the complex interplay between socioeconomic aspirations, cultural values, and individual practices of voluntary family limitation (David 1970).

In 1972, I founded the Transnational Family Research Institute, initially within AIR and subsequently as an independent nonprofit research organization in the behavioral sciences with a focus on reproductive behavior. Cooperative projects and relationships were developed with colleagues on five continents. With our affiliate, Population and Development International, offices were eventually established in Aptos, California; Prague, Copenhagen, Mexico City, Bangkok, Moscow, and Hanoi, always in association with local colleagues.

There is little doubt in my mind that my career choice and subsequent international activities were strongly influenced by my life experiences in the Hitler years. I was educated in Europe and in the United States, was sensitive to diverse cultures, and was strongly attracted to liberal sociopolitical issues. The neglected and often taboo areas of fertility regulation, abortion, and reproductive decision making were traditionally dominated by autocratic patriarchal values. In the postwar period they became important indicators of women's rights, and thus human rights, an area linked to my history, influencing my personal and professional life.

The hostility of the Nazis to sexuality education, contraception, and abortion was always of interest to me. However, to avoid protestations of possible bias, I delayed research until I could elicit the cooperation of an East and a West German colleague. We found that, although thousands of books and monographs had been written about the Nazi period, there was seldom any mention of abortion. A search of numerous German and U.S. archives, research libraries, and indexes of volumes specifically oriented to the experiences of women produced few references related to abortion rates in the Hitler era. We were, however, able to document the increasingly stringent restrictions placed on access to contraceptives and legal abortion. Severe penalties were placed on clandestine procedures, including the imposition of the death penalty near the end of the war. It was rarely noted that the prohibition of abortion did not apply to Jewish women because Jewish fetuses were not considered to be protected by German law (David, Fleischhacker, and Höhn 1988).

Prague

Among the best-known research and policy relevant TFRI projects is the Prague Study, focusing on the long-term development of children unwanted during early pregnancy. Initiated in the late 1960s in Prague, in then Czechoslovakia, the study follows 220 children born in 1961–63 to women twice denied abortion for the same pregnancy and pair-matched controls. Each unwanted pregnancy (UP) child (110 boys and 110 girls) was pair-matched with an accepted pregnancy (AP) child, that is, a child born to parents who wanted to conceive. The unusual circumstances that made the study possible, the matching process, and findings through age thirty are delineated in several publications (David et al. 1988; David 1992; Kubicka et al. 1995).

When first examined at age nine, the subjects obtained similar scores on the Wechsler Intelligence Scale for Children, but the UP children received lower school grades and were rated less favorably in school performance than the AP controls. Differences on all psychological measurements were consistently in disfavor of the UP children. The child of a woman denied abortion seemed to be born into a potentially handicapping situation, a condition consonant with the concept of psychological subdeprivation. The differences widened over time as the UP children rarely appeared on any roster of excellence. A significantly larger number did not continue to secondary school and had contentious relationships with their parents. Around age 21–23, the young adult UP subjects reported less job satisfaction, more conflicts with co-workers and supervisors, and more disappointments in love than the AP controls. By age thirty-five, significant differences in psychiatric morbidity had become apparent.

The still continuing Prague Study, conducted in cooperation with Czech colleagues associated with the Prague Psychiatric Center, has been supported over the years by the U.S. National Institute of Child Health and Human Development, the Czechoslovak State Research Plan, the World Health Organization, the Ford Foundation, the Czech Ministry of Health, and, most recently, the Soros Foundation. I cite it here as a unique longitudinal research project that has provided scientific support for the prevention of unwanted births and documented the effects of psychological subdeprivation on child development. It survived the Soviet occupation of Prague thanks to the persistent courage and scientific dedication of my Czech colleagues in the face of numerous obstacles and personal risks.

When the Velvet Revolution burst forth in Prague in 1989, it was an emotionally moving experience for all of us. Less than two years later, in 1991, I was decorated with the Medal of Charles University in a solemn ceremony in the Carolineum, the hall where the university was founded in 1348. It was a rare honor, which I accepted in the name of our entire research team. My Czech colleagues then told me how concerned they had been about my safety, that my background and Jewish heritage would have provided the perfect ingredients for a communist show trial.

Prague held a special appeal for another reason. The history of Prague Jews was hauntingly fascinating, with periods of splendor and glory intertwined with humiliation and near extinction, from their arrival in the tenth century to their bare survival during the Hitler period of the twentieth century. I had visited the Pincus Synagogue, whose walls are covered with the names of families who perished in the Holocaust. I had seen the thirteenth-century synagogue, one of the oldest in Europe; the densely crowded Jewish cemetery; and the museums displaying Jewish ceremonial art treasures collected there by the Nazis from all over Europe. And I had visited Theresienstadt, the model Nazi concentration camp whose inmates were systematically transported to Auschwitz. The Jewish quarter of Prague had been preserved on Hitler's orders as a memorial to a dead race. Instead it had become a living reminder of Jewish survival.

One day at a meeting of the American Psychological Association my friend and colleague Donald K. Freedheim told me about the Traub Fund administered by the Cleveland Jewish Community Federation. Established by Czech newcomers to the United States, one of its purposes was to preserve the experiences of those fellow Czech Jews who had survived the Holocaust. Joining with my Czech colleagues Zdenek Dytrych and Zdenek Matejcek we persuaded Katerina Biglova, the daughter of survivors and a Ph.D. psychologist-counselor in the Prague Jewish Community Center, to conduct a structured oral history project with thirty-six elderly Jewish women. The initial idea was to record the recollections of their reproductive lives before, during, and after the Hitler period. However, we soon realized that a scientific focus was impossible to maintain amid the onrush of traumatic memories. Katerina's edited interviews and the history of Jewish Prague were summarized and published in an English language monograph, *Remembering: Voices of Prague Jewish Women* (Biglova et al. 1994). It is sold in the Prague Jewish museums, and all royalties are contributed to the Prague Jewish Community Fund for the support of Holocaust survivors, their children, and their grandchildren.

APA and Population Psychology

Throughout my career I maintained close contact with the American Psychological Association. After my return from Geneva I was elected to APA Council by Division Eighteen (Public Service). In October 1969 it was my privilege to introduce a resolution together with the Association for Women Psychologists, declaring that termination of an unwanted pregnancy was a mental health and child welfare issue and thus a legitimate concern of APA. The resolution resolved that termination of pregnancy be considered "a civil right of the pregnant woman," to be handled as any other medical and surgical procedure in consultation with the woman's physician (McKeachie 1970, 37).

At the request of some council members, a second resolution was then moved by Division Eighteen, resolving that APA establish a task force on psychology, family planning, and population policy "for the purpose of preparing a review of the current state of psychological research related to family planning and population policy" and making recommendations for "encouraging greater research and professional service participation by psychologists in this emerging area of social concern" (McKeachie 1970, 34). After only brief discussion, both resolutions passed by a substantial margin, thus placing APA firmly in support of women's reproductive rights well before the January 1973 *Roe v. Wade* Supreme Court decision.

During its tenure the task force, which I served as chair, convened seminars and workshops, produced widely disseminated newsletters, and facilitated publications. Among its several recommendations was one encouraging the establishment of an APA division of population psychology (APA Task Force 1972). Upon meeting the necessary requirements, the division was duly organized in August 1974. An important byproduct of task force efforts was the convening of an interdisciplinary abortion research workshop on the day before the 1973 meeting of the Population Association of America in New Orleans. Over the years, the workshop expanded its scope of interest, and, in 1982, it was renamed the Psychosocial Workshop. Its annual sessions attract a coterie of anthropologists, demographers, economists, psychologists, psychiatrists, sociologists, and other health professionals. How far we have come is apparent in the 1998 APA publication of a book bringing together contributions to the study of abortion by psychologists and colleagues in the social science and health professions to which I contributed the foreword (Beckman and Harvey 1998).

It was also my privilege to serve on the 1969 APA Task Force on the

Status of Women in Psychology, which eventually evolved into APA Division Thirty-five (Psychology of Women). When Surgeon General C. Everett Koop was asked by President Reagan to examine medical and psychological factors in abortion, I served as a consultant to his office, testified before Congress, and was a member of the APA expert panel whose findings were published in *Science* and in the *American Psychologist* (Adler et al. 1990, 1992).

A particular challenge was my service as an APA representative to the International Union of Psychological Science. When the Soviet Union invaded Afghanistan, questions were raised in APA Council as to whether APA should follow the U.S. government example of imposing sanctions and boycotting the Moscow Olympics by boycotting the Twenty-second International Congress of Psychology, scheduled to be held in the German Democratic Republic (GDR) in July 1980. The already difficult situation was made even more difficult by rumors that the GDR would not issue visas to Israeli colleagues because the GDR had no diplomatic relations with the State of Israel and that, even if visas were issued, the flag of Israel would not be flown with those of other participating countries.

I was asked to go to East Berlin and meet with officials of the GDR congress organizing committee. APA made the necessary arrangements. I was met at the airport and immediately driven to the home of the congress president. After lengthy discussion, it was agreed that visas would be issued to the Israelis and that only the flag of the host country would be flown outside or inside the congress. Fortunately, this compromise was accepted by APA Council. Some GDR colleagues commented later that they had not expected APA to be represented by a German-born Jewish psychologist who was free to negotiate a sensitive agreement without concurrent consultation with higher authorities. In subsequent years, as a member and chair of the Committee on International Relations in Psychology, I helped to clarify APA's position on human rights issues and special responsibilities as the world's largest organization of psychologists.

Germany Revisited

In August 1960 my wife and I participated in the Sixteenth International Congress of Psychology in Bonn. We drove to Hagen to revisit the garden where I had spent so many happy childhood hours. The one-family house of my grandparents, reduced to rubble in the war, had been replaced by a four-story apartment building. The only way to enter the garden was through a ground-floor apartment. The name on one of the two ground-floor apartments was that of the family that had purchased the house after the 1938 *Kristallnacht* at a considerably below market price. When I rang the doorbell, an elderly woman answered and seemed somewhat flustered after I had introduced myself and asked her permission to show the garden to my wife. She let us into the apartment and took us to the garden, walking through the dining room, where her family had gathered to eat lunch. After spending a short time admiring the majestic old linden tree, we walked back into the dining room. It was empty, the food untouched on the plates and the people gone. We returned to Bonn after driving past the old synagogue, now a boarded-up building, torched during the *Kristallnacht*.

In subsequent years I had numerous occasions to visit East and West Germany, lecture in German, and meet with German colleagues. Strangers often remarked that I spoke excellent grammatical German but with a very discernible American accent. I smiled, thinking of how I spoke English with a slight German accent. When I was asked where I learned to speak German so well, my reply, that I was born in Germany, usually evoked a stunned silence, generally broken by a follow-up question about the year of my emigration. After that, the story of my past was clear, inducing occasional embarrassment but more frequently a change of subject. There were also some German colleagues who invited me to their homes for the specific purpose of telling their children about the events of the Nazi period. Not infrequently I was the first Jew they had ever met. It was almost as if these parents were trying to inoculate their children against a repetition of the past.

What were my reactions to being in Germany? They continued to be confused and ambivalent. I felt no hatred for all things German. The potato salad and the wurst recalled the enjoyable "good old days" (just as they still do), but the oom-pah-pah music played by beer hall bands in lederhosen recalled the bad times. After three days or so in Germany, I could not leave soon enough. The old images would not remain repressed.

My third return to Hagen came in 1990 when I accepted an invitation from the Society for Christian-Jewish Cooperation. Its chair, Hermann Zabel, and I had already corresponded for a while. A professor of Germanics who grew up during the Hitler period, he had dedicated a great deal of time and effort to compiling the history of the Hagen Jewish community. To my surprise I found in my hotel room a folder with extensive documentation gathered by Professor Zabel about my father and his many contributions to Hagen civic life. I learned that he had received even more votes in his 1933 election campaign than he had in 1929.

In gathering information Professor Zabel encountered considerable hostility from the older generation, reluctant to reveal their participation in events they preferred to forget. The fear of potential incidents was apparent in the committee's decision to give the visitors' names to the press but not to identify the hotel, whose location never appeared in a published story. The lord mayor received us at City Hall and announced that the Social Democratic Party would soon petition city council to find an appropriate way of honoring my father's memory.

Since my wife had felt uncomfortable about returning to Germany, our daughter Gail agreed to accompany me. When we visited the Jewish cemetery, we discovered that the David family plot with the graves of my grandparents and two of their children had been vandalized by the Nazis and could no longer be identified. We found a loose plaque with my grandmother's name that was later attached to a gravestone in an area close to where I believed the family plot had been.

We also arranged to visit the old family garden, entering this time via the other ground-floor apartment. The majestic linden tree was gone, cut down when it threatened to fall. Covering the stump was a planter filled with pansies and marigolds. The tree had died and along with it a part of my childhood.

On our last night Gail and I were invited to services in the new synagogue built by the city of Hagen to replace the original. From the outside, there was no indication that it was a house of Jewish worship—no memorial plaque, no Star of David, no Hebrew inscription. All we could see was a TV monitor over the locked entrance door. The congregation consisted of fewer than twenty families, nearly all immigrants from Eastern Europe. The service was entirely in Hebrew, led by a lay rabbi, assisted by vigorous male chanting. It was all very different from the past when I walked with my father to the synagogue and sat next to him in his pew while my mother sat upstairs with the women.

The previous day I had been invited to give a colloquium at the local university. Gail and I were cordially received and taken to lunch. We talked about the many contributions Jews had made to German psychology, the anti-Semitism that had driven them from their positions, and the fact that only four German professors had lost their jobs due to postwar de-Nazification. As we parted, one colleague said to Gail, "But, you don't look Jewish." Embarrassment ensued when Gail asked what it was that made somebody look Jewish. Old stereotypes still lingered.

My last visit to Hagen was in March 1992 when my wife and I were invited as official guests of the city for the public dedication of the Dr. Ferdinand David Park. An existing park was renamed in honor of my father when the city council approved a petition for a name change initiated by Professor Zabel and endorsed by the major political parties. Beautifully planted, the park is·located about a block from the synagogue and two blocks from City Hall, fronting on the river. After a simple but impressive reception by the lord mayor at City Hall, the representatives of political parties, city government, and local institutions braved the gray, blustery, rainy day to walk the short distance to the park for the solemn dedication ceremony. The street sign was unveiled, stating the name of the park, the dates of my father's life, and a brief mention of who he was. I felt that my father would have been proud.

The next day I was invited to speak to a student assembly at the Fichte Gymnasium where I had been a student over fifty years before. The headmaster of the now coeducational school had searched the records and found the enrollment pages of my attendance, confirming that I had been the last Jewish boy. The student assembly had been selected to assure representation of boys and girls from every school grade, including children of refugees, immigrants, and guest workers from Turkey, Iran, Morocco, and other developing countries. I spoke for about thirty minutes, relating my Hagen history and making comparisons between anti-Semitic propaganda then and antiforeigner sentiments now. Instead of "Jews out!" the neo-Nazi slogan was "Foreigners out!" During the question period, a Moroccan girl noted that she wanted to be friends with German girls but "they don't want us." A German girl replied that "they" (foreigners) only want to be with their own ethnic group. Still another third world girl commented that parents worry about the safety of their daughters if they "mix" with German boys. It all had a familiar ring.

Afterward, in the headmaster's office for coffee, I was surprised when one of the teachers handed me a picture of the garden of my childhood. The teacher had seen my address in the registration book. He and his family had lived in one of the apartments and enjoyed the peace and tranquility the garden had provided to all the residents of the building. On this trip we did not return there. The old linden tree was gone.

There were other meaningful events during this visit, including a private meeting with the lord mayor; a reunion with survivors of the pre-

Hitler Social Democratic Party who recalled their memories of my father; a visit to an exhibit of Jewish religious art collected over many years by another member of the Society for Christian-Jewish cooperation; and a meeting with the son of the surgeon, himself a surgeon, who had saved my father's life, and his wife. There appeared to be a rediscovery of Jews in Germany, from preferential treatment for Russian-Jewish immigrants to renewed cultural interest in Jewish art and history. Yet, despite this intellectual reacceptance of Jews, there seemed to be a fragile ambivalence about how to nurture an evolving rapprochement. In 1997, a gentile German student at Columbia University studying for a Ph.D. in Jewish history taught my granddaughter Sarah's Sunday school class. And, in 1998 three Fichte Gymnasium students wrote to inquire what it was like to be a Jewish student after 1933. They were preparing a term paper on "the dark past."

Reflections

Having celebrated the sixty-third anniversary of my arrival in the United States, approaching age seventy-eight, and writing an autobiography evoke further reflections. Being Jewish was accepted a long time ago. I identify with the traditions of Reform Judaism as does our daughter's family. I never considered myself a Holocaust survivor until the Shoah Foundation asked to interview me on the basis that a survivor was anyone forced to flee his or her homeland under the threat of Nazi persecution. The vexing questions raised by the Holocaust and the riddle of God's existence continue to perplex but are unanswerable for me. Much as my father's first loyalty was to Germany, mine is to the United States. In that sense, I am thoroughly assimilated.

Working internationally with a strong public health/prevention orientation, I have tried to foster transnational cooperation across ideological, cultural, and political barriers and facilitate behavioral research likely to advance reproductive rights and the empowerment of women (e.g., David 1999). The unique opportunities I encountered owe much to circumstances, mentors, and grant makers as well as to host country colleagues who were willing to explore an emerging area of study and assume the personal risks our cooperative efforts sometimes entailed. To them and to my family I express my deepest gratitude for enabling me to chart an unusual career path.

As I write these lines, I am grateful to be alive, grateful to the fate that protected me, and grateful for the sustained and loving support of my life companion for forty-seven years, my wife, with whom I founded a new family in a new land. The terror unleashed by Hitler and Nazi Germany changed my life and its direction. I was one of the lucky ones and no longer ask why.

REFERENCES

Adler, N. E., H. P. David, B. N. Major, S. H. Roth, N. F. Russo, and G. E. Wyatt. 1990. Psychological responses to abortion. *Science* 248:41–44.

———. 1992. Psychological responses in abortion: A review. *American Psychologist* 47:1194–1204.

APA Task Force. 1972. Report of the Task Force on Psychology, Family Planning, and Population Policy. *American Psychologist* 27:1100–1105.

Beckman, L. J., and S. M. Harvey, eds. 1998. *Abortion in the United States: Psychological, social, and political issues.* Washington, DC: American Psychological Association.

Biglova, K., Z. Matejcek, Z. Dytrych, and H. P. David. 1994. *Remembering: Voices of Prague Jewish women.* Prague: Sazba Neptun DTP.

David, H. P. 1970. *Family planning and abortion in the socialist countries of central and Eastern Europe.* New York: Population Council.

———. 1992. Born unwanted: Long term developmental effects of denied abortion. *Journal of Social Issues* 48:163–81.

———. 1999. *From abortion to contraception: A resource to public policies and reproductive behavior in central and Eastern Europe from 1917 to the present.* Westport, CT: Greenwood.

———, ed. 1964a. *Population and mental health.* New York: Springer; Bern: Huber.

———. 1964b. *International resources in clinical psychology.* New York: McGraw-Hill.

———. 1966. *International trends in mental health.* New York: McGraw-Hill.

———. 1972. *Child mental health in international perspective.* New York: Harper and Row.

David, H. P., J. Fleischhacker, and C. Höhn. 1988. Abortion and eugenics in Nazi Germany. *Population and Development Review* 14:81–112.

David, H. P., and J. C. Brengelmann, eds. 1960. *Perspectives in personality research.* New York: Springer; Bern: Huber, 1961.

David, H. P., Z. Dytrych, Z. Matejcek, and V. Schüller, eds. 1988. *Born unwanted: Developmental effects of denied abortion.* New York: Springer. (Also published in Prague: Avicenum, 1988; Mexico City: EDAMEX, 1991).

David, H. P., and H. von Bracken, eds. 1957. *Perspectives in personality theory.* New York: Basic Books. (Also published in London: Tavistock, 1957; Bern: Huber, 1959; Buenos Aires: Eudeba, 1961).

Davie, M. R. 1947. *Refugees in America: Report of the committee for the study of recent immigration from Europe.* New York: Harper and Brothers.

Kubicka, L., Z. Matejcek, H. P. David, Z. Dytrych, W. B. Miller, and Z. Roth. 1995. Children from unwanted pregnancies in Prague, Czech Republic, revisited at age thirty. *Acta Psychiatrica Scandinavica,* 91:361–69.

McKeachie, W. J. 1970. Proceedings of the American Psychological Association for the year 1969: Minutes of the annual meeting of the Council of Representatives. *American Psychologist* 25:13–37.

Dignity and Dehumanization

The Impact of the Holocaust on Central Themes of My Work

Herbert C. Kelman

Biographical Note

Herbert C. Kelman is Richard Clarke Cabot Research Professor of social ethics and director of the Program on International Conflict Analysis and Resolution at Harvard University. He received his Ph.D. in social psychology from Yale and is the author or coauthor of many books and articles. Among the former are International Behavior: A Social-Psychological Analysis, A Time to Speak: On Human Values and Social Research, *and* Crimes of Obedience: Toward a Social Psychology of Authority and Responsibility *(with V. Lee Hamilton). He has been engaged for many years in the development of interactive problem solving and its application to the Arab-Israeli conflict.*

Among Professor Kelman's many awards are the Socio-Psychological Prize of the American Association for the Advancement of Science, the Kurt Lewin Memorial Award, the American Psychological Association Award for Distinguished Contributions to Psychology in the Public Interest, the Gravemeyer Award for Ideas Improving World Order, and the Austrian Medal of Honor for Science and Art, First Class. He has served as president of several professional associations, includ-

ing the International Studies Association, the International Society of Political Psychology, and the Interamerican Society of Psychology.

———————⟶•⟨⟨———————

The Holocaust has been a constant presence and a pervasive influence in my life and work. In this chapter, I reflect on my personal experience in confronting the Holocaust as a social scientist—which is, of course, my particular way of confronting it as a human being. The Holocaust has had an impact—in both obvious and subtle ways—not only on what I chose to study as a social scientist but also on my very choice of this profession as my lifelong career.

Personal Background and Intellectual Choices

I was born in Vienna in 1927 into a Jewish family of east European origin. My parents came to Vienna, separately, from the Tarnopol region in Eastern Galicia during World War I, as young adults. The area in which they were born (and which I visited, with my wife, for the first time in the summer of 1997) is now part of Ukraine. Before World War I it was part of the Austro-Hungarian Empire; between the two wars it was part of Poland; and after World War II it was part of the Soviet Union.

I grew up in a traditional Jewish home, in which I absorbed the religious and cultural values of Judaism. I had a thorough Hebrew and Jewish education, starting at age four and continuing to age twenty. (I received the degree of Bachelor of Hebrew Literature from the Seminary College of Jewish Studies in New York in 1947.) I also had extensive exposure in my childhood to the Yiddish language and the east European culture in which it flourished, through regular attendance at the Yiddish theater in Vienna (which was managed by a cousin) and later through a year spent in Antwerp in a largely Yiddish-speaking environment.

I was eleven years old at the time of the *Anschluss* and lived under Nazi rule for the next year. After the *Anschluss,* my family was evicted from the city housing project in which my father had managed a few years earlier to obtain an apartment (with the help of his status as an Austrian war veteran). My sister and I were expelled from our respective schools but were assigned places in the by then overcrowded Jewish Gymnasium. We experienced the pogrom of November 9–10, 1938—the so-called *Kristallnacht*—in its full force, living by that time in a Jewish neighborhood, around the corner from the Sephardic temple, which (along with all but one of the city's synagogues) was blown up and destroyed on that day. My memories of the *Kristallnacht* are detailed and vivid; I had the opportunity to share them with various Viennese audiences in the fall of 1998, when I took part in the commemoration of the sixtieth anniversary of the event.

In the aftermath of the *Kristallnacht*, it was clear that we had to get out of the country as quickly as possible. The small store that my father owned, in partnership with my aunt and uncle, was closed on November 10, and he never set foot in it again. We had no income and hardly any savings. My sister and I stopped attending school because it was not safe to walk there. (We did, however, manage to find ways of going to meetings of the Zionist youth group that we had joined after the *Anschluss.* I know that my membership in this group, my commitment to Zionism, and my strong Jewish identification in general sustained me during this period and enabled me to hold on to my self-worth in the face of the calculated degradation of the Nazi onslaught.) In addition to being deprived of work, of income, and of schooling, we lived in constant danger. The treatment of Jews, at the hands of bureaucrats, uniformed Nazis, or ordinary citizens, was entirely arbitrary, subject to the whims of the moment. A Jew—of any age and either gender—could be beaten up or forced to wash the sidewalk at any time. My father ran the constant risk of being dragged off to a concentration camp. It was only luck that protected us from beatings or arrests on the two occasions (one of them on November 10, 1938) when storm troopers came to our apartment to search and interrogate us. There was no question, then, that we had to get out. The problem for Jews during that period was not in getting out of Germany but in finding a place that would let them in.

My parents had the foresight to apply for immigrant visas to the United States within a few weeks of the *Anschluss.* We had close relatives in the States who provided the necessary affidavits. Still, in the end, it took two years before our visas were issued, because of the existence of national quotas for immigration to the United States at the time. Although we were Austrian citizens, we were on the Polish quota, since my parents' birthplaces were part of Poland during that period. The Polish quota was relatively small, and it took time for places to become available. I learned later, from a letter written by the U.S. consul in Vienna that I found in my father's papers, that had he delayed applying for the visas by just two or three weeks, the process would have taken an additional year and we would not have been able to escape Nazi-occupied Europe before the Holocaust.

As it was, our problem was to find an interim haven while waiting for our U.S. visas to come through. With the help of a cousin who had escaped to Italy, we managed to obtain illegal visas to Belgium, and we made it to Antwerp in the spring of 1939. The Belgian policy at the time was to allow illegal Jewish refugees from Nazi Germany to register with the police and legalize their stay, provided they did not seek employment. We had no funds, since we were not permitted to take out money or valuables upon departure from Germany. (I remember a very thorough search at the German border.) We were able to subsist, however, with the help of local and U.S. Jewish relief organizations. We stayed in Belgium as refugees for a year—during which, incidentally, I received good schooling and was happily active in my Zionist youth group. At the end of March 1940, our U.S. visas finally came through, and we left Belgium for the United States just a few weeks before Belgium was invaded by German troops. I had my bar mitzvah on the French boat that took us from St. Nazaire to New York, where we arrived on April 8, 1940.

My immediate family was thus saved from the Holocaust. Like so many others, I lost numerous relatives and childhood friends to the Holocaust, and I have lived with the knowledge that it was only by extraordinary luck and by a very slim margin that I escaped the same fate. For many years, I did not think of myself as a Holocaust survivor, because I felt that this title can be claimed only by those who survived in the midst of the Holocaust: in the camps, in the ghettos, in the woods, in the monasteries, or hidden in the cellars and attics of righteous neighbors. I have since learned that the term does apply to me, as a Nazi victim who suffered persecution but managed to escape in time from Nazi-occupied Europe. Accordingly, I have entered my name in the Registry of Holocaust Survivors and submitted information about my family and myself to the database in the Holocaust Museum in Washington.

I do not feel that I have been obsessed by the Holocaust or experienced more than the inevitable and appropriate amount of survivor's guilt. But there is no doubt that the Holocaust has shaped my thinking and my concerns since the end of World War II when we all fully realized the dimensions of the horror that had taken place. There has been scarcely a day, in all of these years, that the Holocaust has not been on my mind in one or another way. And I know that the attempt to confront the Holocaust—to understand it and to contribute to the prevention of future Holocausts, whoever their victims might be—has profoundly affected the discipline I chose to pursue and the topics I have chosen to address within that discipline.

Having noted the pervasive and profound influence of the Holocaust on my life and work, I must enter an important qualification. Just as it is a mistake, in my view, to construct Jewish history and culture entirely around the Holocaust and the experience of persecution over the centuries, it would also be a mistake to construct my own intellectual history entirely around the Holocaust. The Holocaust, as I shall try to show, has had a direct influence on some of the questions I chose to address in my work and has helped to shape the way in which I have addressed some other questions. But there are many other influences—some of which I can articulate better than others—that have played an independent or interacting role in shaping my work. Some of these preceded my encounter with Nazism. Important among these is my early and extensive exposure to Jewish religion and culture, as well as to the Hebrew and Yiddish languages and the environments in which they were rooted. Moreover, at age ten, it seems, I was already heading in the direction of the social-issues-oriented social scientist that I ultimately became: One of my favorite books was a children's text on ethnology; my favorite author was Johann Nestroy, the nineteenth-century Austrian playwright noted for his social criticism; and I was already sensitive to the horrors of war and the irrationality of social prejudice. Other important influences reached me over the years. These included my membership in a religious Zionist youth group, which also introduced me to socialist ideas and kibbutz ideology, my experience with racial segregation in the United States and active involvement in the civil rights movement, my encounters with pacifism and philosophical anarchism, and my exposure to existential philosophy. In short, it would be a mistake to overinterpret the influence of the Holocaust on my work by assigning it a wholly deterministic role.

With these qualifications in mind, I propose that the attempt to confront the issues raised by the Holocaust helped to propel me toward a career in social—and ultimately political—psychology. Within that discipline, it played a significant, if not decisive, role in my choice of four major topics on which my work over the years has focused: conformity and obedience, nationalism and national identity, ethnic conflict and its resolution, and the ethics of social research. My budding interest in the first three of these topics, as I shall elaborate, goes back to the period immediately after the end of World War II, when I was an eighteen-to-nineteen-year-old undergraduate. My interest in the fourth topic emerged in my first year of graduate school, as I was beginning to be socialized into the discipline. A theme that runs through all four of these

topics is the concern with human dignity and the danger of dehumanization—of depriving those placed in the category of "other" of dignity
by denying their identity and excluding them from one's own moral
community, in other words, from the community with whose members
one shares a sense of mutual moral obligation. I shall touch on this
theme as I discuss each of the four topics in turn.

Conformity and Obedience

My work on conformity and obedience shows the most direct influence
of the Holocaust on my research agenda, although it reflects various
other influences as well. My earliest research was concerned with determinants of conformity (Kelman 1950). In my doctoral dissertation (Kelman 1953), carried out within the early tradition of persuasive communication research (see Hovland, Janis, and Kelley 1953), I explored the
conditions conducive to mere public conformity versus genuine attitude
change, that is, private acceptance of the message of the communication. The dissertation research soon led me to the distinction between
three processes of social influence—compliance, identification, and
internalization (Kelman 1958, 1961)—which has continued to serve as
the theoretical foundation of much of my work over the years (see, e.g.,
Kelman and Hamilton 1989). The distinction among the three processes
of influence reflects my abiding concern with the depth, quality, and
durability of change and the degree to which externally derived changes
are integrated with the person's own value system and personal identity
(Kelman 1998b). This focus on the depth and durability of change also
characterizes my later work on international and intergroup conflict,
which draws the distinction between settlement of the conflict, perhaps
in the form of a signed agreement imposed by outside powers, and resolution of the conflict, characterized by responsiveness to the needs of
both parties, by attitudinal and structural changes, and by transformation of the relationship between the parties (Kelman 1996).

The three processes of influence do not represent a strict hierarchy,
moving from a lower to a higher stage, in a moral and developmental
sense. Two or all of the three processes may well occur in the same situation or relationship. All of us, no matter how high our level of moral
development, engage at times in compliance and identification. Indeed,
compliance and identification are often necessary to the maintenance
of personal well-being and social order. Nor is internalization always
"good"; it is possible to internalize destructive attitudes, anchored in a

value system that denies dignity and equality to some categories of human beings. Still, the distinction does have value connotations. It points to the dangers of automatic compliance, without consideration of how self-interest impacts on the interests of others; and of identification without consideration of how a particular relationship impacts on the wider community in which it is embedded. Moreover, the concept of internalization posits the possibility of a process of independent, reflective assessment of external influences in terms of their fit with a personal value system and in terms of their likely human consequences.

My formulation of social influence processes was clearly driven by two interrelated moral concerns.

- Concern about a social order marked by excessive conformity and unwillingness to resist group and authority pressures and by widespread failure to take personal responsibility for national policies, to live up to one's values, and to stand up against evil; and
- Concern about encouraging within the society a process of thoughtful reflection on existing patterns of violence, injustice, and inequality and promoting changes in social attitudes, practices, and institutions in accord with humanistic values.

These concerns were linked to the particular form of social activism to which I had become committed in my late teens—an activism centering on issues of peace, racial equality, and nonviolence and employing conscientious objection and nonviolent direct action as the means of protest and resistance.

When I began my graduate work at Yale in the fall of 1947, I had no idea about the kind of career I wanted to pursue. But I chose social psychology as my field of intellectual endeavor, not only because it intrigued me from the moment I first encountered it but also because I saw it as an appropriate scholarly vehicle for pursuing my moral concerns and my form of social activism. In this connection, it is noteworthy that I joined the Society for the Psychological Study of Social Issues (SPSSI) in 1946, when I was still an undergraduate at Brooklyn College. I was introduced to SPSSI by Daniel Katz, who chaired the psychology department at Brooklyn College at that time and who represented the kind of social psychology that I found appealing: an empirically anchored discipline focusing on the relationship of individuals to larger social structures and historical processes.

Although the moral concerns and social activism that drove my work on social influence were directly related to the dominant social issues of the post–World War II years in the United States, I have no doubt that they were anchored to a considerable degree in my experiences in Nazi-controlled Europe and my confrontation with the Holocaust. The Holocaust sensitized me to the dangers of conformity, to the failures in resisting evil, to the need for socialization patterns conducive to the development of humanistic values and to a readiness to act in accord with such values. The link to the Holocaust became more direct as my work on social influence moved to the study of legitimate authority and destructive obedience. At that point, I was back to the original questions that had haunted me and so many others ever since the full extent of the Holocaust became known: How are such things possible? How can people get to the point of instigating such horrendous crimes, participating in them, or allowing them to happen? And how can one prevent such crimes in the future and build the foundations for resistance to them?

My first attempt to grapple with these questions from a psychological point of view was a forty-page paper for an undergraduate course on the psychology of personality that I took at Brooklyn College in the fall of 1946. The paper, entitled "Towards an Explanation of Nazi Aggression," used the frustration-aggression hypothesis (Dollard et al. 1939) as its primary theoretical framework but also drew extensively on Hadley Cantril's *The Psychology of Social Movements* (1941) and Erich Fromm's *Escape from Freedom* (1941). More than a quarter of a century later, I returned to the same questions in my Kurt Lewin Memorial Address, "Violence without Moral Restraint: Reflections on the Dehumanization of Victims and Victimizers" (Kelman 1973). I argue in this paper that the major instigators for the violence perpetrated in genocide and other sanctioned massacres derive from the policy process and that the key question for psychological analysis is how the usual moral inhibitions against violence become weakened so that large numbers of people are prepared to formulate, participate in, and condone policies that call for the mass killing of defenseless victims. The core of the paper is a discussion of three social processes that help people overcome the moral restraints that would normally deter them from engaging in acts of mass murder, torture, massacre, and other horrendous crimes: authorization, routinization, and dehumanization.

In 1971, two years before I wrote my Lewin address, Lee Hamilton and I started a research project that eventually led to the publication of our book, *Crimes of Obedience: Toward a Social Psychology of Authority and Responsibility* (Kelman and Hamilton 1989). The research began as an attempt to understand the reasons behind the U.S. public's massive out-cry against the conviction of Lieutenant William Calley for the My Lai massacre during the Vietnam War. A national survey that we conducted in the spring of 1971 showed that the majority's disapproval and the minority's approval of the trial and conviction of Lieutenant Calley were strongly related to their differing conceptions of personal responsibility for actions carried out under superior orders. In a subsequent survey, conducted in 1976, we explored individual differences in conceptions of responsibility. How people assign responsibility for actions taken under superior orders is related to their views about authority and their own relationship to authority. In particular, we were interested in the rela-tionship of people's judgments of crimes of obedience to three political orientations—rule orientation, role orientation, and value orientation—that are conceptually linked to the processes of compliance, identifi-cation, and internalization.

Although the empirical data presented in *Crimes of Obedience* are derived from our two surveys, focusing primarily on the My Lai massacre and the Calley trial, the book deals with the general question of how peo-ple determine personal responsibility for actions ordered or authorized by their superiors in a hierarchical relationship. We discuss a variety of historical and contemporary examples of crimes of obedience in differ-ent domains. We conclude the book with a chapter entitled "Breaking the Habit of Unquestioning Obedience," which addresses, in particular, possible policies and strategies for promoting personal responsibility and independent judgment in authority situations. We cast a wide net in identifying crimes of obedience, but the defining case is clearly taken from the Holocaust, whose perpetrators—Adolf Eichmann among oth-ers—often took recourse in the defense of superior orders. For me, this work represented part of my continuing attempt to grapple with the questions that have preoccupied me since the Holocaust: How are such crimes possible, and how can they be prevented?

I am not able in this chapter to elaborate on our definition of crimes of obedience, but I do need to note that the term is not restricted to actions taken strictly out of a sense of obligation or out of fear of pun-ishment. We also include in this category actions that may correspond to the actors' own preferences and are taken in pursuit of some personal or ideological agenda but that the actors *justify* (not just ex post facto but ab initio) by superior orders. These are still crimes of obedience, by our definition, on the presumption that the action would not have been taken without authorization—without the umbrella of superior orders.

Even with this broader definition in mind, I am not proposing that obedience to authority accounts for the Holocaust. To account for the Holocaust, one needs to examine a wide range of factors, including (among others) the historical conditions that provided the context for the rise of Nazism; the political processes that brought the Nazis to power; the sources and implications of the racist ideology and biomedical vision of the Nazi movement; the cultural conditions that made Germany at the time a receptive environment for the promulgation and acceptance of this ideology; the historical circumstances that made Jews a prime target of the Nazi genocidal project; the psychological forces that caused people to participate—passively or actively, with different degrees of enthusiasm—in a genocidal process; and the internal dynamics of the genocidal process once it is set into motion in a society—that is, what Ervin Staub (1989) has called the "steps along a continuum of destruction." Our work on authority and responsibility, and on the processes of authorization, routinization, and dehumanization, provides a small but not insignificant piece of an explanatory framework that can provide an account of the Holocaust and other genocides.

Although I do not claim to be a Holocaust scholar per se, I believe that my work can contribute to how we understand the Holocaust and what we learn from it. In saying this, I am clearly taking a position in the debate about the uniqueness versus generalizability of the Holocaust. In my view, the Holocaust is both unique and a suitable basis for comparative analysis. Every historical event is unique, and the Holocaust clearly has a special place in Jewish history and Jewish theology. Moreover, the Holocaust was an extermination project extreme in its magnitude and unprecedented in its execution. At the same time, the Holocaust is, unfortunately, one of many historical and contemporary cases of genocide that—despite their many unique features—are susceptible to comparative study by social scientists and historians. Studies of different cases can bring us closer to understanding the causes of genocide and the dynamics of the genocidal process and to finding ways of preventing genocide. One of the ways in which my personal experience with the Holocaust influenced my work has been in motivating me to make my own small contribution to this learning process.

Nationalism and National Identity

My work on nationalism and national identity also has old biographical roots. In my childhood, I experienced nationalism both as a destructive and direct oppressive force, in the form of Nazism, and as a personally liberating force, in the form of Zionism. I have already mentioned in passing that my membership in the religious Zionist youth group that I joined at age eleven, shortly after the *Anschluss,* and my strong Jewish identification in general sustained me in the face of the onslaught of the Nazi experience. I credit my Jewish identity for the fact that my self-esteem apparently remained undiminished by the attacks against me and my people. I have no recollection of ever asking myself seriously whether Jews were in some way responsible for or deserving of the anti-Semitism directed at them.

The contrast between the destructive and the liberating sides of nationalism has been a central feature of my earliest thinking and my subsequent research on the subject. I knew from the beginning and had many reasons to confirm that nationalism is a cause or at least a driving force of war and genocide, but I was never prepared to reject it outright because of my awareness of its liberating potential for oppressed people. My very first article (Kelman 1945), written in Hebrew and published in a student magazine in New York, grappled with this issue. The article, entitled "In Defense of Nationalism," distinguishes between positive and negative varieties of nationalism. On the one hand, it describes nationalism as a contribution to the struggle for freedom and against oppression and also, at the psychological level, as a source of cultural identification, self-respect, and personal efficacy. On the other hand, it enumerates the potential evils of nationalism when it becomes chauvinistic, exclusive, and destructive. It is because of these evils, of course, that I felt the need to defend nationalism in the first place.

My subsequent work on nationalism, which began some twenty years after this first piece was published, has always been concerned with the different faces of nationalism. Thus, our empirical work in the 1960s was based on a distinction between different types of nationalism or, more precisely, different patterns of personal involvement in the national system (DeLamater, Katz, and Kelman 1969; Katz, Kelman, and Vassiliou 1969; Kelman 1969). My analysis of nationalism has focused, in particular, on the dualities of nationalist ideology and its object, the nation-state: nationalism both broadens and narrows group loyalties by drawing boundaries that are both inclusive and exclusive, that both unite and divide people; it seeks to build both a state around a nation and a nation around a state; it mobilizes people by both discovering and creating a sense of national identity; it elicits high levels of both selfless and selfish behavior in its followers; and it is both a vehicle for and a barrier to the enhancement of human dignity (Kelman 1997a).

The last point was a central thesis of my presidential address for the International Studies Association (Kelman 1977a), which focused on the conditions, criteria, and dialectics of human dignity. The dialectics of human dignity are a consequence of the contradictory role played by the nation-state in the contemporary world. On the one hand, the nation-state is the primary provider of human dignity to its citizens by protecting their rights, advancing their interests, and giving expression to their group identity. On the other hand, the nation-state often undermines human dignity by erecting barriers to alternative ways of meeting human needs and protecting human rights, alternatives necessitated by the growing interdependence *between* states and the upsurge of ethnic divisions *within* states.

The contradictions of national identity have led me to argue that a group's right to national self-determination by establishing an independent state cannot be automatic (Kelman 1997b). Implementation of that right must be negotiated with those whose needs and interests are affected by the establishment of such a state, particularly minority populations. The central criterion for granting international legitimacy to a quest for an independent state is that it provides absolute guarantees for the protection of minority rights. Thus, even though a state may legitimately be established to fulfill the quest for national self-determination by the majority of the population, it must never claim or strive to be ethnically pure. Any such project, I argue, is automatically suspect as a threat to fundamental human rights and an invitation to ethnic cleansing.

I argue further that "even a group's national identity itself must be 'negotiated,' i.e., explored and discussed, with those who are affected by the group's self-definition" (Kelman 1997b, 331). This is *necessary* because the way a group defines itself often has significant consequences for others; it is *possible* because national identity is a social construction, which can be—and typically is—reconstructed. The negotiation of identity is critical to the resolution of protracted ethnic conflicts, such as the Israeli-Palestinian dispute, in which each group has seen the destruction of the other's identity as necessary for the fulfillment of its own identity (Kelman 1987, 1999). My own work in conflict resolution, which focuses particularly on the Israeli-Palestinian case, is partly designed to encourage the parties to move away from exclusivist and monolithic definitions of identity and to accommodate the other's identity in their own identity

(Kelman 1992, 1998a, 2001). This work will be discussed in the next section.

In concluding this section, let me stress that a theme that permeates my work on nationalism and national identity is the danger of exclusivism. An exclusivistic nationalism can easily slide into dehumanization of the other. When the line that marks off the in-group from the out-group becomes the boundary of one's moral community—the community whose members have a sense of moral obligation to one another—then massacre, torture, rape, ethnic cleansing, and genocide become thinkable and doable. Clearly, the Holocaust, starting with the exclusion of Jews from the moral community of so many Germans and Austrians, which I observed at first hand, sensitized me to this perilous feature of nationalist ideology.

Ethnic Conflict and Its Resolution

My work for some thirty years on ethnic conflict and conflict resolution is directly continuous with my long-standing interest in the study of war and peace and of the social-psychological dimensions of international relations and, in particular, international conflict. I have already mentioned that I went into social psychology because I saw it as a scholarly vehicle for pursuing my moral concerns and my form of social activism. A central part of these concerns and hence of my activism was my attitude toward war and violence.

My interest in peace and nonviolent conflict resolution was propelled by many experiences during my childhood and adolescence. These probably included my father's accounts of his life as a soldier in World War I; the fact that my mother lost two brothers during that war—one on the Italian front and the other in an epidemic; the political unrest in Austria during the 1930s; and finally the horrors of World War II itself. I have no doubt, however, that the experience of Nazi rule and the Holocaust and the lessons I learned from these events played a major role in shaping my views about war and violence. War is a massive exercise in the dehumanization of others—of those defined as the enemy or even as obstacles to the achievement of victory. In war, as in racial persecution and genocide, the targets of aggression are deprived of human dignity by denial of their identity and by their exclusion from one's own moral community. War provides the context for genocide and other gross violations of human rights.

I tried to build the study of war and peace, of international conflict, into my professional agenda from the beginning of my career. In April 1951, when I was just completing my doctoral work at Yale University, Arthur Gladstone and I published a letter in the *American Psychologist* in which we called for the systematic testing of certain assumptions about human behavior that underlie U.S. foreign policy. We pointed out that these assumptions have been challenged by pacifists on the basis of generally accepted psychological principles and that it would be important for psychologists to address these challenges. Reactions to this letter eventually led to the formation of the Research Exchange on the Prevention of War, which was probably the first organizational venture in the peace research movement that began to emerge in the 1950s. The *Bulletin of the Research Exchange on the Prevention of War,* edited by Arthur Gladstone from 1952–56 (I was book review editor), was replaced in 1957 by the more ambitious *Journal of Conflict Resolution,* originally published out of the University of Michigan, which is now in its forty-fifth year of publication.

My own efforts to move my work more actively into the arena of international relations included a research program on the effects of international cultural and educational exchanges (see, e.g., Kelman and Ezekiel 1970), as well as the program on nationalism described in the preceding section, "Nationalism and National Identity." I paid particular attention, in my thinking and writing, to the ways in which social-psychological concepts and methods can contribute to the study of war and peace and of international relations more generally. A major product of this effort was a book I edited for SPSSI, *International Behavior: A Social-Psychological Analysis* (Kelman 1965b). This book, in chapters contributed by social psychologists and political scientists (and one social anthropologist), pulled together the extant knowledge about national and international images and about processes of interaction in international relations. My own introduction and conclusion were particularly focused on the appropriate points of entry for social-psychological analysis—on those points, within a larger theory of international relations, at which social-psychological approaches can make a specifically relevant contribution to understanding and conceptualizing the phenomenon.

My work in this area took a significant new turn in 1966 when I met John Burton, a former senior Australian diplomat and then director of the Centre for the Analysis of Conflict at the University of London. Burton told me about his work in "controlled communication," an unofficial, third-party approach to the resolution of international and intercommunal conflicts that brought together politically influential representatives of parties in conflict for direct, nonbinding, and completely confidential interaction in an academic context (Burton 1969). I was excited about his work because I saw it as a way of putting into practice the social-psychological approach to international conflict that I was grappling with at the theoretical level. The meetings organized by Burton represented to me another point of entry for social-psychological approaches: a point in the larger diplomatic process where social-psychological methods—in the form of face-to-face interactions between selected individuals—can make a specific contribution. I gladly accepted Burton's invitation to an exercise on the Cyprus conflict that took place in London in November 1966.

After that London meeting, I began to think and write about the approach (Kelman 1972a) and eventually to apply it in what we came to call problem-solving workshops. I have worked in collaboration with many colleagues, notably Stephen Cohen in the early years (Cohen et al. 1977) and Nadim Rouhana in recent years (Rouhana and Kelman 1994). Our approach, *interactive problem solving* (Kelman forthcoming), derives directly from the work of John Burton, although it has evolved over the years in line with our practical experience and our social-psychological orientation. I now direct (with Donna Hicks as deputy director) the Program on International Conflict Analysis and Resolution (PICAR) at Harvard University's Weatherhead Center for International Affairs. The program is based on the scholar/practitioner model, which calls for a continuing interaction of practice with research, theory building, and training. PICAR members work on a variety of international and ethnic conflicts, such as those in Sri Lanka, Cyprus, Northern Ireland, and Bosnia. My own work has concentrated, for many years, on the Arab-Israeli conflict and particularly its Israeli-Palestinian component (Kelman 1998c). My personal history can readily account for the fact that my work on war and peace has ultimately gravitated toward the analysis and resolution of conflicts between identity groups and, in particular, the Israeli-Palestinian case.

I began to think about applying John Burton's approach to the Arab-Israeli conflict shortly after I became acquainted with it. The idea came to me in June 1967, as I was watching the news about what turned out to be the Six-Day War. My reaction to the events was one of profound anxiety. The war brought back to me, as it did to many other Jews, memories of the Holocaust and a renewed fear of the annihilation of the Jewish people. The first reaction for so many of us was the question: Is it about to happen again? I felt that the Jewish people could not absorb another Holocaust. The course of the war soon made it clear that this war was not another Holocaust and that Israel and the Jewish people were going to survive. But it was the old concern about Jewish victimization that first impelled me to explore conflict resolution efforts in the Middle East.

At the same time, I had from the beginning been conscious of the fact that there was another people living in the land that the Jews claimed for their national homeland. My second published article—written in Hebrew, like the first, and published in another student magazine (Kelman 1945–46)—was called "On the Question of Jewish-Arab Cooperation," cooperation that I considered both necessary and possible. In the years before the establishment of Israel, I favored the concept of a binational state promoted by minority segments of the Zionist movement. After the establishment of Israel, I was active in American Friends of Ichud, a group identified with the names of Martin Buber and Judah Magnes of the Hebrew University of Jerusalem, which earlier had been among the proponents of a binational state and was now focused on improving Arab-Jewish relations.

The concerns aroused by the 1967 war, along with my commitment to Arab-Jewish cooperation, led me to pursue the feasibility of organizing an unofficial encounter of high-level Arabs and Israelis to explore ideas for resolving the conflict. My efforts, in collaboration with John Burton, did not succeed on this first try. I learned that a great deal of groundwork had to be done before one could successfully recruit participants for such an effort. In particular, it became clear to me that I would have to familiarize myself with the communities involved, especially the Arab world, which I had never visited, and that I would have to establish relationships and connect with relevant networks. Because of other commitments, I was not ready to give this project the kind of attention that it required, and so I put it on the back burner. I did not give up on the idea, however. On a visit to Israel, I discussed it with several colleagues— and received mixed reactions. I thought about the theoretical underpinnings of the approach and wrote my first paper on problem-solving workshops (Kelman 1972a). And, in 1971, Stephen Cohen and I conducted our first workshop with Israelis and Palestinians (Cohen et al. 1977).

It was not until 1973, however, that I committed myself to giving this work my highest priority. I was home recuperating from a heart attack when the October 1973 war broke out. It was a time when, in any event, I had to review my priorities, and this new war convinced me that the Arab-Israeli conflict was the arena in which I must now invest my energies. Increasingly, I immersed myself in the issues of the region. Over the following years, I read about the Middle East, attended numerous meetings and conferences, traveled frequently to Arab countries as well as to Israel, made contacts, built relationships, and became connected with various networks that were crucial to my work. I turned myself into a Middle East specialist. Since 1977 I have chaired the Middle East Seminar at Harvard, which is sponsored by the Center for International Affairs and the Center for Middle Eastern Studies. This kind of immersion in Middle East affairs would not have been possible without the full involvement of my wife, who joined me enthusiastically in workshop activities, in Middle East travels, in the personal relationships that we established through our work (and indeed as part of our work), and in making the Middle East the center of our lives. My only regret is that I decided that I was too old and too busy to learn Arabic when I began this immersion process more than a quarter of a century ago.

During the past quarter century, my colleagues and I have conducted dozens of workshops—mostly with Palestinians and Israelis. Between 1990 and 1993, Nadim Rouhana and I conducted a continuing workshop (Rouhana and Kelman 1994), and since 1994, we have cochaired the Joint Working Group on Israeli-Palestinian Relations, which has produced joint working papers on the final-status issues in the Israeli-Palestinian negotiations. Well over one hundred politically influential Israelis and an equal number of Palestinians have by now participated in one or more of our projects. Although I have done some work with Israelis and Egyptians and have maintained close contacts in Egypt, Jordan, Syria, and Lebanon, I have concentrated my work on the Israeli-Palestinian relationship for several reasons.

- It is the core of the Arab-Israeli conflict, and a stable peace between Israel and its neighbors cannot be achieved without resolution of the Palestinian issue;
- It is the aspect of the conflict about which I care most deeply; and
- It is the aspect of the conflict to which interactive problem solving and my particular social-psychological approach to the negotiation of national identity are uniquely relevant.

In addition to conducting workshops and arranging similar opportunities for interaction between the two sides, I have lectured about the substantive issues in the conflict and have published policy analyses (starting with Kelman 1978) focusing on the social-psychological dimensions of the conflict and approaches to its resolution. These writings have drawn extensively on what I have learned from our workshops, and I have been careful in these writings to avoid compromising my role as a facilitative third party.

The central motivating factors in my work on the Israeli-Palestinian conflict have been my concerns about a secure future for Israel and about justice for the Palestinian people. Both of these concerns are directly linked to my experience with the Holocaust. I feel that I am able to work as a third party in the Israeli-Palestinian conflict because of my deep empathy with both sides and the trust that this engenders in the people who work with me. (I should add here that I have always worked with an ethnically balanced third-party team that includes at least one Arab member; this contributes both to sensitizing the third party to the concerns and perspectives of each side and to assuring the two parties of the third party's evenhandedness.)

On the one hand, I share the Jewish experience of the Israeli members: their memories, their fears, their feeling of connection to the land, their sense of necessity of the Zionist project—particularly in the light of the Holocaust. I am deeply committed to the survival and well-being of Israel. I bring to my efforts at conflict resolution a vision of Israel that is broadly shared by the Israeli participants in our workshops: Israel as a democratic, pluralistic state, living at peace with its Palestinian neighbors without dominating them, enjoying normal relations with the surrounding Arab states, and fully accepted and integrated in the region.

On the other hand, I feel that my own early experiences help me to empathize with the Palestinian experience of displacement, homelessness, statelessness, humiliation, and arbitrary treatment by others who exclude them from their own moral community. Although, as noted earlier, it was my concern about Jewish victimization that impelled me to explore conflict resolution efforts in the Middle East, I was from the beginning and became increasingly concerned about the historical and continuing victimization of the Palestinian people. My own Holocaust experience has sensitized me to acts of exclusion, victimization, and potential dehumanization directed against any group, not only my own group. What makes the victimization of the Palestinians particularly poignant for me is the fact that my own people are the source of that victimization.

The most difficult moments in my Israeli-Palestinian work were those at which I had to confront—within or outside of the context of a workshop—Israeli policies, practices, or isolated acts that involved humiliation, harassment, and arbitrary treatment of Palestinians, depriving them of their dignity and identity. Such moments painfully reminded me of what happened to my own people and what I personally observed in my childhood. I have never, until now, shared these reactions with anyone other than my wife, for fear of being misunderstood. I am not comparing the Palestinian experience to the Holocaust. I have strongly rejected any attempt to draw such an analogy, just as I have rejected the analogy between Palestinian terrorism and Nazi pogroms. But one of the central lessons that I have drawn from the Holocaust is the need to be supremely vigilant to any action that degrades others merely because of the category in which they are placed and excludes them from one's own moral community. Although such actions may be far removed from mass murder or ethnic cleansing, they establish an inexorable logic that readily points in that direction.

The Ethics of Social Research

The fourth and final area of my work that I believe was clearly influenced by my experience and contemplation of the Holocaust was the ethics of social research. I have been concerned with ethical issues raised by social research from the very beginning of my graduate training, as I began to reflect on what I was doing and what kind of knowledge I was producing in the new role into which I was being socialized. Over the years, I have spoken and written extensively about two sets of ethical problems: those relating to the processes of social research and those relating to the products of social research (Kelman 1972b).

In the latter category, an issue that occupied me early on was the manipulation of human behavior. I was concerned that much of the knowledge that applied and basic social research was producing—including the work on persuasive communication and group dynamics that I was personally engaged in—could be used for manipulative purposes. I first spoke about these concerns at a departmental colloquium at Yale when I was still a graduate student; a considerably revised and updated version of that talk was eventually published some fifteen years later (Kelman 1965a). The issue of manipulation was one of a number of issues taken up in a volume on the ethics of social intervention that I coedited in the 1970s (Bermant, Kelman, and Warwick 1978). I have also written about the social uses of research findings in general and about the harmful and dehumanizing uses to which the products of social research can potentially be put in particular domains. In this vein, for example, I have addressed research in developing countries used for counterinsurgency purposes, research on social deviance, research on racial differences in IQ, and research carried out for military or intelligence purposes (see Kelman 1968, 1972b).

As for the processes of social research, a major focus of my writing has been on the ethics of human experimentation. An early article, entitled "Human Use of Human Subjects" (Kelman 1967), dealt with the problems created by the extensive use of deception in social-psychological experiments. In another article (Kelman 1977b), I addressed the issue of invasion of privacy in social and psychological research, starting with an analysis of three different meanings of privacy and the psychological significance of preserving one's privacy in each of these senses. Elsewhere (Kelman 1982b), I reviewed the ethical issues that arise with the use of different social science methods. My analysis, based on a classification of three different types of ethical impact of social research, links up with the distinction between the processes of compliance, identification, and internalization. Finally, in a number of writings (e.g., Kelman 1982a), I have addressed the issue of exploitation of research participants, which arises particularly when Western researchers study populations in developing societies or in other situations in which there is a power differential between the investigators and their subjects. Many of the ethical problems that arise in research can, in fact, be attributed to the power deficiency of the research participants vis-à-vis the investigator and to illegitimate uses of the investigator's power advantage (Kelman 1972b).

In my writings on the ethical issues raised by the processes and the products of social research, a recurrent theme is my concern about their effect on the human dignity of those who are touched by the research. I repeatedly stress the danger that the way the research is carried out— that is, the way the participants are treated in the course of the research—and the way the findings are used may contribute to the deprivation of people's dignity and to the dehumanization that already marks modern life. In a proactive mode, I call for research efforts that contribute to the humanization of society, for the development of participatory research models, and for the democratization of the research community. It is not hard to detect the echoes of the Holocaust in the set of concerns that has prompted my work on the ethics of social research. I have no doubt that the Nazis' abuses in the experimentation with human subjects and their heavy reliance on racial theories propounded by social and biological scientists at the time have contributed significantly to sensitizing me to the ethical issues that I have written about.

Conclusion

I have decided to conclude this chapter with another biographical note. In the section that describes my work on the Israeli-Palestinian conflict, "Ethnic Conflict and Its Resolution," I mentioned that an important turning point in that work occurred in October 1973, when I was home watching the news about the latest Middle East war while recuperating from a heart attack. That heart attack had occurred several weeks earlier, at the Montreal meetings of the American Psychological Association, while I was delivering my Kurt Lewin Memorial Address, "Violence without Moral Restraint: Reflections on the Dehumanization of Victims and Victimizers" (Kelman 1973). I had been working on this address for many months, and I tried to put the finishing touches on it late in the night before it was scheduled for delivery. Although this address dealt with a wide range of cases of sanctioned massacres carried out in the context of a genocidal policy, it clearly represented my attempt to grapple with the meaning of the Holocaust and the social conditions that made it possible. I suspect that the emotional stress associated with writing and delivering this address was a contributing factor to the heart attack. And as I reflect on my decision, in the wake of that heart attack, to dedicate myself to working on resolution of the Israeli-Palestinian conflict, I wonder whether my good fortune in surviving the heart attack came to symbolize, in my mind, my good fortune in surviving the Holocaust.

In my Lewin address, I began the discussion of dehumanization by first asking "what it means to perceive another person as fully human, in the sense of being included in the moral compact that governs human relationships" (48). I proposed that perceiving others as human means according them identity and community, that is, perceiving them as independent and distinct individuals, capable of making choices and entitled to live their own lives on the basis of their own goals and values, and perceiving them as part of one's own interconnected network of individuals who care for each other, recognize each other's individuality, and respect each other's rights. Together, identity and community make up human dignity, "the status of individuals as ends in themselves, rather than as means toward some extraneous ends. . . . The overarching indicator of human dignity in a society is the worth attached to an individual's life" (Kelman 1977a, 531–32). Genocide becomes possible to the extent that we deprive fellow beings of identity and community and thus dehumanize them.

As I have tried to show throughout this chapter, respect for human dignity and counteracting the dangers of dehumanization are the common threads that run through the different areas of my work as a social scientist. The dehumanization of others by depriving them of identity and community—indeed by placing them into the category of "the other"—is at the heart of genocide and crimes of obedience; it is a danger inherent in nationalist ideology; it is the obstacle that must be overcome in efforts toward peacemaking and reconciliation between identity groups; and it is a temptation that must be resisted in the way in which we, as social scientists, conduct our research and allow our findings to be used. The central lesson that I have learned from the Holocaust is that we must never allow any people, any human group, to be excluded from our moral community. I can only hope that, in my own work as a social scientist, I have made a small contribution to this goal by promoting new ways of thinking about individual and social responsibility, about national identity, about conflict resolution, and about the role of the social scientist in society.

REFERENCES

Bermant, G., H. C. Kelman, and D. P. Warwick, eds. 1978. *The ethics of social intervention*. Washington: Hemisphere Publishing.

Burton, J. W. 1969. *Conflict and communication: The use of controlled communication in international relations*. London: MacMillan.

Cantril, H. 1941. *The psychology of social movements*. New York: Wiley.

Cohen, S. P., H. C. Kelman, F. D. Miller, and B. L. Smith. 1977. Evolving intergroup techniques for conflict resolution: An Israeli-Palestinian pilot workshop. *Journal of Social Issues* 33, no. 1:165–89.

DeLamater, J., D. Katz, and H. C. Kelman. 1969. On the nature of national involvement: A preliminary study. *Journal of Conflict Resolution* 13:320–57.

Dollard, J., L. W. Doob, N. E. Miller, O. H. Mowrer, and R. R. Sears. 1939. *Frustration and aggression*. New Haven: Yale University Press.

Fromm, E. 1941. *Escape from freedom*. New York: Holt, Rinehart and Winston.

Hovland, C. I., I. L. Janis, and H. H. Kelley. 1953. *Communication and persuasion*. New Haven: Yale University Press.

Katz, D., H. C. Kelman, and V. Vassiliou. 1969. A comparative approach to the study of nationalism. *Peace Research Society Papers* 14:1–13.

Kelman, H. C. 1945. Lehaganat ha-le'umiut (In defense of nationalism). *Niv* (Hebrew periodical of the Teachers Institute, Yeshiva University, New York).

———. 1945–46. Lishe'elat hishtatfut yehudit-aravit (On the question of Jewish-Arab cooperation). *Niv* (Hebrew periodical of the Teachers Institute, Yeshiva University, New York) 7.

———. 1950. Effects of success and failure on "suggestibility" in the autokinetic situation. *Journal of Abnormal and Social Psychology* 45:267–85.

———. 1953. Attitude change as a function of response restriction. *Human Relations* 6:185–214.

———. 1958. Compliance, identification, and internalization: Three processes of attitude change. *Journal of Conflict Resolution* 2:51–60.

———. 1961. Processes of opinion change. *Public Opinion Quarterly* 25:57–78.

———. 1965a. Manipulation of human behavior: An ethical dilemma for the social scientist. *Journal of Social Issues* 21, no. 2:31–46.

———, ed. 1965b. *International behavior: A social-psychological analysis*. New York: Holt, Rinehart and Winston.

———. 1967. Human use of human subjects: The problem of deception in social psychological experiments. *Psychological Bulletin* 67:1–11.

———. 1968. *A time to speak: On human values and social research*. San Francisco: Jossey-Bass.

———. 1969. Patterns of personal involvement in the national system: A social-psychological analysis of political legitimacy. In *International politics and foreign policy*, rev. ed., edited by J. N. Rosenau, 276–88. New York: Free Press.

———. 1972a. The problem-solving workshop in conflict resolution. In *Communication in international politics*, edited by R. L. Merritt, 168–204. Urbana: University of Illinois Press.

———. 1972b. The rights of the subject in social research: An analysis in terms of relative power and legitimacy. *American Psychologist* 27:989–1016.

———. 1973. Violence without moral restraint: Reflections on the dehumanization of victims and victimizers. *Journal of Social Issues* 29, no. 4:25–61.

———. 1977a. The conditions, criteria, and dialectics of human dignity. *International Studies Quarterly* 21:529–52.

———. 1977b. Privacy and research with human beings. *Journal of Social Issues* 33, no. 3:169–95.

———. 1978. Israelis and Palestinians: Psychological prerequisites for mutual acceptance. *International Security* 3:162–86.

———. 1982a. A changing social science for a changing world: A social psychologist's perspective. In *Indigenous anthropology in non-Western countries*, edited by H. Fahim, 269–83. Durham, NC: Carolina Academic Press.

———. 1982b. Ethical issues in different social science methods. In *Ethical issues in social science research*, edited by T. L. Beauchamp, R. R. Faden, R .J. Wallace Jr., and L. Waters, 40–98. Baltimore: Johns Hopkins University Press.

———. 1987. The political psychology of the Israeli-Palestinian conflict: How can we overcome the barriers to a negotiated solution? *Political Psychology* 8:347–63.

———. 1992. Acknowledging each other's nationhood: How to create a momentum for the Israeli-Palestinian negotiations. *Journal of Palestine Studies* 22, no. 1:18–38.

———. 1996. Negotiation as interactive problem solving. *International Negotiation* 1:99–123.

———. 1997a. Nationalism, patriotism, and national identity: Social-psychological dimensions. In *Patriotism in the life of individuals and nations*, edited by D. Bar-Tal and E. Staub, 165–89. Chicago: Nelson-Hall.

———. 1997b. Negotiating national identity and self-determination in ethnic conflicts: The choice between pluralism and ethnic cleansing. *Negotiation Journal* 13:327–40.

———. 1998a. Building a sustainable peace: The limits of pragmatism in the Israeli-Palestinian negotiations. *Journal of Palestine Studies* 28, no. 1:36–50.

———. 1998b. The place of ethnic identity in the development of personal identity: A challenge for the Jewish family. In *Coping with life and death: Jewish families in the twentieth century*, edited by P. Y. Medding, 3–26. New York and Oxford: Oxford University Press.

———. 1998c. Social-psychological contributions to peacemaking and peace-building in the Middle East. *Applied Psychology: An International Review* 47:5–28.

———. 1999. The interdependence of Israeli and Palestinian national identities: The role of the other in existential conflicts. *Journal of Social Issues* 55, no. 3:581–600.

———. 2001. The role of national identity in conflict resolution: Experiences from Israeli-Palestinian problem-solving workshops. In *Social identity, intergroup conflict, and conflict resolution*, edited by R. D. Ashmore, L. Jussim, and D. Wilder. New York and Oxford: Oxford University Press.

———. Forthcoming. Interactive problem solving: Informal mediation by the scholar/ practitioner. In *Studies in international mediation: Essays in honor of Jeffrey Z. Rubin*, edited by J. Bercovitch. London: Macmillan.

Kelman, H. C., and R. S. Ezekiel, with R. B. Kelman. 1970. *Cross-national encounters*. San Francisco: Jossey-Bass.

Kelman, H. C., and V. L. Hamilton. 1989. *Crimes of obedience: Toward a social psychology of authority and responsibility*. New Haven: Yale University Press.

Rouhana, N. N., and H. C. Kelman. 1994. Promoting joint thinking in international conflicts: An Israeli-Palestinian continuing workshop. *Journal of Social Issues* 50, no. 1:157–78.

Staub, E. 1989. *The roots of evil: The origins of genocide and other group violence*. Cambridge: Cambridge University Press.

Holocaust Influences on a Refugee

Indirect (Pervasive) and Direct (Now You See It, Now You Don't)

Eric Klinger

Biographical Note

Eric Klinger was educated at Harvard and the University of Chicago (Ph.D. in psychology, 1960) and is a licensed clinical psychologist. He is currently professor of psychology at the University of Minnesota, Morris, and a member of the University of Minnesota graduate faculty. He has been a Fulbright scholar and later visiting professor at the Ruhr University of Bochum and visiting professor at the University of Konstanz in Germany. Among his approximately one hundred publications are three books.

He is a fellow of the American Association for the Advancement of Science, the American Psychological Association, and the American Psychological Society. He received the first annual statewide award as the Outstanding Teacher of Undergraduate Psychology from the Minnesota Psychological Association and the Horace T. Morse Amoco Award for contributions to undergraduate education.

Introduction

As an escapee from an early stage of the Holocaust, I am one of the lucky ones. My immediate family suffered but did not perish. I was assaulted but not physically maimed. My life since has been fairly normal and reasonably happy.

How did the Holocaust affect my work? Probably in several ways. First, perhaps, in my overriding interest in—one might almost say vigilance regarding—the causes of human behavior. Second, in its ineradicable, brooding presence in and near my thoughts in whatever I undertake, be it research, friendship, or entertainment. Third, in the international contacts it motivated me to initiate, leading to valued relationships that influenced my scientific thought as well as my personal development. And, fourth, in my latter-day research interests in the nature of hate and paranoia.

There have, of course, also been other likely effects, although it is always hard to know how different the outcome would have been without this specific experience. Without the Holocaust I would probably be writing primarily in German. I would have been less likely to become a professor of psychology. Without a disrupted childhood and embittered parents, I would most likely have been more firmly integrated into my childhood peer groups and been spared some of the developmental problems I encountered in adolescence and early adulthood. I might not be walking around with as profound a sense of hurt (perhaps better expressed in German: *diese bodenlose Kränkung*) over the treatment I can expect from a substantial minority of my fellow humans, a minority that sometimes comes to political power. I might not be as vigilantly involved—though purely at the level of a citizen—in politics and current events.

What follows is a sketch of my experience of the Holocaust and, insofar as I can guess them, its consequences for my work.

My Experience of the Holocaust

Changes in a Child's Life

My first Holocaust-related memory is of my father lying on our sofa in our Vienna apartment, intently listening to the radio. I was about four, and it was probably 1937 or early 1938. It is a scene that must have been replayed many times—it may be a composite memory—but in my memory of this occasion I was struck by the intensity and agitation of my father's expression. I recall no specific content, but I sensed that something momentous was going on.

Soon after the *Anschluss,* the annexation of Austria by the Nazi German government in March 1938, my father was imprisoned. As a Social Democrat, an attorney, and ethnically a Jew, he was a vulnerable target. He had always been a part of our household, and, suddenly, he was gone. So, too, were the maids who had helped my mother with the household tasks and who had been in charge of me for much of each day. And so was my mother's brother, who (so I learned later) left for Brussels the day of the *Anschluss* after being informed by a Nazi employee that he was high on an arrest list. Life had suddenly changed.

My parents and grandparents carefully tried to spare me anxiety over what was transpiring, but the gravity of events suffused the atmosphere of our Vienna, 1938. I remember walking through a park with the woman who had for many months been teaching me English, when, without warning or precedent, a group of teenaged boys began calling us names and throwing stones. The walks in the park ended. Now aged five, I was suddenly enrolled in a Catholic kindergarten. My mother took me there and brought me home, trips that I remember to be, unaccountably to me at the time, filled with tension and a sense of danger. My grandfather came to take me on a visit to the Prater, the Viennese amusement park that was one of my favorite places. There ensued an argument among family members as to whether it was too risky, but my grandfather insisted that neither of us looked Jewish and therefore it was safe. We went without incident but not without foreboding. Once I recall my mother throwing out tin cans with the garbage, insisting that she was not about to save them for Hitler—perhaps the first time I remember hearing the name and the first time I witnessed an act of rebellion, however mild.

The Flight from Vienna

My father was released in October, after more than half a year. Within hours he had left for Paris. My mother began to dispose of our apartment and furniture and crated up those of our possessions that we were allowed to take away, primarily dishes, eating utensils, clothes, and books. In November we moved out and left for Holland—my mother, her mother, and I—to stay with my grandmother's Dutch relatives until we could resolve plans for the future. My maternal grandfather had died years earlier of natural causes. My paternal grandparents had decided to remain in Vienna. He was Jewish; she was not. (Our entire family was a highly assimilated one, much more Austrian and Viennese than Jewish.) My beloved aunt, their daughter, resolved to stay with them, not wishing to abandon them to the dangers ahead. Thus, our family was divided for what would prove to be several years.

The rail trip from Vienna to Amsterdam is a substantial one, but it is normally routine. Much of it runs through Germany. At one longer stop, my mother decided to purchase something, perhaps a newspaper, at the station. As we alighted from the train, a German soldier accosted her and demanded her gold wedding ring. My mother told him that in that case he would have to cut off her finger, because she was unable to remove the band. It was a tense moment, but the soldier relented and let us reboard. This was one instance of my mother's gritty toughness in the face of adversity.

My father quickly decided to take us out of Europe. He had seen, he said, a demoralized-looking, weeping detachment of French troops boarding a train headed for the border with Germany, with which France was still officially at peace, and concluded that he could not entrust them with our safety. But in 1939 getting out of Europe was no easy feat for Jewish refugees. Most countries, including the United States with its virulently anti-Semitic State Department, were erecting whatever barriers they could to keep us out. People made remarkable compromises to leave Europe. Among our family friends, one couple agreed to the condition for admittance to Tanzania (then still colonial Tanganyika) and spent years in the field, living in tents, eradicating tsetse flies. Another couple agreed to employment in a small business in Uruguay. Another moved to Shanghai, there to suffer the Japanese occupation.

We were by some degrees luckier. My father had close relatives in New York who were able to gain his admittance to the United States, but they were unable to obtain my mother's admittance. However, my uncle, who had managed soon after reaching Brussels to emigrate to Australia, was able to arrange admittance there for my mother, their mother, and me. And so, in March 1939, the family split up, my father going to New York, us to Sydney. We would remain apart for four years.

Life in Sydney

Life in Sydney was a mixed blessing. Sydney is one of the world's loveliest cities in one of the world's nicest climates. We found a modest apartment on Bondi Road, which leads to the world-famous Bondi Beach. Before leaving Vienna, my mother had learned the craft of sewing artificial felt flowers, which she now produced in quantity at home with family help and then sold to Sydney department stores. Two little girls, one next door and one down the street, were also German-speaking Jewish refugees who provided something of a support group. Support was important, because to many of our Australian peers we were damned on two grounds. The two parts of "German Jew"—the epithet by whose endless repetition we were derided and isolated—were to them neither exculpatory nor pitiable but additively despicable. Insofar as our teachers were aware of this process, they appeared to accept it as the natural course of events. Had I been more assertive and thick skinned, I could eventually have compelled the respect of my peers and, probably, joined them, but as an only child with limited experience relating to peers, I withdrew. During my first three years in Sydney, I did not have a single child friend beyond our little refugee community. The workings of the Holocaust were not confined to areas under German occupation.

It was, of course, a godsend that I had arrived in Sydney with a smattering of English. I entered first grade in 1939 some months into the school year, which in Australia begins early in the calendar year, and spent most of the first three school years in Bellevue Hill School. Bellevue Hill, aptly named, overlooks Bondi Beach and the South Pacific on the east and Sydney Harbor on the west, where we could sometimes watch the *Queen Mary*, converted to a troop ship, at anchor. Despite the natural beauty, and apart from participating in occasional games of marbles, however, my recollections of school life there are of total social isolation.

Perhaps it was this isolation, which thrust me onto my own resources, that led me to a lifelong pattern of going my own way. More likely, it strengthened a genetically prepared disposition. In any event, far from entering new or changed situations with a careful eye on what others did or thought, I took my bearings internally and barged ahead. Others' values, judgments, and ideologies had far less impact on me than they had on my age-mates. Even then I tended to think for myself. This is consistent with my behavior later, when I began academic jobs oblivious of the local ideologies, status hierarchies, and requirements for obeisance and when I undertook research directions that were widely considered by the behaviorist establishment as taboo.

During 1942, my mother, feeling burdened by child care but earning a decent living with artificial flowers, enrolled me for fourth grade in Epping Grammar School, a boarding school on a tiny farm just outside Sydney that was run on the British model. Epping is now a Sydney suburb, and the school has disappeared seemingly without a trace, presumably under a suburban housing development. It was my first enforced, intimate integration into a native peer group, at first an intensely unhappy experience that I tried my best to escape; but gradually, without my recognizing it at the time, it began to take hold. I took part in some of my schoolmates' activities, such as building a sled (for use on a grassy slope—there is no snow in Sydney) and stoically getting caned for it by the headmaster—a bonding experience with my playmates! I began to compete in track, began an individual friendship, experienced an intellectual awakening, and won an award for performance in science.

As remote as Nazism and war seemed at first, their existence gradually became pervasive even in Sydney. The German invasion of Poland on September 1, 1939 reverberated through the world. After the United Kingdom went to war, so perforce did its Australian colony. My aunt's husband, who had declined to remain with her and her parents in Vienna, had entered Australia and was suddenly inducted into the Australian army. After Japan entered the war, there were air-raid drills, blackout requirements, and Yankee troops playing baseball in Sydney parks. Some kinds of food became scarce. Rationing set in. And when my Epping playmates began to build "crystal sets"—primitive radios—I was officially forbidden to do so on security grounds: I was an "enemy alien"! The evening when a Japanese two-person submarine stole into Sydney Harbor and proceeded to shell an apartment building before being blasted out of the water, Epping Grammar School pupils and staff were rushed into the basement shelter to sing patriotic songs and Church of England hymns while waiting for the all-clear siren.

The Epping experience should have continued beyond the first year—I would have benefited greatly—but during the Australian summer holidays my mother managed to obtain immigration papers for the United States, with departure planned for March 1943. I was held out of school until then. After a month at sea with my mother on a Swedish freighter, we landed in Los Angeles and continued on to Bridgeport, Connecticut, where I would live until beginning college.

I arrived in Bridgeport with an Aussie accent and with beginning skills in cricket and field hockey but not in baseball, basketball, or American football. I was back to square one—an immigrant Aussie German Jew—and I was again being chased down the street by hostile natives! This time, however, teachers intervened, and I immediately learned to appreciate the traditions of American democracy and official tolerance.

Growing up in America

When my father arrived in New York in 1938, a recently successful Viennese attorney without English-language skills, he accepted his only job offer, a placement on an assembly line at $5 a day. He was subjected to his share of humiliations at the hands of an intolerant supervisor and was eventually fired. During the months at the factory, however, he had begun trying to sell Watkins products door-to-door, and he eventually earned more as a part-time Watkins dealer than at his full-time factory job, which he lost with little regret. In 1942 he became a Watkins distributor who sold to dealers, and although this was never a lucrative success, he continued this type of work until his retirement.

There was a certain exhilaration in having lost everything, hitting bottom, and bouncing back, but the psychological wounds of my parents were immense. My father, a gifted amateur pianist, cellist, and composer in pre-*Anschluss* Vienna, a man who played in amateur chamber groups, a man with numerous professional relationships and a growing reputation as a defense attorney, member of a Social Democratic chess club— my father found himself after the *Anschluss* deserted and excluded by all of his non-Jewish friends and acquaintances. He witnessed the substantial crowds who welcomed the German troops and the many who eagerly seized on the opportunities to strip Jews of their property, livelihoods, and homes. It was an experience that permanently embittered him, that he could never forgive. He relentlessly turned his back on his former life, became as Americanized as possible, and refused to have a piano in the house. He never made music again.

When my mother and I arrived in April 1943, there must have been a bit of joy, because my brother, Roger, was conceived immediately. Soon, however, my parents began to bicker, or, more precisely, my father persistently criticized my mother, and she persistently argued back. He regularly attacked me as well, so that the tenor of home life in Bridgeport became intolerably hostile. My father recruited all of us to help in "the business"—for my mother it was virtually a full-time job—because we lived for many years on very meager revenues. Unionized postwar factory jobs would have paid much better, but the thought of working again for someone else was for my father anathema. He worked himself and my mother to exhaustion, got our bills paid, and provided the essentials; and he supported opportunities for my intellectual growth. After nearly twenty years, he was able to afford some luxuries, such as vacations in Florida. But home life was for me so utterly unhappy that I escaped it as much and as soon as I could. The escape was partly into schoolwork and nonfiction reading, which my father in particular strongly encouraged; partly into scouting, which became a large part of my life; and partly into individual friendships with non-Jews, one of them the son of a Methodist minister. When I graduated from high school a few weeks after turning seventeen, I left.

This is not the place for a full autobiography. To at least indicate the rest of the story, I obtained a bachelor's degree at Harvard and a Ph.D. at the University of Chicago; entered into intense relationships with women to whose supportiveness, kindness, and therapeutic effects I am forever in debt; married well; fathered three children, who suffered somewhat but not terminally from the carryover of my own upbringing; gained tenure; and continue to teach, research, and write. In middle adulthood I was to some extent reconciled with my father, though without ever saying so out loud; my mother, alas, died too soon for that.

The Holocaust Revealed

During World War II, communication with my paternal grandparents and aunt was extremely difficult. We did receive rare letters, subject, of course, to wartime censorship. We learned of the confiscation of my grandparents' business and apartment and their forced relocation into a ghetto and received hints of their privations. Only with the liberation of Vienna and of the Nazi concentration camps did we gradually learn the full truth. My grandparents, aunt, and a cousin of my father survived—my grandparents in Vienna, my aunt in hiding in Budapest, my father's cousin in hiding at first and, finally, by outliving his confinement to a concentration camp. The others who stayed had died in the camps—my grandfather's brothers, my mother's best friend, and numerous other family friends and relatives, including the Dutch couple who had sheltered us in 1938–39, whose children died in the Dutch resistance.

We saw the films of the newly liberated concentration camps and shared in the all-but-universal horror but with the addition of the oppressive knowledge that much of our extended family died in those camps—that, had we stayed, we would most likely have shared their fate, a fate that many of our fellow Austrians wished on us. Thereafter, my more anti-Semitic U.S. schoolmates found a new taunt: The trouble with Hitler was that he didn't kill enough Jews!

This awful, nightmarish knowledge of what took place, and that it was directed at us as well, weighs heavily on all Jews of our generation and on everyone else who can identify with the victims. It raises such fundamental questions regarding the depth of evil and the limitless human capacity for cruelty as to wipe out any tendency toward innocent trust in our fellow humans or in human institutions. The Holocaust is a defining event for the nature of human nature, not because human nature is in any sense limited to such evils but because it has under given conditions proven capable of them. The Holocaust has many precedents—it is unique in Jewish history primarily in its magnitude—but it will serve forever as a symbolic reference point for the shadow side of being human.

Impacts on Thought: The Years of Ambivalence and Holocaust Avoidance

Without realizing it, I began to look for the causes of what had happened to us. Blame marked the Zeitgeist of Holocaust explanation in the 1940s: it was Hitler's fault; it was the fault of the German national culture, of the authoritarian personality supposedly fostered by it. As a student in high school, in the antisocialist and anticommunist atmosphere of that time, I noticed that "Nazi" was short for "National Socialist" and explained the Holocaust as the result, among other things, of the forced conformism that I imagined was part of socialism. People incapable of extreme individualism would fall prey to group phenomena such as anti-Jewish hysteria. It was a somewhat naive first intellectual response, but it launched me into larger questions. When I entered Harvard, it was with the intention of studying the causes of human behavior and subsequently international law so that I could become an effective diplomat on the international scene. I wanted to be able to save humankind from the international imbroglios that lead to war. I imagined that the answers lay in political science, and I enrolled in political science courses as a freshman. I also joined the Harvard chapter of World Federalists.

The Harvard Years

William Yandell Elliot taught his introductory government course ("Gov 1a") as a *philosophy* of government course that began with Plato and worked its way through the leading nineteenth-century European philosophers of society and human nature. The world of intellectual possibilities opened much wider than I had ever imagined. I saw instantly that to explain political events I would need to include economics and social processes.

As a sophomore I enrolled in the corresponding courses. Harvard, however, had just launched an experiment in redefining disciplinary boundaries. Under the intellectual leadership of Talcott Parsons, Gordon Allport, and others, it had combined the socially most relevant parts of psychology with sociology and social and cultural anthropology to form a new Department of Social Relations. When I took my first course in the area ("Soc Rel 1a"), my instructor was psychologist Gordon Allport, and the textbook in the course was, rather audaciously in retrospect, his 1937 book, *Personality*. I was entranced and became a major in social relations.

Much of my time at Harvard was spent in a kind of divided consciousness. On the one hand, I enrolled in a German writing course, wrote Holocaust-related short stories (that earned C's!) in an intermediate English writing course, and was easily drawn into conversations about the Holocaust and the war. On the other hand, I stayed away from Hillel House and other Jewish activities after one disappointing encounter, became an agnostic, took my only history courses in British history, ignored the fact that at that time Gordon Allport was writing his classic book on prejudice, and generally acted as if the Holocaust had little to do with me. It was not that I felt nothing emotional about it—on the contrary, it was a profoundly painful subject, and I implicitly learned to avoid it. Except for the summer after freshman year, when I lived at home but spent little time there, I also distanced myself from my parents and other relatives. On one of the infrequent weekends that I spent at home, I brought along my Kirkland House suite mate, Ludger Schnippenkötter, a towering six-foot-three, blond German-Catholic exchange student, who just about terrified my parents! In retrospect, it was a period of partial denial that stretched out for decades.

Correspondingly, I completed my major in social relations with little reference to the Holocaust. The summer after junior year I remained in Cambridge on a Social Science Research Council undergraduate fellowship, whose purpose was to support my undergraduate research on Allport's ascendance-submission dimension of personality, testing a rather obscure hypothesis that respondents scoring on the submissive end of the scale would show less variability in their item scores (because of greater rigidity due to greater defensiveness) than those scoring at the ascendant (dominant) end. The results supported the hypothesis and made my honors thesis.

On the surface, within the field of personality, this research direction was about as far from the Holocaust as one could get. Nevertheless, it is perhaps no accident that, of all the research problems I might have gravitated toward, it was dominance/submission that attracted me. It was the dimension that stimulated my clearest hypotheses of the time. My first investigation of it was of its role in roommate relationships. I hypothesized that liking between roommates would be greater as their ascendance-submission scores better complemented each other. Thus, two intermediate scorers or a very dominant partner paired with a very submissive partner would be most likely to get along. The results were spectacularly confirmatory and forever hooked me on behavioral research! But in other contexts, dominance/submission was under discussion (mistakenly, I now believe) as the critically important dimension in German society that made the Holocaust possible. The "authoritarian personality," after all, was marked by an affinity for dominance or submission. It is not a connection I consciously made then.

Doing research gave me the greatest pleasure of any sustained activity that I had ever experienced. I reconsidered my plans for law school. After the Strong Vocational Interest Blank gave me equal "A" scores in psychology and law, I decided to do what I knew to be enjoyable and applied to graduate school instead.

The Chicago Years

By the time I reached graduate school at the University of Chicago, I had decided to become an academic personality psychologist. Independently of what little advice I received, I mapped out a program that included developmental, psychometric, clinical, and biopsychological components along with personality, as well as a clinical internship. Although I originated little research, I assisted briefly with a thematic apperception test (TAT) validation project and a social-competence project and spent most of the six years up to the Ph.D. as a research assistant and then research associate with Helen Hofer Gee, a recent Minnesota psychometrics Ph.D., at the Association of American Medical Colleges (AAMC). There I was part of a massive, ultimately unsuccessful project to improve prediction of medical student grades by adding to the Medical College Admission Test (MCAT) some of the newer personality measures of the time. With Helen Gee's encouragement and the supportive guidance of my adviser, Donald W. Fiske, I wrote my dissertation as part of this project.

During this time, the only reminders of my prewar background came through passing the language requirement for the degree in German and reading an article by Kurt Lewin in the original language. I studied Freud, as did my fellow students, in English. My principal friendships and romances were, with few exceptions and only one lasting exception, with non-Jews.

Toward the end of this period, I met and married my wife, Karla Ann Michelke, the agnostic daughter of a Lutheran pastor, all four of whose Lutheran grandparents had emigrated from northern Germany to the U.S. upper Midwest. The potential irony of this was not lost on us at the time. We explained the ease with which we fit together as the result of our both having roots in Germanic culture. I had emigrated more recently, but Karla's parents had grown up, even though in South Dakota and Minnesota, in German-speaking households and partly German-speaking communities. In any event, it was a marriage that has lasted and produced three sterling offspring.

The Building of a Research Program

Spring of 1960 was a time of major change. We married; I received and accepted a job offer from the University of Wisconsin in Madison; and I finished my dissertation, passed my orals, and received my Ph.D. In August we moved to Madison, Wisconsin.

In September I faced the first classes I had ever taught, having had zero experience even as a teaching assistant before that. They were a graduate course in intermediate statistics and experimental design and an advanced undergraduate course in clinical psychology, two courses that I had myself never taken, although I had most of the necessary academic preparation for them. During the two years I spent in Madison, I also taught introductory human adjustment and an advanced undergraduate course in individual differences, two more that I had never taken. The latter course was part of my undoing at Madison.

Coming in with no teaching experience to teach four courses that I had never taken, much less taught, made for an intensely busy year of course preparation and execution. Especially after the failure of my dissertation project, it was hard to get a research program going, but research was my primary reason for entering university life and was essential for success in that department. At first I prepared and submitted an article based on research completed previously at the Veterans Administration (VA) on diagnosing schizophrenia with Rorschach patterns, coauthored a statistical note on calculating Fisher's Exact Test, and wrote up a data set originally collected by my new colleague Mavis Hetherington on an experimental analysis of psychopathy. It was a heterogeneous group of articles, all of which were eventually published, that held little indication of a central programmatic thrust. They did, however, betray (I use the word advisedly!) an interest in individual differences, an interest I confirmed when I volunteered to teach the course on individual differences that was still in the catalog but had not been taught in anybody's memory.

The programmatic thrust was alive but hidden. I had made the decision not to publish my dissertation, which essentially showed that the unsuccessful personality predictors (from the Edwards Personal Preference Schedule and Allport-Vernon-Lindzey Study of Values) not only did little to predict success in medical school but also failed to interact with characteristics of the medical schools. Instead, I decided to pursue the reasons for the failure, which I attributed to shortcomings in the assessment tools. My University of Chicago adviser, Donald W. Fiske, was working on his critique of such measures, and some of his skepticism belatedly rubbed off on me. I planned, but never executed, an elaborate empirical study to see whether varying the forms of items, especially to take into account situational contexts, might make the measures better at confirming hypotheses regarding their interactions with other variables. In preparation, I reviewed several years of personality journals and compiled a statistical relationship between the type of item in a personality measure (or its status as a projective method) and its success rate in confirming the authors' hypotheses regarding interactions with other variables. As I expected, there was a significant relationship. To my surprise, however, the results showed that variables drawn from projective tests, such as the Rorschach Inkblot Test and Thematic Apperception test, yielded significantly better confirmations of interaction hypotheses than did traditional psychometric variables. Because the type of measure was heavily and inextricably confounded with the type of construct being measured (e.g., anxiety was measured psychometrically, need for achievement projectively), I ill-advisedly decided against trying to publish this study, but it launched me on the next stage of inquiry: what might account for the superiority of projective measures in confirming interaction hypotheses? Projective measures were widely regarded as "fantasy" measures, but theories of fantasy of that time were entirely inadequate for answering my question. What I needed to do, I decided, was to devise an adequate theory of fantasy; and to prepare for that, I would undertake parametric studies of how fantasy scores responded to various kinds of experimental conditions.

This pursuit would occupy the next decade and shape my research for the rest of my life. It is a pursuit that arose organically out of the logical sequence of events—of questions and data—that emerged from my participation in the AAMC prediction project. I can detect in it no trace of *direct* Holocaust influence.

The chemistry between me and the Department of Psychology in Madison quickly soured. The fact that for several years I had concentrated my efforts in Chicago on the AAMC research project and on my

VA clinical traineeship had taken me out of the academic loop. I arrived in Madison largely naive as to how departments operate and with little preparation for empathizing with the situation of their decision makers. I did little to inform myself as to how the department functioned or about its operative values. I also freely injected myself into its discussions of policy issues. It was thus rather belatedly that I learned of what amounted to its ideology: experimental methods are scientifically good; correlational methods are scientifically worse than useless. Anyone who does not understand this is a dope. But the study of individual differences largely proceeds correlationally, and both my initial research interests, including my dissertation, and my volunteering to teach a course on individual differences established me as scientifically unrespectable. The department was also ideologically behaviorist, as was nearly every major department in the country. To harbor an interest in fantasy as such was bound to be suspect.

To make matters worse, I chafed under the entrenched, rather heavy-handed leadership of the department and its seeming disregard of student interests. When Carl Rogers wrote his scathing critique of graduate education, it was this department that he was in the process of leaving. Distinguished as the department was and remains, it was at that time highly demoralizing for students and junior faculty alike. I was reappointed, but in my second year I went into the job market to seek another position.

The Morris Years of Productive Theory Building

Early in 1962 I learned of an opening at the University of Minnesota, Morris (UMM). The campus had been opened in 1960 as an experiment with a tiny freshman class and thirteen faculty. It was a move that the University of Minnesota regents took independently of the Minnesota legislature, which had repeatedly refused to fund it. The regents decided to try it anyway for two years. If the campus succeeded, it would be continued, otherwise not. By 1962, when it became apparent that the campus would succeed, the legislature relented and appropriated funds for it. I would arrive as the first full-time teaching psychologist on the campus just as the first UMM students became juniors. My assignment would be first to start recruiting the next psychologist and then to teach six three-credit courses a year (two per quarter), propose a curriculum, organize a laboratory, and participate in the building of a new college. The lure of this relative independence and responsibility—to be able to shape an educational program, to research without fear of ideological censure—and the contrast with my tenuous situation at Wisconsin were irresistible. When Rod Briggs, UMM's supremely dynamic dean, drove down to Madison to interview me over beers in the student union's Rathskeller, I agreed to come up for a look, and I signed on.

This college had its own educational ideology: undergraduate liberal education, exclusively, for a selected, bright population of students drawn from a broad region; a moderate teaching load for its faculty, as befits a University of Minnesota entity; and an emphasis on quality. Unlike many campuses of multicampus universities, UMM was, except geographically, an integral part of the University of Minnesota. UMM faculty participated in the overall university's governance and access to facilities and funds. That the college was located in a town of about four thousand people 100 miles from the nearest city of more than fifteen thousand and 150 or so road miles from the nearest metropolis of Minneapolis-St. Paul and was situated in sparsely populated, largely agricultural plains did not faze its planners!

From a Holocaust standpoint, it was not a logical location. Madison had moved me inside the area of perhaps the heaviest German immigration in the United States. In Morris, I was beyond its center. Apart from UMM, the only Morris individual still known as a Jew had converted to Lutheranism decades earlier. The nearest synagogue was two hours away. The mayor, welcoming new faculty, lauded the cosmopolitan diversity of Morris: why, there were not only Germans but Norwegians, Swedes, Danes, even Icelanders! He was dead serious.

But to me, it mattered little. From the standpoint of urban living, Madison had already been a huge comedown from Chicago. Our real downtown became Minneapolis, three hours away. Building a psychology program, a research program, and a campus—and, eventually, a family—would keep me too busy to care very much.

Despite the many challenges of the new position, I soon plunged into my new research program, the parametric analysis of TAT need-for-achievement scores. Before leaving Wisconsin, I had conducted the first investigation in this direction—ironically, a completely experimental study. To obtain parametric data on the properties of fantasy, I decided to investigate the projective variable that at that time was the most heavily studied and hence best understood, TAT need-for-achievement scores, along with TAT need for affiliation. The extensive, impressive research of David C. McClelland and his colleagues had shown that these scores were influenced by motivational sets induced in participants by experimenters' verbal instructions. In the belief that these scores might respond just to nonverbal modeling effects, I clipped scenes from a film, one modeling achievement and the other modeling affiliation, showed them soundlessly to research participants, and then asked them to write TAT stories. The achievement and affiliation scores were significantly influenced by the films.

This was a small pilot study that shaped my empirical research program for ten years. With generous support for eight years from the National Science Foundation, professional actors—live at first, later on film—portrayed researchers as they administered some tests, including the TAT. They portrayed three kinds of experimenters: achievement oriented, warmly affiliative, and neutral. Participants in the same room with them gave the expected results in that their stories reflected the motivational sets that the experimenters induced with their verbal instructions; but others, who saw these experimenters over closed-circuit television or on film but could not hear what was said, also wrote stories that significantly reflected the kind of personality the actors portrayed. This meant that the effects were not due primarily to the verbal instructions, as had been assumed, but to the nonverbal aspects of the experimenters' demeanor. The "fantasies" represented by participants' stories reflected a modeling effect of the experimenters.

Obviously, this program, like its predecessors, shows no particular Holocaust influence. It grew out of the inner logic of scientific events. However, in 1965 I began to outline a projected book, which grew into *Structure and Functions of Fantasy* (1971). By 1968, I began to write it. Among the literature that I needed to review was the work of philosopher Johann Friedrich Herbart, some of which was unavailable in English. As I struggled through his work in German, I became aware of how much German competency I had lost (and also how much I had never gained!). It was a surprisingly painful discovery that stuck in my craw. I was forced at long last to confront a part of my identity that I had for many years neglected.

Nevertheless, like the empirical research program it accompanied, my book shows no particular Holocaust influence. It reviewed a very large literature on play, dreams, daydreams, and projective methods; and it laid out a comprehensive, systematic theory of fantasy. It introduced the motivational theory of current concerns—the influence of people's goals on how they respond to the many stimuli they encounter, in particular how concern-related stimuli trigger thoughts related to the concern. It also introduced the probable role of emotional responses in mediating that influence. These ideas grew out of the literature I had read, out of my own data, and out of my subjective inner experience, with little direct connection to my personal history.

Tranforming Experiences: Reconnection with Holocaust and *Heimat*

My connection to the Holocaust reemerged as the result of three further transforming experiences. One was the start of my friendship with my German colleague, Heinz Heckhausen, in 1967. The second was the United States' role in the Vietnam War. The third was a Fulbright semester in Heckhausen's department of psychology at the Ruhr University of Bochum in 1975–76.

Heinz Heckhausen

Heckhausen had come into my life at an American Psychological Association (APA) meeting in 1966, when we were introduced as sharing interests in achievement motivation. We also had in common that he was the first psychologist hired at the then brand new Ruhr University of Bochum and he, too, was helping to build a campus and a psychology program. We hit it off, and when he traveled to Lincoln to participate in the Nebraska Symposium on Motivation in spring of 1967, he stopped off in Morris for a few days on his way back. It was the start of a lifelong friendship.

Heinz was fluent in English, having spent part of World War II with an Iowa farm family as a prisoner of war; but when our conversations seemed to remain purely English, he encouraged me to speak with him in German. It was the first German conversation I had tried to hold since my teens—my conversations with my parents had gradually become purely English on my side. It was intensely uncomfortable. I had lost a lot of ground in the language, a fact that disturbed me greatly.

Inevitably, the conversation gravitated toward our wartime experiences. In fact, all of my nonperfunctory conversations with Germans of about that generation or older always eventually came to address the war and the Holocaust. If I did not bring it up, as I usually did not, my conversation partners did. It was as if we had to know each other's experiences and our stance on the major issues of the war and to assess the nature and extent of our mutual suffering; and the suffering *was* mutual. Apart from suffering through combat and the destruction of a huge percentage of the males of a couple of generations, including many friends and relatives, people such as Heinz returned to a Germany devastated by Allied bombing and battle and subject to enormous levels of privation. Most of the historic city cores and many outlying historic buildings had been destroyed or severely damaged—not only the factories, military facilities, and railways but also opera houses, cathedrals, museums, universities, medieval quarters, palaces, castles, and many of the cities' residential areas and their inhabitants. Central Bochum, as a heavily industrialized city, was almost completely leveled. Infrastructure was laid to waste, and hunger and cold were part of many people's lot. Yet, Heinz was among the lucky ones, having survived without serious injury. There were emotional hurt and an inevitable residue of bitterness on all sides of the catastrophes of Nazism and World War II.

With Heinz Heckhausen I had reengaged to some extent with what I had left behind and from a far fuller perspective. Europe, and in particular Germany and Austria, became a more concrete presence in my mind. Heinz and I continued intermittently to correspond, though we did not meet again for over eight years. I continued to reject suggestions by wife and friends that it would be fun to vacation in Europe. I had seen a lot of the world as a child, I replied, and had little need or desire to travel so far now. Actually, the idea nearly terrified me. Just contemplating it stirred up such intense feelings of hurt and rage that I could not imagine subjecting myself to such a reimmersion in the continent of my birth.

The Vietnam War

The second transforming event, which enabled me to moderate these feelings, was the Vietnam War. I had escaped all military service—too young for World War II, in college during the Korean War on a 2-S deferment, and too old to be inducted by the time I finished my Ph.D. On account of this, I at first felt some lack of credibility in opposing the Vietnam War; but when, by 1967, I realized the enormity of what the war was doing to the Vietnamese population, I became an informed critic and an active political opponent. I also began to reflect on certain parallels between this war and the Holocaust. Hundreds of thousands of Vietnamese civilians were losing their lives, as well as the combatants on both sides. Largely motivated by my empathy for them, made easier through my brush with the Holocaust, I became convinced that the war was wrong, and I protested by letter, march, and speech. I organized support within our county for Senator Eugene McCarthy for president in 1968, with two-thirds of the Stevens County Democratic-Farmer-Labor convention eventually voting in his favor. But in the United States of America of that time this kind of protest was perfectly safe. I had risked nothing and lost little through protest. I could have done more—after all, hundreds were dying every day, visible on the television tube—and yet I continued to pay my taxes, to devote most of my time to my academic activities, to live in the United States, and to avoid anything resembling civil disobedience or sabotage. I continued, in other words, to be a "good American," even as my taxes and my implicit consent were contributing to the gruesome deaths of innocent civilians. I did not care enough about their suffering to uproot my life or to oppose my adopted country more vigorously.

If that was so, and if I could think of myself as a reasonably upright individual, how much outrage was I warranted in directing at the German and Austrian populations, for whom the slightest opposition, let alone resistance, would have been immeasurably more costly? Already in the 1930s, German courts were ruling that offenses such as refusing to use the "German greeting" (the stiff-arm salute) or to sing the "Horst Wessel" song constituted an "important reason" for an employer to fire an employee, regardless of prior contractual agreements (Rüthers 1991). This was especially the case for public employees but extended to all other groups as well. Employing a Jew was sufficient legal grounds for suppliers and customers to boycott an "Aryan" business, even if that meant breaking a contract. Eventually, continuing to do business with those flouting Nazi racial policies was itself considered a sanctionable offense. The entire economic, social, and legal system was rigged to exact enormous costs from those unsupportive of Nazi doctrine. It constituted the pervasive corruption of an entire society through manipulation of everyone's incentive structure.

Although the non-Jewish population was from nearly the beginning certainly aware of extreme hardships and indignities imposed on Jews, the basest cruelties were officially kept from the public. Eventually, many people had heard of them, but for most these were wartime rumors. The Final Solution, the Nazi program for the complete annihilation of Europe's Jews, was probably begun in the summer of 1941 and officially, though secretly, propagated and coordinated at a conference of top Nazi officials in the Berlin suburb of Wannsee on January 20, 1942 (Shirer 1960). It was again explicitly not publicized, and its procedures were to some extent disguised. For much of the war, therefore, many a loyal "good German" could resist drawing the correct conclusions.

This is not to deny or condone the complicity of millions of citizens with the Holocaust. Rather, it is to indicate the motivational matrix for the decision making of average citizens. If my motivational matrix kept me from taking stronger action while fully informed of what my government was doing and while fully disapproving of it, I was in a position to comprehend some of what had happened to average Germans and Austrians. My hurt and rage, still present, became manageable. By the early 1970s, I could contemplate going back.

Perhaps this shift in feeling also made other kinds of thinking more likely. In 1972 I launched into a formal statement of a theory that had been gathering shape in my mind, a theory of the consequences of encountering an obstacle to an important goal—of loss and failure. Fed by observation of my own subjective experiences, as well as of the literature, it broadened into a larger motivational theory, with the concept of current concerns still at its core, though in much elaborated form. I published this in the *Psychological Review* (Klinger 1975) but also launched into writing a book to explore the theory more fully, especially its implications. Doing so constituted opening up to emotional considerations far more fully than I had done before.

The book (Klinger 1977) took its title (*Meaning and Void*) and its leitmotiv from the writings of Viktor Frankl, especially *Man's Search for Meaning* (1963), with its detailed account of life and death in a concentration camp; but my book was written in the empirical tradition and literature of U.S. and German experimental psychology. It focuses extensively on anger, depression, alienation, addiction, and suicide. It is, in a way, a synthesis of the disparate influences on my life, and it confronts from a scientific perspective the dark emotions associated with forced emigration—with economic and cultural dispossession.

The Return and Its Aftermath

The third transforming event consisted of going back. I obtained a senior Fulbright award to fund a research semester with Heinz Heckhausen at the Ruhr University of Bochum. Objectively speaking, we cotaught a seminar on the theory of current concerns and related topics, assisted with each other's publications in progress, and talked about motivational theory; and my family and I did a fair amount of sight-seeing. Subjectively, the experience excavated a large component of my psychological being that had slid out of sight, buried by Americanization, with which it had no cultural fit. Reclaiming this component thereby amended my identity.

To anyone who has not experienced something similar, it is hard to communicate the depth of feeling entailed in my initial return. Because the terms of the Fulbright award required traveling by Lufthansa, the experience really began in New York. Announcements now were in German as well as English. I began to experience a welling up of emotion. This emotion cannot be characterized as pleasant or unpleasant, merely as intense arousal that seemed to fill my chest and throat. There was a tingling quality to it, almost a shiver. My eyes moistened. It gained in intensity, with almost a sense of shock, when we disembarked in Frankfurt and stepped into a fully German atmosphere. The accents and mannerisms were not quite the right ones, Hessian rather than Viennese, but their effects were very significant. I felt both a sense of being close to home and of hazard, a returning minority individual whom many of those around me at the airport would not welcome back. However, the welcome in Bochum—by Heinz; his wife, Christa, and their children; and his staff and colleagues at the university—was warm and effusive. My fears were allayed.

My wife and children, who had arrived later on an Icelandic flight, and I soon boarded the train to Locarno, Switzerland, to visit my late mother's brother, and then on to Vienna (nach Wien!) via Zurich. In Zurich, we boarded an Austrian train staffed by an Austrian crew. Now the accents were right, and there was a general sense of the *rightness* of it all. The encompassing feeling welled up again to new heights. Through that long, alpine train ride to Vienna, I sat transfixed, consumed with emotion that rose steadily the closer we got to our destination. About an hour from Vienna I had to leave my family and sit alone. They were excited, and they knew something was happening to me, but they could not possibly know what I was feeling, and I was in no condition to talk about it. At that moment, I felt completely disconnected from them. So I sat by myself, staring out into the gathering darkness and completely immersed in feeling. It was, without exaggeration, the most intense emotional experience of my life.

In some degree, the feeling remained with me throughout that week in Vienna. It peaked again when the widow who then occupied the apartment of my first five years graciously welcomed me to enter it and stay as long as I liked—and after less than half an hour I departed, unable any longer to contain the feeling it evoked. I had certainly not anticipated anything like this. I expected an emotional reaction but not that one. How to explain it? It had to do with reunion, not with particular people but with a culture—with language styles, characteristic expressions, phrasing, and hard-to-translate concepts; with gestures, expressions, and expectations; with particular attitudes and folk wisdom; with neighborhoods, favorite parks, and walks; with music. It all had its counterpart in me, the part with which I had recorded it and had learned to respond to it, a part buried from decades of disuse because there was nothing for it to fit with. It was an implicit part, which I could not have described or perhaps even acknowledged. I believe that the resurrection of this buried subself was what unleashed the emotion. Perhaps if someone very close had died, been mourned, relegated to the past, and then encountered again alive, the encounter would unleash a similar tide of feeling. It felt like two sundered parts of me had reunited.

This experience is almost surely not specific to Holocaust refugees. It most likely happens to those torn from their cultures at certain ages who much later return. But in this instance, it was the impending Holocaust that tore us away. It thereby became a Holocaust effect.

On arrival in Vienna, we were met by our last remaining relatives there, the family of my father's cousin, who had survived ghetto brutality, hiding, and a concentration camp to become a Viennese police detective and subsequently a real estate manager. He, his wife, and their two daughters, then of college age, looked after us and reinstated a family connection that has strengthened with time. It was one more bond to my homeland. I have returned for visits more than a dozen times since then, having never lost my affection and sense of connection with the place, although now it feels more simply like home—really, the first of my several homes.

Back in Bochum, I could focus among other things on my inadequacy in my native tongue. Not only had I lost fluency, but I had never learned to express myself in academic German, had never studied psychology in German, had never needed to express complex ideas in German. I formed the long-term goal of gaining complete fluency at an academic level, shedding a certain Americanization of my Viennese accent, and being able to "pass" as the native speaker I originally was. With a good deal of attention and effort, what I had lost began to come back, and I also began to extend my vocabulary to the academic enterprise. With considerable help, I could function credibly in our seminar. By November, with intensive language preparation and notes, I could deliver a colloquium talk in German. However, during that semester I never attained the competency to pass as a native speaker. It was apparent that this would be a longer project.

For whatever its significance, by December I had become ill and would be dogged by a succession of internal infections, from which I fully recovered only two years later. I ascribed it to a long period of overwork, beginning well before Bochum; but overwork was not new to me. Had it merely caught up with me, perhaps as I had gotten further into middle age, or was the emotional strain of returning taking its toll?

The cross-fertilization of ideas between Heinz Heckhausen, along with his capable scientific staff and students, and me was highly fruitful. Both of us subsequently evolved theoretical structures that have had some influence and that show the traces of our interchange. We retained a close scientific connection that has passed, especially after his untimely death in 1988, to his former students, several now themselves distinguished professors.

A Binational Identity

The Bochum experience created a new, undissolvable tie to the German-speaking part of the world. My next trip there, in summer of 1979, was a six-week vacation. It was lovely, but I discovered that my lack of effort to maintain my language gains since 1976 had led to massive backsliding. Upon my return to the States, I resolved to read some German each day, at least a few pages, beginning with a history of Austria, and to maximize opportunities to listen and converse in it. I also resolved to become an amateur Austrianist. I have maintained this program. In 1981, it coincided with my burgeoning interests in imagery methods in psychotherapy; I spent a spring quarter leave with Hanscarl Leuner in Göttingen. The leave resulted in a number of publications and, back in Minnesota, a series of graduate seminars.

In 1983, Heckhausen accepted an offer to join the new Max Planck Institute for Psychological Research in Munich. With no teaching obligations, though with the possibility of teaching and dissertation advising at the University of Munich, with a large staff, space, and generous funding, he would be able to launch a new, larger phase of his already distinguished research program. However, with his leaving on short notice, his institute in Bochum needed an interim professor to serve until a permanent replacement could be hired. He phoned and asked whether I would consider serving. I gratefully accepted and spent 1983–84 in full-time teaching as the interim occupant of his professorial chair. I formed close ties with some students and colleagues, among the latter especially Michael Bock and Reiner Nikula, whose collaboration sent my research program into new, more cognitive directions. This time, I was accompanied by my wife and our youngest son during the first part of the year but spent the latter part alone. With little occasion to use English and steady demands to function in German, surrounded by German speech live and in the media, I gradually arrived at the point I had striven for: ability to pass, at least under some conditions, fleetingly, as a native speaker. It was an enormously satisfying moment.

Thereafter I became a frequent visitor to Germany and Austria. In part this was to visit friends from my previous sojourns there, but in 1985 I was invited to join the Scientific Advisory Council that assesses and advises the Max Planck Institute of which Heckhausen was part. I served on it for twelve stimulating years, leading to intensive intellectual exchanges especially with Jürgen Beckmann and Peter Gollwitzer from Heckhausen's unit and, in the course of the council's work, with its members—especially its chair, Hans-Jochen Kornadt—and with the other research directors, Franz Weinert and Wolfgang Prinz, and their staffs. The council met annually at first and then biennially, with occasional extra sessions. In 1995, at the gracious invitation of Gisela Trommsdorff, I spent a month as a visiting professor at the University of Konstanz. My assignments there included a workshop on hate. Along with other occasions to travel to Germany, I have averaged about one trip there per year and have spent cumulatively over two years there.

Other Impacts on Work and Thought

These various contacts resulted in a widening circle of contacts and some collaborations: with Julius Kuhl of the University of Osnabrück and his students, especially Arno Fuhrmann; and with Frantisek Man and Iva Stuchlíková of the University of South Bohemia. Man and Stuchlíková have joined my long-term collaboration with Miles Cox and Joseph Blount in investigating the Motivational Structure Questionnaire (MSQ) in relation to alcohol use and other variables. Stuchlíková and Leo Stuchlik, a skilled programmer, produced a computer-administered version of the MSQ. It may seem strange to count these as Holocaust influences, but without my burning desire for some reintegration with the culture of my birth, it is far less likely that these contacts and collaborations would have come about. They are part of the branching, indirect consequences.

There is one more direct consequence. By the mid-1980s, I had become intensely interested in the phenomenon of hate. It arose against the ever-present backdrop in my mind of the Holocaust, out of my continuing sense of hurt and wariness as a past and possibly future victim of hate, but also out of the repeated evidences of hate, from the mass murders of Cambodia to the official Iranian-Shiite hatred of the West; the old hatreds of the Middle East; South Africa's nationalists; Hutus versus Tutsis; the American Nazi factions; the chronic racial, ethnic, and religious tensions of the United States; the persecution of homosexuals; and so many others. With my chief research assistant in Bochum, Jutta Bott, I began to think about hate more systematically and eventually developed a small collaborative research project with her, which was extended with undergraduates at Morris. I have also led two graduate seminars at Minnesota related to the topic, the first of them with Bott's strong contribution, and a workshop on hate at the University of Konstanz. All of this work is still unpublished, although some was presented in Brussels at the International Congress of Psychology in 1992. I view it as still preliminary, but it is a start.

The central theme of my thinking about hate is to cast it as an innate human disposition that lies latent until evoked. The threshold for evoking it varies greatly from one person to the next and in accordance with certain potentiating conditions. It is an adaptive disposition under some circumstances but one that lends itself to being perverted. Surely the Holocaust is the quintessential example of its perversion.

My primary research program remains focused on two main directions: (1) motivational and emotional influences on cognitive processing (currently pursued with evoked-potential methods; Klinger 1996; Klinger et al. 1996) and (2) topics related to motivational structure: its assessment (principally with the MSQ; Klinger, Cox, and Blount 1995), relation to substance use (Cox and Klinger 1988), and modification through Systematic Motivational Counseling (Cox, Klinger, and Blount 1992). The first of these, conducted since the 1960s with an extraordinary team of UMM undergraduates and graduates, is driven by the internal logic of theory and data; it has no perceptible relationship to Holocaust experiences.

The second grew out of a chapter in *Meaning and Void* that builds on those aspects of the book that I take to be influenced by Holocaust experiences. Insofar as that is the case, it can count as indirectly Holocaust influenced. That chapter attracted Miles Cox and led to, so far, two decades of collaboration on alcohol- and other substance-related issues, which has become autonomous of any direct Holocaust influence.

Conclusion

These, then, are the impacts of the Holocaust on my work as I see it—no doubt an imperfect vision. The indirect influences are pervasive, just as diverting a river affects the path of the water thereafter. The sundering of my connection with the culture of my birth made an American out of me, which shaped my being and my thought; and my hunger for reconnection, once awakened, shaped me in new ways and led to a host of personal and professional relationships. These, in turn, influenced my thinking and offered opportunities for research collaboration that my wish for reconnection inclined me to pursue.

The direct influences of the Holocaust on my work are more intermittent and harder to identify with confidence. For years, I avoided—virtually resisted—direct influence. When I was able to confront my feelings and work through them, Holocaust-relevant themes entered my work: I became preoccupied with theory relating to loss and meaning, to anger, depression, and alienation; the book presenting these took as its point of departure the work of Viktor Frankl, especially as it grew out of his concentration-camp experiences. I made a study, though unsystematic, of relevant German and Austrian history and literature and strove to reestablish my German-language competency, which in turn introduced me to contacts and literature I would not otherwise have experienced. I turned to a systematic study of hate and established the beginnings of a potentially long-term research program.

A psychoanalyst (which I am decidedly not) would detect elements here of identification with the aggressor, of undoing, of regressive yearnings, and, of course, Oedipal features. One might identify counterphobic activity, repetition-compulsion, and other psychodynamic echoes of fleeing the Holocaust. Descriptively speaking, perhaps so. No doubt there are others. So be it.

REFERENCES

Cox, W. M., and E. Klinger. 1988. A motivational model of alcohol use. *Journal of Abnormal Psychology* 97:168–80.

Cox, W. M., E. Klinger, and J. P. Blount. 1992. Systematic Motivational Counseling: A treatment manual. Manuscript.

Frankl, V. E. 1963. *Man's search for meaning: An introduction to logotherapy.* New York: Washington Square.

Klinger, E. 1971. *Structure and functions of fantasy.* New York: Wiley.

———. 1975. Consequences of commitment to and disengagement from incentives. *Psychological Review* 82:125.

———. 1977. *Meaning and void: Inner experience and the incentives in people's lives.* Minneapolis: University of Minnesota Press.

———. 1996. Emotional influences on cognitive processing, with implications for theories of both. In *The psychology of action: Linking cognition and motivation to behavior,* edited by J. A. Bargh and P. M. Gollwitzer, 168–89. New York: Guilford.

Klinger, E., W. M. Cox, and J. P. Blount. 1995. The Motivational Structure Questionnaire. In *Assessing alcohol problems: A guide for clinicians and researchers,* edited by J. P. Allen, 399–411. Bethesda, MD: National Institute on Alcohol Abuse and Alcoholism.

Klinger, E., E. S. Goetzman, T. Hughes, and T. L. Seppelt. 1996. *Microinfluences of protoemotional reactions and motivation on cognitive processing.* Invited paper presented at the annual meeting of the Midwestern Psychological Association, Chicago, May 1996.

Rüthers, B. 1991. *Die unbegrenzte Auslegung: Zum Wandel der Privatrechtsordnung im Nationalsozialismus,* 4th ed. Heidelberg: C. F. Müller.

Shirer, W. L. 1960. *The rise and fall of the Third Reich.* New York: Crest/Fawcett.

The Holocaust and Social Science: A Personal Odyssey

Richard Ned Lebow

Biographical Note

R. Ned Lebow is professor of political science, history, and psychology and director of the Mershon Center at Ohio State University. He was educated at the University of Chicago, Yale University, and the City University of New York (Ph.D., political science, 1968). His previous positions included appointments as professor of strategy at the Naval and National War Colleges and professor of political science at the City University of New York, the Bologna Center of Johns Hopkins University, and Cornell. He has received fellowships from the Council on Foreign Relations; Carnegie Corporation; MacArthur, Rockefeller, Volkswagen, and Hewlett Foundations; German Marshall Fund; Danish National Research Council; and U.S. Institute of Peace.

His research is concerned with international relations theory, psychological models of foreign policy, bargaining and negotiation, and strategies of conflict management. He is the author or coauthor of six books and editor or coeditor of six others. His most recent books are The Art of Bargaining, We All Lost the Cold War, *coauthored with Janice Gross Stein (selected by* Choice *as one of the best academic books of 1994), and* International Relations Theory and the End of the Cold War, *coedited with Thomas Risse-Kappen.*

Introduction

We have been asked to analyze how the Holocaust influenced or even determined our choice of careers and continues to affect our professional lives. For some of us, the links between life experiences, political beliefs, and research agendas are strong and self-evident. For me, the Holocaust is a root source of my commitment to use science as a tool to build peace, tolerance, and social justice.

Like every story, mine has its twist. My knowledge about my origins is incomplete and uncertain. I always knew I was adopted but had no information about my previous life until adulthood. I developed my interest in conflict resolution and chose my career before discovering a possible, personal connection with the Holocaust. As my narrative makes clear, my professional interests and choice of career were nevertheless a direct response to the Holocaust and World War II. I am therefore something of an anomaly, at least in comparison to the other authors. I hope my experience will put theirs into a sharper light.

Our collective experience also provides an interesting point of entry into the epistemological controversy about the nature of science—social science in particular—and how it proceeds. Our experiences help to illustrate what I call the psychology of discovery. This is a critical component of science that is undervalued and largely ignored by logical positivism and other "unity of science" approaches (Kratochwil 1995).

My chapter is divided into four parts. I begin with a short overview and critique of unity of science approaches. My argument highlights the need to study the life experiences of scientists to understand their research agendas, their theories, and, most important, how they frame problems. This will tell us a lot about how discoveries are made and the way in which science progresses.

In part two, I attempt such an analysis, using myself as a case study. I reconstruct my early life and analyze how family and environment shaped my political consciousness, which, filtered through my personality, led to a career in international relations with a focus on conflict management resolution. I show how my life experiences made me particularly receptive to psychological approaches that attempt to understand the causes and consequences of nonrational behavior.

Part three describes the remarkable rescue of one hundred Jewish children from occupied France in the summer of 1942 and how I learned, more than forty years later, that I might have been one of them. I analyze the consequences of this discovery for my identity and what it further reveals about the complex relationship between identity and professional commitment.

Finally, I return to the problem of science. I take up the question of the proper goals of social science and show how it can be both political in purpose and scientific in method. Using the experience and careers of my fellow panelists as a model, I argue for an approach to social science at odds with both unity of science and postmodernism.

The Psychology of Discovery

Philosophers of modern science have tried to rid science of any primordial influences and turn it into a set of true statements about the world. Logical positivism, and related conceptions, attempts to do this by directing attention to the logic of justification: the rules by which statements can be judged to be true. Sophisticated logical positivists acknowledge that ideas come from all over the place but do not consider their genesis important. Science is the process of validation.

Logical positivism misrepresents how science actually functions in two important ways. Working scientists rarely accept or reject propositions on the basis of formal rules; they do so with reference to practices and arguments that they and their colleagues find persuasive. This has led some philosophers to maintain that science is best understood as a "practice" whose expectations and norms of validation evolve over time.

Logical positivism and other unity of science approaches further assert that the progress of science is independent of the culture, life experiences, and personalities of scientists. Science responds to its own imperatives; previous discoveries unearth anomalies or open up promising lines of inquiry that are investigated by subsequent scientists. Many times this happens. But ideas that propel science to the next stage rarely grow out of existing science. Thomas Kuhn and others have shown how revolutions in science are triggered by fundamental shifts in gestalt that identify new problems and new kinds of solutions to them. To explain these gestalt shifts, one must go outside of science.

There are other compelling reasons for rejecting logical positivism's single-minded focus on the logic of justification. Even mundane science that builds on previous research is driven by creativity. To understand creativity, and, by extension, science, we need to develop a psychology of discovery.

The logic of justification cannot help us distinguish between crazy suggestions and creative ideas that may advance knowledge. This is a daunting but inescapable task. The scientific community continually makes decisions about which areas of inquiry or projects to fund or seek resources for and which researchers to hire, tenure, or promote. Such decisions reflect judgments about the fruitfulness of different paths of inquiry or the creativity of individual researchers. These decisions shape science; over time they move inquiry down one path as opposed to another. Surprisingly little research has been devoted to understanding how these decisions are made or whether the criteria on which they are based are appropriate.

Science reduced to the logic of justification will overvalue technicalities and formalization and will privilege research problems that generate easily validated but not necessarily significant propositions. It will also encourage tautologies, that is, systems of thought that can be true but uninformative. Rational choice is a striking example. It has been defined in a way that makes it unfalsifiable, and, I believe, has generated few novel insights or explanations. For the most part, it has restated existing understandings in a different language. It has nevertheless found disciples in many fields. A concept of science that focuses entirely on the logic of validation ultimately threatens to turn social science into a scholastic enterprise.

For all of these reasons the psychology of discovery needs to be recognized as a critical component of the practice and understanding of science. The first step in this direction is to acknowledge that the process that Kuhn calls "puzzle creation" is not the result of existential choice or random walks. It is conditioned by the values, life experiences, and personalities of scientists and the broader social and broader cultural setting in which they take shape.

A Case Study

My research on deterrence offers a minor but interesting illustration of the psychology of discovery. In the early 1970s, I embarked upon a study of international crisis. The impetus was the Cuban missile crisis and the threat of nuclear annihilation it raised. I wanted to know how such crises might be prevented or more safely managed. I put together a data set of acute twentieth-century crises and spent about a year reading the scholarly literature on crisis management and secondary accounts of individual crises. Much of this literature stressed the critical role of deterrence and compellence and argued that political-military challenges such as Czechoslovakia (1938), Korea (1950), and Cuba (1963) were due to the defender's failure to display adequate resolve. It attributed Kennedy's success in beating back challenges in Berlin and Cuba to the combination of military capability and resolve.

These explanations seemed to make sense, so I set out to ascertain why defenders had not shown adequate resolve and how committed defenders could more effectively communicate resolve. I gathered data on twenty-six crises and used them to determine the extent to which defenders had met the four requirements of deterrence: clearly defined, carefully communicated, defensible commitments backed by efforts to show resolve to defend them. My data were puzzling. Many seemingly credible commitments had been challenged.

I sought to resolve this apparent contradiction by taking a deeper look at the calculations of the challengers. I was able to identify three different kinds of crises. In the first two (justification of hostility and spin-off crises), leaders challenged adversarial commitments because they wanted war or sought an objective so critical that they were prepared to go to war to attain it. The failure of deterrence presented here was theoretically unproblematic. In the third and most common kind of crisis (brinkmanship), initiators did not want war; they sought political gains and fully expected their adversary to back down when challenged. In two-thirds of these cases the defender stood firm, and the initiator had to back down or fight an unintended war. This dramatic and unexpected finding compelled me—reluctantly at first—to question the efficacy of deterrence as a theory and strategy of conflict management.

I went back to my cases and found a striking pattern. In every brinkmanship crisis where the initiator had miscalculated its adversary's response, their leaders had framed the problem as one of loss avoidance. They had envisaged their challenge as a way to cope with a combination of grave domestic and foreign problems. Because they felt compelled to pursue a challenge, they rationalized the conditions for its success. Focused on their own problems and interests, they were correspondingly insensitive to the interests of their adversaries and efforts by the adversaries' leaders to signal resolve. Deterrence had been defeated by motivated bias. In some cases, deterrence had helped to provoke a challenge by aggravating the internal or foreign problems to which the initiators were responding.

My discoveries generated a research program that occupied my attention for the next decade (Lebow 1981; Jervis, Lebow, and Stein 1984; Lebow and Stein 1987). Much of this research was undertaken in collaboration with Janice Gross Stein. We have investigated the links between domestic problems and foreign policy, the motives and calculations behind political-military challenges, and the implications of these findings for theory building in psychology and political science. We have also explored the efficacy of alternative strategies of conflict management and the conditions in which they are appropriate. Our most recent joint publication, *We All Lost the Cold War* (1994), uses previously classified documents and interviews with former Soviet and U.S. policymakers to explore the consequences of deterrence and compellence during the Cold War.

The psychology of my discovery raises interesting questions. Conflict and its resolution have been the focus of my research for more than thirty years. My investigation of crisis was preceded by studies of ethnic conflict and divided nations and followed by work on how and why conflicts, international and internal, move away from violent confrontation. Why have I dedicated my professional life to such a depressing subject that brings me into contact with the worst and least rational side of human nature?

Many of my colleagues pursue theory as an end in itself. My research is theoretical but driven by real world problems. I want to develop theory that can serve as a guide for more enlightened and successful foreign policies. This is what brought me to the study of crisis. Why do I have no interest in model building and research that are unconnected to any broader social commitment?

The field of international relations, and social science more generally, is dominated by structural theories that assume rational actors with ordered preferences and understandings of their environment limited only by the information available. I am critical of these approaches. My research emphasizes the important, independent role of leaders. I believe they do more than respond to the constraints and opportunities of their environments. Foreign policies are significantly shaped by leaders' goals and mediated by their highly subjective, and often seriously flawed, understandings of context. They are constantly cross pressured and pushed toward difficult trade-offs. They frequently violate the norms of rationality, especially when it comes to decisions about war and peace. These beliefs grew out of my research but also reflect an earlier sensitivity and concern for the irrational. This sensitivity may have made me more receptive than other researchers to the anomalies of deterrence.

I believe there are compelling, scientific reasons for my theoretical orientation. But they do not explain why I see and respond to the world the way I do—or why rational choice theorists see it differently. Our contrasting orientations reflect our values, life experiences, and personalities. To understand my science, it is necessary to understand me.

New York, 1942–58

My parents were married in 1927 and unable to have children. For years they tried to adopt and finally succeeded when they received me in the fall of 1942. They adopted a second child, my brother, Robert, within weeks of his birth in New York City in October 1945. Beyond the assurance that my birth mother was Jewish the adoption agency provided no information. My parents told me that I had been seriously ill with an ulcerlike condition that had been improperly diagnosed and treated. They remembered that the adoption agency had named me David, the same name they had picked for a son. They promptly renamed me Richard, so I would be "theirs." My middle name, Ned, was after my mother's father, whom both my parents had adored.

On a conscious level my adoption was unproblematic. I never doubted that I was a wanted child or that my parents loved me and my younger brother as they would any biological children. We loved them in return. When I was old enough to make comparisons I realized that my parents were more nurturing and supportive than those of many of my friends. From time to time, somebody would remark that Rob (a blond, blue-eyed giant with the build of a linebacker) and I (with dark hair and eyes and neither as tall nor as solid) bore little resemblance to each other or to our petite parents. Rob or I would explain that we were adopted, and thus it became known to all our friends.

I can only remember a couple of occasions on which adoption came up in anything other than a positive way. The most dramatic incident involved a ninth grade English assignment. We had to write an autobiography, and I started with the story of my adoption. The teacher read my description aloud to the class and asked why I had invented the story. Didn't I know that adopted children grew up disturbed and many became criminals? Why would I want to invent such a tale? I was more amazed than angered. My cousin Steve, not adopted, was my classmate and furious, and he gave the teacher a tongue-lashing. We were both sent to the principal's office. Our parents, summoned to school, explained that we had told the truth and pressed the somewhat chagrined principal for an apology.

During early adolescence some of my friends went through a period of wondering if they had been adopted but never told by their parents. I reassured several of them that their concern was probably misplaced but that if they were adopted it was something to be proud of. At around this age I began to have fantasies of my own. Knowing nothing about my origins I could give free rein to my creativity. Most of these fantasies revolved around the Holocaust, with hard-pressed parents fleeing the Nazis making the wrenching decision to save their son by handing him over to the underground or some other agent of mercy. I was the son of a famous German-Jewish physicist or Viennese conductor. My favorite variant was French. I was the scion of Rothschilds who had been smuggled out of the country by faithful family retainers. After the war, the Rothschilds hired France's foremost detective to track me down and restore me to my rightful patrimony. I waited impatiently to be liberated from the ennui of 1950s suburbia. Years later I realized the Rothschilds must have entrusted this all-important task to Inspector Jacques Clouseau.

On one level, these fantasies, like those of my friends, helped to cope with the stress of adolescence. They resurfaced in my late twenties, after the breakup of my first marriage, another difficult time in my life. Even as an adolescent, it occurred to me that the fantasies also addressed a deeper psychological need. Why else would I occasionally pass them off as the truth to my friends? Already the budding social scientist, I considered several hypotheses.

The Rothschild, nuclear physicist, conductor aspect of the fantasies posed no analytical challenge. Like that of many adolescents, my self-esteem was woefully low, and here was an effective and harmless way of giving it a quick boost. The most obvious explanation that occurred to me for the fantasies as a whole was legitimization. Many, if not most, adopted children are born out of wedlock and in former times carried the stigma of being called bastards. I had a great-aunt who referred to me as such, although never to my face, and I only found out about it years later and that it had caused a rupture with my parents. It is hard to probe one's psyche, but when I did, the motive of legitimization did not strike me as compelling. The possibility that I might have been conceived in a spasm of illicit passion, in the backseat of a car or in a hotel room, I found more exciting than troubling. After all, I was desperately trying to get a little action of this kind myself. I could readily imagine the scene: a GI, his unit about to be shipped off to England, spending his last leave with his girl in New York, taking her dancing at Birdland and afterward . . .

My parents represented two strands of U.S. Jewish life. My father,

Joseph, was born in 1902 or 1903. The Social Security Administration records show 1902, but Dad, who was robust and in full command of his mental facilities until he died in the summer of 1998, insisted that it was 1903. He saw first light in either Minsk or New York. His parents died when he was young, and his three older sisters could never agree among themselves whether he was born before or after they left Russia. The Brooklyn courthouse that might have resolved the controversy burned down many decades ago, and its records were lost. Uncertainty about origins seems to run in the family.

As a child my father lived from hand to mouth and until recently was very reluctant to talk about this painful and emotionally barren part of his life. He supported himself by selling apples from a pushcart and worked in a cigar store, as a bellhop, and, during World War I, as part of a riveting team in the Fore River Shipyard south of Boston, where he built destroyers for the British navy. He started at the bottom of the riveting ladder as the coke heater and progressed through rivet transporter to rivet thrower to the man on the deck who caught the red hot rivet in a cone and held it in place for the riveter.

After the war, my father took evening courses to develop his considerable artistic talent. His confidence buoyed and credentials in hand he answered several ads in New York papers for commercial artists. He had several interviews but was rejected because he was Jewish. He persevered and was finally hired by the Manhattan Shirt Company. He had made it into the middle class.

My mother, Ruth, who died at age eighty-six, was born into a German-Jewish family that had come to the United States early in the nineteenth century. When Napoleon's armies tore down the ghetto walls of Baden-Baden, young Abraham and Sarah took advantage of their freedom to set out for the New World. Their offspring prospered. One son accompanied Frémont's expedition to California; Frémont had sought a Hebrew speaker in expectation of discovering the Ten Lost Tribes. Two grandsons served in the Civil War—on opposite sides—and survived desperate combat between their regiments at Bloody Angle at Gettysburg. The Union veteran, my mother's maternal grandfather, speculated in New York real estate, sired thirteen children, and built an elegant townhouse on the upper East Side. He lost his money and house in the crash of 1893.

My mother, raised in genteel poverty in Jamaica, Queens, regaled us with stories about this stern patriarch and his family. She was a capable student and was admitted to Hunter High School, one of New York City's most select secondary educational institutions. After graduation, her parents urged her to go to teacher's college, but she went to work instead—as my father's secretary at the Manhattan Shirt Company. Dad was immediately smitten by this dark, buxom beauty and wooed her with love letters mailed in hand painted envelopes depicting events in "Rufie's" life. The flow of handmade cards and announcements was unremitting for the next sixty-six years and commemorated birthdays, anniversaries, and other joyous occasions in their love-filled and uncommonly cordial relationship.

My father was also taken with my mother's parents, Ned and Estelle Newman, who provided him with the parental love and attention he had so sorely missed as a child. He joined the family and adopted their religious, political, and social values. In the 1920s, the religious and social ill will between German-American Jews and their eastern European cousins was still great. German Jews were assimilated and relatively well off, and, to the extent that they practiced their religion, they did so in Reformed synagogues where services were conducted largely in English and often accompanied by organ and choir. The two communities were further divided by politics. Jews from the Russian Empire brought with them their Zionism and socialism. German-American Jews were overwhelmingly Republican and regarded Zionism and its commitment to the restoration of Israel as grist for the mill of anti-Semites who described Jews as undesirable, unassimilable, and un-American.

The Newmans belonged to Rabbi Stephen Wise's Free Synagogue but do not seem to have been active members. Their religion posed no problem for my father. He had an Orthodox upbringing but never felt drawn to religion. When his father died, he sat shivah for the requisite period of time and for many years afterward never set foot in synagogue. My parents did not hide their origins and made me aware of my Jewish identity at a very young age.

I may have been Jewish, but I was not raised in a Jewish home. We did not celebrate the Sabbath, nor, until my teenage years, did we have a Passover seder. We had a Christmas tree and exchanged Christmas presents. When I turned ten, my parents joined a synagogue, enrolled me in Hebrew school, and later sent me to bar mitzvah lessons. I thought the whole business hypocritical and suspected that my parents forced this ordeal on me to maintain their social standing in the Jewish community. I practiced passive resistance until Jerome, my mother's more sophisticated brother, took me aside to explain what he thought was going on. When my father had turned thirteen and been bar mitzvah, he had no family with whom to share this *mechiah* (blessing). He went by himself with a bottle of wine to a storefront synagogue and was called to the Torah. For much of his adult life he fantasized about having a son or sons who would be bar mitzvah in the presence of proud parents, other relatives, and friends.

My mother disapproved of the Zionism and the Democratic politics of our neighbors. My father had somehow convinced her to vote for Roosevelt, which she did four times, but both then voted for Dewey and Eisenhower. I threatened to disown them if they voted for Nixon, and suitably chastised, they returned to the Democratic fold in 1960. My father never felt threatened by Zionism, or shared my mother's embarrassment at hearing someone speak with even the slightest Yiddish inflection. Poma, as we later called her, was seriously concerned that I would pick up the local patois and pronounce "Long Island" as one slurred word with the emphasis on the *G*.

To explain my Jewish identity, interest in the Holocaust, and subsequent career in international relations we also need to look outside my home. My formative years were spent in Forest Hills, Queens, in a middle–middle class neighborhood of newly built row houses and red brick apartments. There were also farms that had been granted a temporary stay of execution by the halt in housing construction imposed by the war. The hub of my existence was our block. It consisted of two rows of compact two-story row houses with driveways in the middle of the block leading down to alleys where residents could park their cars. A vacant lot stood at the top of our side of the block and served as a communal playground and victory garden. Every afternoon mothers gathered on the benches, and we children played in and around a sandbox. On weekends, our fathers tended the garden and cleared it of ever encroaching "fascist weeds."

My neighbors were first generation Americans and immigrants. Most of the latter had fled the Nazis, fascists, communists, or two of the three in the case of one Polish family. Our immediate neighbors, the Bodenheimers, came from a small town near Basel, on the German-Swiss border, and had made it to the United States on the eve of the war. Their teenage son, Burt, my baby-sitter and idol, told me how their Swiss teacher—Burt and his sister were not allowed to attend a German school—conspired with their parents to get some of their assets out of the country. Every so often their parents put gold and money inside a hollowed out schoolbook that Burt or Inge would carry across the border past mocking but generally lax guards. Another contemporary, from

Genoa, had a more dramatic story. The boat his family had come over on had been torpedoed, and they were adrift in a lifeboat for almost a day before being picked up by a destroyer. His proudest possession was a patch given to him by one of the ship's officers.

The war was omnipresent. Every night there was a blackout, and we drew oilskin curtains over the windows to hide the city from German bombers that never came. My father was a block warden and often carried me on his shoulders when he made his evening rounds. I "contributed" to the war effort by following the bigger children around with my little wagon to help collect scrap metal, tin cans, and other recyclables. I had a large bulletin board in my room with photographs of the Brooklyn Dodgers on one side and a map of Europe on the other. After D day, Dad and I used colored pins to mark the progress of the Allied armies in France, Italy, and eastern Europe as they closed in on the Third Reich.

On occasional weekends, my father would use some of his precious gasoline ration to drive us down the hill to what is now La Guardia airport to watch the military aircraft. I knew them all—I even had spotter charts for German warplanes—and was thrilled by the sight of sleek, twin-engine P-38's taking off to fly cover for convoys. Sometimes we would venture further afield to lower Manhattan to watch merchantmen, flying flags from all over the world, take on cargo or slip out of their berths to join a convoy forming off Sandy Hook or Coney Island. My most dramatic memory is of watching, again from my perch on Dad's shoulder, as part of a large and silent crowd, the *Benjamin Franklin*—the fuselage and tail of a "Zeke" still protruding from its superstructure—escorted up the East River by a fleet of tugs. The carrier had been pummeled by kamikaze at Leyte Gulf but somehow limped back to Pearl Harbor. The San Diego Navy Yard, where it had been sent for repairs, had admitted defeat, announcing that this was a job that only the Brooklyn Yard could do. We New Yorkers were very proud.

On our block the Pacific War was a sideshow. The real fight was against the Nazis. Their conquests and atrocities affected our lives directly. Many block residents worried about family in Europe, and Jews were particularly anxious as stories began to filter in about the death camps. Many of the men on the block had been deferred from military service on the grounds of age, like my father, or because they worked in vital war industries. Most of their children were too young to serve. There were exceptions, among them two brothers from a German Catholic immigrant family. One of them had been shot down on a bombing mission over Europe. In May 1945, a staff car pulled up to their house across the street, and an officer got out, rang the family's bell, and disappeared into the house. My mother and I observed the scene from a second-story window. She gripped my arm more tightly when the officer emerged and drove off. Moments later, our neighbor came out of the house screaming. My mother ran out to console her and discovered that she was crying from joy; her son had been liberated from a German stalag, was in good health, and had been given the highest priority for transport home. A couple of days later, at the block VE Day party, I was more rambunctious than usual and cadged sips of beer from celebrants' mugs until, blotto, I collapsed into my father's arms.

I was not yet four when the war ended. The fact that I remember so much is indicative of the enormous impact it had on me. Much of the impact was psychological. I knew the Nazis were evil and out to get me because I was Jewish. It made no sense. I was a nice boy; my parents were wonderful people; and we were no different from anybody else on the block. And as far as I could detect, nobody on the block treated us any differently. Why did a whole group of people hate us so much that they wanted to kill us? One afternoon, Burt and I listened to a speech—I think it was by Goebbels—on a shortwave radio. I did not understand a word, and even Burt, a native German speaker, had some difficulty because of the crackle, static, and periodic fading of the signal. But I did not have to understand German to feel the passion and hatred. It was frightening and irrational.

My understanding of the concept of irrationality could not have been very developed at the time—I doubt I even knew the word. But the radio broadcast, and the broader enigma posed by Nazi Germany, brought home the realization that grownups, and, worse still, those in positions of authority, could behave in crazy ways. I may have concluded, although I have no direct recollection of this, that to understand the Nazis and, more important, to protect myself, I needed to know more about this kind of behavior.

My interest in irrationality—and fear of it—was reinforced by another incident. On Sunday, April 12, 1945, I was in the car with both my parents, returning from yet another visit to the airport. My father had turned on the radio so I could listen to *Daniel Boone,* one of my favorite programs. Before the episode even began it was interrupted by a special news bulletin. President Roosevelt had suffered a stroke in Warm Springs, Georgia. Shortly afterward, the announcer informed us of his death. My parents were stunned, and they were not alone. Cars all along the Grand Central Parkway began to pull over to the grassy sward along the side of the road. We followed suit, and I watched as people climbed out, their radios blaring, to seek solace in one another's company. In the eyes of a three year old, it was a disturbing scene. People were sobbing, hugging one another, or perched on their running boards listening to the latest bulletins. The adults to whom I looked for guidance and protection were utterly confused and at a loss to know what to do.

These events aside, I felt secure personally. I knew that the United States was strong and Germany far away. My father and Burt had assured me that the blackouts were just a precaution. I had a vivid sense of what bombings could do. One of my friends, Allen, had survived the London blitz and had a badly scarred face from burns he had incurred when his house and block had been hit by incendiaries. Another, a slightly older Estonian boy, dived under a table, or whatever was handy, whenever he heard a loud noise. He lay there trembling and had to be coaxed out gently.

Subconsciously I felt less secure. One morning I awoke early with the Nazis on my mind—I do not remember if it was before or after listening to Goebbels. I sat on the floor and drew pictures of swastikas and Iron Crosses and hid all the drawings behind my bed. The incident, long forgotten, came back to mind in college in the course of reading a monograph about an African village in which the residents exorcised the power of threatening and evil spirits by hiding representations of them in a cave.

If the war aroused interest and insecurity, the immediate postwar years provoked interest and guilt. The interest requires no special explanation. These were event-filled years, and I was an avid newspaper reader, the *Herald Tribune* in the morning and the *Telegram* or *PM* in the afternoon. I was also an addict of *Movietone News,* which I saw on Saturday mornings at the local movie theater between episodes of *Flash Gordon, Don Winslow of the Navy,* and other riveting serials. I was fascinated by the Nuremberg proceedings, the beginning of the cold war, and the Berlin blockade and airlift. But what really engaged my attention was the founding of Israel, its ingathering of refugees, and its courageous struggle for survival during the War of Independence. To my mother's consternation, I helped my friend Penny, on whom I had a desperate crush, and her older sister, Susan, the real organizer of our effort, to sell "shekels" to raise money for Israel.

The guilt was more complicated. The newspapers carried stories and photographs of liberated concentration and death camps. The newsreels had more graphic footage. Later, in the 1950s, I watched television documentaries and read diaries, such as those of William Shirer, and more scholarly analyses, not only of the Final Solution but of the whole Nazi saga. I also encountered survivors, some of whom began to trickle into our neighborhood after the war. One of my school bus drivers had numbers tattooed on his arm, and I would cast furtive glances at them.

Six million Jews had been killed, and a disproportionate percentage of them had been children. The numbers were overwhelming but did not have the emotional impact of individual stories. I was deeply moved by the *Diary of Anne Frank* and even more by the Broadway play, to which my parents took me. I contrasted my fate with Anne Frank's and with that of all the other children who had been slaughtered. I belonged to that extraordinarily fortunate minority of Jewish children who had survived the war.

I had not only survived, I had lived well. There had been rationing, and meat and dairy products had been in short supply. But we had been less affected than many urban dwellers because my mother's brother Jerome, a master sergeant in the Quartermaster Corps, worked in the Reading Market in Philadelphia and brought hard-to-find foods to us on his frequent furloughs. My parents were also aware of their good fortune and grateful to the United States and Jerome. One of the few times my father really lost his temper with me—that is, before I became a teenager—was over a glass of freshly squeezed orange juice that I absolutely refused to drink because of all the "disgusting" pulp in the glass. I had never seen oranges before, and Jerome had brought us a few as a special treat. My father squeezed them with great care and was furious when I grimaced and pushed away the glass. I got a stern lecture on how lucky I was in contrast to all the starving children of Europe.

Emotions are hard to reconstruct, especially those of childhood, and it is almost impossible to pinpoint their origins unless there are well-remembered triggering events. My guilt took shape only slowly, in response to numerous external stimuli, some of which I have described, and all of which were refracted through my hyperactive intellect. My guilt sneaked up on me, and I was not really aware of it until later in life. In retrospect, I can only reconstruct it through its manifestations and offer an explanation that I find emotionally and intellectually convincing.

The fundamental cause of my guilt was my survival. Millions of Jewish children had been butchered while I refused to drink orange juice with pulp and slept soundly every night in my comfortable bed. I knew about the war and Hitler's persecutions, although not about the death camps, and had treated the war as an amusement and a sporting event. I got a big thrill out of watching convoys and warplanes and never really considered the unpleasant truth that all the sailors and pilots were risking, and sometimes losing, their lives to protect me and other civilians. I knew that more was at stake than a pennant or flag but rooted for the Allies, the "home team," the way I did for the Brooklyn Dodgers.

I was not just any child, but an adopted child, plucked from his sickbed in an orphanage by two loving and caring parents. This made the comparison to the Jewish children of Europe all the more striking. What had I done to deserve this extraordinary good fortune? Nothing that I could think of. Here was the source of my guilt.

It is often said that a little knowledge is dangerous. For my age I knew a lot about the wider world, perhaps too much, and lacked the experience and maturity to make reasonable sense of all this information. It was obviously ridiculous to feel guilt about whatever pleasure I derived from the war; no sheltered three year old could be expected to have anything like an adult understanding of war. Adoption was also nothing to feel guilty about; my parents wanted me as much as I needed them. But then identities are rarely built on rational foundations.

My guilt may explain my Holocaust associations. My adolescent fantasies did more than buttress my self-esteem; they may have been a primitive attempt to address my guilt through direct identification with the victims who lay at its root. By assuming their identity, and, by extension, their burdens, I could try to lay mine to rest.

A child who constructs an identity for himself as a survivor unwittingly assumes a heavy burden. Like many real survivors, he may feel the need to live life not only for himself but for others who did not have the opportunity. This can take many different forms. In my case, it may be reflected in my optimism and drive to enjoy life to the fullest extent possible within the confines of the law, morality, and, I would like to think, good taste.

More important for our purposes, this identity has also led to a commitment to justify survival by making a contribution to society. Given my early interest in World War II, and its consequences for my identity, the choice was obvious. I would study the causes of ethnic conflict and war and what could be done to alleviate and prevent them. If such knowledge were put to good use, it might prevent another generation of children from becoming victims of prejudice and hatred. I would also learn something about myself in the process.

When I was very young I wanted to be a baseball player or a crooning cowboy. At about the age of eleven, I developed what would become an enduring interest in physics, especially cosmology. The latter was romantic, challenged the imagination, and addressed fundamental questions of the universe. It was—I hesitate to say—concerned with origins. Alas, my skills in all these areas, except perhaps baseball, were pedestrian. My younger brother would scream for me to stop whenever I sang in the shower. But lack of talent was not the decisive consideration. My interest in World War II and conflict in general had deepened and led me to read widely in European and Jewish history. Certainly by the age of thirteen I knew I was going to be a social scientist. Physics was interesting, but so was social science, and, more important, it addressed my personal responsibility in a way that physical science did not.

My career has more or less followed the course I charted as an adolescent. My research has focused on the origins of war and ethnic conflict and on strategies for preventing, containing, and ameliorating them. Not surprisingly, it has emphasized the nonrational elements of human behavior and sought to build bridges between history and political science and between both of them and psychology. My current research examines why some international and ethnic conflicts move away from violent confrontation. The small contribution I have made to understanding these problems is a source of satisfaction and an incentive to continue my research. I nevertheless feel frustrated by the fact that knowledge about conflict and its causes seems only rarely to lead to more enlightened policies. But that is another story.

Paris, 1942

At 4 A.M. on July 16, 1942 (*Jeudi noir*—Black Thursday), Paris police raided apartments and houses in and around the city in an attempt to arrest 27,388 Jewish immigrants from Germany, eastern Europe, and the Soviet Union. Many of the 12,884 Jews who were actually arrested were sent to Drancy for subsequent deportation to Auschwitz. Children and adults with children were held at the Vélodrome d'Hiver, a glass-covered sports stadium in the fifteenth arrondissement. More than 8,000 people were crowded into the inadequately ventilated and suffocatingly hot stadium and fed only soup supplied by the Red Cross and Quakers. The water in the sinks had been turned off, and the available toilets promptly jammed. Survivors, and there were only a few, remember an unbearable stench, constant noise, and a complete lack of privacy.

The police had their hands full. Few Jews had illusions about their fate even before they were marched out of the Vél d'Hiv to a nearby rail siding for transport to Auschwitz in rank cattle cars. One woman went berserk and was handcuffed to a stretcher. There were several suicides, and one mother tried to kill her child with a broken bottle. Another lacerated her son's veins. Some of the police were sickened by the scene of wailing mothers, screaming children, and baton-wielding police. In defiance of orders, one contingent managed somehow to protect a handful of young children, including a several-month-old baby. That baby may have been me.

The police handed the children over to a group of well-placed, French-born Jewish women who banded together to provide refuge for them and other, mostly older, children who had escaped the roundup. Native French Jews remained at liberty until November 1943 but risked their lives by hiding "foreign" Jews marked for deportation. One of the women rescuers, Paulette Fink, was the daughter of the chief rabbi of France and mother of two young girls. Her husband, a reserve officer, was a prisoner of war, as were the husbands of several of the other women she mobilized to care for what were now almost one hundred children.

Madame Fink and her friends knew that it was only a matter of time before they were discovered by the *Milice* (the national police). Something had to be done to get the children out of Paris and, better yet, out of France. A priest known to one of the women offered to hide them temporarily in his village. He told his parishioners that it was their Christian responsibility to protect the children, and they did so for several weeks under the nose of Nazi occupation forces. Everybody in the village knew what was going on and kept quiet.

Madame Fink had made contact with the Zionist underground and sought to enlist them in her scheme to send the children to the United States. The Zionists were initially hostile to the idea; Jewish children should go to Palestine. This was impossible in 1942, and the Zionists finally agreed to smuggle as many of the children as possible out of France. They set up two escape routes, both of them via Vichy, the unoccupied part of France governed by the collaborationist regime of Marshal Pétain. The first group went south to Marseilles, by boat to the Algerian port of Oran, by train to Tangier, across the Strait of Gibraltar by ferry, and by train again to Lisbon. The second group went south to Bordeaux, where Aristides de Sousa Mendes, the Portuguese consul, provided passports to Jewish refugees. He continued to do so until German pressure led Lisbon to recall and expel him from the foreign service. From Bordeaux, the group went to Biarritz and then over the Pyrenees at night into Spain. Once in Spain, everyone could breathe freely and without subterfuge board a train for Lisbon.

The capital of neutral Portugal, Lisbon was filled with refugees seeking transit to the new world. Visas and berths were hard to come by, and there was a thriving black market in both commodities. Once again the children were lucky. A U.S. Jewish group, contacted by Madame Fink, made arrangements to bring everyone to the United States. They somehow managed to get a Liberty ship to stop in Lisbon on its return trip from Britain. The children crowded into the holds and slept on hammocks slung between cases of Johnny Walker whiskey that the British, desperate for hard currency, were exporting to the States in the form of ballast. It is conceivable that one of the destroyers my father built—they saw service in both wars—escorted the convoy through the submarine-infested waters of the North Atlantic.

The ship and its convoy reached New York harbor without incident. Its human cargo was unloaded at night while compliant immigration officials looked the other way. Illegal immigrants all, the children were rushed off to orphanages and foster homes throughout the metropolitan area. In due course, they were adopted by U.S. Jewish families.

Back in France, Madame Fink and her colleagues continued their efforts to protect children, an extraordinarily difficult operation after French Jews began to be rounded up and sent off to death camps. By the war's end, they were still at work and had saved almost eight thousand Jewish children, most of whom were placed with Catholic families or institutions in France as it was no longer feasible to smuggle children out of the country. Madame Fink's husband escaped from his prison camp and joined the resistance but was captured and killed by the Nazis.

Identity Reconsidered

What an irony to construct an identity as a Holocaust survivor and then to find out years later that you may actually be one. This is a plot line worthy of Dickens or da Ponte!

In *Le Nozze di Figaro*, Figaro is saved from marrying his mother, reunited with Susannah, and lifted from his station as a servant by the discovery of a birthmark. Nothing quite so dramatic happened to me, but the catalyst for my discovery was a birthmark of sorts. I met Madame Fink in Palm Springs, California, and over drinks and dinner listened to her describe her efforts to rescue children during the war and her subsequent difficulties in reclaiming many of them from the Catholic orphanages or homes where they had been stashed. I was naturally intrigued by her account of how she and her friends had managed to arrange the escape of a group of children from France in the summer of 1942.

No possible personal connection crossed my mind until she mentioned the name of the U.S. group and adoption agency who had helped to arrange the passage and subsequently placed the children with U.S. parents. It was my adoption agency. The timing was about right too. When I told the story to my parents, my mother told me that the agency had no children at all in 1941 and much of 1942. Then they received an unexpected call announcing that children were available and that they would be allowed to choose one from among them. My mother further remembered that some of the youngsters they met were older and spoke languages other than English. Former social workers I subsequently spoke to confirmed that the agency laundered a group of Jewish children from France and provided their adoptive parents with cover stories about their origins.

The circumstantial evidence seems compelling, but there is no way of ascertaining if I was indeed one of these children. For obvious reasons no official records were kept. The French Jews who arranged the rescue—I have spoken to several of them—had more reason not to keep records. Not that records would do any good, as the *flics* who saved the infant would not have had a clue about the mother's identity, although one of them might have remembered if there were any siblings.

My encounter with Madame Fink and other participants in the rescue operation has affected me deeply. I am awed by their courage, selflessness, and collective accomplishment. That all these people, many of them not even Jewish, would risk their lives or careers for children with whom they had no personal connection says something wonderful about the human capacity for empathy and altruism. Their actions seem especially poignant against the contemporary backdrops of Yugoslavia, Burundi, Rwanda, and Zaire. One can only hope that similar stories of protection and rescue from these horrendous conflicts will come to light in due course.

The consequences of the saga for me personally were more difficult to assess. I was certainly receptive to the possibility that I was the baby tossed to the *flic*. It was a wonderfully dramatic saga, at least as good as any of my teenage fantasies. It also reinforced my long-standing identity as a Holocaust survivor. Upon investigation, I recognized that I could never establish with any certainty my connection to these events. I also realized that the truth of the matter is inconsequential. My identity and my feelings about it are independent of whether I crossed the Atlantic or merely the East River in 1942. They require no escape from the Nazis to legitimize them.

Madame Fink and her associates undeniably played a role in my liberation but not necessarily the role they or I first envisaged. Their story was a catalyst for me to think more deeply about my identity and its origins. I replayed my childhood experiences and emotions and came to understand more fully the reasons why the Holocaust was so central to my identity. I no longer feel guilt about surviving—whether in Paris or New York—but retain an undiminished commitment to contribute to the general welfare through my research and writing. I also realized that this commitment long ago freed itself from whatever guilt-driven origins it might have had and endures for more compelling and adult reasons. If it turns out that I was born in France my identity will have come full circle, but in the intervening decades I have moved on.

Social Science and the World

Writing this chapter has not been easy. The joy of liberation from footnotes has been more than offset by the challenge of personal introspection. I am ambivalent about making the chapter public. I am not a psychological exhibitionist; I get no kick from displaying my psyche before an audience. Quite the reverse. Why then did I accept the assignment?

I did so for personal and professional reasons. The personal reasons should by now be obvious. Writing the chapter offered me an opportunity to work through more fully the sources of my identity and how they influenced my commitment to social science. Thirty years of teaching have taught me that you only really come to understand something when you have to lecture or, better yet, write about it.

A second reason, personal and professional, was Peter Suedfeld's worthy premise. Studies of Holocaust survivors and their children have invariably stressed the emotional scars of that experience and the behavioral pathologies and coping difficulties it engenders. Trauma can also serve as a catalyst for creativity and commitment, as indeed the Holocaust has for all of the authors and for many other survivors who have pursued productive lives in a variety of professions. It is essential to document this response and, by doing so, acknowledge and reaffirm the remarkable potential of human beings to fashion hope and good works out of the detritus of evil and destruction. Finally, I hoped I could exploit my life experience to reflect upon the nature and purpose of social science. I began this chapter with a broadside against logical positivism and other unity of science conceptions for their exclusive focus on the logic of justification and total disregard of the psychology of discovery. I want to extend my criticism to postmodernism and argue that both kinds of approaches constitute serious threats to science.

Unity of science's pretension that objective social science can produce universal laws and generalizations has always struck me as absurd. Social understanding is inherently subjective. Research agendas, theories, and methods are conditioned by culture, beliefs, and life experiences. So too is receptivity to research findings. Recognition of this truth has led postmodernists to interpret science as a political process and cloak for individual and group claims to privilege. This view of science is equally flawed because it ignores the barriers erected by the scientific method against theories and propositions that cannot be falsified or are demonstrably false.

The scientific method does not always prevail over politics and prejudice. The problem is sometimes the scientists themselves. Nineteenth-century biological and anthropological studies of cranial capacity "proved" the superiority of the Caucasian "race." Some contemporary researchers are still trying to do this with data from intelligence tests. Well-founded scientific claims can also encounter resistance from the wider community. The theory of evolution continues to provoke widespread opposition from fundamentalist Christians. Claims by medical researchers that smoking is harmful, and, more recently, by environmental scientists that the waste products of industrial society threaten an irreversible transformation of the environment, have encountered predictable opposition from industries with profits at stake. The tobacco companies and some major polluters support scientists who dispute these claims.

The scientific method is also a subject of controversy. Positivists contend that propositions must be carefully specified and empirically falsifiable and be derived from, or assist in building, theories that explain and predict. They argue over what constitutes adequate specification and testing and even more about the nature and goals of scientific theory. Attempts to provide definitive answers to these questions, like those of Karl Popper, inevitably fail and risk substituting dogma for the ongoing questioning, inquiry, and debate that constitute the core commitment of science. These controversies render scientific truth uncertain, but working scientists, invoking the techniques and skills they have learned, generally have little difficulty in distinguishing good from bad science.

The scientific method in many ways resembles the Bill of Rights of the U.S. Constitution. Its meaning is also best interpreted through practice. Like the scientific method, it has not always been interpreted or applied fairly. The Bill of Rights has sometimes failed to protect political, religious, and so-called racial minorities from the ravages of prejudice. In 1898, *Plessy v. Ferguson* established the principle of separate and equal education for African Americans that endured until *Brown v. Board of Education of Topeka* in 1954. De facto segregated education continues to this day in some locales. The Supreme Court decision in *Brown v. Board of Education* reflected changing attitudes toward African Americans and the Constitution itself. Another impetus was extensive social science research that demonstrated that separate education was inherently unequal. Despite continuous controversy about the meaning of the Constitution and periodic failures to apply its principles in practice, there is an overwhelming consensus that the Bill of Rights remains the most important guarantee of individual freedoms. The scientific method is an imperfect but essential bulwark against many of the same kinds of passions.

There is an important distinction to be made in science between the questions we ask and the ways in which we answer them. What distinguishes us from ideologues is our commitment to finding and evaluating answers by means of the scientific method. Our research agendas, especially those of social scientists, are shaped by political beliefs, life experiences, and desires for professional recognition. There is nothing wrong with these motives. Good social science should be motivated by personal involvement in the burning issues of the day. Research can clarify these issues, put new issues on the agenda, and propose and evaluate the consequences of different responses. It can also influence the way people conceive of themselves, frame problems, and relate to the social order.

Positivism and other unity of science approaches would make social science sterile in its search for passionless, abstract truths and discourage interest in policy-related research. Postmodernism would make social science irrelevant by its rejection of the scientific method and insistence that all "readings" of texts and the world at large have equal standing. Social scientists need to confront both of these dangers by reaffirming and explaining their twin commitments to social progress and the scientific method. The links between ourselves and our research do not undercut our claim to be practicing science; they make us better scientists and better human beings.

REFERENCES

Green, D. P., and I. Shapiro. 1994. *Pathologies of rational choice.* New Haven: Yale University Press.

Jervis, R., R. N. Lebow, and J. G. Stein. 1984. *Psychology and deterrence.* Baltimore: Johns Hopkins University Press.

Kratochwil, F. 1988. Regimes, interpretation, and the "science" of politics. *Millennium* 17 (summer): 263–84.

———. 1995. Why Sisyphus is happy: Reflections on the "Third Debate" and on theorizing as a vocation. *Sejong Review* 3 (November): 3–36.

Kuhn, T. S. 1962. *The structure of scientific revolutions.* Chicago: University of Chicago Press.

Lebow, R. N. 1981. *Between peace and war: The nature of international crisis.* Baltimore: Johns Hopkins University Press.

Lebow, R. N., and J. G. Stein. 1987. *Journal of Social Issues* 43, no. 4. Special issue, Beyond deterrence.

———. 1994. *We all lost the cold war.* Princeton: Princeton University Press.

March, J. G., and J. P. Olson. 1988. *Rediscovering institutions,* 77–78. New York: Free Press.

Rouse, J. 1987. *Knowledge and power: Toward a political philosophy of science.* Ithaca: Cornell University Press.

Zuccotti, S. 1993. *The Holocaust, the French, and the Jews.* New York: Basic Books.

Linking the Present and the Past

A Personal Story

Gerda Lederer

Biographical Note

Gerda Lederer was born in Vienna in 1926 and emigrated to the United States in 1939 after a year in Paris. She earned degrees in physics and mathematics from New York University (NYU) in 1947 and in mathematics education from NYU in 1967 and a doctorate in sociology and comparative international education from Columbia University in 1980. She has taught mathematics in high schools and colleges in the United States and in Germany and since 1978 has been engaged in an international comparative study of authoritarianism among adolescents. Her research has been published in numerous books and journals in both countries and both languages.

She has been a member of the International Society of Political Psychology since its founding in 1978, has held offices including the vice presidentship, and was the first recipient of the Society's Erik Erikson Award for distinguished early-career contributions to the field. Since 1987, she has taught courses in political and social psychology at universities in Germany and the United States. She is currently teaching courses in political psychology in the classroom and on the Internet for the New School University, formerly The New School for Social

Research. She has pioneered a program of cross-cultural Internet teaching, bringing together students and teachers from abroad and from the United States in the virtual classroom.

⟹•⟸

Introduction

In the course of one of the many films containing interviews with Holocaust survivors (*We Were So Beloved,* written and produced by Manfred Kircheimer), a man looks back at his childhood in the German countryside and recalls that he admired and envied the German SS men he saw, handsome and trim in their shiny black boots and their tailored uniforms. He was then a boy of eight, and his envy had been his guilty secret.

This episode made me look back at my own feelings, in Vienna in March 1938. That spring I turned twelve, Hitler's army marched into Austria, and the democratic state of Austria became part of Germany's Third Reich. Had I perhaps also been a little envious of the people whom this event made so happy, perhaps unwilling to admit these feelings even to myself? I wrote in my diary that I was glad that I was among the persecuted; had I not been among them, I feared that I would have been among the others. Those others were elated; they seemed to be in a joyous trance. There must have been some who were apprehensive, but I was not aware of them at the time. I pondered a poem by Goethe that an older friend had written into my leather-bound autograph album.

> *Du musst steigen oder sinken,*
> *Du musst herrschen und gewinnen,*
> *Oder dienen und verlieren,*
> *Leiden oder triumphieren,*
> *Amboss oder Hammer sein.*

> [You must rise or fall,
> Reign and win,
> Or serve and lose,
> Suffer or triumph,
> Be anvil or hammer.]

(my translation)

Were those really the only alternatives?

Background and Childhood in Vienna, 1926–38

My parents did not discuss politics with my sister and myself. Most families I knew wanted to protect their children and keep "the dirty business of politics" from them as long as possible.

My father, born in Vienna in 1889, was a Jewish Austrian (not an Austrian Jew). He loved Austria, especially Vienna. He felt close to Emperor Franz Joseph (1830–1916), who passed my father's retail store and residence on Mariahilferstrasse when he made his way in the royal coach each morning from Schloss Schoenbrunn on the outskirts of Vienna to the Hofburg in Vienna's center. My father told me that he, along with many others, would stand in the street and watch the emperor's carriage go by. As my father would have it, they greeted each other. In fact, Emperor Franz Joseph was a friend of the Jews of Vienna.

I think my father was conservative and not politically involved. He had been a soldier in World War I and was proud of it, and he loved Austria. And my mother thought whatever my father thought or at least never mentioned it to me if she had a different opinion. She was a businesswoman, which was unusual for a woman of her circumstances. She loved life, and she loved music. She played the piano; she sang well and often; and I thought her very pretty.

In July 1934 an event of such proportions shook Austria that it imprinted itself on my memory. Chancellor Dollfuss was assassinated. I had to think of that event when John F. Kennedy was shot in 1963. My youngest daughter was then about the same age as I had been in 1934. It was a shock for her—as it had been for me, twenty-nine years earlier—the violent death of the country's leader, the sadness and the pomp and circumstance, the loss of a symbolic father figure. I think I decided that I had loved the little man (Dollfuss was not quite five feet tall), especially after he was dead. Kurt von Schuschnigg ascended to power and continued the semifascist order in Austria.

If I was largely unaware of politics before 1938 it was probably because the political system did not intrude on my life. Like most of my friends, I belonged to an upper-middle-class assimilated Jewish family. We attended a public elementary school. That is also the reason that we did not have Orthodox Jewish classmates.

Besides my parents and our governess, the most important adult in my life during the first three of the four years of elementary school was Lehrer (teacher) Feigl. This teacher taught us all subjects except religion. He always taught with vigor and enthusiasm, and I can remember that he devised a very effective method for teaching set theory when he taught us arithmetic. But he loved teaching German best. He inspired us with his diction and his enunciation. He often slipped into the role of the Burgtheater actor he wished he had become; we were his audience. He was passionate and extremely authoritarian. I loved him, and I feared him. And I acquired at that time a deep feeling for the German language.

Religion was taught to Austrian public school pupils during the school day. Unless the parents had requested exemption from all religious instruction, that is, had declared the child *konfessionslos* (having no religion), instruction in one of the three major religions was provided. For one hour twice a week the children in our class went either to a Protestant minister or to a teacher of Jewish religion (in higher grades to a rabbi) or stayed in the room with the majority to await the Catholic priest who would come to instruct them.

I remember the two teachers of religion I had in the lower grades as beautiful, gentle, and understanding young women who taught the (Old) Testament as wondrous stories and who encouraged religious observance at home. Attendance at the Saturday afternoon children's service at the local synagogue was also required. As proof of attendance one had to bring the program card that was distributed there. Under the influence of the school's religious instruction my sister and I besieged my mother to light Shabbat candles on Friday night, a custom we observed from then on throughout the years we spent in Vienna.

Like many of the other Jewish families in Vienna, practicing the Jewish faith meant observing the major Jewish holy days with family and friends. These repeated rituals left me with warm memories. For example, we always celebrated Passover with Aunt Cilly, actually an aunt of my father. As I try to reconstruct the event, the atmosphere of closeness and warmth suggests to me for the first time that perhaps Aunt Cilly's apartment was small. That thought never crossed my mind then. I remember some humorous repartee about possible abbreviations of the predinner prayer service spoken by my father and an uncle; I remember being allowed to taste wine (not particularly to my taste but so grown up); and I remember waiting for Prophet Elijah to come through the door that had been left ajar in order to drink from the wine goblet that had been filled for him. I also remember asking the four questions, an integral part of the Passover ritual. It is the responsibility of the youngest son to rise and, in Hebrew, ask such questions as, Why is this night different from all other nights? This honor fell to me, and I felt very important. I was allowed this participation in spite of the fact that I was a girl, but then there were no younger boys in the family.

We lived near a Catholic church, and I remember being taken there from time to time by the family cook. I loved the smell of incense, the statues, and the cool quiet. I also remember a picture of Christ on the cross in a small shop window that I passed every Saturday on my return from the visit to my synagogue. It said under the picture that if you looked at it intently for two minutes, Christ's eyes would open. I stopped there every week and waited for Christ to open his eyes. Once I leaned against the glass so hard that the window broke, and I ran home, my heart pounding.

I loved the Christkindlmarkt, the stalls erected around St. Stephen's Cathedral at Christmastime, with their toys and sweets and wonderful smells. I don't recall that I ever wished that we had a Christmas tree. I think I felt integrated in the Vienna of my childhood, secure in my identity.

When did I first become aware of anti-Semitism? I recall two incidents quite clearly. In the first case I conclude that I was only four years old since my sister was six, in 1930. She had entered first grade in the village near Vienna where we had a summer home. Soon thereafter, my parents withdrew her, and we moved back to Vienna. Anti-Semitic comments and perhaps acts had prompted this decision. It is too late to ask what had actually happened; there are no longer witnesses to this time in my life.

The second incident I recall happened in 1934, when I was eight. I had been attending the same public elementary school in Vienna since first grade and had several good friends. In third grade, I made a new friend. Her name was Irmgard. I loved and admired her, and she reciprocated my friendship. We planned one day that I should visit her after school, and when I asked my parents' permission, they did not grant it. My mother had telephoned Irmgard's parents and had been told that they did not approve of such a close friendship with Jews. I remember being as surprised as I was hurt. Only then did I become conscious of the fact that my other friends were Jewish and Irmgard was not.

Discrimination, Persecution, and Exodus, 1938–39

At 6 P.M. on March 11, 1938 my family listened as Chancellor Schuschnigg held a radio address in which he said good-bye to his Austrian countrymen. His speech was followed by the Austrian national anthem, played like a funeral dirge. Though I was not quite twelve years old, that event and many of those in the six months that followed before we left Austria have remained surprisingly vivid in my memory.

As mentioned at the beginning of this chapter, I witnessed Austria's reaction to the *Anschluss*. There was an ecstasy of acclamation and joy. Years later, the mendacious postwar self-portrayal of Austria as Hitler's first victim was to make me cynical regarding historical accounts and, incidentally, lay the groundwork for my interest in political psychology.

But back to 1938. The manifest racist anti-Semitism that had taken five years to develop in Germany was accomplished in as many months in Austria. Upon my return to school two days after the *Anschluss*, the twelve Jewish children of my seventh grade class of thirty-six were segregated to the rear of the classroom. Aryan children could not be expected to sit next to Jews, was the explanation. Some of our teachers were in silent empathy with us; many were not; some were openly hostile and aggressive. In art, the projects we were working on were discontinued. A picture of Hitler was displayed, and the assignment was to draw a likeness. Jewish children were not permitted to draw Hitler's portrait, however. In music, Nazi songs were learned. We had to stand but were not allowed to sing as our classmates intoned, "Wenn das Judenblut vom Messer spritzt" (when Jewish blood spurts from the knife).

The streets were full of flags adorned with swastikas and also full of uniforms. One morning, as I started on my way to school, I saw that the windows of our store had been smeared with swastikas and the words *Jude* and *Juda verrecke* (Jew, croak). One of the employees was busily scrubbing away at the paint so that my father would not see it or have to clean it upon his arrival.

Movie theaters, swimming pools, and even park benches were off limits for Jews. I remember one Sunday when my parents took us to the Jewish cemetery to play, the one place from which we were not barred.

My uncle was driving in Vienna when his car was stopped and confiscated. He was sent to the concentration camp Dachau. He was a man in his sixties, hard of hearing and a diabetic. His failure to hear and promptly obey orders caused him to be singled out for torment beyond his endurance. He was very ill by the time his family was able to achieve his release.

My sixteen-year-old cousin Ernst was strong-armed into joining a group of Jews who had to scrub political symbols of other parties from the street. When pushed to the ground by one of the young Nazis, he got up and slugged his tormentor. Thereupon a few of the men beat my cousin without mercy and left him unconscious in the gutter. When he recovered consciousness, he hid in a doorway until dark and then made his way to our house. His arrival contributed to my father's realization that we had to leave Austria.

Up to that time, my father had maintained that he had no enemies. He had fought for Austria in World War I. Vienna was his home. He had never harmed anyone, had on the contrary helped many people. He could not conceive of leaving Austria.

Though my father had found the thought of leaving Austria preposterous in March, he knew by the summer of 1938 that we had to go if we were to have a chance. He joined the lines seeking visas to distant countries. England, the United States, and Australia were his first, second, and third choices. In the end he filed applications for each of these countries but felt we could not wait for the visas to be granted, a lengthy process. He bought visas for us to enter the Dominican Republic and purchased passage on an ocean liner. With these documents in hand, my father obtained three-week transit visas for France. He sold the family stores to Aryan buyers for a pittance, paid that pittance as *Reichsfluchtsteuer* (tax for fleeing the Reich), and left Vienna with his family in late September 1938, just before the *Kristallnacht*.

How does a child of twelve experience this upheaval? I was aware of the pall that hung over our lives, the lurking danger as we prepared to leave Vienna, the fear when crossing the border on the way from Vienna to Paris. But the experience was also a lark, an exciting adventure. I am convinced that I did not experience real terror solely because I was never separated from my parents. The childhood illusion that they were there to protect me from harm allowed me to remain a child, secure in the knowledge that my parents would stand between me and the evil that threatened the world.

Of the ten months we lived in Paris, I was only able to attend school for three. My sister and I had to withdraw from public school when the school asked that documents be brought to show legal residence status. Later, each of my parents and my sister attended courses that were supposed to make it possible for them to earn money to support us in the country of our immigration. I stayed home, minded a two-year-old cousin, and shopped and cooked. Since my vocabulary was as limited as my culinary skills, my extended family, for whom I cooked, had to make do with two simple alternating menus.

There was an additional important event of a personal nature that took place during that year. When I turned thirteen in an apartment hotel in Paris I lost my faith. It was the year I learned French; read *Der*

Zauberberg, by Thomas Mann; and memorized ballads of Goethe, Schiller, and Heine. My belief in a deity had been getting weaker, but I thought that only God could explain the wonderful formations in even the smallest snowflake of the universe. When I found scientific explanations that could account for the patterns of nature I became an agnostic.

We continued to wait in vain for visas. When it seemed that the French would refuse to extend our permits yet another time and they threatened to send us back to Germany, where concentration camps awaited us, we decided to leave for the Dominican Republic. At that inopportune moment that country declared our visas invalid. By great good fortune we were notified shortly thereafter that the U.S. visas had been granted, and we left for the United States as quickly as possible.

I remember that we traveled to New York in great style on one of the French Line's huge steamers, the *Ile de France,* having been able to use the tickets previously purchased for travel to the Dominican Republic. For myself at thirteen, it was a wondrous experience. The steamer trunk that carried our possessions was recently accepted for exhibit at New York's new Museum of Jewish Heritage. This made me feel a little like a relic of the past myself.

The American Years, 1939–73

We arrived in New York shortly before the outbreak of World War II in Europe. I was now thirteen, facing the twin problems of adolescence and cultural integration while my parents faced those of economic survival. I don't remember experiencing serious difficulties learning a second foreign language within a year (though I remember French remaining my favorite for quite a while). The scholastic demands, first in seventh grade, then skipping right into the second year at Evander Childs High School, did not seem overwhelming. When I had academic problems, my sister helped me solve them. I enjoyed learning and got along well with my teachers. I earned good grades and was even awarded some academic honors. My parents, strangers to that world and preoccupied with their struggle to earn a living, had to be informed that these were in fact achievements to be savored.

During those years I also remember loneliness. Though I know that this is a frequent experience in adolescence, I attributed mine to the cultural dislocation, to the disinterest among my classmates in the serious political issues that had so dramatically affected my life. But who knows, I might have been equally alone as an awkward thirteen in Austria. Looking back, I think that my life would have taken a different course if I had been more popular with U.S. teenagers. Like other young refugees from Nazi Europe, I would have turned my back on the culture and language of the country of my birth that had treated us so badly, and I would have embraced all things American with passion.

However, since I found only a few casual friends in my high school, I tried clubs and groups outside of school and finally found a safe haven in an Austrian youth group whose members had come through life experiences similar to mine. It gave me a chance to become politically active, to commune with nature, to practice sports, and to contribute to the war effort. Some friendships that were formed there have lasted a lifetime. This group was my world until it disbanded sometime after the end of World War II.

Some of the decisions that shaped my life were made relatively casually during that time. I remember selecting my future course of study and thus a professional direction by a process of elimination. I picked mathematics and physics over art and English, for example, because I enjoyed the work and could do it as well as the best students in those courses, whereas I was not so sure of my talent in the other subjects.

In spite of our economic situation, my sister and I both achieved the coveted college education. She took secretarial courses to learn the skill that would support her during her college years, moved to New York, and attended Hunter College. When she passed away some years ago, she was the head of Adelphi University's Science Library.

I entered New York University at age sixteen with a partial tuition scholarship, studying at night, and, like my sister, I earned my way. I remember spending my days working for Bell Laboratories in a sprawling city block between Bank and Bethune Streets in downtown New York. I was proud to be one of fourteen technical assistants, working forty hours a week for $18 and frequently putting in overtime. I enjoyed the work. When we were dismissed in 1945 at the end of the war to make room for the traditional males to fill our places I became a disenchanted feminist.

During the next four years I had a succession of jobs. A "mathematician" was sought by a box company, and I was hired. I had to calculate endless series of measurements for knocked-down cardboard boxes. I was disillusioned, but I calculated until I was laid off. I was hired by a radio factory as a junior physicist. I had to spot-check radio sets selected at random from the assembly line. I remember that a number of sets failed to meet standards. As a result, the tolerances were increased. Full of moral indignation, I kept checking.

I lectured for Brookhaven National Laboratories at an exhibit at the New York Museum of Natural History on atomic energy. While I was holding forth to about twenty visitors, between the Van der Graaff globe and a model of atomic fission, the love of my life, also a member of the Austro-American Youth Group, proposed to me. We were married in April 1948.

Around that time, I started work as a technical editor for the McGraw-Hill Book Company. At the time my first daughter was born, I was copy-editing the manuscript of a textbook on optics. My husband finished it with my help, sitting in my hospital room. (At that time, it was customary to allow a five-day hospital stay for childbirth.) After her birth, I started editing at home—not only for McGraw-Hill but also for D. Van Nostrand, Prentice-Hall, Academic Press, and others. My second daughter came between *Differential Equations Made Easy* and *Mathematics: A Topical Approach*.

In 1954, we moved to the Catskills. The reason we bought that house on that meadow was that it reminded us of Austria. My husband had left Austria at eighteen; I had been twelve. We had acquired U.S. citizenship; we spoke English with each other; we were Americans. Yet each of us had internalized a longing for the mountains and the meadows of our childhoods, and when we found the blue gentian and the chanterelles, we stayed. That is where our youngest daughter was born.

Taking only a very brief look at the next fifteen years, I can report that as our three daughters grew up, we felt it best for the family to leave our rural Shangri-la. We returned to civilization in a New York suburb; I became a mathematics teacher; and the marriage I had considered ideal for many years fell apart. In 1973, my husband and I decided to try a year's separation. All three girls were away at college, and after twenty-five years of marriage, it seemed possible and wise not to sever the marriage immediately but to try life apart.

For the consumption of friends and relatives—and because there was more than a kernel of truth to this version—I said I was setting out to discover why mathematics instruction abroad produced considerably better mathematics knowledge and comprehension than our efforts in the United States. This conclusion had been reached by the International Project for the Evaluation of Education Achievement (IEA) in their multinational study of mathematics achievement (Husen 1967), which concluded that U.S. thirteen and seventeen year olds placed eleventh and twelfth, respectively, with respect to the twelve industrialized nations examined.

A colleague gave me a newspaper clipping announcing a search for German-speaking U.S. teachers of mathematics to come for two years to teach in Hamburg, Germany, where there was a sudden shortage of teachers of mathematics. I was interviewed for the position and was hired, even though I could only stay a year, having only been granted a one-year leave of absence from my teaching job. My fluent knowledge of German sold the hiring committee. With a group of other U.S. teachers of science and mathematics, I was scheduled to leave for West Germany in July 1973.

Pivotal Experiences, 1973–74

How did I feel about going to Germany? Some of my Jewish friends were shocked and looked at me askance. Among the other twenty-three teachers accepting the German offer of positions, there was only one Jewish couple, and they were not refugees from Nazi Germany. I was excited to be off on this adventure, to break out of a marriage that had become unendurable and to be on my own, free of the responsibilities for a family. I had originally been offered a job in Switzerland, but when this did not work out and I found myself headed for Germany, I was a little anxious and quite curious about the former aggressor.

I would not have wanted to go to Austria. I had been back to visit Austria a number of times since 1938. The Austrians were known to be anti-Semitic, with many clinging to a political mind-set not so different from that of the prewar years and probably the war years. My feelings for Austria were a mixture of yearning and loathing, and I had no desire to teach Austrian children.

And Germany? Where National Socialism had its origins, where even little children spoke that "high German" I had learned to love as a child? What was the source of my fascination? What did I expect to find by entering the lion's lair? By 1973, World War II was part of the past for Americans, especially for those whose families had not been devastated by the Holocaust. I expected this to be the case in Germany, too, though I anticipated the massive devastation of the German cities to have left physical and psychological scars. I thought the Nazi period a taboo subject. In their hearts, I expected the Germans to be more or less unchanged, to be what they had been in the 1930s. When had losing a fight ever changed a combatant's opinion? What would have made the Germans change in those twenty-eight years since their defeat at the hands of the Allies?

These largely unconscious expectations were based on my visits to Austria, where the Nazi era was never talked about except when oblique references alluded to the suffering they, the Austrians, had had to endure ("You were lucky . . .") or to sotto voce comments about things that had been better "under Hitler."

I was to teach German children; I had contact with their German parents and with my German fellow faculty members. My students were born about thirteen years after the end of World War II. Most of their parents, especially the mothers, enjoyed *die Gnade der spaeten Geburt* (the grace of the late birth), to borrow a phrase later coined by Chancellor Kohl to point out the automatic innocence of all that happened under Hitler of those born too late to have experienced the Third Reich as adults. It soon became clear to me, however, that this generation was also deeply affected, in many ways, by the period of National Socialism and World War II, which they had experienced as children and through their parents. A symbolic example comes to mind. On a class trip (*Klassenreise*) traditionally held at the beginning of the school year, for students to get to know one another better, the chaperoning parents proved unable to produce even a single German song to go with the evening's campfire. A self-conscious censorship found the songs that came to mind politically tainted. With relief we finally sang the ever popular "Hoch auf dem gelben Wagen," a song that had recently been sung by Foreign Minister Scheel, and some of the most popular songs of the folk group Peter, Paul, and Mary.

There were many paradoxes. Considering Germany's traditional tripartite system of education undemocratic, the Federal Republic of Germany tried to move away from the division of students according to aptitude (into *Hauptschule, Realschule,* and *Gymnasium*) to a system of comprehensive schools (*Gesamtschulen*). The model was the U.S. high school or a similar plan implemented in Sweden. However, feelings in the population were split. Especially parents of bright and capable students did not want to give up their dream of a strictly academic education for their children. And to implement the structural change in the face of opposition struck the Germans as authoritarian, even if the aim was a more democratic system. *Gesamtschulen* were established not instead of but in addition to the conventional schools. The new system did not work out as well as it might have because the top students continued to attend the academic secondary schools as before. One of the few remaining democratizations left from this era is the decision-making process concerning the selection of students for the gymnasium. No longer does a single examination at the age of ten decide a child's educational future. Performance over a period of one or two years, teacher recommendation, and parental wishes play a significant part in the school choice, and there is a "second way" of attaining the baccalaureate at a later time in the educational process.

While economic conditions in suburban Hamburg, where I had come to teach, were quite similar to those I had left behind in Westchester, New York, the behavior of the students was markedly different in a number of respects. I was busy recording anecdotes and observations. Overnight, I had become a "participant observer." I was interested in the experiences of my fellow teachers from the United States and compiled, distributed, and analyzed my first questionnaires.

The U.S. teachers were scattered among quite a number of schools in the area. I was the only U.S. teacher at my school. I now depended for social contacts on my new colleagues. I had said nothing about my background and discovered that my German fellow teachers had decided that I might have been an Austrian war bride. Since I wanted to assess the prevalence of anti-Semitism in my environment, I decided to leave this image in place. I thought I would learn more if people were not aware of my Jewish background. A test of residual anti-Semitic attitudes came in the form of two new students who were admitted during the school year. The boy and girl came from Israel. Their father had emigrated before the war and now returned, uninhibited in his display of great wealth. The children frequently arrived at school by chauffeur-driven limousine; they were exempt from writing on Saturdays; they were often unprepared; and they tended to be fresh and self-righteous. And these were the only Jews at this school, among the relatively small number of Jews living in Hamburg. I listened carefully to the teachers and also to the custodian (*Hauswart*), a man with little education and much power, a typical situation in German schools. I heard criticism of the children but never in reference to their background or to Israel. This seemed to me almost unnatural, as if everyone was under the spell of a taboo. I imagined that a similar situation in the United States, especially in the U.S. Midwest, would have elicited other comments.

I had been told that North Germans were cold and distant, hard to get to know, and that Germans in contrast to Americans had few intimate friends and were not very interested in expanding this limited circle. I remember that my own reception was warm and friendly, not only when measured against the warnings and expectations of friends.

I remember that the teachers were divided into two groups, ostensibly the smokers in the teachers' smoking room and the nonsmokers in the other. Actually it was a political division, running also along age lines. It took me a while to discover that this resulted in the presence of some coughing nonsmokers suffering in the teachers' smoking room. There was little social contact between the two groups. As an older nonsmoker (I was then forty-seven), I landed at a table with conservative older women.

As the year progressed, I decided to change my image. Not having heard anti-Semitic comments when I was thought to have been a (non-Jewish) war bride, I decided to set the record straight. I casually remarked to some teachers that I was Jewish. I had been treated with warmth before this revelation. Now my colleagues started to vie for my friendship. I felt that I was encountering philosemitism, and I didn't know how to react. I tried to imagine myself in the place of the Germans I was encountering, and I decided that it would be very difficult to react "normally" under the circumstances, assuming that anyone could suggest what "normal" might be after the Holocaust.

Sometime during that year I met a German approximately my age, and we became friends. Like my husband and myself, he and his wife had recently separated after a long marriage, and they had three children. We were surprised at how much we had in common. We met for long walks. Together we explored Hamburg and we talked. It was difficult for me to hear him talk about his life experiences in the Hitler Youth. At the age of sixteen he had been drafted into the army with his tenth grade class and his teachers. He was a soldier for six weeks and a prisoner of war of the Americans for a year. I don't know whether I was the first Jew he had ever met; I certainly was the first one he got to know well.

We visited the memorial at the site of the former concentration camp Bergen-Belsen together. I placed a stone on one of the memorial gravestones, a Jewish gesture of respect dating back to biblical times. He did not know whether it would be sacrilegious for him do the same. He stood as if paralyzed and cried.

The people among whom I had decided to live for a year had stopped being "the Germans"; they had become individuals. And my expectations of what I would find and experience had proved false.

At the end of the academic year I returned to New York. I had made many friends and had a great variety of impressions. I felt a need to discuss my experiences and their implications with my U.S. friends and colleagues. When I did that, however, I found that many had their own picture of Germany and the Germans. They seemed disinterested and unwilling to consider revising it. On the occasion of a lecture I held at my U.S. high school about the mathematics curriculum and my experiences in the German classroom, one of the parents in the audience told me that my observations were incorrect, that I had been deluded.

I found myself in a strange situation. Having previously spoken about the Holocaust and the Nazis to inform Americans about the greatest genocide of all time, I suddenly found myself perversely trying to set the picture straight regarding the Federal Republic of Germany, thirty years after the end of World War II. And I found that many U.S. Jews were content to live with the stereotype of "the Germans" as "the Nazis." They did not feel the need to reexamine reality. It was bewildering for me to discover that a positive attitude toward "the Germans" prevailed only among those who harbored secret sympathies for the Germany of the 1930s.

Looking for Answers, 1975–80

My first marriage had ended. I resumed my position teaching mathematics in the United States. But the German experience pursued me. The motion pictures shown late at night, in which all Germans conformed to a Nazi stereotype; the unquestioning behavior of U.S. students and teachers when they pledged allegiance to the flag displayed in each classroom; the words of parents telling their children to do as they were told: I saw them all with a different awareness. I felt as if I were living in two worlds and had two distinct and irreconcilable forms of perception.

What was this quality that had prevailed in Germany and that had undergone such change? And had it really? Or had my limited experience produced a delusion, as had been suggested?

In the ensuing year, my two worlds met. Teachers from the German gymnasium where I had taught followed the invitation of my Westchester high school, my U.S. colleagues, and the parents of our students and visited with us for two weeks. The visitors were touched by the warmth, the friendliness, and the generosity of their hosts and by the Americans they met in general. And for me, some of the cultural differences between the visiting Germans and my U.S. colleagues became even clearer.

The German visitors were also more than a little bewildered by social customs unfamiliar to them. For example, our U.S. high school principal, who welcomed them personally in his office upon their arrival, shook hands with each one, addressed each by first name, and introduced himself similarly. The German teachers were taken aback. Some had worked at their school with colleagues for a dozen years or more and still addressed them in the formal manner (with "Sie" or as "Frau" or "Herr Schmidt"). They were suddenly called upon to call this foreign principal the equivalent of "Du." It was almost unthinkable for them, at the very least awkward.

I began to realize that such conventions of a culture were not coincidental. They reflected cultural values that, in turn, were an integral part of what makes Germans German and Americans American. In his book entitled *Society and Democracy in Germany* Ralf Dahrendorf (1967) writes about pivotal differences in value attitudes and role expectations between the Federal Republic of Germany and the United States. He calls them the private and the public virtues (285) and says about them that the private virtues, dear to the Germans, provide the individual with standards for his own perfection, whereas the public virtues prized in the United States are of greatest importance in societies whose aim is the frictionless mastery of relationships between men (286). Perhaps the single maxim that best characterizes public virtues is "keep smiling"—make things easy for the others, even if this is hard for you (287).

How true, I thought. Many Germans I had met basically misunderstood the "superficial" friendliness of Americans and especially criticized what seemed to them the hypocrisy of "keep smiling." As a little social experiment, try smiling at a toddler in a supermarket in two different locales: Atlanta and Frankfurt. In Atlanta, the parent will return your smile and make you feel that you have made a friend. In Frankfurt, the parent is likely to stare you down with an angry frown, silently criticizing your intrusive behavior.

My sensitivity to cultural nuances became finely tuned. The more I thought and read, the more there seemed to be to know. I decided to embark on a new course of study evenings, after my teaching job.

When I entered Columbia University in 1976 to study sociology and social psychology, I was almost fifty years old. I had a master's degree and twenty years of experience teaching mathematics. Teaching in Germany for a year had awakened the memories of the first years of my life in Austria and raised questions I wanted to answer. My training in mathematics helped determine the choice of approach.

As my studies progressed, I became familiar with Kurt Lewin and Erik Erikson, with Erich Fromm and Wilhelm Reich. I realized that much of the material I was studying was already familiar to me, in some instances from earlier studies and in other cases seemingly as if I had known these things since childhood.

Goethe—and "the Germans"—had thought that one had to rule or serve ("Du musst herrschen und gewinnen, Oder dienen und verlieren"). The "bicyclist's syndrome" had prevailed, in Germany even more pronounced than elsewhere: stepping down on those below as you bowed to those above you—a pervasive pecking order. I marveled how well Heinrich Mann had described this in a historical setting in *Der Untertan* (1918). I read about the authoritarian German father and typical German family constellations in Bertram Schaffner's *Father Land* (1948). I read *The Authoritarian Personality* (Adorno et al. 1950) as if it were a thriller. Rokeach's *Open and Closed Mind* (1950) was a revelation. I was fascinated by David Mantell's analysis of Green Berets and conscientious objectors during the Vietnam War (1972–74).

For my dissertation I posed the questions, Are young Germans of the Federal Republic of Germany fundamentally less authoritarian now, thirty-two years after the end of World War II, than the German sixteen year olds of 1945; and how do they differ from their U.S. contemporaries?

I found research carried out by psychologists who had asked questions about German and U.S. sixteen year olds at the end of World War II (McGranahan 1946) and by a number of investigators in subsequent decades. I studied novel theories by psychologists such as Thomas Ziehe (1975) about the new personality types growing up in the Federal Republic of Germany and I added my research to the work in progress, replicating earlier surveys of German and U.S. adolescents with broader samples and a many-faceted questionnaire.

When it became necessary to produce a German version of a previously used English questionnaire, I tested the quality of the translation with a special small-scale study. The questionnaire was administered to eighty bilingual students twice, the second time after a two-week interval. While a control group completed the questionnaire twice in the same language, half the students received the questionnaires first in one language, the second time in the other. Inquiring into occasional discrepancies led us to discover that children who are at home in two cultures and two languages think very differently about some things when they are thinking in a different language.

The results of the analysis within cultures over time and across cultures showed a diminution of intercultural differences and a sharper reduction of authoritarianism among German adolescents than among U.S. adolescents since 1945. The data also revealed significant correlations between authoritarianism, pseudopatriotism, ethnocentrism, and dogmatism in both cultures.

I completed my dissertation in 1980 and received the Ph.D. from Columbia University. Soon thereafter, I translated the research into German, and it was published as *Jugend und Autoritaet* (1983).

In a way I felt that I had come full circle when I was asked by the Institute for Conflict Research in Vienna to carry out an empirical survey similar to the German one in Austria, to throw light on the adolescents in Austria and for the purpose of cross-cultural comparison.

In the years between 1978 and 1987, my three daughters grew up to be successful and fulfilled professional women. During that time, I took leaves of absence from my high school twice—first for a year to collect data and experience in order to write my dissertation and then for two years to work in my new field in Germany. I continued with my research on comparative authoritarianism and investigated the causes and expressions of youthful protest and aggression.

In June 1987, I retired from teaching mathematics in New York in order to pursue my new profession. I moved to Germany and worked for some time at the recently founded Institute for Anti-Semitism Research in Berlin. At that time, I also taught some courses at universities in Berlin and Hamburg. In my private life, I had taken the big step and had married my German partner of many years, the man I had met in 1973 during my "German year." Living in Germany now, I had a front row seat at that great upheaval, the political and symbolic fall of the wall between the East and the West in 1989.

With the desire to document the events that were happening in terms of attitudes and opinions of the young people experiencing them, I was able to replicate and expand my research in the Federal Republic of Germany, the United States, Austria, the German Democratic Republic, and Moscow.

Since 1992, my husband and I have lived in New York. I continue to work in the field of political psychology, where sociology, psychology, and political science come together. My interest in adolescents and their development in society and in the field of authoritarianism continue to challenge me (see Stone, Lederer, and Christie 1992 and Lederer and Schmidt 1995). Perhaps the roots of this interest lie in my adolescent experiences with fascism and persecution. Perhaps it is because progress is so uncertain, at best tenuous.

I believe and try to teach that we cannot afford to think in clichés if we want to prevent genocide in the future. Teaching on the Internet for the New School University, a university forged by refugee scholars in the 1930s and 1940s, I have been able to bring together descendants of the victims in the United States and of the perpetrators of the Holocaust in Austria in "virtual classrooms" in the effort to help them confront and understand the past.

My composite identity—Austrian, Jewish, American—augmented by the perspective of my German partner, has helped me see the world from a wider angle. The recognition that my work has received has been very gratifying. After a hiatus of nearly half a lifetime, I have turned to the questions raised by the experiences of the early years of my life. It is a quest I am still pursuing.

REFERENCES

Adorno, T. W., E. Frenkel-Brunswik, D. J. Levinson, and R. N. Sanford. 1950. *The authoritarian personality*. New York: Harper and Row.

Dahrendorf, R. 1967. *Society and democracy in Germany*. Garden City and New York: Doubleday & Company.

Husen, T. 1967. *International study of achievement in mathematics: A comparison of twelve countries*. New York: Wiley.

Lederer, G. 1983. *Jugend und Autoritaet: Ueber den Einstellungswandel zum Autoritarismus in der Bundesrepublik Deutschland und den USA*. Opladen: Westdeutscher Verlag.

Lederer, G., and P. Schmidt, eds. 1995. *Autoritarismus und Gesellschaft*. Opladen: Leske und Budrich.

Mann, H. [1918] 1982. *Der Untertan*. Munich: Deutscher Taschenbuch Verlag.

Mantell, D. M. 1972–74. *Familie und Aggression*. 1978. Reprint, Frankfurt am Main: Fischer Taschenbuch Verlag.

McGranahan, D. V. 1946. A comparison of social attitudes among American and German youth. *Journal of Abnormal and Social Psychology* 41: 245–57.

Rokeach, M. 1960. *The open and the closed mind*. New York: Basic Books.

Schaffner, B. 1948. *Father Land, a study of authoritarianism in the German family*. New York: Columbia University Press.

Stone, W., G. Lederer, and R. Christie, eds. 1992. *Strength and weakness: The authoritarian personality today*. New York: Springer.

Ziehe, T. 1975. *Pubertaet und Narzissmus*. Frankfurt am Main: Europaeische Verlagsanstalt.

A Wandering Jew as a Social Scientist

The Convergence of Historical and Professional Life Lines

Jacob Lomranz

Biographical Note

Born in Germany and raised in China, Jacob Lomranz has spent most of his life in Israel. He received his B.A. from Tel Aviv University and his Ph.D. from Duke University. He is currently at Tel Aviv University as professor of psychology, academic director of the Herczeg Institute of Aging (of which he was founding director), and director of the Frankel Fund for Holocaust Research. He also founded and directed the university's Research Units of Severe Brain Injury and Psychology of Adulthood and established a clinical psychology service in homes for the aged.

    Professor Lomranz's research has concentrated on personality, clinical psychology, group dynamics, creativity, life-span development and gerontology, and the long-term effects of trauma. He has published three books and over one hundred scholarly articles and chapters and is president of the Gerontological Society of Israel.

Introduction

In writing this chapter, I adopted a twofold approach. First, my mode of expression is that of the personal essay (Epstein 1997) as narrative

(Suedfeld et al. 1997), in which life and story cannot be distinguished and are in a continuous relationship, enriching one another. Since the chapter's basic points of departure are the past atrocities of war, uprootedness, and persecution, a developmental framework incorporated in a historical perspective is required.

Second, the orientation of the chapter is that of *science as scientists* (Robinson 1976). The creation of scientific work often encompasses a variety of personal, autobiographical, ethical, and cultural needs (Lubow 1977). Merton (1973) explores the ways in which knowledge is shaped by the scientist's existential condition, experience, values, and culture. He views science as a subsystem of culture and elaborates the concept of "scientific community." In addition to the scientific norms shared by all scientists in the world, there exists a subculture of scientists, to which I perhaps belong, comprised mainly of Jewish people, first and second generations of immigrants, as well as those who experienced World War II and were affected by Nazi brutality. While I don't have a sense of belonging to such a group in my routine life or daily work, I am aware of the existence of this kind of "group culture."

Biographical Synopsis

In the summer of 1997, when I was leisurely touring the Canadian Rockies, the editor contacted me and asked me to contribute a chapter to this volume, a request I found both challenging and intriguing. I had just left my position as founder and director of the Herczeg Institute on Aging at Tel Aviv University, the first of its kind in Israel, and the offer seemed relevant to my reflective and future-planning mind-set. About twelve years ago, in line with my own age and personal development, I somewhat shifted my professional interest. I concentrated on adult development with the dual purpose of contributing to needed changes in the concept of development (from child centered to adult and life span) and deriving implications for clinical psychology. In 1987, I was able to establish a novel university-associated mental health clinic that officially functioned as a psychological service in two major homes for the aged in Tel Aviv and also served as a formal training placement center for graduates of clinical psychology (Lomranz and Bar-tur 1998). Much of my searching in the field and the stimulation it gave me may also be related to the launching of my children and to my friends' and my own aging and especially that of my mother.

The academic world has been my major habitat throughout my scientific career, offering me an environment conducive to the development of my intellectual abilities. The potentials for research, teaching, curriculum development, and clinical training at Tel Aviv University provided major satisfying avenues for my interests. I usually develop informal relationships with my students, aiming for an atmosphere conducive to learning. As the director of the clinical program between the mid-1970s and 1980s, I found an arena receptive to the introduction of my ideas about academic-psychological education as well as the optimal combination of U.S. and European university structure and goals. At that time, I also established a research unit on the psychology of adulthood and aging and introduced curriculum changes in the department of psychology, making adult development an integral part of that curriculum.

I have always been involved in educational matters and have succeeded in modifying and implementing educational and cultural programs outside the university, too, in the community. Some of my activities in these areas include my contribution to the implementation of teaching adult development in Israeli high schools; active membership in the Israeli and European gerontological societies; and investments in organizing public seminars in adulthood and aging. I have a sense of "mission" in dealing with aging and gerontology.

During the early 1970s, as if anticipating the Yom Kippur War, I established a psychological clinic for severely brain-injured soldiers. This happened very soon after I returned, in 1970, with my wife and two children, to Israel from my graduate studies in the United States, to face political and economic turmoil and wars in Israel. My participation in the Yom Kippur War had a profound impact on me. My involvement in treating traumatized soldiers was so engrossing that I did not realize, for several days, that I had a high fever and had contracted pneumonia. This was my firsthand professional experience with trauma and PTSD. (It dawns upon me that wars could serve as "markers" on my life line: I was born close to World War II; fled to China where I experienced the Japanese occupation and the American-Japanese war; emigrated to Israel while its War of Independence was still going on; in Israel lived through the Sinai War, the Six-Day War, and the war of attrition, participated in the Yom Kippur War and the Lebanon War, and experienced the Gulf War). My years in the United States, as a graduate student, between 1966 and 1970, when my son was born, were enriching, exciting and rewarding, personally, interpersonally and educationally. The fact that I feel at home when visiting the United States is evidence of this positive experience.

I earned my B.A. in 1965, having begun my undergraduate studies at Tel Aviv University in 1960, in philosophy and psychology. I became an assistant in the Department of Psychology. The university, investing in "future young faculty," granted me fellowships that enabled me to travel and study for my Ph.D. in clinical psychology in the United States. Upon returning to Israel, I joined, at the age of thirty-three, the Department of Psychology, where I continue to work at the present.

Before my undergraduate studies, I worked in a bank, served in the army, got married in 1958, returned to work in the bank, and became a father to my daughter. Not having gone to high school, due to the death of my father and the difficult years in Israel, I worked during the day and studied at night for the "matriculation" diploma that is a requirement for admission to the university. I entered the university at the relatively late age of twenty-four, having postponed my studies because, among other reasons, I aspired to become a writer and believed that a university education was superfluous in achieving such a goal. As an undergraduate, I supported myself by teaching and preparing blind army veterans for their high school matriculation examinations.

I have worked all my life, since the age of fifteen. During most of the 1950s, I worked in various jobs, as an electrician, at a newspaper, and then in a bank. As an adolescent, I earned the money needed to support myself and my mother, after the death of my father in 1954, and later, after my marriage, also to support my newly established family. My mother's financial situation changed drastically when she received German reparation monies. This money was accepted with great ambivalence, and as I look back today, I think that given the situation, the culture, and personal needs, it was almost impossible not to accept it, but from a different perspective, I believe it was morally wrong. My late adolescent and young adulthood years were exciting and stimulating. In time, my work in the bank, despite my success there, became meaningless to me. Each day I found myself spending eight hours at work and then rushing off, changing my clothes, and enjoying myself with friends in cafés, leading a bohemian life for the next ten hours.

Israel, where I arrived with my parents from Shanghai early in 1949 and where, in the early 1950s, I experienced my preadolescence, presented dual qualities of existence. It was then a young state, having fought a devastating war to gain its independence, grieving for its dead, almost crushed by very poor economic conditions, but at the same time bursting with energy and hope for an ideal future. The country was at that time engaged in absorbing hundreds of thousands of refugees and

Holocaust survivors from postwar Europe and Middle Eastern countries. Immigrants soon overwhelmingly outnumbered the local population, and profound ethnic tensions were created between "eastern" (Asia/ Africa) and "western" (European) Jews, a friction that plagues Israel to this very day. The conditions for adjustment were extremely harsh. My father in particular found he was unable to adjust financially, and to a certain extent socially and culturally, and attempted to emigrate to the United States. For him, Israel became a temporary stopover. In fact, living through the war and experiencing social-economic hardships, uprooting, and persecutions created a family atmosphere permeated by the desire to reach the light at the end of the tunnel, namely, "the American dream." At the same time it imbued much of my life with a sense of continuously "sitting on suitcases," in transit stations. For me, however, even the hard years in Israel were a marvelous time, growing up in an exciting period, curious about a strange yet close people and a country marked by a spirit of freedom, ideology, and hopes of establishing a model state.

I had lost schooltime due to World War II and the prolonged but exciting journey by ship from Shanghai to Haifa in Israel. However, I recall my two and a half years at an elementary school in a Tel Aviv suburb, which had previously been an Arab village, as thrilling and precious. Due to the mass immigration to Israel, my classmates came from about fifteen countries. The years from my bar mitzvah throughout my adolescence were both very stimulating and character building. Those were the years in which I also devoured an incredible number of books. My love for literature, poetry, and the arts has remained with me to this day. My father, reconciled to his disappointment at my refusal to study in a *Yeshiva* (institute for religious studies), insisted that I master an occupation that would ensure my livelihood. Little did he know how constructive that instruction was, because, in 1954, half a year after I finished elementary school, when we were finally granted immigration visas to the United States, he suddenly passed away.

My earlier childhood and formative years, however, took place in Shanghai, China, which I reached after being uprooted from my German birthplace at the age of about two and where I grew up until I was nearly twelve. Shanghai was an international port city made up of various "quarters" (British, French, Chinese, etc.). One of its most striking features was the diversity of its people, architecture, and cultures. I do remember that, between the ages of four and nine, due to the war, I often had to stay at home alone, during air raids and curfews, since both my parents had to go out to work. I had some frightening childhood experiences because I was often alone, and I was also afraid of the Chinese and even more of the Japanese soldiers. Up to the fifth grade, with interruptions caused by the war, I attended a secular, English-speaking Jewish school from morning till 2 P.M. After school I rushed to the synagogue, where I remained until the early evening hours, studying the Jewish Scriptures in an authentic *cheder* (a traditional small classroom where a rabbi taught children using Orthodox teaching methods). I believe these Jewish studies (for about six years beginning with basic Hebrew and going on to biblical and finally to talmudic studies) had a great impact on me, not only in terms of their content, which enriched my imagination and feelings, but also on my mode of thought and analytic ability. I should emphasize that my father, whom I would term a modern Jewish scholar, always surrounded by books of religion, created a learning atmosphere in our home. He valued learning and took delight in discovering interpretations of Hebrew Scriptures. He was, however, no less immersed in the secular world of intellectuality, art, and culture. A major influence of my father was that his inquisitive nature, spiritual orientation, optimism, and good-natured attitude toward life taught me, amid the war-related experiences, to ponder and ask questions instead of complaining. The environment, people's lives, and social events, as well as misery, all became thought-provoking subjects and later in life served as grist to the mill of my mind.

Children may experience growing up in the shadow of war very differently than adults. As a child I never regarded life in Shanghai as a disaster, but in retrospect, I realize that it certainly involved many serious hardships and affliction. When we arrived as refugees, the Chinese welcomed us; when we left they threw stones at us. At first, we lived in the western, more elegant quarters of the city and were free to move and commute. Two years later, in the early 1940s, with the strengthening of the German-Japanese treaty and especially after the Japanese attack on Pearl Harbor, the Japanese, who then occupied China, imposed martial law and restricted us to a ghetto in the older, impoverished parts of the city. During the war years, living conditions in Shanghai were harsh. Sanctions were imposed; housing was crowded; the surroundings were often unfriendly or hostile; it was hard to find work; the supply of food and boiled water was limited; schools were frequently closed; and travel was restricted. Four times we had to move and relocate our living quarters. We suffered under an oppressive military regime in wartime conditions. Commuting was restricted and depended on military permits; special, yellow-striped identification cards for Jews were issued; we lived under constant curfew conditions; and life became onerous. As the American-Japanese war intensified, the early and mid-1940s brought increasing American bombing raids on Shanghai, causing heavy damage and death, and, simultaneously, the Japanese occupation grew even harsher.

I remember both my parents as good spirited. In those years the two of them worked hard and barely made a living, while sicknesses such as dysentery and tuberculosis were widespread in the community. In Shanghai, even as a child I witnessed death, certainly as a result of the bombings and the destruction they caused, but I was even more affected by continually seeing Chinese dying on the streets. Homelessness was part of the daily scene, and the streets were overcrowded with starving beggars, many of them dying there. Furthermore, I remember that even after the war, on my daily rides to school in a rickshaw, we would pass a crematorium where dozens of bundles containing dead children were heaped up. The situation began to change when at the age of nine I stood, squeezed between an enthusiastic crowd on the docks of Shanghai, welcoming the liberating U.S. Sixth Fleet commanded by General MacArthur. Liberation also brought with it the horrible, unbelievable news that six million Jews had been massacred and gassed and that our entire family (my mother had five siblings, my father eleven) had been murdered by the Nazis. Except for my two children, I know of no one who carries my family name. The enormous impact of the Holocaust was then imprinted on my mind, mainly through the reactions of my mother. A delicate, sociable, caring, and giving person, she was nearly devastated by the news of the Holocaust and the losses she had experienced. She reacted with prolonged and extreme grief, which, I believe, caused a significant personality change in her and had a major impact on me. Her reaction constitutes the core of my experience, attitude, and involvement in all Holocaust-related phenomena. After the war, we found ourselves again "sitting on our suitcases" hoping to leave China for—where else?—the United States. That was a tense waiting period, the pressure being exacerbated by the advancing forces of the Red Army headed by Mao Tse-tung in the late 1940s. But as the reader already knows, at the end of my "Shanghai chapter" we were not greeted by the Statue of Liberty but by Mount Carmel in Israel.

Before the outbreak of World War II, Shanghai was an open international port, where no visa was required. Hence, it became the last refuge for many of Europe's persecuted Jews and took in and saved over twenty thousand Jewish refugees from Austria, Germany, and Poland. Among the last to flee Germany, after all our property had been confiscated by the Nazis, we arrived in Shanghai as refugees in the summer of 1939. Life in Germany had become unbearable. All the well-known restrictions on Jews were enforced. I remember my mother recalling how she, with me as a baby, was on her way home on what turned out to be *Kristallnacht*, when synagogues and books were burned, windows were smashed, houses and apartments occupied by Jews were damaged, there was rioting on the streets, and every Jewish passerby was brutally beaten. In a state of shock, she fled with me in her arms from alley to alley until she safely reached home. After that my father and his brother tried to smuggle themselves over the Belgian border in an attempt to reach Britain, which would enable them, under British law, to bring over their families. They were caught and arrested, and my mother, in my presence and alone, was interrogated by the SS. My father spent weeks in a German jail, and just before he was to be deported to a concentration camp, my mother miraculously was able to buy us passage (from a Jew who at the last moment changed his mind) on a ship to Shanghai, at a time when the Germans still allowed Jews to leave the country if they had somewhere to go. Both of my Polish-born parents had arrived in Germany in 1929. They met and married in 1932, hoping to build a family and a good life in Germany, believing that conditions would improve and that the Nazi regime would be short lived. I was born, their only child, in Leipzig, Germany, on the morning of January 10, 1937.

While further biographical information will be interwoven in the coming sections, I wish this biographical sketch to stand as a reference to which the reader can return to comprehend the logic of some later connections that I make and, preferably, to arrive at some of his or her own novel insights.

Intermezzo

Now that I have outlined my selective biography, the basic questions are, How can one comprehend the psychological impact of persecution, uprootedness, migrations, and relocations upon one's life span? What happens to an individual's identity, sense of self, and mode of personal existence when the historical and cultural narrative changes abruptly? How does one go about the task of relating the two: the biographical and professional life lines?

Life narratives interweave individual experience with social reality.

Therefore, life and work lines, as stories within stories in my narrative, are, necessarily, at times separately presented, but they are basically dialectic and inseparable, residing in a unified, organismic context. Many narrativists argue that the conditions for a narrative include continuity and coherence since the narrative is the unity of a person's life. To my mind this, however, is open to discussion and dependent on one's hermeneutic point of view. I would argue that stories, always conceived in a present context, are endlessly associated with new contextual elements, and are, like life, intertextual and deconstructed, the origin of their meaning open to different interpretations and change. Owing to such perpetually changing, unperfected, novel possibilities—in addition to the variance between persons and their attitudes toward inconsistencies—coherence and continuity are not prerequisites for personal identity and narrative.

I will, in the following pages, present the professional-biographical interrelationships in two sections: first epistemology organized and later content organized in larger cogent circles of my scientific work. Finally, in the last part of this chapter, I will delineate some basic concepts, such as "refugee" and "wandering Jew," all lending possible meaning to the transformations in my life story.

Epistemological-Biographical Components and My Scientific Work

A person approaches his or her productions, including research, with the equipment he or she carries: knowledge, abilities, and skills. That equipment, while certainly containing a genetic element, also evolves through one's socialization and history. I refer here to epistemology and its classical components as an underlying basis, a constitution, molded through my personal history, resulting in the characterization of my thinking and feeling and the interpretation of my experience, including my work experience.

Space

I grew up and lived in different, crowded and spacious, spatial environments. I do not mind density, either with people or objects, but also love to roam in open spaces. Boundaries may be invisible. Distances are never conceived as barriers to contact or cooperation. The manner in which different people—diverse in cogent aspects of personality, language, cul-

ture, and modes of spatial contact—arrange matters, build close relationships, and constructively produce common products has always
intrigued me.

Complementing my interest in interpersonal communication is my
interest in how people communicate nonverbally. One early memory I
have is from Shanghai. When we could barely manage financially, my
father went with a friend to the local, very crowded market, stood there
waving a scarf of my mother's and some other cloth, under the watchful
eyes of Japanese soldiers, and without knowing a word of Chinese, only
with gestures, sold the garments and made a profit. Arabic, Chinese, and
Jewish "contact cultures," perhaps in contrast to German and Anglo-
American "noncontact" cultures, as well as the crowded conditions in
the Shanghai ghetto, all may have been influences that fostered my interest in the study of *touching behavior and personal space* (e.g., Lomranz et al.
1975) as major components in interpersonal communication varying
across developmental, gender, and cross-cultural perspectives.

Time

The context of time for dislocated people may produce specific patterns
of living and raises fascinating questions. What can time mean for wanderers and refugees, who have no stable and consistent territory of their
own, who repeatedly are uprooted and relocated? For whom normative
time expectations are interrupted and then continued in drastically different contexts? For whom the issues of survival and death already are
cardinal at a very early age?

I am keenly aware of the different aspects of temporality (Eyal 1996):
the "objective," linear, nonreversible, additive, and measurable aspects
of time as well as the "subjective," reversible, nonadditive, and unmeasurable aspects. I detect the results of living in subjective time in my
lesser emphasis on materialism, pragmatism, and socially imposed func-
tionalism, accompanied by a noncompliant attitude toward norms and a
fascination with the theoretical and abstract. One strategy for successfully dealing with the inconsistent and complex qualities of temporality
may be to stay young at heart, not to be threatened by the passage of time
and often to experience a sense of timelessness. With such characteristics of temporality one may be able to attend to the present and yet have
a broad, extended future perspective. Or, one may be able to work on an
urgent task as if all the time in the world were available (important for
clinical psychologists); but this may also entail piling up tasks, being

unable to complete them, and experiencing constant time pressure. For many wanderers or refugees many future goals may never materialize; yet these same people may continue to be motivated by such a future, remain basically optimistic, and continue to believe that goals will be achieved and dreams will come true. Many of these characteristics have been, and still are, features of my own sense of time.

The synchronicity or asynchronicity between personal and social time, and the imposed structures of time, have an important impact on behavior and mental health. Refugees, dislocated people, and Holocaust survivors that I have encountered often experience being "off time" instead of "on time." Personally, my internal clock dominates the external clock. In fact, all my life I have found the different life lines colliding more than complementing one another; my work line has interrupted my developmental line (having had to go to work in preadolescence) and was itself disrupted by economic necessities (e.g., determining the kind of work I had to do, hindering career development), and my family line did not coincide with my career line.

Another source of my own fascination with the study of time may be my early encounters with death. If newborn children, in the Shanghai ghetto, were already dead, then obviously a person need not go through the passage of time and age in order to die. The life span (Eyal 1997), age, and time have been a fascinating triangle. I have learned that being close to death, as Holocaust survivors were, for instance, may color one's attitude toward time. This may be the connection I find between my triple interest in Holocaust survivors, time and gerontology, and scientific work. The *personal meaning of time* has accompanied me since my student years and has become central in my scientific work. I have studied the beliefs and attitudes toward time (e.g., Lomranz, Shmotkin, and Vardi 1991), time as related to various personality traits and behaviors, the meaning of time-related concepts across the life span, the passage of time, perceived properties of time, and time perspective in Holocaust survivors (e.g., Lomranz et al. 1985).

Complexity, Perception, Cognition, and Ideology

I have always felt constrained by Aristotelian logic and at home with complexity as a cognitive style (Suedfeld and Bluck 1993). Complexity is not limited to perceptual/cognitive styles but may also find expression in one's philosophy of life, for example, the acceptance of diversity, contrasts, the ideology of democracy, freedom of choice, and letting people

"evolve" on their own, all also ingrained in my work as a scientist, an educator, and a clinical psychologist. These may be related to my refugee
and immigration experiences, where choices could not always be made,
preferences could often not be obtained, and seemingly contradictory
states had to be lived with. It may well be that my tendency to accept complexity and diversity constitutes a way of problem solving and a mode by
which conflict can be solved and contradictions accepted. The epistemological essence of complexity has evolved to become part of my scientific interest as reflected in my work on the image of man, the concept
of aintegration (e.g., Lomranz 1998b), and the notion of the wandering
Jew outlined subsequently.

Constancy, Continuity, Discontinuity, and Change

While constancy has a strongly felt presence in the experience and perception of my Self and the world, I am also at home with the notion of
nonconstancy and change characterized by discontinuity. The maintenance and consistency of the Self are a particularly intriguing question
with relation to disruptive historical and developmental experiences. As
psychologists, many of us learn that chaos or sharp disruptions in the
individual, society, or culture destroy the coherence of the Self. If so,
how, for instance, are we to understand the posttraumatic Holocaust survivors who experienced disruption on almost every conceivable level and
yet most of whom function adequately and experience themselves as
"whole" people? Herein lies my specific interest in the study of change
associated with discontinuity as well as the study of Holocaust survivors
and elderly people.

A personal sense of continuity may be associated with a generational
one, based to a great extent on a social heritage, the flow of age grades
and generational transmissions. Couched in these terms, I would expect
to experience discontinuity in my life. As a Jewish refugee, I was robbed
of the rich Jewish-German-Yiddish culture of my family, of its language
and even of its geographical existence. A collective memory needs a
geography, but I am not able to tell my children: go visit the birthplaces
of your ancestors or that of your grandfathers, since those have been
wiped out. I recall that for years I had what almost amounted to an urge
to buy a piece of land to have as my own. Wandering between countries
not my own has contributed to my versatility and flexibility in regard to
the functions of continuity and coherence. Again, all these find expression in my scientific work (Lomranz, 1998).

Toward People

While I cherish my individualism, I have also always felt an affinity to Karen Horney's "towards people" concept (Horney 1950). While such individual inclinations may be related to the fact that I had no siblings and, as an only child, had to learn to be self-absorbed and thus, perhaps, to combat loneliness, the social and people-oriented aspects may also be related to my parents and my life as a refugee. My parents liked people and developed close friendships, and active community involvement was central in their existence.

As a clinical psychologist and researcher, I tended to treat the more severely suffering populations (e.g., psychotics, the brain injured, post-traumatic survivors, the aged afflicted with various problems). The various university-based institutions I established were geared toward people under stress or undergoing transitions (e.g., Holocaust survivors, the aged, the brain injured). I am continuously engaged in initiating new centers, building bridges between theory and practice, between the ivory tower university and the community, and carrying a heavy load of administrative work in an attempt to initiate change. Such inclinations also found expression in my efforts to improve interpersonal sensitivity and alleviate intergroup conflict, in my work on conflict resolution between Arabs and Jews (Lakin, Lomranz, Lieberman 1969), my research on values (e.g., Pazy and Lomranz 1980), and my ongoing work as a clinical psychologist.

Time, space, territory, perceptual and cognitive modes, values, and social involvement are powerfully interrelated. In many instances, the separation between these entities or the absence of one, for instance, territory, may, among other things, create or increase a sense of absence, longing, or loneliness. The issues of separation, loss, and growth run, like a thread, through most of my research and are central in the research on Holocaust survivors and midlife couples. In fact, one of my articles on launching is titled (after Rilke) "And Thus We Live, Forever Separating." By definition, the previously outlined epistemological characteristics must necessarily be dispersed in all of my scientific work.

The Cogent Fields of My Scientific Work

At this point, I would like to assemble my scientific work, dispersed under the various epistemological components, into four centralizing areas, all of which, of course, also reflect the basic traces of my personal history and perhaps bear out more forcefully some of those noted earlier.

Human Nature and the Image of Man: The Field of Personality Theory

The Jewish prayer (recited especially at funerals) that asks, "Who are you? Where did you come from? Where are you going? And to whom will you be giving your life's account?" seems to encompass the essential questions about the human condition, personality theory, and human nature.

I believe it is time to supplement the present personality research, focusing on "variables," with more basic questions about human nature and to engage in the formulation of broader theoretical questions. However, a basic required shift in the field requires a shift in our comprehension of human nature, a needed change in the image of Western man. This change in image is not just philosophical; it also has vital, essential implications in the world of science. After Auschwitz and now that postmodernism characterizes most domains of life, such a change in the human image and in our language and the conception of culture, science, and human beings seems to be a necessity.

Almost all of my mentioned research interests find their core in my investigations in the field of personality theory and my efforts to formulate inclusive theories or concepts about personality (e.g., Lomranz 1986). Western culture was, to a great extent, built, rather strictly, on such principles as harmony, integration, Aristotelian logic, causality, homogeneity, synchronization, consistency, and continuity. These were also the underlying principles in comprehending human nature and the image of man. My recent work on aintegration (1998a), based on an expanded notion of the human image, indicates that people may live with contradictions, discontinuity, and paradox. In this work, I emphasize human strength and the capacity to endure difficulties, hardships, and inconsistencies, enabling people to absorb events that do not make sense, to be bewildered cognitively and frustrated emotionally, and yet to maintain mental health. Perhaps a paradigmatic shift is necessary if we are to conceive of the human condition in its totality, including the ability to age, suffer, enjoy, endure, and grow, all at the same time.

Clinical Psychology

My early *research on groups* focused on group dynamics, on personal growth, and on the diversities of methodology and leader typology in such groups (e.g., Lomranz, Lakin, and Schiffman 1972). I was also intrigued by the brain-behavior relationship, and my interest in *psychoneurology* found expression in the treatment of severely brain-injured people. My clinical research interest in *trauma* and *depression* was manifested in my application of systematically ongoing measures of depressive mood reactions to a life-span sample, investigating how the public mood in Israel changes along time and relates to significant and stressful events, such as the Lebanon War or the Gulf War. My work in clinical psychology is best divided into two interrelated sections: theoretical and research interests and work as a practicing clinical psychologist.

Clinical psychology is a multifaceted discipline and profession. It has relevance to the life sciences, the health sciences, medicine, the arts, the humanities, and the social sciences. Its methods include empiricism, phenomenology, and cognitive and experiential sciences. Such a wide array of relevances is well suited to my intellectual tendencies, my love of art, and my scientific and social endeavors. In clinical psychology I see a field in which the conception of art and science as the two different cultures can be challenged and disproved.

My personal history and experiences as an immigrant, a refugee, and a wanderer instilled in me, among other things, a certain degree of curiosity, compassion for people, universality as an outlook, the acceptance of complexity and diversity, a certain measure of altruism, and a belief that changes can be for the better. These have become absorbed into my ongoing behaviors as well as those traits and acts that constitute the basic and classic processes in psychotherapy—listening, empathy, transference, working through resistance, countertransference, striving for understanding, grieving for loss and creating new possibilities, containing excitement, enduring sorrow, experiencing compassion, and providing support. I also assume that my history has placed me in an "in-between" cultural position that, together with the ability to distance oneself, is in many ways a required position for a psychotherapist. Being able to experience personal growth, then to separate and yet feel enriched, is a major result of constructive psychotherapy, just as it may also be for wanderers and immigrants.

Personally, performing exclusively individual psychotherapy was always insufficient for me. I therefore was always involved in creating clinical institutional frameworks through which help could be extended to those in need. It is in that light that I view the establishment of a unit for the treatment and study of severely brain-injured Israeli soldiers and their families. The unit had an exciting, pioneering, and experimental atmosphere, and its programs and treatment techniques have been disseminated to other Israeli institutes for the brain damaged. The creation of a psychological service for the aged (Lomranz and Bar-tur 1998) and the Herczeg Institute on Aging can be conceived in the same light.

Living Despite Trauma

For several years I refrained from investigating Holocaust survivors, which coincided with my refusal to visit Germany. However, my profound interest in this subject area came about through my conviction that a different approach and attitude toward Holocaust survivors must come to the fore and that this can be achieved only on the basis of a different research approach. For one, I wished to focus on the strength of survivors. Their wounds may be permanent but their strength to cope with them and live normal, rewarding, and fruitful lives is as yet a wonder. I attempt to comprehend the survivor more inclusively, in a broad coping and living context, actually humanizing the image of survivors. A comprehensively existential approach to survivors necessitates, however, a differential as well as an integrative approach. The life-span-oriented, theoretical, multidimensional model (Lomranz 1990, 1995), which I developed, includes the long-term impact of the trauma and the manner in which its influence may vibrate across the years; the impact on the survivors' developmental line and their developmental stages and tasks; the impact of historical events; the resulting stress upon the survivors; and finally, the various resources at their disposal to cope with the trauma: their personality configurations and personal, interpersonal, and environmental resources. Some of our major investigations with survivors included the themes of hope, cognitive operations, defense mechanisms, and the role of interpersonal relationships in the death camps and afterward as revealed in posttraumatic processes. This work also has an integrative quality in that it relates Holocaust research to the general body of research in personality theories, adult development, and coping with stress. In terms of methodology, I utilize nomothetic as well as idiographic approaches (Suedfeld et al. 1997). In light of that model, my research focused on normal samples of survivors (as opposed to clinical ones) and introduced differentiation as to the nature of the traumatic experience (e.g., death camps, working camps, hiding, etc.; or age at onset of trauma, gender, etc.). I believe that many of my biographical and epistemological aspects, with which the reader is by now familiar, were all blended as they found a meaningful channel in the study of survivorship in general and specifically that of the Holocaust survivor.

Adult Development and Gerontology

I adopted the developmental life-span perspective in my investigations of *mid-life couples, separating,* and *the launching process* (e.g., Lomranz et al. 1996). Further along the life span lies my interest in *gerontology* (including elderly Holocaust survivors). My interests here focused on mental health and aging in general (e.g., Lomranz 1998a), as well as that in homes for the aged. However, this interest grows out of an array of far broader interests. In adult development and gerontology I also find the conflation of many of my basic interests (e.g., time, personal space, personality theory, long-term adaptation to traumatic stress, mental health, death). Currently, my efforts are focused on gerontological theory and educational and clinical gerontology. These have found expression in the establishment of a unique model clinic; in a psychological service for the elderly in homes for the aged (Lomranz and Bartur 1998); and in my efforts to develop a graduate program in gerontology, as well as in my private practice, where most of my patients are elderly. I have to admit that my work in gerontology also is imbued with "missionary" zeal, since I wish to contribute to societal change, to the position of the elderly in our culture, to educating the general public, and to "gerontologizing" scientists so that many more of them will be dedicated to work in this field, all endeavors that will lead to the humanization of aging.

Despite great progress in recent years by the elderly in integrating into society, they are still far behind and are considered marginal "limbo" people (Hazan 1980). In fact, there are striking similarities, in certain respects, between the elderly and refugees. Both have often been torn away from their roots, "processed" in terms of human and geographical ecology, and coerced into accepting new roles. Both are marginal, residing on the fringes, outsiders, suffering the larger society's approach to them as a minority group. Both groups may project a set of values no longer relevant to their present surroundings and culture, and both may have to talk in a "double voice" (Hazan 1996). Here, however, the resemblance may end since refugees and immigrants have, in general, better opportunities to grow and develop, especially in Western societies, where they often become the major force leading to progress and change. The elderly may want to feel committed to their respective societies, but those societies, while paying them lip service in calling them "senior citizens," at the same time expel them and render them outsiders. Old age is penalized, and injustice prevails. I feel we are confronted with waste and injustice that undermine our claim of humanness as a society.

My own history and identification as a refugee may have constructively contributed to my development in the field of gerontology. I also recognize a further feature of mine that has an element of rebellion. I often find myself in professional and social opposition to the dealings of institutions, organizations, and governments as well as to policies and societal structures. Can we detect here a refugee mentality of the "wandering Jew," a person who, in order to survive successfully, can not identify with institutions and authority and so rebels against, evades, or mocks them? Finally, aging and death, as Lévi-Strauss (1963) argues, are both natural and anticultural. It seems to me that my work in gerontology, which has perhaps incorporated my encounters with death, occupies precisely that space between the natural and the anticultural, a space that provides me with an arena for committed scientific work in gerontology.

In the preceding discussion, personal and academic/professional histories have been dwelt upon and at times interrelated. I leave it to the reader, at this point, to draw his or her own further conclusions about motivational or guiding connections between history and scientific endeavors and products. As we continue, I attempt to provide more integrating inferences of this material through some broader and relevant conceptualizations.

Some Unifying Cogent Concepts

The question to be asked in this section is, Which concepts may interrelate existential and professional life lines? In many ways this chapter (as well as the others in this book) serves as a testimony, demonstrating how a constructive life is carved out in spite of catastrophe. In an attempt to better understand the intricate processes of such adjustment and growth, I will try to explicate some notions that I believe bridge, and to a certain extent integrate, the various life events, histories, and biographies. I feel free here to weave a tapestry of various concepts, offering schemas to explain the interweaving of scientific and career development in light of the personal histories of displaced people. I therefore focus on umbrella concepts such as immigrant, refugee, and especially wandering Jew. I should state that at different times in my life I felt I was residing in each of these concepts and in fact now feel I incorporate them all.

Basic Concepts

Immigration

Roget's *International Thesaurus* (1962) places the terms *migration* and *immigrant* under the category of "travel," "wandering" (including wandering Jew), and "traveler." Grinberg and Grinberg (1989) state that "migration" refers to the geographic mobility of people who move from one place to another but caution that "Those who emigrate and the conditions of their migration are of an infinite variety" (16). However, even in the best of cases, that is, when it occurs out of a person's free will, immigration is a complex process and has personal, interpersonal, social, economic, and cultural repercussions. This is even truer when immigration is a consequence of forced, involuntary migration, as in my own case and that of millions of others. Then one would designate these people as *refugees,* defined as "person[s] taking shelter in another country, from war, persecution, natural disaster or trouble" (*Oxford Dictionary of Current English* 1996). Frequent, accumulating immigrations, like those that were part of my history, involve a repetitive cycle of uprooting, relocating, and readjusting. They involve wandering, experiencing hardships and separation, finding temporary refuge, adapting culturally, paying a high physical and mental cost when coping with stress, and then repeating and, in many ways, reliving the whole process.

Refugees as an in-between, "Desert Generation"

The refugee reenacts the state of transition as an existential state. Experiencing a continuous state of transition may give one a sense of "almost" belonging to a particular culture but, at the same time, being a stranger to it. The result is that one seems to be residing in an "in-between" culture: living in more then one culture, between positions, between identities, and between political systems. An in-between position may provide broader perspectives, but it also prevents one from becoming a full partner. It may, moreover, become an existence characterized by a constant striving, which is never realized. In association with the in-between state, I recall the notion of "seeing the beloved country from the mountain but never reaching it" as a psychological-existential metaphor. Even more powerful may be the concept of "the generation of the desert." Its origin is in the Bible (Exodus); the desert generation had to wander forty years in the desert not because of the distance from Egypt to Israel but because this, although liberated, was a generation of slaves, with a slave mentality. Hence, Moses feared they could not serve as the founders of a new, free people. In fact such a generation of refugees may, perhaps, be unable to become an integral part of the new state; they may not even be able to identify with it despite the fact that they strove for it. This was a generation between the old culture and the new; between new and old values; between their memories of and homesickness for Egypt, the known past, and their anticipation of the promised land, Israel, the future dream. While their fate was cruel, to wander until they died, their transitional position was clear: the task of readjusting and integrating was beyond their ability. Generalizing this metaphor, many immigrants and refugees may have a similar fate, and only their children, or grand-children, may achieve full partnership in their host countries. This may also be part of the dynamics of generational gaps; the elderly, the greater part of their lives behind them, may indefinitely carry the mark of the "stranger." They may not be able to adapt and utilize to the utmost the possibilities in their new environment, while their children may be able to do so.

A Refugee Disposition

Notions such as "homeland," "my" country, or "exile" may, for some peo-ple, carry an anachronistic meaning. However, who can conceive the depth of insult and injury resulting from being torn from the body—country or home—with which one so profoundly identifies? Such insults to the psyche may have long-lasting impacts on one's personality. In the battles of survival and adjustment, the denial of the present may be used, the present then possibly becoming frozen between a past, usually mythologized, and a future. Even after a refugee feels more comfortable and even enjoys what the new culture has to offer, therefore realizing the old culture would anyhow not be a place he or she would want to return to, the refugee still does not feel more a part of the host culture. The realization only leaves him or her with sadness about being uprooted, with pain and confusion. All these result in a psychological habitat, which I term *a refugee disposition.*

I define a *refugee disposition* as a state of mind characterized by a sense of uprootedness, the awareness of one's inability to identify with and feel part of the culture ("I will never be a real American/Frenchman," etc.), its people and norms; by the feeling that what matters is temporal and transient; by emotional blocks to involvement, experiencing the ambiva-lence of wanting to belong but fearing to be immersed in the new cul-ture and, thus, experiencing estrangement and alienation. It may well be that such an attitude, which has the effect of distancing, is, in part, a conducive stance for a scientist or psychologist.

The Wandering Jew: Definition and Characterization

I propose to focus on the concept of the "wandering Jew," a concept related to and at times overlapping with the concept of refugee, yet one that is rich in its specific characteristics and meanings and therefore merits separate attention in an understanding of how my personal and professional histories have converged. Despite its historically Christian-Jewish legacy and basis, I believe that the concept of "wandering Jew" in a postmodern society is not confined to Jews but is relevant to the personal comprehension of perhaps millions of people in the Western world.

Historically, the Christian legend "The Wandering Jew" is assumed to have been finally composed in Constantinople in the fourth century and first appears in literature in the West in the thirteenth century. The story tells of a Jerusalem cobbler called Ahasuerus, who was condemned to wander eternally for having taunted Jesus on his journey to the crucifixion. While the original legend refers to one Jew, it later was applied to Jews in general and was anti-Semitic in nature. Clearly the legend that Jews are by nature wanderers is false (in fact they wished to strike roots and stay in their various countries); but their history is a series of expulsions from the countries they lived in, and their wanderings seem to aptly describe the conditions under which Jews actually lived for thousand of years.

This Jewish-related concept (at times interchanged with the term *eternal Jew*), which I regard here as representing a human psychological condition, a state of mind, is well known in the world and has been popular, especially in the European literature, for ages. Jewish and Christian writers and philosophers have depicted the wandering Jew in major works. These include, among others (Baron 1985): Guillaume Apollinaire (who portrayed the wandering Jew as a jester enjoying his wanderings); Buber (as craving and cheerful); Byron, George Eliot, and Louis Golding (as following his fate); Goethe (as sarcastic and observing misfortunes with irony); Robert Hemerling (as Cain who is denied death); Kierkegaard (as forever enduring), Potok (as a personality synonymous with wandering); Shelley (as a Promethean atheist); and Wordsworth (as craving rest). Keeping such literary and artistic portrayals in mind, I would like to add further characterizations of the wandering Jew (including some that are distinct from those of the refugee), in the area of personality, internal dynamics, and sociocultural spheres.

Some Personality Characteristics

Risk Taking

It seems that the wandering Jew has learned to live immersed in a situation of constant danger without being disabled by it. He or she is forced and at times is willing to take risks despite constant danger. The wandering Jew may be at home with the concept of "fate," which in many ways may guide him or her to differentiate between what can or cannot be changed. It may aid the wanderer in an attempt to turn matters to personal benefit even under oppressing circumstances.

Curiosity

Curiosity may well be reinforced and enhanced by a life of wandering in childhood, given the fact that children often react differently than adults, with curiosity and excitement, to relocations and new places. Personal curiosity and wandering may enrich each other.

For most scientists, curiosity may be a necessary condition. For me, the tendencies to "expect," to "long for," and to "crave" are somehow associated with curiosity. These fuel further expectations, strivings, and ambitions for future plans, dreams to be actualized, discoveries, and scientific work. Inherent in wandering, moving from one place to another, is the possibility of finding something new. As scientists move from subject to subject, a potential for new creative acts may come to the fore.

Restlessness, Sustenance, Breadth, and Work

Scientists, in many cases, are required to be "gray workers," engaged in formalized and at times routine work (Kuhn 1962). This may be an obstacle for some scientists-as-wandering-Jews, who experience restlessness, for whom single-track mindedness may be boring, and who find it difficult to sustain interest in one subject and maintain consistent work patterns as their interests change. Such tendencies may result from the wanderers' experience of interruptions in their schooling, work, and lifestyles.

All these may result in an inability to achieve adequate goals and may also jeopardize further gains in those scientific areas with which the scientist is preoccupied. On the other hand, broad-mindedness, tolerance, open-mindedness, the ability to utilize opportunities, and wide perspectives may be the other side of this coin. A history of wandering and diverse experiences may also magnify one's interest in the global and the gestalt rather than in the details, in the macro rather than in the micro. The same scientist, then, who is unable to pursue a very defined, specific course may tend to be dialectic and produce integration between related issues and fields or find a niche in, for example, the history of ideas.

Practical versus Philosophical

H. N. Bialik (1873–1934), who is regarded as the national poet of Israel, described his father as a man "with his feet on the ground and his head in the sky." This characterization may fit many of the Diaspora Jews who were engrossed in practical doings, seeking work and earning a livelihood, but were also, in light of their value system, culture, and tradition, inclined to sit in synagogues and study the Holy Scriptures. As we turn to Jewish immigrants, refugees, and wanderers and superimpose that background on their condition, we see that at least in some of them, this has led to an intensified conflict between the so-called practical and the philosophical. The wanderer, rich in the experience of expulsions and resettling, may, due to considerations of survival and adjustment, decide in favor of the practical. The abilities to succeed, to comprehend priorities, to calculate correctly what will produce positive results and change are also all in the interest of social scientists (many of them being applied scientists).

Humor

Humor can be considered as experiences a person encounters and laughs at, as a defense mechanism, and, in a broader sense, as part of a worldview or an approach to life. Humor entails the unity of contrasts, and antithetical thoughts can be unified in a joke. Humor can also enable coping even if negative emotions are involved. Humor, as Valliant (1993) claims, "like hope, permits one to focus upon and to bear what is too terrible to be borne" (73). Jews, on the whole, have used humor to cope and have contributed remarkably to this field. It is no accident that having been persecuted for thousands of years, Jews have turned humor into a cultural value, well developed and integrated into their being, as reflected especially in the Yiddish language.

As a component in one's worldview, humor enables one to be aware of contradictions yet to feel above them, to be persecuted and yet experience a certain superiority as well as sympathy or compassion. It may permit self-criticism without self-deprecation and self-harm. As an approach to life, it may foster openness and lead to distancing from extremism and tolerance. As a cognitive style, it includes the appreciation of paradox, the use of wit, the use of dialectics, and the ability to synthesize. The reader will recognize here some attributes of scientists. However, I should add that the life experiences of wandering— witnessing frequent changes, learning that facts are not necessarily eternal, that time continuously brings about vicissitudes, and that diversity and different perspectives always exist—all may contribute to the cultivation of humor.

Identity and Its Sources

Do not migration and wandering pose a threat to the sense of identity? Identification results from the continual interaction between spatial, temporal, and social integrative links (Grinberg and Grinberg 1989) and necessitates sources of reference to each of those. With what source or reference group can the wandering Jew actually identify as he or she moves from country to country, changing professions or interests, social environments, cultural settings, and the human scene? Where does the wanderer turn to in order to fill the needs required for self-identity and its maintenance?

Interpersonal Resources

Given the wanderer's predicament, it is only natural that his or her *intimate circle*, family and significant others, plays a crucial role. It is here that he or she invests, and in return that circle functions as a buffer against stress. The wanderer may not even expect or ascribe importance to acceptance by the larger culture. Such acceptance may even entail the danger of loss of self-identity. While refugees may strive to incorporate the values of their new environment, the wanderer adheres to personal values, based on a belief system (e.g., religion or worldview) and the principles operating in his or her family and community life.

Psychosocial and Cultural Resources

Erikson (1956) conceives identity as the relationship between an individual and the group. Various aspects of *reference groups* relevant to our discussion should be noted (Hyman and Singer 1968). For the wanderer, two potentially contrasting groups come to mind. One is the local and sectoral reference group to which the wanderer perceives him- or herself as belonging; the other refers to the wider, "external" surrounding (e.g., authorities, government, etc.) groups or agents. In fact, this potential contrast finds an almost metaphoric expression nowadays in public and political opinion in the State of Israel, as some quote the statement of the first prime minister, Ben Gurion, that it is not important what the "Gentiles say but what the Jews do," while others take the opposite stand, that what the international community thinks is what counts.

It certainly must be extremely terrifying to belong to an ethnic group that is being persecuted or systematically exterminated. However, a common fate fosters cohesion, solidarity, and identity. The wandering Jew, also known as a storyteller, may experience identification with a group with whom he or she continuously constructs a narrative, the narrative of the wandering Jew. As noted by Funkenstein (1993), "The identity of an individual and the identity of a group consists of the construction of a narrative, internal and external: the narrative constructed *by* and the narrative constructed *about* the subject" (23). Other identification resources may lie in adherence to a belief in an unchanging entity, such as the belief in God, a sense of uniqueness that puts a person apart from social and cultural surroundings, or a stress on that person's unique attributes in contrast to those of other individuals (e.g., "I cherish learning more than those around me," etc.).

Belongingness: National, Cultural, and Territorial
The immigrant building a new life in a very specific territory wants to relate, identify, belong, and become part of that place and culture. This may be part of his or her attempt to relinquish a sense of discontinuity. Erikson (1956) explicates how the attainment of identity necessitates a sense of belongingness that, in turn, in every transitional situation, always involves a change in norms, values, and behaviors. This may not always hold true for the wanderer. He or she may not experience marginality and may not yearn to become part of the host or refugee society or wish to belong to it. The wanderer may identify with various parts of the values or norms of the host culture, but that is not a necessity since the wanderer is not threatened by discontinuity. The wanderer fears being swallowed up by the host culture, while the immigrant may wish for it. In contrast to the refugee who, not feeling belongingness, is upset and constructs his or her "nostalgic" places of worship, stores, social circles, and so on, which are needed since their absence may be disruptive to the refugee's identity, for the wandering Jew the sense of specific, local belongingness is irrelevant. Thus in various ways, the wanderer may be, paradoxically, much more a part of the host country. The wanderer

finds the "expectable environment" wherever he or she is, in a constructed ecology (which may consist of the books the wanderer reads, the special food or drink consumed, friends, various cultural and artistic rituals, specific connections with the host culture, etc.). Not being completely integrated and, furthermore, taking pride in that situation, the wanderer may be self-content. He or she feels content and does not want to give up the identity of a wandering Jew. In many ways the wanderer does not want to, or knows it will not be possible to, strike permanent roots in the new place. The wanderer's sense of time is different because of the knowledge that he or she will have to—because of external or internal reasons—separate and wander again.

Acceptance of an Internal Exile

While exile, an intriguing, multidisciplinary concept, may be thought of as relevant mainly to political refugees, I prefer a broader approach. Felman and Laub (1992) claim that "In its strong sense, exile is not merely a departure but an act of self-expropriation and renunciation of one's origins" (35). In this definition, one may find removal from a natural, original location, and yet it also casts light on the Self as an active actor and perhaps as covertly accepting the state of exile. Part of the wandering Jew's state of mind may be characterized as a constant "internal exile." He or she may accept it as a personal ontology. Such acceptance as part of the Self may also be a prerequisite for the success and growth of the exiled in exile. Examples can be found in the arts (e.g., Chagall, Chopin, Hindemith, etc.), in science, (e.g., Einstein, Kurt Lewin, etc.), and in fact in the flourishing of culturally rich centers designated as exile or Diaspora (e.g., the Jews in Babylon, Moslem Spain, Germany, and the contemporary United States; the Indians in South Africa, etc.). So while exile comes about through eruption and persecution, it is also associated with growth, success, and happiness. Furthermore, as a core concept in Judaism, a positive meaning was attributed to exile. It has been considered by many Jewish religious thinkers and philosophers as the state that has enabled, through the suffering it brings upon the Jewish people, the uniqueness, the strong religious faith, and the high spiritual level of Jews. Many have argued for the eternal perpetuation of Jewish exile, at least until the coming of the Messiah. The point to be made is that exile, for the wandering Jew as well as for many scientists, may, in a very profound sense, be considered not as a disaster to be undone but as a proper habitat or state of being. The wanderer perhaps functions in line with a "transitional ecology," that is, an ecology that is in constant transition, ever moving, an ecology that one makes oneself belong to but does not have a possessive feeling about. This comes close to a transcendent relationship, a sense of universality, or an Eastern sense of "cosmology."

It should be interesting to relate these components to the scientific way of life. The scientific community is international. As I go through my own habitats, I count that during my lifetime I have lived (the measure being at least one year or more in a place) in twenty homes, as I assume many a wandering Jew has. The life of a scientist is seldom localized. He or she, like the wandering Jew, has to be a member of an international community.

Summary

I have mapped the contours of the concept of the wandering Jew. On the basis of that description we can demarcate the personality configuration of the wandering Jew as someone who does not experience a commitment to territorial roots, perhaps perceives dislocations as a matter of destiny, and may also take a certain pride in his or her condition. The wanderer may feel him- or herself a "universal person," forever enduring, with a broad perspective and conscious of the many surrounding worlds. The wanderer's personality characteristics include curiosity, risk taking, humor, and open-mindedness; these in fact may counterbalance the element of loneliness that is an inseparable part of wandering. He or she may be well rehearsed in seizing opportunities, combining practicality with spirituality, searching for novelty yet feeling restless and experiencing difficulties in sustaining an ongoing interest or committing to superficialities. The sources and reference groups for the wanderer's identity are family and an intimate circle. He or she is a person for whom Exile is an internalized global space, a person who is able to bear the distance of not belonging locally but basically feeling belongingness to a different essence. The wanderer is able to create a personal ecology in different places. Being equipped with all these attributes enables him or her to adjust, experience considerable well-being, and succeed in work, career tracks, and life.

The personality dynamics embedded in the wandering Jew present a specific case of how, despite a background of persecution, uprooting, and dislocations, constructive modes of existence may develop. Among those many modes may also be the one characterized by the life of a scientist and his or her specific productions and achievements. Furthermore, later gains can be related to earlier hardships. Persecution may sharpen sensitivities; uprootedness may result in flexibility; wandering may engender the tendency to differentiate and seek alternative perspectives; the struggle to survive may foster useful coping capabilities; and distress may nurture the seeds of creativity. Thus, it is the constructive powers of human beings, even those with a catastrophic background, that I wish to emphasize.

The contours of the wandering Jew I have outlined cannot be separated from my personal worldview formulated in the course of my history. I not only deem the wandering Jew concept significant in comprehending the convergence of my personal and professional life lines but also consider its descriptions to be important as we attempt to comprehend the lives of immigrants, refugees, and "foreign workers" around the world who were able to build constructive lives, as scientists or otherwise. Now, traumas, genocide, uprooting, and relocations are not the fate of only the few; rather they characterize the condition of many millions. The wandering Jew's qualities have become universal to many because of the characteristics of postmodern society, in which both mobility and uprootedness have become universal trademarks found in the histories of many nations. Thus, "wandering Jew" should be comprehended beyond its Jewish signification and understood in universal terms, as some literary writings actually conceived of it.

I wrote this chapter while residing in Chelsea and in New York City, time and space reflecting again the wandering Jew's state of mind and habitat. For me personally, the terms *immigrant, refugee,* and *wandering Jew* are historically-developmentally grounded and actually genetically pronounced in my being. I have projected the concept of the wandering Jew, including developmental and dynamic experiences of persecution and hardships, as well as those of lifestyle and growth, onto my own history to serve as a core framework in which the specific areas of my scientific work can be understood. It may serve as the arena in which the specific biographical components incorporated in my work, as demonstrated in the sections on the various disciplines I engage in, have been played out. In many ways the sum total of my experiences as a child, an adolescent, and an adult resulted in characteristics similar to those of the wandering Jew, characteristics also reflected in my life, including my life's productions and scientific gains.

Epilogue: Understanding Lives as a Combination of Factors

The intelligent reader will not assume a direct relationship between mass historical events and the exact nature of a career line. The conglomeration of factors, processes, and dynamics is far too large to enable causal relationships. Yet I have suggested here possible personal and professional connections, which I leave for the reader to judge. Moreover, even with the present limited information at the reader's disposal, I would encourage him or her to further relate to the various personal and historical events and the interaction between them.

One's narrative, despite its reliance on past selective memory, also reflects a substantive existence. I lived through the hardships described and am a victim of World War II and its atrocities. The catastrophe in my life and my losses as well as my building experiences in the postwar years all had a powerful impact, and the attempt to comprehend their influence on my mode of existence is a challenge. The goal in this chapter was to comprehend how events in the flow of life accumulate, bring forth behaviors and additional events, and create developments and how, after all, the past is interwoven in the present, as Freud (1916) aspired to understand. Ultimately I think we are interested here in the existential-professional combination and its interrelatedness with the sweep of unfortunate history, because it tells us something about our private selves and at the same time about human abilities and nature. My preoccupation with this chapter brought home to me, perhaps even more forcefully, that *who* I am, including my personal development as a scientist, is inextricably intertwined with *what* I experienced, including the experience of trauma and uprootedness. The contemplation of such interrelated processes of personal history and work is an essential ingredient in self-knowledge, which I believe, in the tradition of Socrates, can be shared so that it becomes communal knowledge. I can only hope that the reader detects these processes in the present discourse, becomes engaged in a personal discourse of relating and integrating his or her personal experience, and in fact, in that manner, produces his or her own additional contribution to the communal knowledge presented here.

NOTE

The author gratefully acknowledges the support of the Naftali Frankel Fund for Holocaust Research.

REFERENCES

Baron, J. 1985. *A treasury of Jewish quotations.* London: Jason Aronson.

Epstein, J. 1997. The personal essay: A form of discovery. In *The Norton book of personal essays,* edited by J. Epstein, 11–24. New York: Norton.

Erikson, E. 1956. The problem of ego identity. *Journal of the American Psychoanalytic Association* 4:19–27.

Eyal, N. 1996. *Real time: The personal experience of time.* Tel Aviv: Aryeh Nir.

———. 1997. *As the river runs: A psychological journey.* Tel-Aviv: Miskal-Yedioth Achronoth.

Felman, S., and D. Laub. 1992. *Testimony: Crises of witnessing in literature, psychoanalysis, and history.* New York: Routledge.

Freud, S. 1916. *Mourning and melancholia. The standard edition of the complete works of Sigmund Freud,* 14:239–58. London: Hogarth.

Funkenstein, A. 1993. The incomprehensible catastrophe: Memory and narrative. In *The narrative study of lives,* edited by R. Josellson and A. Lieblich, 21–29. London: Sage.

Grinberg, L., and R. Grinberg. 1989. *Psychoanalytic perspectives on migration and exile.* New Haven: Yale University Press.

Hazan, H. 1980. *The limbo people: A study of the constitution of the time universe among the aged.* London: Routledge and Kegan Paul.

———. 1996. *From first principles: An experiment in ageing.* London: Bergin and Garvey.

Horney, K. 1950. *Neurosis and human growth.* New York: Norton.

Hyman, H., and E. Singer. 1968. *Reading in reference theory and research.* New York: Free Press.

Kuhn, T. 1962. *The structure of scientific revolutions.* Chicago: University of Chicago Press.

Lakin, M., H. J. Lomranz, and M. Lieberman. 1969. Arab and Jew in Israel: A human relations training approach to conflict. *NTL Institute for Applied Behavioral Science. Exploration in Applied Behavioral Science,* vol. 1. Washington, DC: Library of Congress, catalog no. 76-95235.

Levi-Strauss, C. 1963. *Structural anthropology.* New York: Basic Books.

Lomranz, J. 1986. Personality theory: Position and derived teaching implications for clinical psychology. *Professional Psychology: Research and Practice* 17, no. 6:551–59.

———. 1990. Long-term adaptation to traumatic stress in light of adult development and aging perspectives. In *Stress and coping in later life families,* edited by M. A. Parris Stephens, S. E. Crowther, S. Hobfoll, and D. L. Tennenbaum, 99–121. Washington, DC: Hemisphere.

———. 1995. Endurance and living: Long-term effects of the Holocaust. In *Extreme stress and communities: Impact and intervention,* edited by S. Hobfoll and M. De Vries, 325–52. Boston: Kluwer.

———, ed. 1998a. *Handbook of aging and mental health: An integrative approach.* New York: Plenum.

————. 1998b. An image of aging and the concept of aintegration: Coping and mental health implications. In *Handbook of aging and mental health: An integrative approach,* edited by J. Lomranz. New York: Plenum.

Lomranz, J., and L. Bar-tur. 1998. Nursing home care and consultation. In *Comprehensive clinical psychology,* edited by B. Edelstein. Amsterdam: Elsevier Science.

Lomranz, J., M. Lakin, and H. Schiffman. 1972. Variants of sensitivity training and encounter: Diversity or fragmentation. *Journal of Applied Behavioral Science* 8, no. 4:339–420.

Lomranz, J., and A. Pazy. 1980. Cultural aspects in conceptions of values. *Megamot Behavioral Science Quarterly* 25, no. 3:341–50 (in Hebrew).

Lomranz, J., A. Shapira, N. Horesh, and Y. Gilat. 1975. Children's personal space as a function of age and sex. *Developmental Psychology* 11, no. 5:541–45.

Lomranz, J., D. Shmotkin, N. Eyal, and Y. Zohar. 1996. Launching themes in Israeli fathers and mothers. *Journal of Adult Development* 3, no. 3:159–70.

Lomranz, J., D. Shmotkin, and R. Vardi. 1991. The equivocal meaning of time: Exploratory and structural analyses. *Current Psychology: Research and Reviews* 10, nos. 1 and 2:3–20.

Lomranz, J., D. Shmotkin, A. Zechovoy, and E. Rosenberg. 1985. Time orientation in Nazi concentration camp survivors: Forty years after. *American Journal of Orthopsychiatry* 55:230–36.

Lubow, R. 1977. *The war animals.* New York: Doubleday.

Merton, G. 1973. *The sociology of science.* Chicago: University of Chicago Press.

Oxford dictionary of current English. New York: Oxford University Press.

Pazy, A., and J. Lomranz. 1980. Value conceptions of American and Israeli youth. *Journal of Social Psychology* 111:181–87.

Robinson, D. 1976. *An intellectual history of psychology.* New York: Macmillan.

Roget's International Thesaurus. New York: Crowell.

Suedfeld, P., and S. Bluck. 1993. Changes in integrative complexity accompanying significant life events: Historical evidence. *Journal of Personality and Social Psychology* 64, no. 1:124–30.

Suedfeld, P., R. Krell, R. Wiebe, and G. Steel. 1997. Coping strategies in the narratives of Holocaust survivors. *Anxiety, Stress, and Coping* 10:153–79.

Vaillant, G. 1993. *The wisdom of the ego.* Cambridge: Harvard University Press.

Reflecting on Memories and Professional Pursuits

Roberta S. Sigel

Biographical Note

Roberta S. Sigel is professor of political science, emerita, at Rutgers University. She has been a guest professor and lecturer at several European universities and has held numerous offices in various professional organizations, among them the presidency of the International Society of Political Psychology. She is now vice president of the American Political Science Association.

Professor Sigel's research interests focus on the interaction among social structure, major societal events, and political structure and on how this interaction affects the formation and change of individual and group attitudes and behaviors. She has written and edited books on the political socialization of youths and adults. More recently, she has become interested in gender relations, and she is currently involved in a study of the impact of the women's movement on two generations of women from the same family.

It has often been said that much writing essentially is autobiography. Comments are frequently made to the effect that what poets and novelists write about can be traced more or less directly to the ways in which they experience life. Suggestions that the same might hold for scientists, especially social scientists, are far less common. Careful examination, however, not infrequently reveals that the questions that scientists choose to address in their research actually have deep, intricate roots in personal experiences and life events that preceded the choice of work. Needless to say, scientists and other researchers are frequently quite unaware of these roots, if for no other reason than that they may not be in the habit of asking themselves such introspective questions, preferring instead to think of themselves as aloof and objective investigators whose personal experiences have nothing to do with their research. This volume, however, asks the contributors to engage in just such an enterprise of introspection or reflection. It asks them to examine the connection they might discover between their own early life experiences and the nature of their research, and it asks that the exploration be made within the context of a very specific event, namely, the Holocaust.

In my own case, I have to confess that when I began to tackle the assigned task of introspection, I suddenly realized that up to that time I had never given the matter any thought. I had simply assumed that the Holocaust was unrelated to my choice of a profession or the topics I chose to investigate. Initially I doubted that the two could possibly be connected. To be sure, in my private life not a day passes that I do not think of the Holocaust. It simply has become an ever-present part of my daily life, shaping my reactions to so many situations and events. But until now I had always thought—when I thought about it at all—that my personal emotions were a thing apart from my "scientific" work. Only after I began to reflect seriously and with some pain on the task ahead of me did I begin to realize that my two worlds—the world of memory and the world of professional pursuits—probably do not constitute two completely separate worlds. And because they are not as separate as I had originally assumed, I decided that for me the most straightforward way of coping with the topic would be to become quite autobiographical—an approach I generally seek to avoid.

I was more fortunate than many who are contributing to this volume in that I left Germany before the full fury of the Holocaust was unleashed. At the time the National Socialists came to power, I was still a student in a Berlin high school, spending my busy but relatively carefree days in much the same way most middle-class youngsters spent their time in those days. In a few years, I felt certain, I would enter one of the German universities and begin my studies in economics. As I now look back upon my childhood and adolescence, I would say it was a rather uneventful, secure, and relatively happy period of my life. By the time the infamous *Kristallnacht* of 1938 took place, foreshadowing the full horror of state-sponsored anti-Semitism about to follow, I was already safely settled in the United States and bound for college. I was thus spared the direct victimization, terror, and persecution suffered by many of the contributors to this volume, especially those who were children at the time and had to cope as best they could with the personal abuse, fear, terror, and violence of that cataclysmic event.

To this day I remember vividly the day and the place where I learned that Hitler had been appointed chancellor of the German republic. I was meeting a cousin at a subway exit where we picked up the noonday paper and, as was our custom, began to look at the news. Bold headlines virtually screamed at us that President Hindenburg had appointed Adolf Hitler to become the country's *Reichskanzler* (prime minister). Incredulity followed and soon after gave rise to our conviction that his tenure in office would not last, it was sure to be a temporary aberration. Parliament and the cabinet would refuse to ratify the decision made by the president, who was believed to be fairly senile by then. While we soon had to learn that our prediction was not about to prove correct, at first not much change seemed to take place in our lives. Certainly not in our high school. For quite some time the curriculum, the assignments, and the activities proceeded along their customary course. So I and my Jewish classmates continued our studies alongside our gentile classmates without untoward incidents. We visited in each others' homes and joined each other in all the things adolescents are wont to engage in. During those first few years my life, mercifully, was not permeated by premonitions of the horror that was to come soon after.

That is not to say that the changing and increasingly nasty atmosphere left me untouched. Gradually some classmates began to come to school in the uniform of the Hitler Youth (though their interactions with their Jewish classmates remained unchanged), and some formerly outspoken teachers refrained from commenting on current events, up to then a fairly frequent occurrence. During my last school year a mandatory course on race (*Rassenkunde*) was introduced into the curriculum. Cloaked in scientific or pseudoscientific jargon, it purported to demonstrate the superiority of the Aryan "race" and to denigrate all others. I have no recollection of how the course affected me emotionally (or how it affected my classmates) or whether it even affected me. Nowadays I frequently puzzle over that gap in my memory and its significance. Soon it became quite clear that I would have to abandon my hope of obtaining the university education I so desired. Still, on the surface the daily pattern of my family's life continued along its customary path for quite a while.

Not long after completing my baccalaureate (*Abitur*), I left Germany on a visitor's visa and came to the United States. Although by then the ominous signs had begun to accelerate, and notwithstanding the pain of having to leave my family behind under these threatening circumstances, I honestly believe that at the time I had not the slightest premonition of the horror that would descend in just a few more years on all those left behind. Naively, I continued to cling to the belief that what was then transpiring was probably temporary and certainly was uncharacteristically German; it did not represent the Germany of which I was fond and that I admired. At that time I still felt thoroughly German, much as did many other assimilated German Jews.

But it was not too long after my arrival in the United States that the catastrophic signs (beginning with the *Kristallnacht*) became unmistakable. They severely shook my earlier beliefs. I began to ask myself over and over again the question, How could such a cataclysmic nightmare be possible in a civilized country like Germany? How could the good people I knew and liked possibly be involved in such horrendous acts?

Within a year of my arrival in the United States I was offered a fellowship to attend college. In my rush to become a thoroughly Americanized coed on the campus of a southern women's college, the urgency of that painful unanswered question gradually began to fade into the background. Or was it perhaps deliberately even though unconsciously repressed? Why else would I have refused to speak German even when coaxed by classmates to do so? Eventually, as the news from abroad became ever more awful, I no longer wanted to reflect on my initial question; I was done—I thought—with my past. I wanted to be and feel like an American. After graduating from college, I began studying for a master's degree in history with much emphasis on U.S. history and some work in intellectual history. I made no effort to take courses in German history, past or present, courses that might have provided answers to my troubling question. That, as I thought, had become a closed chapter for me. Finis.

Then came the work on the Ph.D. that I took in history, again with some emphasis on intellectual history. So what did I choose for a dissertation topic? Nothing remotely related to my fields of study. Instead I wrote on U.S. attitudes toward Germany and the Germans as expressed in large-circulation U.S. family magazines. In it I traced how U.S. attitudes changed from the onset of the Nazi regime to the outbreak of the war; how in the beginning the magazines made a sharp distinction between the German people, whom they greatly admired and liked, and the political regime, which they censured severely; and how toward the end they no longer made any distinctions but despised and condemned both with equal vigor. At the time I never reflected on the reasons behind my choice of dissertation topic. Had I been asked, I probably would have attributed it strictly to convenience. The materials were readily available in the stacks of Harper Library at the University of Chicago (where I then lived) and required neither travel time nor financial outlay but just a short walk across Chicago's Midway.

If that had been the real or at least the only reason, why did I not give the dissertation to my committee for approval as soon as I had completed the analysis of U.S. public opinion? Why did I feel compelled to add a component on German opinion to it? Why did I spend many additional months analyzing the vast collection of public opinion surveys that the U.S. army of occupation had conducted in Germany after the war? What significance could the opinions of the postwar German populace possibly have for my dissertation topic, which after all dealt with U.S., not German, public opinion? At the time I never reflected on that question. In retrospect I begin to understand what I had hoped to find in these documents, even though I certainly was not aware of it at the time. The surveys—at least as I interpreted them—gave ample evidence that robust majorities of that generation of Germans had always been and still were essentially authoritarian. Germany as the epitome of authoritarianism, was that perhaps the answer I had hoped to find, the answer to the question I thought I had left behind? Or did I perhaps hope to convince U.S. scholars that Germany was unregenerated and required their watchful attention? Even today I still can't be sure what my motivation was. Be that as it may, after completion of this phase of my research, I quickly wrote up my analysis and interpretation of the German data and made it the last chapter of the dissertation.

If my memory of the chapter is correct, it was a gloomy and very angry one. Was I really unaware that this last chapter had absolutely nothing whatsoever to do with the theme of my dissertation? Apparently so. My dissertation committee, of course, immediately recognized its irrelevance. The members, quite correctly, insisted that the last chapter be omitted from the dissertation though they accepted the rest of it as presented. Needless to say, I felt compelled to drop the chapter that was so dear to my heart. But I was deeply disappointed and utterly unable to let go of the ideas expressed in it. Hence I was much relieved when in the following year *Commentary* published it as an article in their section titled "The Study of Man." With that publication my catharsis was completed, and my research turned to other topics, mostly in U.S. politics.

In the 1960s (after a ten-year period devoted exclusively to raising a family), I returned to academic life and with it to active research. The unanswered question, though deliberately ignored in the interim, apparently was never completely forgotten and soon kept occupying center stage in my research, though it was formulated in a vastly different and far more general framework. Some of the dramatic events of that period (race disturbances, assassinations, flagrant miscarriages of justice, etc.) prompted me to channel my research away from the study of political institutions and direct it to the study of human behavior and to the contexts or conditions under which specific behaviors, social as well as antisocial, were most likely to evolve. I became particularly interested in investigating what circumstances may prompt perfectly ordinary and otherwise decent human beings to engage in flagrantly antisocial behaviors and what prompts others to stand by passively rather than prevent such acts.

To that end I began to study political socialization, and that topic became the major focus of my research for the next two decades. I had become convinced that the democratic and cooperative behavior of individuals is neither innate nor occurs by chance but that its success depends in no small measure on the extent to which people see it practiced, valued, and rewarded in many spheres of life. I attached much importance to the relevance of these civic characteristics for the political system because the events of my youth had taught me that even the most democratic system cannot endure without the help of democratic citizens who are willing, should the need arise, to become actively involved in the life of the polis. And because I believed that a sense of civic responsibility as well as cooperation, tolerance, and other hallmarks of democratic behaviors can be taught but has to be taught fairly early in life, I directed my attention to the study of children and adolescents. In my early research I observed that most youngsters professed great love of liberty and democracy but that even adolescents really did not seem to understand what democracy involved and what it expected of its citizens. In fact, many seemed to value democracy mostly for the personal freedom it afforded them but to ignore or be oblivious to the responsibilities it entailed. With this problem before me, I began to devote particular attention to the study of the democratic orientations of children—their understanding of the concept *democracy*, the extent to which they might be willing to become politically involved in adulthood, and what lessons home and school had conveyed to them. Above all, I began to focus on two dimensions: (1) the impact certain public events exert over young people's trust in government and their willingness to participate in it and (2) the social circumstances of their lives and how these affect their political attitudes and behaviors.

The results of my research convinced me that even fairly young children are affected by dramatic public events that occur around them, and I was quite struck by the drop in trust I observed among them in the wake of the political assassinations and the racial disturbances of the 1960s. Ten years later, during the denouement of the Watergate episode, I was equally struck by the political indifference and apathy, bordering on alienation, that in the interim had developed among adolescents. Gone apparently were the deep trust and intense, uncritical patriotism that had characterized earlier generations of youth. It was as though the tragic events of the preceding decade had inured them against feeling involved. A small longitudinal study begun in more benign times but completed during more turbulent ones showed that the idealistic and trusting children I had interviewed previously had in the interim lost their trust and any inclination to render public service, let alone enter politics upon reaching adulthood. These results kept me wondering what kind of behaviors and commitments we ought to anticipate when this cohort, so completely preoccupied with self, would reach adulthood.

If even young children could show such sensitivity to public events, how much more plausible would it be to assume that adults' attitudes and behaviors might change in response to social, economic, and political developments! My research interests, therefore, began to turn to the study of adult political socialization. At the time I began that work, the field of political socialization research had focused primarily on children and adolescents, based on the assumption that most aspects of personal development have become more or less fixed once an individual reaches adulthood, if not earlier. That proposition became more and more questionable to me as I familiarized myself with the recollections of Holocaust victims; read the memoirs of the victims of the Stalinist regime; and, in the wake of the Vietnam War, learned about post-traumatic stress. I became increasingly certain that our knowledge of the political development of youth, though useful, was inadequate for understanding adults' political behavior under conditions of tremendous personal and social stress. The work of psychologists and gerontologists informed me that we tend to underestimate the potential for intellectual and emotional growth and development as well as deterioration all through the life cycle. So why should the same observation not also hold for adults' political attitudes and behaviors? At first my preoccupation with individual responses to survival under conditions of political horror led me to contemplate editing a volume dedicated exclusively to that topic, and I collected much information on the impact of political persecution, terror, and torture on their victims and on their perpetrators. But as I began working on that project, I realized that also less dramatic, more mundane, but far-reaching changes could leave their marks on people, and I became interested in examining how adults cope with such less traumatic changes in their lives. Of particular interest to me was the impact of recent societal changes, changes that differed in significant ways from what people had been led to expect of life. How, for example, do adults react when confronted with new social movements that advocate changes in time-honored social relations, such as the Civil Rights and the Women's Liberation movements? My growing interest in the ways adults cope or fail to cope under these conditions of social change as well as under more adverse and stressful ones eventually led to an edited volume on the topic of adult political socialization.

I shall close with a brief comment on the research that preoccupies me these days. It deals with gender relations in the wake of the modern Women's Liberation movement. It too, like my previous work, focuses on people's capacity to deal with new social and political developments. The recent changes in women's economic and social position call for adaptations of a magnitude both genders may have thought inconceivable not so long ago. At the center of my current work lies the question, How do men and women both in the United States and abroad negotiate their change in gender roles? How do men and women cope with the conflicts bound to arise under these conditions?

The tragic and often bloody events of the last few years have only strengthened me in my opinion that information about adult socialization, especially under conditions of change, is urgently needed. The current world scene with all its interethnic warfare, genocides, and similar forms of violence illustrates all too painfully that the question that I asked myself as I left Germany and for which I never found a meaningful answer is not restricted to that country. It really is a universal question, namely, how can we account for some of the savagery and inhumanity that perfectly decent and normal people seem capable of committing? What are the conditions, the restraints, and the opportunities that encourage people in or inhibit them from engaging in a whole range of political acts from the altruistic to the heinous, the humane to the inhumane? The growing literature directed toward answering that question—the current volume is an example of that kind—bears witness to the perpetual timeliness of the question.

At the time that Peter Suedfeld asked me to contribute a chapter to the volume he was editing, I was reluctant to do so because I failed to see how my work on changes in gender relations and the stress to which they give rise as well as my earlier work on youth during benign and somewhat less benign times could be in any way related to having spent part of my youth under fascism. I was honestly convinced, as I stated earlier, that my work as an adult was totally unrelated to these early experiences. Only when I began to reflect seriously on the charge he had given us did I realize that the theme that runs through much of my work, namely, humans' response to conditions of political suffering and upheaval, is probably not unrelated to having previously been witness to an event of unspeakable horror. I am deeply grateful to Peter Suedfeld for having afforded me this insight into my professional work.

Remembering the Holocaust

Snapshots from a Cognitive Science Perspective

Herbert Weingartner

Biographical Note

Herbert Weingartner is chief of the Cognitive Neurosciences Section, Laboratory of Cognitive Sciences, and special assistant, National Institute on Drug Abuse, National Institutes of Health, and concurrently adjunct professor of cognitive science at the Johns Hopkins University (where he received both his Ph.D. in experimental psychology and his postdoctoral training in clinical psychology). He has previously held a number of academic, research, and administrative positions in universities and government in the Washington, DC, area.

Dr. Weingartner is a founding fellow of the American Psychological Society and a fellow of several other professional and scientific organizations. His research, reported in some three hundred articles and book chapters, deals with the psychobiology of cognitive dysfunctions, especially memory, related to mood disorders, Alzheimer's disease, brain lesions, amnestic disorders, and "normal" aging. More recently, he has turned to the application of cognitive science and cognitive neuroscience to the development of more effective learning environments.

Summary

A cognitive science perspective is used to help interpret my sense of the consequences of my limited Holocaust experience. Cognitive styles, our signature of how we deal with life themes such as loss, self-worth, risk taking, the nature of our relationships (with children, spouse, parents, friends, and colleagues), and the affective tone that colors our interactions, are just some of the aspects of who we are that would logically be linked to our early developmental history. While cognitive models and theories have proven useful in describing and accounting for how the typical individual thinks, attends, learns, and remembers events, these same heuristics may be of value in appreciating/describing the impact of significant personal-individual events that shape who we are (including our choice of career).

In trying to recapture my early history and projecting it forward to the present, I have chosen to use a writing style that is impressionistic, in the form of a series of short sketches. I felt that a scientific journal style was inappropriate, while that of an essay would give the impression of having developed a kind of closure and structure in considering these events. This is not the case. They remain a patchwork of fragmented experiences that must still be appreciated.

Introduction and Overview

Don't Write This Chapter

I was very reluctant to write this chapter. First of all, I don't have any right to talk about my Holocaust experience. I escaped one of the defining events of the twentieth century at the age of four. The big tragic parade proceeded without me or my immediate family. I did have an early vague sense that things were terribly wrong and that the world was dangerous and violent. I also grew up with a strong dose of impending doom, of danger that was just around the corner of time or space. But that is not the same as actually meeting up with the threat to life, loss, helplessness in the flesh. Some of my family did not escape in time or couldn't get the papers of passage, and they disappeared somewhere unknown or, in other instances, in camps and circumstances that could be partially identified. They were certainly forgotten in our daily lives in our new home, the Washington Heights of New York City. That neighborhood was home to many other refugees who "got out." We renamed the neighborhood the Fourth Reich.

The second reason for not wanting to write this chapter is because I did not want to look back at my own early history, a history that I had put away and sealed over. After all, I left Germany in the spring of 1939, at the age of four, and children that young have little conscious memory of the events that may have shaped their lives. Of course, that is nonsense when viewed from a cognitive perspective of how knowledge is laid down early in development. Furthermore the refugee experience of fleeing, and looking back at those left behind, the tone of family life for my family having just escaped, the reliving of the experiences of the surviving relatives and friends who joined us after the war also occurred so very long ago. Again I remind myself that I was only a youngster at the time.

Why Did I Have to Write This Chapter?

First, I owed myself an opportunity to look back at my history. I have in the past muffled the sound of what I heard in my head as I considered those early events of leaving Germany and the nature of what it was like growing up with a pervasive sense of fear and foreboding that marked family life at least up to my early adolescence. I also wrote this chapter because five years ago my wife died after battling a cancer that finally won. I still can't get myself to give away her clothes, nor have I been able to alter my (our) home. I have considered the possibility—no, concluded—that my early experiences just before and after leaving Germany have left me particularly unskilled at dealing with loss (i.e., I dread it and am overwhelmed in expecting loss and dealing with it). So, writing the chapter and examining my early history were a way of working through my experience in helping my wife deal with her disease and her dying and finally for me to obtain closure after her death. Third, I had to write this chapter for my two sons, Eric and Michael. It has taken me forever to let them get a look underneath their father's skin, at what may account for his fears and his need to overprotect and at why he finds it so difficult to simply let go, to experience unbridled joy. So the work necessary to complete the chapter had to be done for me, for my sons, and so that I can finally bury Liz.

Incidentally, I also wrote the chapter because it afforded me yet another look at, a personal view, of my work as a cognitive researcher. I have spent my career reducing problems into digestible bits, the ones that can be studied in the laboratory. Furthermore I have successfully avoided problems for which we do not have readily available relatively clean methods and procedures for picking apart mental events. Can one get anything useful from using these cognitive laboratory methods and models in order to understand the cognitive consequences of specific individualized experiences as opposed to unearthing general "laws" that govern how we think, learn, remember, attend? Can nomothetic methods be useful in teaching us anything about cognitive functions? Can one use the growing wealth of knowledge about the neuroanatomy and neurochemistry of mental events, along with what is available from the many scores of studies that have provided a functional analysis of specific cognitive functions, to understand our own developmental history? At first blush all of these questions are answered with a nay, since we don't know enough. So I have provided yet another disclaimer to this chapter. I wrote it anyway.

The section following the introduction provides a cameo of who I am. I thought that would be useful, so I put it there, to put what follows in the context of the characteristics of the reporter. Also, I sense that, like solving a problem, knowing what the solution looks like (what I became) provides clues about how I might have gotten there. In the next section I provide a brief sampling, sketches, of some of the events I associate with my experience of the Holocaust. The third section of the chapter briefly considers how cognitive models might be used to interpret and understand the impact of a Holocaust experience on what is stored in memory, forms of remembering and the interpretation of what is remembered. In that section I also insert some personal vignettes, in which I make use of some of these cognitive perspectives in interpreting how my early history may have shaped who I am.

Peeking at Who We Are (or a second look at myself)

We all look at who we are, in our fashion. Squinting, sometimes even staring, at our histories and what we are about is just part of being alive. How we look is an important facet of that introspective experience. So, the adage, don't tell me about yourself but let us watch what you do, how you respond to events. That tells us a good deal more about who we are than the actual events in our history and the stories we tell about those events. We are multiple selves.

I "chose" cognitive psychology as a career and have spent most of my time studying the psychobiological mechanisms of normal and impaired cognitive functions (primarily memory-related phenomena). I have used drugs as tools along with methods and models of experimental psychology in order to understand cognitive failure and to develop treatments that might reverse these dysfunctions (such as in the case of Alzheimer's disease). Like many others interested in the life sciences, I have tried to understand normal functions, such as components of memory, by studying impaired cognition. I started out as a physicist and went on to study memory and by doing so perhaps, maybe, possibly, avoided looking at my memory of the past. After all, it is easier to consider the properties and characteristics of a model than the actual phenomena and events that are modeled.

What makes someone choose to train and work as a cognitivist? After you get past the reflex answers such as, the mind is extraordinary and it defines who we are, of course the study of minds is inherently exciting— but then again, not everyone studies brains and what they can do. All of the contributors to this book were asked to comment on how our early experience may have helped define career choice. Of course, all of our early experiences shape what we do; but dismissing the question takes nothing away from the fact that it is a tough question and deserves an answer (albeit a speculative one).

I started out with a degree in physics and only then went on to do graduate work in experimental psychology. The primary reason that dictated that choice at the time was that I was interested in behavior, in cognition, from a hard science perspective. In retrospect I was also attracted to the vagueness of cognitive models and theories. I think I experienced a sense of comfort that almost any metaphor for reality was a possibility in the world of cognitive science. One could live out one's fantasy; one could live in the world of math and metaphor without touching reality. Concrete answers about exactly how, for example, memory really works were beyond our capability, and the area was therefore attractive. I did not have a history of enjoying reality. In addition, I have spent my life first listening to "mind chatter" dealing with who I am and how I got that way and then studying cognitive phenomena that even remotely might allow me to peek at some of these issues. I would suspect that I share that motivation for career choice with many psychologists, including those who are reductionist researchers. Cognitive science is a particularly attractive field for personalizing the asking and answering of scientific questions.

I see myself as a minimalist. I have had great difficulty expecting much support and recognition in professional settings even when it would have been appropriate. My mind-set has been that not wanting or needing much leaves one less vulnerable, allows one to survive.

The theme of loss is one that has always haunted me. Just one constant expression of that is being overly concerned about my two sons' welfare. I spend a good deal of time making sure that their safety is made of steel cables. In fact they are accomplished and complete, and they are forever trying to convince me that I need not worry about them.

Throughout my early years, and also as a young adult, reflexively, automatically, looking for a place to hide in new surroundings. Blending in was important. That meant not looking like a refugee child, trying to get my parents to appear like everyone else, to lose their strong accents (which never happened), to look like and act like everyone else. I have always been quite conscious that I am a Jew in a world that can turn hostile at any moment. My father taught me that view and reinforced it throughout my life even though I half-heartedly tried to talk him out of that position. My sense was that impending danger was everywhere. Somehow I felt that it was my role to protect my parents and especially my brother, and this was an emotionally trying commitment.

In contrast, injustice or scapegoating that would leave someone humiliated would often drive me to act without considering risk. It is the one type of stimulus that could and has driven me into a rage that would force me to abandon my real or imagined hiding place. It was a rage that would overwhelm fear and a need to hide. This was the case starting early in my life in response to being called a "dirty kike" (where I remember almost killing the kid who shouted that at me) to experiences in my professional career where I made someone else's injustice my cause because I experienced their humiliation in personal terms. These are just a few facets of who I am that come to mind.

What do I make of all this? In terms of outward appearances I have been very successful; appropriate; effective in my career; a warm, open, loving, and unconditionally committed father and husband, and this style was also evident in my relationships with friends and colleagues. I am described as always appearing at ease and having a quick and ready wit. What is missing in this picture of successful socialization is an enormous need to hide who I am as well as my skills along with shortcomings. Starting with my earliest sense of self, I needed to make sure that this private picture was undiscovered. Internally, I experienced heavy and frequent doses of gloom, sense of a lack of value, helplessness, and an enormous need to control and anticipate a perception of impending doom. The trick was to be forever vigilant and "silent." Ironically, I am someone that often looks at threat with peripheral rather than central vision. I "choose" to blur what may be threatening and use my imagination to transform and neutralize threat. This strategy, this cognitive style, proved to be somewhat useful in helping my wife and me, as well as our sons, to live life as normally as possible rather than to be overwhelmed by the experience of multiple recurrences of breast cancer over a period of eighteen years. Enough already.

Historical Snapshots

My Family

I was born April 4, 1935, in Flehingen, Germany, three years after Hitler officially took power. My brother, Werner, was born April 28, 1936 (so much for not getting pregnant while nursing). My grandmother was furious that my parents were so irresponsible that they would bring us into a world that was rapidly closing in around us and that dug its teeth into every facet of our lives. My father left in mid-1938 with the hopes of obtaining papers that could deliver the rest of his family. In the meantime, events marched on, and my mother became an expert both in protecting my brother and me and also in learning startle, fear, constant vigilance. She learned how to listen and correctly interpret every sight and sound. Everything depended on being right and careful. My brother and I used our child's minds to think about and learn her skill of being afraid and made it our own. We left Germany in the spring of 1939. We had missed the "grand parade," or had we?

My father, Hugo, was born in Flehingen, as were his father, grandfather, and great-grandfather. He went to school in this village and became a modestly successful *Viehändler* (cattle dealer), just like his father, uncle, cousins. He loved what he did. He enjoyed rural life, the culture of the villages, of southwest Germany, the farmers he dealt with, and the smell of fresh dung on an early spring morning. He was ten years older than my mother, Erna, who came from the nearby village of Klein-Eichholzheim (population three hundred). Both Hugo and Erna and their families, like the others in the village, were little concerned with world politics. When they were teenagers, access to worldly information was minimal—of greater concern were the well-being of the cattle and the village daily life news. Their lives had been similar, simple and straightforward. Their parents made decisions for them (probably including who was a suitable mate), and they followed the rural lifestyle into which they had been born, looking to get married and have children. At twenty-two Erna marries and was immediately pregnant with her first child; three months after the birth of Herbert, she was pregnant again (with my brother, Werner).

The world surrounding Hugo and Erna (our world) was changing rapidly. The security of the village, the centuries of tradition, and the history of family that had nurtured them were replaced by an environment of daily fear. Relations with neighbors moved from intimacy to hostility. We Jews were the pariahs, and there was no place to hide. There was also a sense of disbelief that all this was happening, mixed with a fantasy that the oppression and terror would somehow evaporate. This was not to be. Instead, finally, Erna was left on her own with two young infants; her husband (my father) voyaged to the United States to find papers for the family. Her life was terrorized, and there was no one in her family without fear. Along with all of the other Jews in 1938–39 Germany, children as well as adults, we became practiced experts at tasting fear and dealing with it in some fashion. There was only one solution, to leave Germany, which required waiting, papers, luck, silence, ducking; and sometimes someone available to listen to the fears, someone to say that things will turn out all right. What I remember of my mother is growing fear, being held, and feeling her tremble in the dark. Each sound in the street sets off another alarm. And the fear builds during the first four years of my life.

I still can't believe that I am in the picture, along with my brother, holding our grandfather Heinrich's hands, in our knit hats, our shorts, and our high socks, staring out toward the camera, standing in front of the burned-out synagogue, in the center of the village of Flehingen in southwest Germany. The picture was taken in February 1939, just before my fourth birthday and a few weeks before we had the papers that allowed us to leave for the United States. I can't read any emotion in those faces. On the other hand, I am sure that even by my fourth birthday I had grown accustomed to the nature of the startle response. When I think of my mother, virtually the first thing that comes to mind is fright, being held close to her and while being enveloped experiencing her overwhelming *Erschreckung.* I have blurred memories of *Kristallnacht,* the basis of the picture behind the picture. Perhaps I have made up the memory of shouting, crashing furniture, of being pushed aside, hiding in a rabbit hutch. And what did I ask my mother as all of this was happening . . . and what were her answers, and were they a comfort? It is all rather vague. These are events that happened so long ago and perhaps are generated by my imagination rather than events that I really experienced. The growing feeling of doom-gloom-fear, helplessness, in a vague, poorly labeled form is what I remember. I think I could virtually taste and feel it in the air and in my mother's touch as she would hold my hand . . . but the associated images are dim and perhaps never occurred. After all, I can't remember. On the other hand, the child looking out of the photograph, the one that is part of my history, was aware of what was going on, and it made a lasting impression. I got to know that child rather well.

Many but by no means all of the Jews of Baden-Würtemburg who remained in Germany in 1940 were sent to concentration camps in France (de Gurs and Rivesaltes). My maternal grandparents, uncle, and cousin Berndt remained in Klein-Eichholzheim until their deportation to Camp de Gurs, on October 22, 1940. My grandmother died in Gurs, while my uncle Günther died after being sent from de Gurs to Auschwitz. My cousin Berndt survived, as did my aunt Bettie (in Gurs) as did survivors who joined the family such as those orphaned by the Holocaust; Ilsie, who married Henry Weingartner; and Edith, who somehow got out of Gurs and was then hidden in Annecy and married my cousin Kurt.

According to my aunt Bettie, in a recent interview given to a reporter for a weekly newspaper called the *Aufbau,* "Our Christian neighbors in Klein-Eichholzheim were always close to the Jews." My sense is a bit different. When I returned to the village for the first time, there was little interest in or knowledge about what had happened to their Jewish neighbors (so much for being close). *Kristallnacht* had its impact on Klein-Eichholzheim, with the willing participation of its citizens. Here, as was the case throughout Germany, the synagogues were burned and Jews deported and murdered. How could the villagers of Klein-Eichholzheim plead ignorance, with a population of 286, where a burp at one end of town could be distinctly heard at the other end?

The New World

On the boat over to the United States I told the deckhand, "Der Werner hat in die Hose geschissen," and my brother Werner, my "arch rival," said, "Und der Herbert auch." (I said, "Werner crapped in his pants," and Werner's reply was "So did Herbert.") We were scared to the core of our beings.

My father's parents arrived and came to live with us in 1941 after escaping through Portugal. My mother's family couldn't get out. The issue of choices is a nasty one. If you have limited numbers of papers, who gets a ticket, and who is left in the back of the queue? I had a sense of what that meant rather early in my childhood. Bottom line: none of my mother's efforts to provide the paper bridge for her parents, brother's family, other relatives worked out. In its place, I experienced at a distance her overwhelming foreboding. My mother would often say aloud, "Why didn't they at least let the Jews leave even without any of their possessions?" (but then again, no one wanted us).

I know that, at least in some form, my brother and I comprehended some of the dynamics of the refugee experience on our lives. For example, I had a child's sense of the choices that had to be made: who received the limited number of affidavits, papers, and signatures guaranteeing support for prospective refugees; who might get out. I also had a sense of some of the unfairness in the choices that left others behind, for example, my maternal family, including grandparents, aunt, uncle, cousin. The importance of the trivial, such as a piece of paper, a stamp on a document, or passing a physical at the consulate in Stuttgart (which apparently I almost failed, since it turned out that something suspicious was spotted in my throat that turned out to be nothing).

Everything Matters

What was it like growing up in Washington Heights, in New York, the site we labeled the Fourth Reich? At home we spoke German, and that was also the language heard on the streets and in the shops and in the *Schule* (Orthodox synagogues). Everywhere one felt the atmosphere of gloom, doom, and *Verzweiflung* (despair). It was a community of refugees, many of whom had left Germany with nothing and were struggling to make it. Their children were caught up in the palette of the emotions of that community. Even as young children we appreciated and understood the predominant mood of our community. It was also where I learned a great deal about the nature of generosity and commitment in terms of the way people would try to help each other. The sense of foreboding crept into many activities. For example, I remember the reaction to my brother and me playing and making noise during a Saturday morning service: one of the congregants leaned over to tell us, "If you don't behave we will give you to Hitler." It wasn't funny. Fun came much later, well after the war was over. In the meantime we continued to hone our skills at being vigilant, controlled, and private. One source of protection was to fit into the new culture. My brother and I were completely committed to that task as well as our role in dragging our parents along with us (such as trying to get them to speak English and lose their accents).

Early on, my brother and I learned and then knew, took for granted, that Jews as individuals or as a group were alone, on their own, and that no one gave a damn, that we had to duck, and that meant blending into the surrounding woodwork. And yet, our parents' accents identified us as refugees loud and clear. That was unsettling and made it difficult to blend in, to hide. How one looked mattered to both Werner and me. Blending in meant a great deal to us.

Signs of the Times

Hiding, staying out of sight, blending in: themes that strike a chord that has played out in various ways throughout my life. Ironically, in contrast, I have taken risks as a cognitive psychologist that are in sharp contrast with this mode of operation. That is, rather than studying traditional themes in cognition and using the standard methods of experimental psychology to answer cognitive questions, I have instead opted for using drugs as tools for modeling and mimicking cognitive phenomena. I did this type of work before it became somewhat fashionable. I guess academic risks are not in the same league as those that influence our safety and ability to survive.

There is something special in being right out there. For many centuries Jews have been recipients of a rich set of markers, signs of who they were, badges that would identify them as special. In fifteenth- to sixteenth-century France, Jews were required to wear a *rota*—a badge in the shape of a wheel in either very visible yellow, white, or red. In Sicily, blue badges were the rage. In Rome, Jews were required to wear a red cape, while in Spain they were honored to wear a pointed hood. A pointed hat (often in the shape of a Star of David) served as a Jew marker in Germany, France, and England, while a black hat was also sometimes used for that purpose in, for example, Germany and the Papal States. Nice to know you can always be noticed in a crowd.

Cognitive Models and a Way of Thinking about Mental Functions: A Framework for Understanding the Impact of Early Experience on Memory and Forms of Remembering or as a Vehicle for Keeping Personal Experience at a Distance

Overview and Agenda of Cognitive Science

The major goal of cognitive science research is to understand in both behavioral and neurobiological terms the specific component operations that are necessary, that are responsible for carrying out mental functions such as attention, perception, memory, and learning. Once one has taken apart the components of the mind, parallel cognitive research is designed to try to put the parts back together again, in order to appreciate the integrative functions of the central nervous system. Only then can we begin to understand how what we sense is perceived and how the bits and pieces of our memory are experienced as recapitulations of our past—and how that knowledge is used to evaluate our past and present and to plan future courses of action.

Some aspects of cognitive research may be particularly useful in thinking about personal histories. For example, we have learned that memory is not unitary but instead is expressed in many different forms. The findings that have been used to characterize different types of memory come from many sources, such as brain imaging studies, patients with discrete brain lesions, drugs that selectively disrupt various brain systems, behavioral manipulations in normal volunteers and in cognitively impaired patient populations, and studies of how memory and related cognitive functions are acquired and altered during development. Some of the forms of memory include the following: memory with "conscious" awareness of the context in which that remembered knowledge was acquired (explicit memory); memory without conscious awareness of the source of knowledge, such as memory for rules and skills, or knowledge in memory that is inferred on the basis of our reactions to events (implicit memory); knowledge in memory that is the result of a good deal of thinking—well-processed information, compared to poorly encoded experiences; working or short-term memory; memories that are formed on the basis of simple conditioning; "hot" emotionally meaningful memories as opposed to "cool" remembered knowledge . . . and the list of distinctions continues to grow.

We have learned a good deal about the brain systems that are responsible for carrying out these different types of cognition/memory. For example, it is likely that cool, conceptual memory operations are based upon operations performed in the hippocampus (along with the temporal lobe and frontal lobes). Hot emotional memories are likely to result not so much from our thinking about events but rather from our immediate reaction to events, which then results in the storage of knowledge of those events through activation of a part of the brain that has for some time been associated with the experience of emotion, namely, the amygdala. Hot memories are often fragmentary rather than conceptually organized. These memories, such as what has been learned under conditions of stress, may be particularly likely to be memorable, particularly after periods of delay (i.e., there is a stress-induced memory advantage for emotional material; Cahill et al. 1994, 1995).

However, memories of traumatic events often occur in fragments (such as in the form of snippets of images, olfactory and kinesthetic sensations), and they are often poorly organized and not well encoded, at least not in a semantic form. The memories lack coherence. The neurobiology of emotional learning and memory has been well worked out for fear conditioning (Damasio 1998; Adolphs 1995; LeDoux 1995; Armory et al. 1995; Rogan et al. 1997), and some work has also provided the broad outline of the integration of the hot and cold memory systems (Cahill and McGaugh 1998).

One of the dominant themes in cognitive research has been the role of conscious versus unconscious processes in the expression of various cognitive activities such as memory and attention. This issue may be particularly pertinent when one asks questions about our historical past that depend on awareness of the context and source of knowledge as opposed to inferring histories on the basis of how we react to events and our behavior. Debates about the reconstructive processes involved in memory, the generation of false memories, often revolve around issues of consciousness and awareness of the context of what is remembered. Hundreds of volumes and papers have been written about this topic, with the result of some modest new knowledge and a great deal of emotion about what may be responsible for false versus veridical remembering.

The reader should, however, appreciate that the many distinct forms of cognitive functions that have been "uncovered" are also overlapping functions and that sometimes differences in concepts are merely a means for describing the same cognitive behavior using different metaphors. For example, simple associative (classical) conditioned responses can be "remembered" without subjects being aware of the source of their knowledge, that is, why they respond as they do. In that sense remembering only in the presence of some cue, such as an odor (cue-dependent remembering), can be described as conditioned responding (learning) and also as implicit remembering (when subjects are unaware of the basis of their response in some situation). Likewise, the role of implicit knowledge in decision making has been studied in detail because it provides yet another vehicle for examining the important role of knowledge in and outside of awareness.

Obviously, the multi-jargon-laden forms of labeling different kinds of learning and remembering are as confusing as they are uninteresting to those outside the field of cognitive science. Also, while we have made enormous progress in appreciating the differentiated nature of all kinds of cognitive functions this appreciation is expressed at the level of modal functioning, functioning in the typical subject. This is very different from attempting to use cognitive models and theory for accounting for individual and idiosyncratic cognitive experiences.

Cues, Context, Individual Differences, and Cognitive Styles

Circumstances, situations, along with individualized cognitive styles, dictate how we interact with our environment, how we learn, how we organize our experience, what we do and do not attend to, how we remember, and what aspects of previous experience and knowledge we remember. What comes to mind, what we are capable of retrieving from our memory, is often circumstance dependent or cue dependent. In addition, we place the foot-/handprint of our cognitive processing styles on how we deal with all kinds of events, including the scenarios we make up about who we are. The notion of specificity of cognitive functioning (modularity of functioning) is even expressed in functions often misidentified as global characteristics such as intellectual capacity. It is rather apparent that intelligence, intellectual functioning, is not one entity. This specificity is also expressed in the cognitive styles we use to interact with our world.

For example, the psychologist Howard Gardner has proposed that some of us use a cognitive style, or form of intelligence, such as reliance on a linguistic logical-mathematical style of processing; while others think spatially, or have a particularly well-developed musical sense, or have a keen awareness of body and kinesthetics, or have developed particularly effective interpersonal schemes of functioning; while some of us are particularly likely and perhaps talented at intrapersonal scanning of inner self. Other cognitive science classification schemes differentiate between top-down versus bottom-up thinking. Top-down processing is processing in which an a priori conceptual strategy is used to react to events, to process information. That is, a conceptual scheme is in place and is used to scan and organize information. Bottom-up processing is stimulus or event driven. The subject processes stimulus information and uses this information to build or form a conceptual scheme for organizing information or scanning a visual field. Yet another classification scheme that is commonly used is that of controlled versus automatic cognitive operations. For example, many attention deficit disorder children express impairments in cognitive functions that require control and monitoring skills but are unimpaired in carrying out cognitive operations that can be accomplished automatically. Older, more clinically driven views of the cognitive styles include field-dependent versus field-independent responders, concrete versus abstract thinkers. Finally, there remains an old legacy from a psychodynamic view of mental functions that uses terms and concepts such as *denial, dystonia* (inability to track feeling states), *repression,* and *suppression* to describe aberrant cognitive styles for dealing with ourselves in interaction with our environment.

Uncovering Our Cognitive Makeup through the Use of Challenge Paradigms

Physicians often use challenge paradigms to uncover underlying pathology (e.g., cardiac stress tests). Challenge paradigms have also been used to unearth forms of cognitive pathology. For example, the cognitive response to anticholinergic drugs such as scopolamine may be useful in identifying elderly subjects who may be particularly at risk to develop Alzheimer's disease. That is, elderly people who are cognitively unimpaired but are at risk for Alzheimer's disease, when administered low doses of a drug such as scopolamine (a cholinergic antagonist), demonstrate some of the cognitive features of patients with mild to moderate Alzheimer's disease. In contrast, normal elderly controls when administered the same drug also express impaired memory, but the form of that response is qualitatively different from the one that mimics Alzheimer's disease (Molchan et al. 1992).

Similarly, individuals with histories of post-traumatic stress disorder (PTSD) are much more likely to respond with acute anxiety than is the case in normal controls without such a history when administered a drug such as yohimbine (a β_2 antagonist that stimulates norepinephrine release in the brain, a neurotransmitter known to be involved in the stress response) as well as several other drugs (for a recent review and new findings in this area of research see Bremner et al. 1997; Bremner et al. 1995). Parallel findings demonstrate that when PTSD subjects view material that is relevant to their previously experienced stressors, their cerebral response to such material also distinguishes them from normal volunteers. Regional cerebral blood flow is increased in these patients in the ventral anterior cingulate gyrus and right amygdala while subjects generate mental images of stress-related pictures. Likewise, individuals at risk for developing alcoholism or other forms of drug abuse are more likely to express impairments in reflective (control) cognitive processes when administered drugs such as alcohol or benzodiazepine. These impairments in reflective cognitive function are not ordinarily apparent. The point is that it may be necessary to behaviorally or pharmacologically challenge someone in order to obtain a picture of his or her cognitive makeup.

Learning and Priming of Simple Associative Emotional Responses (stimulus-response)

Conditioning learning and "remembering" have been demonstrated in even the simplest organisms. In humans, we have loads of evidence of simple conditioning taking place in the fetus and in all kinds of infant experience. It is also clear that conditioned responses even in days-old infants can persist for a very long time, perhaps throughout life. Furthermore, conditioned associative learning can occur in a single trial or event. This type of knowledge (associative conditioning) can be, and often is, expressed outside of awareness and can be extremely difficult to unlearn (extinguish).

Along with conditioning of associative responses, we have also learned a good deal about the generalization and discrimination that are associated with conditioned learning. The role of generalization of simple associative learning, such as fear conditioning, has been one of the themes in the century-old study of classical conditioning. One of the sub-themes in this research has concerned conditions that exaggerate and diminish generalization. Children who do not as yet have well-developed language skills are more likely to generalize responses, such as fear, to a wider range of stimuli than adults who can use acquired knowledge to discriminate between similar stimuli.

This theme in memory research continues to provide us with new knowledge about the role of nurture in shaping who we are. For example, in a paper that recently appeared in *Lancet,* cognitivists compared previously circumcised and noncircumcised infants in terms of their response to being inoculated at four months of age. The response of the two groups to this brief modest pain was highly discriminable both behaviorally and in terms of physiology (Taddio et al. 1997). I am not surprised by this type of finding, as a good deal of single-trial learning takes place throughout our lives. Nevertheless, I find it extraordinary that a single brief event early in life is encoded well enough to alter behavior months later. Other research has documented some of the neural systems that may explain why it is so incredibly difficult to extinguish conditioned fear (Armory et al. 1995; LeDoux 1995). Appreciating how memories are established is a formidable task, but so is our understanding of how we might erase memories.

Another related growing body of research has defined in detail the behavioral, physiological (including hormonal), and neurobiological responses to acute and chronic stressors and their impact on learning, memory, and modes of responding. Changes in the same neurochemical events that have been known for years to alter the establishment and consolidation of memories are also associated with the stress response. The emotional response to stress provides a particularly favorable biological milieu for the formation of consolidated memory traces, memories that are especially likely to survive and be accessed efficiently. For example, glucocorticoids, adrenocorticotropic hormone (ACTH), vasopressin have all been shown to affect the consolidation of memory traces (McGaugh 1990; McGaugh 1992; Weingartner and Parker 1984). Furthermore, glucocorticoids, released during stress, are known to have particularly toxic damaging effects on the hippocampus—a structure that has for decades been considered one of the more important brain systems involved in the formation and retrieval of many forms of memory. The toxic effects of stress on the central nervous system are particularly likely to occur during early development. The neurobiological impact of early stress has been captured in some recently completed brain imaging studies (Bremner et al. 1997; Bremner et al. 1995).

Stimuli associated with stressors can also serve to cue the recapitulation of stress, as in post-traumatic stress disorders. One of the expressions of the induction, by appropriate cues, of post-traumatic stress disorder is intrusions in thinking. For example, Baum and his colleagues have studied the short- and long-term impact of all kinds of disasters such as hurricanes and have demonstrated that the impact of such stressors is expressed in dramatic, "spontaneous," robust, and frequent intrusions in thinking and perception along with hormonal-brain stress responses for experiences associated with those disasters. Rapid hormonal and brain changes and learning take place under the original stressor conditions, and the knowledge consolidated in memory is associated with a whole array of stimuli that can implicitly elicit that knowledge. That knowledge can be retrieved and expressed in many forms, including the occurrence of stressor situation–relevant intrusions in thinking.

Using a Cognitive Perspective in Considering Individual Life Events

Events That Trigger Top-Down and Bottom-Up Thinking in Dealing with Threat

The concept of denial has been used, as well as trivialized, for well over a century. I would argue that, in cognitive terms, one form of denial can be characterized in terms of the interplay and sequencing of two types of operations. Threatening (potentially overwhelming) events (stimuli) trigger a fragmented and immediate response that may well be outside of awareness. This is processing that would be seen as bottom-up stimulus-driven processing. This then induces a second type of cognitive response, based on top-down thinking, that is manifested in the form of a selective retrieval of a knowledge template that biases how those events continue to be processed. This template may include selective filtering, encoding, and attending to those events and ultimately may encompass how events are interpreted and stored in memory.

Several types of personal Holocaust-related experiences in my own life come to mind where I used this type of denial (this mode of thinking and remembering).

When I was young, my father would say to me (in German mixed with Hebrew), "You think you can trust them [the Gentiles], but don't count on it. They all have *Riches* [Hebrew for anti-Semitic bigotry]." That was his sense of how the world worked. On the other hand, I have always found that position very personally threatening and—perhaps with exaggerated intensity—disagreed. I did not want to agree or to acknowledge evidence of not so much outright obvious bigotry but the more subtle, less explicit forms of *Riches* directed at Jews, African Americans, and others. It took me a lifetime to begin to note the not-so-obvious signals of hate in particular and in general to observe other forms of threat around me. I had to learn that one could survive despite acknowledging threat and hate. To acknowledge the *Riches* and other forms of threat required that I learn two things. First, I was not helpless. Second, on the contrary, not acknowledging *Riches*/threat is dangerous.

It is interesting to speculate about what "acknowledge" means in cognitive terms. We know so much and so little about the nature of cognitive functions, and yet when we try to understand real world questions/issues in cognitive terms we often draw a blank. So we revert to the vernacular of the lay language rather than cognitive science in grappling with denial of personal threat. I have some cognitive terms, such as *knowledge outside of awareness, cues, priming,* but none of them really provides new insights into, for example, response to threat in the form of situations that may be demeaning or dehumanizing to me or someone else, even a stranger. For me, this can really fuel anger in ways that I often have trouble controlling. Human dignity is most important, and this has been the case both in and outside my professional life. Most people value human dignity, but I suspect (although I am certainly not sure) that its value for me is linked to experiences of my childhood.

Another form of a top-down cognitive template that is used to deal with life events is one of not acknowledging my own needs and preferences, in effect, requiring and needing nothing. I would describe this in noncognitive terms as being a minimalist. This has been evident in all facets of my life, including how I have functioned as a professional. Of course I share this with many others who have learned this style of functioning based on their unique developmental histories. I have figured out ways of not needing anything, not needing anyone, not needing resources to accomplish my science. Right now, at this very minute, I know, if I had to, I could scrape by with virtually no resources. I have very often thought through what it would take to survive hiding in some attic, in the woods, in any setting. The essential ingredient is keeping needs to a bare minimum.

Cue, Context, and Remembering

A great deal of memory research has been concerned with the role of cueing and context in both explicit (conscious) remembering and implicit ("unconscious") remembering. Some of this research has also been extended to studies in which context is defined in terms of a mood or a drug state or an environmental setting and the specific match of encoding and retrieval demands. Memory for previously acquired knowledge (experience) is in part a function of the extent to which remembering conditions match the context in which the information was first acquired. Context influences how information is interpreted, encoded, organized in memory. The types of information that are most likely to be temporarily "lost" in recall are those for which the effort to remember occurs in a context that is very different from the encoding-processing context at the time of acquisition. This inability to access information that nevertheless is available in memory is particularly likely for information that is poorly elaborated or encoded. It includes information about mood, emotions, or poorly understood events. In addition, state-dependent retrieval failures are especially likely to occur when remembering is attempted explicitly under free recall conditions rather than in the presence of cues (such as in recognition memory). Consequently, there are many conditions in which knowledge in memory is inaccessible although available (Eich et al. 1997; Waller, Putnam, and Carlson 1996).

All of us have many experiences that illustrate facets of cue-dependent or context-dependent remembering and forgetting. On a personal note that is relevant to the theme of this chapter, several examples of context- and cue-dependent retrieval of knowledge easily come to mind. I often think of words in German, particularly around affective themes, especially themes having to do with fear, startle, shame. I can picture the words and the conditions under which they evoke images of discomfort.

The smell of pine and musk struck a note of familiarity as I came through the front door of my house in Flehingen as an adult. Also vaguely familiar were the pitch and roll of the small streets, the creek that ran through the center of the town, the backyard, the barn next to the house, the smell of dung; these all were familiar, and yet part of me thought that it was my imagination that triggered these thoughts-memories. Moving from room to room through the house of my early childhood, up the stairs, yes, it made some sense, and it brought me back, in bits and pieces of memory, as I wandered about.

In another venue for cue- or context-dependent remembering, one that remains vivid in memory is my mother's response of *Verzweiflung* that would serve as a powerful trigger for eliciting childhood helplessness and foreboding. For me that meant that I would somehow need to be the rescuer and protector, yet I felt that I would not be effective in either role. So, instead, I used my skills to somehow get all of us, my mother, brother, and father, to blend into the woodwork and thereby find some release from danger. I didn't always get their cooperation, nor did I know how to communicate my experience of helplessness, since I had neither words to describe what was going on nor the will to share my own private discomfort.

Priming of Loss-Related Associations and Intrusions in Memory

I took a trip with my two sons shortly after my wife died. It was December 27, 1993. Eric and Michael (then twenty-three and twenty-one years old, respectively) had asked whether it might not be a good idea to travel back with me to Flehingen, Germany. We needed some time together. We flew into Frankfurt on December 24; stayed in "my" village, Flehingen, on Christmas Eve; and the next day headed over to Strasbourg, France, where we visited some relatives and then slowly headed toward Paris, where we had planned to meet my sister-in-law and nephew. And so it was that we spent the night in Dijon on our way to Paris. When we arrived in Dijon in the middle of the afternoon, we parked our rented car at the center of the city. Michael was going to cash some traveler's checks at a bank and would meet Eric and me back at the car in about ten minutes. Eric and I waited, talked about our relatives back in Strasbourg, about Flehingen, and about the rest of our trip toward Paris.

Time went by. It was now twenty and then thirty minutes since Michael left us. Where was Michael? Cashing a traveler's check should take five or ten minutes. It was now forty minutes later (during which time it turned out that Michael was shopping—inquiring of several banks to get the best rate of exchange). Eric kept chatting about all kinds of things, and I panicked. What intruded into my thinking, Germany when I was a young child, while vague, was nonetheless powerful and overwhelming: Where was Michael? Where could he be? Was he trapped? Would I ever see him again? What intruded into my thinking was that Michael was lost, was helpless in Dijon; and dread, fear, filled my consciousness. At the same time, I kept up an outward appearance that I thought effectively masked my sense of foreboding. Where was he? He was lost, trapped, helpless, swallowed up somewhere in Dijon, and I could hear trains and see the look on his face as he was swallowed up. It became harder and harder to disguise the panic, and Eric picked it up and knew what it was about. He understood, only partially, but just enough to appreciate my fear. I vaguely knew where the panic came from and knew how to try to control it, but it leaked out, and there it was. Only on Michael's return could I smile and seal the lid on the experience, and we laughed about it.

I knew, or at least thought I knew, where these intrusive thoughts came from. I have been there hundreds of times before. I could experience the dread of loss, of helplessness, and do so without losing a step, while smiling and carrying on a conversation. And yet the feelings would give me away. I was a good actor but not good enough to disguise everything.

Much later Eric asked me about the experience. He asked me about my brother, Werner, his idiosyncracies, his anxieties and the odd ways about him, his phobias. He asked if it was possible that the way Werner was and, by implication, my propensity to startle, my inability to "let go," the need to control, the difficulty that I have in allowing myself unrestricted, free, uncensored joy might be inherited or acquired and, if so, to what extent. Should he worry about the heritability of this angst for his children? I am more concerned about what we learn from one another, what we do and don't do, the opportunities we have missed to share who we are in ways that enrich us.

Challenges That Reveal What Isn't Ordinarily Discernible

Perhaps provocative behavioral events also tell us something about the underlying cognitive programs and knowledge that govern our functioning in ways that are not apparent in everyday life. In some ways this theme also may be seen as another example of stimulus-specific responding with all of its theoretical implications. I think all of the events associated with my wife's dying and death were a kind of challenge paradigm that helped me to express some of the knowledge that was stored in my memory, knowledge that was first acquired during my early years of life. The experience or possibility of loss is a powerful theme, which is expressed in so many ways in dealing with my wife's death. It is now several years later, and the house looks the same as when Liz was alive. Her clothes hang in the closet, and I find it so very difficult to close the door behind me and to acknowledge that she will not return.

I wrote some notes about my feelings and thoughts about Liz some months after she died. As was the case throughout her dying, I didn't let my children take a look at what was going on inside their father's skin. I experience an overriding propensity to be overwhelmed when confronting loss and the related strong need to remain attached to relationships and, by default, one's past, including the things associated with the lives of those who are part of my life. I would label this with the German word *anhänglich*. I also associate a need to be overprotective, not just of my children but also of postdocs that have come to the National Institutes of Health (NIH) to work with me. Consequently, even a hint of threat or possible harm triggers an exaggerated response of being overprotective. That is part of being overly *anhänglich* as opposed to having a healthy detachment. This is also associated with what I would label unrealistic rescue fantasies, for example, around my NIH colleagues who are struggling to make it.

I still can't accept her death. Five years later I have changed little in the house. I keep morsels and mementos, clothes, notes, I keep it all as if I could bring her back in some magical way by keeping her things around the house. Yes, tomorrow she might walk through the front door. But then there are the images of her last months, days, hours, the moments after she had just died when I held her in my arms and kept holding her even as the funeral staff came to pick up her body, as they placed her in a body bag, zipped it up, and carried her out of the house.

I haven't edited this section in some time, and I don't want to do it now either. I still find all this difficult to deal with. Based on my version of priming and my early history, this represented my worst nightmare, one that I could recall having had in my head as a very young child, one that persisted as a theme through my adolescence. The theme was one in which, in various situations, I would be helpless and could not save someone whom I loved. Here I could do many things that made life bearable for Liz as she fought her cancer, but ultimately I was helpless as a disease took its course. This disease would not listen to arguments, pleas, treatments. It just marched on, each day shouting in my ear, and all I could do was to look on, hold my wife's hand, and try to let her know that things would be all right. I got to be pretty good at putting a hopeful spin on what was happening. Enough of this.

Nature and the Expression of Nurture (so my brother, Werner, and I are pretty much alike)

The issue of nature versus nurture has been a classic theme for debate for well over a century in accounting for issues ranging from the nature of intelligence to behavioral traits, forms of psychopathology, special skills and lack of skills, and so on. One of the challenges of twenty-first-century behavioral-neurobiological science will be not simply to uncover the genetics of specific behaviors but to reveal the distinctive environmental conditions that allow that genetic information to be expressed. It is the interaction of the acquired and inherited knowledge that will continue to grow as the foundation of a new psychobiology of behavior.

Some things strike me as being obvious. I don't understand why a developmental perspective has taken so long to excite cognitivists. What appears to be obvious is that a developmental point of view is ideally suited to look at so many important issues. Likewise, a systematic understanding of how experiences are laid down as knowledge in memory, from a developmental perspective, parallels the exploding interest in brain plasticity from reductionistic, molecular, and comparative phylogenetic perspectives. Where knowledge comes from, and how new knowledge is acquired, are tantalizing questions to ask with regard to the very young.

Sorry, Eric and Michael. I wish I knew more. I don't know the answer regarding the factors that got me to turn out the way I am. If I knew I would tell you. My bet is that most of the "squirrelly stuff" is acquired, but I am just not sure. Anyway, look at all the great things you got from Mom and me: looks, brains, charm. You can't go wrong with all this. Also, and most important, I am unconditionally and totally committed to both of you. That also allows us to explore all kinds of issues of who all of us are and who we become.

It is only now, late in my life, that I have been ready to look at and examine my early history. I don't experience any sense of closure in terms of those early events that shaped me and whose legacy has been handed down to my sons. What I do appreciate, at many levels, is that our history is reflected in how we respond to things, what we think about, how we organize our universe. I am not all that interested in what you tell me about what you know, what your associations are; in your ability, on demand, to tell me stories, scientific stories, news items, what you had for breakfast. I would rather watch who you are, how you respond, and that will tell me a little of your history. That is also relevant in evaluating the consequences of early experience. We remain rather limited in our ability to project forward the combined effects of nature and nurture in the context of development; so we end up with conjecture, hints of things that may be correct, vague ideas, and a need to learn and know more.

Overview and Conclusions

So where are we at the end of this rather tentative, sketchy story? Personally, I have learned something from completing this chapter. It does not surprise me that I try, where possible, to consider autobiographical events by looking down at them through the abstract lenses of some model. If that is not sufficient to blur the images of what I am looking at, I make certain that I don't stare at my history with foveal vision but rather peripherally and then only briefly (an impressionist's sketch).

As psychologists, we can obtain a consensus on several points. In an age of reductionistic biology, we have been able to note enormous gains in our knowledge in the life sciences, especially genetics. We are still struggling to obtain even a fuzzy picture of the psychobiology and mechanisms (even in functional terms) that account for many facets of normal or impaired behavior. However, we are moving, ever more rapidly, in a direction that will allow us to effectively study broadly defined phenomena such as behavior from a developmental perspective; cognition (not just in a fragmented form but as it occurs in complex interactions with the environment); emotion; and the representation and expression of different forms of knowledge, including how different forms of knowledge are acquired. Questions of nature versus nurture have always been asked, but now we have the tools to begin to answer them for all kinds of problems, and furthermore we have successfully applied this knowledge.

This type of research will tell us about modal processes and operations in the average person or in the average patient with a particular form of pathology. Scientific strategies that we have available are not nearly sophisticated enough to solve problems such as psychological accounts of the events and the consequences of those events in our personal histories. On the other hand, we have available conceptual tools for asking questions in interesting ways and useful interpretive schemes for interpreting autobiographical events. We can, and should, make use of them, while appreciating the limitations of our theories, knowledge, and models in providing us with "answers" about our behavior and its underlying neurobiology. However, the need to examine who we are, who our cotravelers are, and where we have come from is irresistible.

I returned to Klein-Eichholzheim, to Flehingen, on several occasions and wandered about for a few hours, but I couldn't wait to leave. I would then return several years later, poke around, go to the town hall, talk to some people, go out to the Jewish cemetery at the edge of town, and when my discomfort had risen would head back across the French border. I listened to a piece by Haydn and was suddenly confronted with the melody of "Deutschland über alles"; I winced, and the music was turned off in my head. I heard pieces of the same music in a wonderful, melodious part of a Beethoven trio, and again my head was jarred back from the beauty of the strings.

My brother, Werner, never went back to Germany. He has spent most of life skittish, frightened of many things. Many years ago he set up a small bank account in Switzerland for himself; for me; for my sons and my wife, Liz, just in case. . . .

What do I make of these snippets of facts and reactions, feelings, styles of living in both my professional life and my personal private life? How much of all this is nature rather than nurture? Surely it will all turn out to be a complex interaction of nature and nurture. There are so many uncontrolled variables to consider that in the end it is difficult to conclude how, or even if, these early experiences are important in defining who I am. Methods and models of cognitive science are not powerful enough to provide answers to questions about the veracity and impact of early experience-knowledge on how we function as adults.

One final note. Last year about this time, my friend Shlomo Breznitz and I put a *mezuzah* on my door. It contains the traditional message, along with one of our own creation, a credo of how we might best live our lives. It seems as if it took me forever to mark who lives here.

REFERENCES

Adolphs, R., D. Tranel, H. Damasio, and A. R. Damasio. 1995. Fear and the human amygdala. *Journal of Neuroscience* 15, no. 9 (Sept.): 5879–91.
Armory, J. L., J. D. Cohen, D. Servan-Schreiber, and J. E. LeDoux. 1995. An anatomically constrained neural network model of fear conditioning. *Behavioral Neuroscience* 109:246–57.
Bremner, J. D., P. Randall, E. Vermetten, L. Staib, R. A. Broner, C. Mazure, S. Capelli, G. McCarthy, R. Innis, and D. S. Charney. 1997. Magnetic imaging–based measurement of hippocampal volume in posttraumatic stress disorder related to childhood physical and sexual abuse—A preliminary report. *Biological Psychiatry* 41:23–32.
Bremner, J. D., P. R. Randall, S. Capelli, T. Scott, G. McCarthy, and D. S. Charney. 1995. Deficits in short-term memory in adult survivors of childhood abuse. *Psychiatry Research* 59:97–107.
Cahill, L., R. Babinsky, H. J. Markowitsch, and J. L. McGaugh. 1995. The amygdala and emotional memory. *Nature* 377, no. 6547 (Sept.): 295–96.
Cahill, L., and J. L. McGaugh. 1998. Mechanisms of emotional arousal and lasting declarative memory. *Trends in Neurosciences* 21, no. 7 (July): 294–99.
Cahill, L., B. Prins, M. Weber, and J. L. McGaugh. 1994. β-Adrenergic activation and memory for emotional events. *Nature* 371, no. 6499 (Oct.): 702–4.
Damasio, A. R. 1998. Emotion in the perspective of an integrated nervous system. *Brain Research Reviews* 26, nos. 2–3 (May): 83–86.
Eich, E., D. Macaulay, R. J. Lowenstein, and P. H. Dihle. 1997. Memory, amnesia, and multiple personality disorder. *Psychological Science* 8, no. 6:417–22.
LeDoux, J. E. 1995. Emotion: Clues from the brain. *Annual Review of Psychology* 46:209–35.
McGaugh, J. L. 1990. Significance and remembrance: The role of neuromodulatory systems. *Psychological Science* 1, no. 1:15–25.
McGaugh, J. L. 1992. Affect, neuromodulatory systems, and memory storage. In *The handbook of emotion and memory research and theory*, edited by S.-A. Christianson, 245–69. Hillsdale, NJ: Lawrence Erlbaum Associates.
Molchan, S. E., A. Hill, H. J. Weingartner, J. L. Mellow, B. Vitello, R. Martinez, and T. Sunderland. 1992. Increased cognitive sensitivity to scopolamine with age and a perspective on the scopolamine model. *Brain Research Review* 17:215–26.
Rogan, M. T., U. V. Staeubli, and J. E. LeDoux. 1997. Fear conditioning induces

associative long-term potentiation in the amygdala. *Nature* 390, no. 6660 (Dec.): 604–7.

Taddio, A., J. Katz, A. L. Ilerissch, and G. Koren. 1997. Effect of neonatal circumcision on pain response during subsequent routine vaccination. *Lancet* 349:599–603.

Waller, N. G., F. W. Putnam, and E. B. Carlson. 1996. Types of dissociation and dissociative types: A taxometric analysis of dissociative experiences. *Psychological Methods* 1, no. 3:300–321.

Weingartner, H., and E. S. Parker. 1984. Memory consolidation: Cognitive perspective. In *Memory Consolidation: Psychobiology of Cognition,* edited by H. Weingartner and E. S. Parker, 1–12. Hillsdale, NJ: LEA Press.

Part 3

Targets of
Political Persecution

Coming Full Circle

Learning from the Experience of Emigration and Ethnic Prejudice

Karl W. Butzer

Biographical Note

Karl Wilhelm Butzer received the BSc (honors in mathematics) and MSc in meteorology and geography from McGill University, and Dr.rer. nat. in physical geography, minor in ancient history, from the University of Bonn. He has held professorships at the University of Chicago and the Swiss Federal Institute of Technology (ETH) in Zurich, as well as a Guggenheim Fellowship in Britain and Africa. He is now centennial professor of liberal arts at the University of Texas, Austin. He has conducted extensive field research in Europe, Africa, and Latin America, some in collaboration with his wife, Elisabeth Butzer. His work established the age of Homo sapiens sapiens *sites as older than one hundred thousand years, three times the age previously accepted, setting the stage for biomolecular studies proposing the "out of Africa" model of humanization.*

Professor Butzer has published two hundred articles and fourteen books, monographs, and edited volumes, of which the most recent is The Americas before and after 1492 *(Cambridge, MA, 1992). His many honors include the*

Busk Medal of the Royal Geographic Society (1979), the Fryxell Medal of the Society for American Archaeology (1981), the Henry Stopes Medal of the Geologists' Association of London (1982), and the Pomerance Medal of the Archaeological Institute of America (1991). He is an honorary fellow of the American Geographical Society and has been elected to both the American Academy of Arts and Sciences and the National Academy of Sciences.

Introduction

The twentieth century has been marred by extirpation and expulsion of national minorities on an unprecedented scale. Yet, as the century draws to a close, television screens relentlessly remind us that senseless and inhumane atrocities are not a thing of the past, that rabid ethnic prejudices in the guise of nationalism lurk just beneath the surface in all too many places. I am haunted by the traumatized faces of lost innocence, of Muslim children from Bosnia and Kosovo, who have witnessed their homes burned, their fathers killed, and their sisters or mothers raped. We are tempted to point the finger at other places or peoples, but deep-seated ethnic prejudice is far more pervasive and plays itself out much closer to home. Its most vulnerable victims are the children.

Indeed, there is a silent violence, not played out on TV news, about which most people are uninformed. For decades, children from Spanish-speaking homes in Texas were ridiculed and punished by their teachers for speaking Spanish in class or on the school grounds. As recently as the early 1980s, Hispanics and African Americans were beaten to death in sheriffs' offices. Generations of people with Spanish surnames have been imbued with the stigma that their Mexican culture and biological heritage were inferior. Undereducated, with few successful models to look up to, they could not shake the burden of shame, as they saw it. The spirit of countless children would be sapped, even before they entered high school, as they and their parents saw themselves culturally and genetically predetermined to failure in all but the most menial of roles.

Ethnic prejudice, particularly in conjunction with incidents of violence, is so cruel to the individual, in the form of an imposed collective guilt or ritual public denigration by the empowered group. Whether for personal gain or ideological zealotry, political, religious, and educational leaders have time and again sought to capitalize on societal insecurities by identifying ethnic scapegoats and fanning the flames of latent prejudice or even mass hysteria. The results have sometimes been horrific, at whatever scale a pogrom or ethnic cleansing.

What burdens me just as much, however, is the endless hurt done to children the world over, in everyday situations, through the spite or careless disdain of mainly "nice" people of a dominant group. Recently I was astounded, watching "The Great War" on public television, to see a film clip of 1917 showing U.S. schoolchildren carrying books about Germany out of a library to throw into a bonfire, with the smiling approval of the librarian and of their elders. One can only speculate how the social attitudes and values of those proud little grade-schoolers were twisted, or how a third-generation German-American pupil may have been scarred for life, by such a book burning. It is the defenseless and vulnerable child who must bear the pain of stigmatization, unequal opportunities, and hopelessness, ashamed of who he or she is. Such a childhood all too often projects into a demeaning life without higher goals or fulfillment.

I come to this subject not as a Holocaust survivor but as a member of a German Catholic family that chose, and was able, to emigrate illegally in 1937. As a six year old in England I experienced plainclothes police entering our home, ransacking our library, and taking away my father. That trauma continued for ten years, as I grew up in wartime and postwar Canada. But unlike the voiceless child of an underclass, I received the support of my cohesive, middle-class family, which gave me the means and will to fight back and, above all, to compete and succeed. I later repressed most of the memories, but there was just enough scar tissue to make me hypersensitive to ethnic prejudice around me, whether it be a mere slight or a serious injustice to an "outsider," particularly if that person lacked the articulate family support and education that had sustained me. And at midlife I began a disciplinary shift from environmental history to cultural themes that eventually led to university courses on ethnicity. It was here that I recognized that I had come full circle, drawing now on my early experiences to try to instill tolerance in my students.

But the purpose of this essay is didactic, not autobiographical. It attempts to use a personal narrative to illuminate the insidious nature of authoritarian repression, the experience of emigration, and the impact of ethnic prejudice and stereotyping on the children of minority groups.

Cultural Conformity in the Nation-State

The consolidation of the Western nation-state during the eighteenth and nineteenth centuries went hand-in-hand with the direct or indirect reduction of "regional" variety in terms of custom, language, and culture or religion. The most effective tool was the system of public schools that enforced monolingual education and projected a monolithic national identity. Acceptable cultural difference was reduced to the realm of folklore, be it the ethnic dinner-dance at the church or a parade. In some countries the transformation was incremental and peaceful, in others it was not. Homogenization from above and the elimination of cultural difference are central to understanding the complexities of ethnicity, particularly because most Anglo-Americans believe that the "ethnic succession" of the melting-pot model is essentially a benign process.

Long after most European countries had been transformed into nation-states, Germany had resisted unification under either the Catholic Hapsburgs (Austria) or the Protestant Hohenzollerns (Prussia). But between 1814 and 1866, Prussia acquired direct control, or hegemony, and in 1871 the king of Prussia became the German emperor. Berlin displaced Vienna as primate city, Austria was excluded from the new Germany, and "Prussia" came to represent both a powerful bureaucracy and a military caste that projected a nationalist ideology. We were Rhinelanders and Catholics, as well as Germans, but Prussians against our will. Our heritage included a century of resistance against centralization, first by Prussia, then by Prussia's Nazi successors.

The distribution of Catholics and Protestants in the German-speaking part of Europe is grounded in the religious wars of the sixteenth and seventeenth centuries that highlighted older cultural differences and led to divergent development after 1648. The west and south, including the Rhine country, Bavaria, and Austria, were Catholic, coinciding roughly with the former Roman provinces. Here the world outlook was distinctly western European. German Catholics remained loyal to a universal church and, based on their traditional lore, recognized common roots with the Low Countries and France in the empire of Charlemagne. At the same time, the northern and eastern parts of Germany cut off their ties to Rome during the Reformation and reinforced their orientation toward Scandinavia and the East.

In 1815 the autonomous statelets of the Rhineland, which were 70 percent Catholic, were incorporated into Protestant Prussia, with its traditions of militarism and expansion. A vigorous policy of Prussianization was soon implemented, designed to replace the civil service, to "appropriate" the upper classes and so reduce Catholics to the same underclass they were to become in Prussian Poland. Unlike the French occupation of 1794–1814, which had abolished serfdom and created permanent rural leaseholders, Prussian rule was long perceived as foreign domination. That helps explain the irony that my paternal grandparents had a print of Napoleon on their bedroom wall.

The smoldering resentment came to a head in 1872–79, after German unification under Prussia, to the total exclusion of Austria. Bismarck first disbanded or expelled the Jesuits and other religious orders. He then demanded that all priests take government examinations before being able to exercise office and effectively closed down Catholic worship and education. The archbishop of Cologne was imprisoned and parts of the clergy exiled. Catholic resistance was mobilized by the Zentrum, the Catholic Centrist Party that cut across socioeconomic class lines. Electoral solidarity was translated into political protest, the emergence of an articulate press, and civil disobedience by both clergy and laity. Known as the *Kulturkampf* or culture war, the confrontation reinforced Rhenish identity in particular. Bismarck eventually came to recognize that sustained confrontation with a third of the population made little political sense, and the penal laws against Catholics were finally removed in 1890. But the clergy and Catholic politicians continued to be scourged in the national press as "Roman" sympathizers, and Catholics were still bypassed for higher government appointments or university positions. The "establishment" was and remained German rather than European and was very much Protestant.

Catholic mobilization continued after the culture war. Both the Zentrum and the bishops joined the Polish clergy of Prussian Poland in their fight for Polish-language schools. Together with the socialists, they also opposed the ever-increasing military budgets. After World War I, Catholic voters did not join the growing ranks of support for the Nazi economic platform, custom tailored to a nation coping with six million unemployed during the Great Depression.

Electoral analyses of the Nazi vote from 1928–33 consistently show that Nazism had little appeal for Catholics.[1] Nazism represented a belligerent, antireligious movement, extolling a motley collage of "Germanic virtues" all too reminiscent of the Prussian past. Furthermore, Catholic society was strongly organized in socializing and supportive networks for different age and occupational groups. Once in power, but holding only 35 percent of the popular vote, the Nazis gained absolute control through existing "emergency" laws. Whereas the socialists and communists were promptly battered with brutal efficiency, the Nazis chose a more subtle and insidious strategy to curb religious freedom and practice. Sunday worshipers were harassed and ridiculed by uniformed Nazis on church steps; crucifixes were removed from Catholic classrooms; sermons were interrupted by organized hecklers; and outspoken preachers were threatened, placed under house arrest, or imprisoned.

Although some of the discourse on the ambiguous role of Pope Pius XII in regard to Nazi atrocities alleges that the German Catholic hierarchy were accomplices by silence, this was far from the truth. Martin Niemöller and the Protestant "Confessing Church" are familiar abroad and justly so. Less well known but more broadly based was Catholic opposition. It included Bishop Clemens von Galen, who unleashed a strong protest against the new culture war in his Easter pastoral letter of 1934. Despite all efforts to muzzle him, he and many others continued to speak out forcibly against totalitarianism, the persecution of Jews, and the campaign to undermine religion in society. In 1941, he was able to almost halt the Nazi eugenics program that had taken 70,000 victims. Yet von Galen is only one more familiar example of the testimony of conscience. Of the 12,100 Catholic priests in Germany, over half were in some way under surveillance, intimidated, arrested, fined, or imprisoned for "subversion." They served 2,400 jail sentences, and 417 of them, including army chaplains, were sent to concentration camps. One hundred seven lost their lives.[2]

In the end, however, there was no winner against the police state, which operated through media control, intimidation, informants, and random denunciations. The Prussian penchant for by-the-book law enforcement, long the butt of Rhenish jokes, had a more disturbing downside: the middle class felt constrained to obey unjust or immoral laws, particularly when dependent on government salaries or support in any capacity.[3] Conformity became a matter of economic survival. Nazi sympathizers permeated some academic disciplines, and the acquiescence or compromise of the establishment was achieved through various small perks. After twelve years of terror and an apocalypse, the many components of German society had been atomized, the traditional bonds of solidarity broken.[4]

Despite a stream of Cold War movies on international espionage, the average North American has no clue what everyday life is like in a police state, such as Castro's Cuba, Ceausescu's Romania, or the Baltic states under the Soviet Union. He or she can relate to the protesters of Tienanmen Square, but the long stream of refugees from Guatemala and El Salvador was mistrusted as a category of essentially "economic" migrants. Although each ideological "media dictatorship," of the left or the right, has different parameters, the common thread is physical intimidation by a state that assumes absolute control, muzzling freedom of thought and expression and leaving its populace impotent. Just how determined the Nazis were to dominate was obvious after the "Night of the Long Knives" of mid-1934, when all perceived competitors from within were murdered, or in the vengeful vendetta after the attempt on Hitler's life a decade later that saw five thousand military and intellectuals, including the wives and children of mere suspects, tortured and condemned by "people's courts" or executed without the pretense of trial.[5]

My Parents

The preceeding outline of the culture wars reflects the legacy of my father, Paul Anton Butzer (1893–1984). He was not a talkative man, but when I was in my teens he broached the subject frequently, developing various points that supported or elaborated the general argument. In retrospect, I realized that this was the most important thing he felt that I should know about himself and, by extension, about who I was. For him, the first culture war was living history. During the 1870s his grandfather, then a relatively prosperous farmer, had provided a safe house to hide fugitive priests, who were being secreted across the Prussian border. His family was politically aware and active and uncompromisingly anti-Prussian. My paternal grandmother, Margaretha, née Brabender (1866–1950), with no more than a primary school education, took after her father, as did my father; she was a strong and informed woman. Her brother, Wilhelm Brabender, was her counterpart, serving as an oblate missionary in rural Saskatchewan in 1905–31. He was my godfather, a burly and gregarious man who preached in English, French, and Cree and who reputedly never spoke ill of anyone.

In the second culture war, the family was unflinchingly anti-Nazi, but there was very little they could do. Thirteen of them voted "no" in the plebiscite to confirm Hitler as president in 1934—which required the conspicuous use of a different voting booth for dissenters; but when the local election results were published, that precinct reported 100 percent "yes" votes.

Years later, in a professional capacity, I recognized that the Catholic Rhinelanders of my father's memory and family heritage met all the criteria of mobilizing behavior in an ethnic group. A mythical origin in Charlemagne's "united Europe"—the goal of the visionary French politician, Robert Schuman, in the 1950s—represented the primordial roots. During the early nineteenth century, in the absence of a unifying political structure, the Catholic institutions became a "popular" (rather than "established") church, which led and defended its communities. In the more complex political maelstrom after 1871, a parallel, secular organization, the Zentrum, provided political organization and a voice in Berlin. Together, Zentrum and the popular church mobilized the various socioeconomic classes, all age cohorts, and both sexes to assure social reproduction. Religion was a matter of social bonding, not theological imperative.

It was my father who, through consistent example, taught me to respect "the other." Yet he came from an impoverished family that had lost its substantial farmland to speculators in one generation and was engulfed by the industrial revolution in the next. As the second of eleven children, he left school in 1907 at thirteen to work in a factory when his own father fell sick and later died with acid-corroded lungs. As fortune would have it, he did not end up in a production line but as an apprentice in a company that manufactured parts for steel rolling mills: that offered opportunities for advancement. His mother raised the younger children, with the help of his meager wages, by growing flowers to sell at market in Benrath, now a suburb of Düsseldorf. Despite the long working hours he arranged for private lessons at night, beginning with English and French, a remarkable priority for a teenage factory apprentice in that day. On holidays he took the train to some starting point and went hiking, crossing the border to Belgium and perhaps France. Later in life he was nostalgic for the time before 1914, "when you could cross any border without a passport."

Father was drafted soon after World War I broke out and received the Iron Cross (Third Class, of course) in France but then came down with typhoid in Poland, on the Russian front. After a long convalescence and garrison duty in Berlin, he was decommissioned in July 1916 ("the happiest day of my life"). He was returned to civilian life because his technical talents had been apparent in the steel mill, and he was now needed at a time when German industry was moved into high gear to meet the demands of the war. By 1921 he had taken a sufficient number of night courses to gain admittance to the Technological University (TH) of Aachen as a special student, receiving a three-year leave of absence from the Schloemann Steel Works in Düsseldorf. During that time he earned a high school equivalency on the side, while completing the work toward a university engineering degree in late 1924. He also met my mother, the first female student in mathematics at the TH, and they married in 1925. He was then thirty-two years old.

Upward mobility was a formidable task in that time and place, which speaks for his determination. But that does not explain a young factory worker's fascination with history and politics. He once confessed to me that in another life he would have become an archaeologist, to excavate in Egypt or Greece, like Heinrich Schliemann. He was enthusiastic about Leo Frobenius, from which I infer that he attended a public lecture on African ethnography. He recalled conversations with the parish priest in Benrath, who was a local history buff. From his early efforts to learn English, I speculate that he may have once thought of emigrating to the United States—or to Canada, from where his favorite uncle, Wilhelm, gave glowing reports. It truly was an unusual family, as I found out when I got to know them better in 1954: many of his siblings, despite their limited education, read newspapers regularly and discussed political events in a big way.

One of Father's stories impressed me greatly. He went to France in the 1930s to find the grave of my mother's oldest brother, Karl, who had fallen near Verdun in 1916. There, he related, he ran into a Frenchman who helped him, and they spent half an afternoon musing on the folly of war. I don't remember that my father ever spoke French, and he was by no means a gifted linguist. Like myself, he just went out and "communicated." But I still have his expensive French-German dictionary, which looks used, and he had a well-worn self-help book for Russian when I was growing up. His vision was global, as I always knew. My mother related to me that in 1925, when Field-Marshall Hindenburg (cosponsor of the military dictatorship in 1917–18) won the German presidency, Father predicted that Hindenburg would favor the right-wing militarists, who in turn would bring on a second war. In 1933 it was indeed Hindenburg and his clique who invited Hitler to form the cabinet.

My mother, Wilhelmine, née Hansen (1902–86), also worked her way up in difficult times. Her father, Franz Hansen (1858–1914), was the last guild master of cabinetmakers and wood-carvers in Aachen and had sculpted altars for churches as far away as Hungary. But he went bankrupt a year after her birth, too stubborn to adapt to industrial furniture making. Yet, working as a school custodian, he was the impetus to get three of five children through the senior matriculation at elite schools, and Mother went on to break gender barriers at university, while her brother Karl received a teaching certificate before going to war. Whereas my father was staunchly anti Prussian, Mother had a residual nostalgia for the monarchy, perhaps because brother Karl had received a prize "from the Kaiser" upon his graduation. She spoke fluent English and French and greatly admired French culture. Her cooking, in fact, was more French than stereotypically German, reflecting the fact that Aachen is culturally midway between Cologne and Brussels. Mother was fearlessly outspoken. That trait ran in her family, right or wrong. Her willingness to fight for what she believed was right significantly complemented my father's idealism.

Whereas I learned my regional particularism and anti-establishmentarianism from my father, it was my mother who instilled a German ethnicity in me before I was ten. She always talked about the fine, tall soldiers who had marched through Aachen at the outbreak of the war; they had all died, as did her favorite brother. Those who came back after the armistice were small and emaciated or maimed. Being German to me became synonymous with sharing in a national tragedy, a collective loss that would never be healed. I suppose that my father had similarly resolved the contradictions between Rhenish loyalties and a broader German ethnicity. Much like the emergence of a single U.S. identity between the Civil War and 1945, the autonomous segments of Germany's intricate regional mosaic appear to have fused in the firestorm of two world wars.[6]

Emigration

The early Nazi years were a looming disaster in my parents' eyes. Most people took the anti-Semitic rantings as a cheap political ploy or as a thunderstorm that would soon pass by. But as early as April 1933, a carefully formulated decree required expulsion of most Jewish Germans from the civil service and universities, and a second edict of September 1935 stripped even people of partial Jewish ancestry of full citizenship. After that my father managed to persuade two good Jewish friends of his, J. Loewy and Hugo Lorant, then fellow engineers at Thyssen A.G. in Mülheim an der Ruhr, to emigrate to England. They founded Loewy Engineering in London. Little did Father know how important that would prove to be.

Other Germans also found their civil rights sharply curtailed. An insidious network of informants sowed suspicion everywhere, abetting the secret police, so that people who simply spoke their minds could be railroaded by "people's courts" for "endangering public welfare." The capitulation of the judiciary, as an institution, allowed a redefinition of "justice" that left the accused little hope of legal redress. Public pressures for conformity were intense, especially in the industrial and administrative centers.[7] Even schoolchildren were encouraged to report on their teachers and classmates. My father, as an engineer at Thyssen—an industrial giant—was under constant peer and company pressure to "set a good example" for the workforce, but every morning he refused to return the "Heil Hitler" salute of the twelve-year-old Hitler Youth at the company gate. Neither did he march in the First of May worker parades. In 1935 the secret police inquired about his failure to do so, and in 1936 they threatened action if he failed to march the next year.

There had also been an incident at school, where my then eight-year-old brother, Paul, had loudly refused to stay when the Nazi flag was raised in the schoolyard, in front of the assembled children and the principal. A sympathetic teacher warned my parents that the principal was a militant Nazi and that the secret police would conclude that our parents had "the wrong attitude," a real liability because they intended to keep Paul from joining the Hitler Youth at age ten. Adamantly unwilling to compromise, my parents were deeply concerned about their children growing up in a police state environment, forced to repress themselves at every turn by fear. It would surely stunt our moral and intellectual growth. Added to that was the Nazi military occupation of the Rhineland in 1936, breaking the peace convention; Father was now convinced that another catastrophic war was only a matter of time and that his children would be consumed in it.

Legal emigration was impossible, so flight was the only alternative. But that option was not for the fainthearted. Not only was it difficult and perilous, but it meant giving up an upper-middle-class lifestyle for total uncertainty—at a time of global unemployment. The countries of the free world were reluctant to admit emigrants, particularly those without visas and a clear prospect of employment. It is not necessary to elaborate upon how many Jewish refugees were refused admittance by England or the United States in the late 1930s, including a Jewish professor of my parents who subsequently died in a concentration camp.

It was a very difficult decision, but my father decided to risk all. He resigned at Thyssen to take a fictive job with a small company in Aachen, owned by one of my uncles. On Easter Saturday he went to the Netherlands, with a briefcase and a one-day exit permit, to attend an electrical engineering exhibition in Arnhem. He had only been allowed to take ten marks and his return train ticket out of Germany. Once there he went to a modest hotel and wired to Loewy Engineering, asking whether they could provide him with a job in England and arrange for his entry permit. But that London office was closed until the next Tuesday, because it was Saturday and the following Monday was a bank holiday. Penniless and already in default on his expected return to Germany, he waited with dwindling hopes. But on Tuesday a telegram arrived at the hotel from London, telling him he had a job and wiring him £80 for his trip. My father then paid his hotel bill and bought a one-way ticket to London. He did *not* march on May 1, 1937.

The first step in a great gamble had paid off. Father's Jewish friends in London, whom he had first contacted in November 1936, had come through for him. They had not only reciprocated with extreme generosity but over subsequent years provided loyal support and displayed great kindness. Mr. Loewy was a saint to us children. He died early, but Mr. Lorant and my father were still in touch by mail, exchanging photographs, for years after both had retired. They had been friends since 1913.

Meanwhile, my mother and we children were sequestered in Grandmother's home in Aachen until two weeks later she received a cryptic message, a signal that she could now join Father in London. The next day she crossed the Dutch border on a "short shopping trip" but went on to London. My brother and I were smuggled out, hidden under seats of a schoolgirls' bus, and taken to a nunnery in Gemmenich, just across the border in Belgium. Here arrangements had been made to keep us until Mother found a place to live in England. Grandmother used some pretext to stay with the nuns for the duration, to keep an eye on us.

Detailing the preconditions and the flight elucidates how difficult such decisions were. If anything had gone wrong, the outcome would have been disastrous. Lacking outside assistance, it would all have been impossible. Without their international outlook, my parents could not even have contemplated emigration. For the average German dissenter, emigration or flight simply was no option.

Professionally, our emigration adventure left an indelible impression on me. I have a deep empathy for international refugees—who lose everything, with uncertain prospects—and sympathy for their plight. I accept current arguments that "economic" immigration, whether legal or illegal, strongly selects for people with vision, conviction, and initiative. It is a "good" selection, which will contribute richly to a host country over generations to come. It also illustrates how vital support networks are for vulnerable individual immigrants in a foreign land. And it angers me that immigrants almost everywhere continue to be scapegoated as salient contributors to economic or social problems.

Trauma

At two and a half years of age, I had no idea what was going on. That probably heightened my trauma of spending four months in a convent with officious nuns, who would not let me sleep in the same room as my grandmother. It is the earliest coherent data set in my memory bank, and I still recall many details vividly. At night I cried and threw up regularly, desperately seeking motherly comfort. During the day I barely ate and felt resentment for my surroundings. My only beacon was my grandmother, but she seems to have been powerless to intervene more effectively.

Grandmother spent time in the mornings at the village church in Gemmenich, and occasionally she took me there for mass. My greatest independent feat was running away from the convent one morning. I well remember getting out onto the road, with some relief, and then deliberately honing in on the church tower perhaps a half mile away. There were cows grazing on one side of me, cars passing on the other, but I felt exultant rather than afraid. Eventually I got to the church and sat down in the pew next to my grandmother. She was dumbfounded. The nuns watched me even more closely thereafter, but I felt I had made a statement.

In 1987 my brother took me to revisit the convent in Gemmenich, and I promptly got my bearings. He smilingly let me show him exactly where we had played together on the grounds and where I had taken off down the road as a toddler. But I also felt the anger resurface and then thought about how unfortunate orphans, be they ever so little, must feel under much more hostile circumstances. My father saved the Belgian stamps from the correspondence between my mother in London and Grandmother, mailing her letters from Gemmenich or nearby Moresnet. I still keep them, as mementos of a page in my life.

My family reunited in a London suburb in mid-August 1937, and I went back to being a child. Then the war broke out. We crisscrossed masking tape across all glass windowpanes to impede flying glass, and when the bombs fell, we huddled together under the oak dining table. Who was bombing us? The Germans, I was told, our people. Why were they doing that? Because those are the bad Germans that we were running away from.

At the end of 1939, Loewy Engineering was relocated to Bournemouth, on the south coast of England, and we rented a nice little house in what seemed to be heaven. There were so much open space and nature, and on Sundays Father took us to the sandy beaches, especially on the Isle of Wight. The blitz was beginning to heat up, and every day I saw the clusters of little white fish in the sky—German planes with smoke screens—heading for London. I soon learned to distinguish English and

German aircraft by their distinctive engine noise. You could tell who was approaching, and from what direction, before you could see them, just from that distant but distinctive roar of motors. Those planes with the undulating engine noise were my people. But if they won and "got" us, my people would hurt us. So I hoped the raspy British engines would win.

That simple analysis was shattered when the British secret police showed up at our door one morning while we were getting dressed for breakfast, probably in June 1940. They were tight lipped and unfriendly as they searched the house. They pulled the books out of our bookshelf until one of them waved one book in his hand. "*Mein Kampf*!" he gloated. Actually it was F. Dahn's history of the Visigoths, *Ein Kampf um Rom*. But that didn't matter. In a matter of minutes my father was hustled out carrying only a handbag. I ran screaming after the car, "My daddy!" But they had taken him away.

German refugees were being "interned" as potential spies. Father's group was carried in open, flatbed trucks to camp out in tents on a soggy field somewhere in Lancashire. He was one of the lucky ones. He got out after three weeks, because Mr. Loewy was very persuasive to the wartime authorities that Father was indispensable for the British war industries. But when he arrived back in Bournemouth, we were gone.

A week or two later "they" came back for us, again unannounced. Mother had an hour to pack one regular and two small suitcases. When I regained my bearings we were in a huge institutional basement in Bristol, together with some fifty other people. Except for an Englishwoman married to a German, with an infant child, they were all Jewish. My mother explained that the Jewish people shouldn't really be imprisoned, because Hitler had wanted to kill them. They were friends of England. I realized then that we somehow didn't fit that category. They were such friendly women that I was full of wonderment as to why they had been arrested. My brother remembers how Mother spoke indignantly to a warden, saying that someone should take the children outside so that the women could undress for bed. Eighteen of us youngsters were taken for a walk around the building, accompanied by twelve guards. The irony didn't escape my brother. We all got a sandwich and slept on the floor on what impressed me as thin mattresses.

After a few days we were off to Liverpool, by train as my brother recalls. Since the carriage compartments all had doors, both to the corridor and to the outside, an Englishwoman sat in each one, next to that outside door. Our Englishwoman served us a delightful box lunch.

When my mother expressed her appreciation for the care we were receiving, she was told that no food had actually been provided; the woman herself had decided to pack something to eat, just in case. That story has reminded me, in a small way, how in a hostile world there always are some humane people who see foreign women and children for the women and children they are. Many of the Jewish women went hungry that day, because their wardens hadn't brought a lunch.

In Liverpool, our number had swelled to over two hundred, with detainees from elsewhere, and we were transported in a convoy of buses. But we could hardly make it to our destination, because the streets were jammed with people, raising their fists, faces distorted, screaming, "Kill them!" I couldn't know that Liverpool had recently been bombed by the Germans and that those angry people had sustained terrible losses. I was only a child, and I was horrified to see such livid hate for the first time. That image has never left me, and each time I cannot help reflecting on how that hate had been misdirected at two hundred poor Jewish refugees.

Eventually we were put up in a disused old sailors' home in the slums of Liverpool. There was dust everywhere, almost a quarter inch thick. Outside there still were chanting crowds, but I felt more secure once inside the building. We each got a slice of bread with peanut butter and jelly, but I was still very hungry.

Days later we were taken by ship to the Isle of Man, in the middle of the Irish Sea. It was a lovely place, and we were distributed in a series of houses in what normally was a summer seaside resort. We were often hungry, but the woman who owned the house did what she could. Later she told my mother that after five weeks she still hadn't been paid anything by the government for the requisitioning of her house or for our upkeep. There was an old fisherman on the wharf who had a white beard, and he was also very nice to me. But a block away there was barbed wire.

After perhaps six weeks of internment we were suddenly back in Bournemouth. Mr. Loewy had worked another miracle on our behalf. But those two hundred Jewish women and children didn't have a Mr. Loewy, and although they shouldn't have been there at all, they stayed on the island. When the weather turned cold and gales battered the Manx coast, the detainees were caught there without any winter clothing. They froze, as one new friend had written my mother, who then sent them a big box of warm clothes, including her own winter coat. Mother was an impulsive giver. But those unfortunates on Man still had a long trail of woe ahead of them, twice victims of prejudice. In 1942 they were shipped out to Australia, their husbands and fathers to Canada. So much for justice.

Bournemouth was a changed place on our return. It was the height of the blitz. The beaches were empty, closed off with multiple rolls of barbed wire, to anticipate a possible German invasion. Day after day the German planes churned by overhead, and once a bomb was dropped near our place; the explosion was deafening, and later I tried to locate the impact spot but couldn't find it. I did find a German plane that had been shot down and was displayed next to the main road. I looked it over very carefully: it was so small and had an open cockpit (an observation or weather reporting plane). What shocked me was the primitive steel seat. How uncomfortable and cold it must have been for the pilot. He had bailed out and was badly wounded. He also was German like six-year-old me, and now it didn't matter whether he was a good or a bad German. I felt very sad about him.

Every English person here seemed nice to us, despite the war, and there were good times again, because the family was together. Several small friends and I found an abandoned dugout encampment at the end of our block, and we combed over what little was left behind. Mother explained that Canadian soldiers had been posted there (during the summer of 1940) to protect England from invasion. But our neighbors had commented on how messy they were and that the English had to provide them with proper uniforms and train them. Mother thought it odd that young men who had volunteered to come out and help were put down like that, simply because they came "from the colonies."

I added that impression to the growing list of inconsistencies of that first eventful year since the war began. Nothing seemed to make much sense, and nothing was predictable. Most English people were warm and kind, but police people were not, and a lot of people in Liverpool wanted to kill me. Jewish people were being hurt by English people, but they were poor refugees and should have been helped instead. Mr. Loewy and Mr. Lorant were Jewish and good to us, but the bad Germans were hurting Jewish people. I was German, but I was supposed to wish the bad Germans to lose the war. Canadian soldiers were good people and spoke English, but they were looked down upon. Daddy loved England, but he didn't seem happy. I wondered about all these strange things a great deal.

Much later it began to make sense. These were the ambiguities and contradictions of ethnic behavior. There weren't any categories of "good" versus "bad" people. Individuals, some good, some not so good, were found in any group. And there were both bullies and victims. For me, 1939–40 was a formative year. I had had my first crash course in ethnicity. Despite the trauma, I had been very fortunate. But my identity was being thrust upon me by events, at too early an age.

Canada

I had now learned where Canada was, and on my first day in school I was fascinated to hear about a Columbus who had sailed across the sea with a fleet of three small boats to discover the New World. The images in my mind then are still there, and of course it never dawned on me that fifty years later I would be doing research on Columbus as a scholar. The next thing I knew, my parents were talking about going overseas to that New World, to Canada. In reality, we didn't seem to have any choice. Loewy Engineering was opening a branch office in Montreal, Canada, and my father was to be transferred because of some government directive.

It was an incredibly exciting journey. We saw endless shipbuilding yards as we embarked on the *Warwick Castle* in Glasgow, and we sailed straight into a howling midwinter gale. Father and I tried walking on deck every day, and for much of the trip we seemed to be the only guests in the dining room. We arrived in St. John, New Brunswick, during the night of January 24, 1941. I went on deck with all my clothes on, but it was bitingly cold—twenty degrees below zero. The next night we were on a train, rumbling between snowdrifts that were as high as the train. I understood that we had started a new life, and every year on January 24 each of us, together or privately, remembered that day. It conferred on us the title of "Landed Immigrant," the Canadian equivalent of a "green card."

We moved out to a very simple home in western Notre Dame de Grace, on a street half built up by one of the Canadian railways before the Great Depression halted everything. Most of the neighbors identified themselves as "Scots" or "Irish," and few of them were friendly. I loved the big open spaces outdoors, but it was a social environment that we were not familiar with—lower middle class, unlike our former neighborhoods. My father found himself with an effective cut in salary, compared with England, and we bought used furniture. My parents read a lot of library books together and befriended some of the Jesuits who ran a high school and college adjacent to the parish church. For two years the Jesuits came over for coffee and cakes and seemed to enjoy some good conversations.

My father's new boss and his wife were Jewish, German speakers from Czechoslovakia. "Tante Clacha," as we called her, was nice and motherly, but the boss was no Mr. Loewy and did not appreciate Father's talents. The saving grace for my father was Imy Jaffé, who had come over from the London office with her parents, the Sachses, an old Jewish couple who had emigrated from Poznan and also spoke German at home. Mrs. Jaffé and the Sachses were our dear friends. They had relatives in Europe who had escaped via France to Madrid. Father was always given the Spanish stamps from their correspondence, and I still have them. Over the years I have looked at them several times with a curious feeling of affection.

A kind of preview to our new social environment came during the one parish picnic that we attended in the spring of 1941. Father had entered a footrace and was about to win, when someone deliberately tripped him. As he fell, a lot of people broke out in cheers. It was apparent to all of us that the "rules" in Canada were different than in England. I connect this incident with my lifelong dislike for the puffed up, officious ushers I found at the Sunday masses in most old, established Catholic communities in Canada and the United States.

Outside the home, things turned nasty in the fall of 1941. I was being called names in second grade, and then a gang of more than a dozen boys jumped me on my way back from school. I wasn't really physically hurt but was humiliated and terrified. I told the principal, and he scolded them in his office the next day. When the boys filed back into class, the young teacher, Mrs. Brawley, asked if they had gotten the "strap." They replied no, and then she said, "Good. You didn't deserve it." That gave them the license to do what they wanted, and it became a year of terror. I became afraid to go out on the playground during the breaks, and after school I was stalked by a gang of boys who regularly followed me home to line up in front of the house, shouting, "Heil Hitler!" My grades plummeted, and I slipped from third in a class of twenty to second or third last: every month we shifted class seats according to rank, the best performers sitting up front. I was regularly sitting in the last row now and began to lose my sense of self-esteem. I became ashamed of my origins.

In the summer of 1942, my parents felt they had to get me into new surroundings. So we spent some weeks at a sort of vacation motel near Lachute. It was a relief, and we met a group of empathetic people who were really nice to me. They were bilingual French Canadians, and I recognized that they were different. My parents noticed that too, and later that summer we went to a small French hotel in Fourteen-Island Lake, in the Laurentian Mountains near Shawbridge (now named Prévost). The owners, the St. Pierres, were farm people and had five bilingual children. They became my first friends in the New World.

That fall my parents kept me out of school, and I went to Mrs. Shaw, the retired principal of my school, for home tutoring. Totally isolated now, I really felt ostracized and finally told Mother that I wanted to go back to school, even if the kids beat me up. I did, and although I was still afraid to go out on the playground, the third grade teacher had her class under control, and there were no more incidents, despite the overt hostility of most of the boys.

When she thought she was alone, Mother cried a lot. She explained that Aachen had been heavily bombed, and she was afraid that her own mother had been hurt. She might never see her again. My father was also in bad spirits. Later, I learned that he had deliberately switched from designing machines to sales. When he had started working for the war effort, he was helping save England from German attack. Now the mills were grinding out aluminum to build planes that killed civilians in German cities. He just couldn't handle that, as a matter of conscience.

In the summers of 1943 and 1944 we rented a summer cottage in Fourteen-Island Lake, and I began to experience life as a child should. I played with the smaller St. Pierre boys and worked with the bigger ones on the farm. I learned how to cut and bale hay, milk cows, and fork manure. I learned to dance to the jukebox tune of "Stardust" at the Dew-Drop Inn with thirteen-year old Cécile, blonde and adorable to a nine-year old boy. I also learned to speak French. Our family became insiders in the little French Canadian community of five families. We were told about Mr. Dujardin, who always watched the door, that he was on the run for evading conscription. Once he jumped out of the back window of the Dew-Drop Inn as the police came in the front door. As French Canadians, they told us, they didn't want to fight England's war, so we were not "the enemy." They tended to see us as friends, perhaps as fellow underdogs. Our friendship with the St. Pierres lasted for life. The oldest boy, Raymond, later went to work in Montreal, and Father sometimes had lunch with him when they worked in the same district. The two of them remained in periodic correspondence until my father's death. Ironically the St. Pierres were bicultural too, as I comprehended later. Their grandmother had been a vivacious Irishwoman.

In fourth grade a school inspector came into every class once a month. After rustling through some papers behind the teacher's desk, he would ask about the children's ethnicity. All the "English" children had to stand up, and so forth.[8] Finally he would ask, "Are there any foreigners?" Now I had to stand up in the aisle. "What are you?" he would ask. "German," I had to say. Every month the same routine, with the same effect. The other children were reminded, and the hostility, bullying, and name-calling flared up again. I remember wondering, with growing anger, why he had to do this even though he already knew the facts.

There is another incident, one of only a few that I have recounted to others, that is very applicable. When a pencil or an eraser went "missing" in class, the teacher promptly came down to search through my desk and that of Paul Laberge, the only French Canadian in the class. But eventually it turned out that Charlie Benson had the item. That happened not once but several times—the teacher predictably pounced on the desks of the only two minority students, but the stolen trinket was always in Charlie's. This was a classic reflex—you're not one of us; therefore you must look dishonest and disreputable; and so you're the obvious suspect. That is probably why police selectively stop or pick up African American motorists for "suspicious behavior."

Whenever I was in Montreal I had nightmares about children beating me up, and my mother started taking me to a chiropractor. He was French Canadian, and he was very kind. I enjoyed the visits and the manipulations and felt that they really calmed my jangled nerves. We began to use only French-speaking professionals; it made such a difference. Some of them were unfriendly, but it wasn't directed at us. The English-speaking Jesuits no longer came over, leaving my mother wondering why. Instead three German Jesuits, who had been in Canada when the war broke out, started visiting. One of them, who was a dreadful bore, tried talking to me in German on his first visit. I understood perfectly but couldn't find the words to respond. It made me aware that I was always answering my parents in English, and that now irritated me so much that I began to try to speak in German again.

It had become evident to all of us that we were socially isolated except for a very small circle of German, Jewish, and French Canadian friends. Something important happened after the Normandy invasion in 1944. Father began listening closely to the radio when he was home; this was so unusual that Mother had to explain why he was on edge. After all those years of wishing for an Allied victory, the impending destruction of

Germany was quite another matter for him. It was a two-edged sword, and I immediately understood. Having been told for as long as I could remember that the Nazis must be defeated, it gave me a palpable sense of relief to discover that my father was also tortured by the contradictions of loving Germany while also hoping for victory over Nazi Germany. Yes, it was all right to feel for Germany. No matter how bad it was, it was my country. My ethnicity had become clear to me.

Things also began to change at school. I had been an unaggressive child, never fighting back when picked on. At age eleven, beginning my preadolescent growth spurt, I was ragged once too often and threw a few punches. It was one of the stronger boys, and I was surprised to see that his nose was bloodied, because I had gone for his face, instead of his chest, as was conventional in schoolyard scuffles. He was shaken too, and we just stood there and looked at each other. After that, the class pecking order was turned topsy-turvy.

One day the boring Jesuit came in with a magazine that had pictures of piles of Jewish bodies in a death camp. I remember how stunned we were. On another occasion he had magazine pictures of raped German women, dead on the streets of Berlin. I didn't get to see those pictures, but hearing about it made me very angry. The next time Tante Clacha visited, for the last time, she told my mother that if any of her relatives in Prague proved to have been killed, she would go over and distribute poisoned candy to German children. I was shaken but couldn't believe it. It was a loss of innocence for me, because she was such a kind person. Yet since I was already beginning to grasp the enormity of what was later called the Holocaust, I somehow understood that she was in anguish, had said something she didn't mean, and didn't intend to hurt us. Nonetheless I felt that our circle of friends was becoming smaller still.

The postwar years were different in that I went from the defensive to the offensive. I was fighting a lot, getting good grades, and allowed to be chummy with some of the "holdover" teens retaking seventh grade. In high school I would get belligerent when somebody asked me about my nationality: "A bloody (expletive) German! What about it?" My alienation was turning into defiance. I put together a makeshift punching bag and spent hours, it seemed, in the basement pummeling it. Every summer there were three glorious months at our country house, exploring the bush around Fourteen-Island Lake. I devoured Western novels and received a .22-caliber rifle that saw a lot of use. My nightmares of victimization turned into recurrent dreams of violence. At home I never argued with my parents. For them it was an easy passage of adolescence within the house, except for the pounding in the basement. My anger was directed to the outside.

Prejudice was now directed top-down. Two examples, both of whom happened to be Jesuits, will make the point. As a college junior, my brother heard his professor of philosophy make the following dramatic statement in class: "For the last century, no, for the last three hundred years—the Germans have been the curse of the world!" Then there was my third-year high school teacher, an *American* Jesuit, as it was emphasized. Father Kelly constantly used body language and metaphors as if he were a Notre Dame football coach. One day, in theology class, he made eye contact with me and made some derisive remark about "German geniuses." Then he almost snarled, "Moral fortitude! The Germans didn't have moral fortitude, and that's why the Americans went out and"—some sort of euphemism for "beat the guts out of them" followed, while he continued glaring at me without a blink. He had no personal reason to be that spiteful, and the next day I was in the dean's office with my mother.

The dean was a nice person, shy and soft spoken, and he always seemed to have a gentle twinkle in his eye when he saw me. He made no argument but immediately discussed alternative solutions. He recommended against switching me to another third-year class, because the same priest taught religion class (!) in all of them. Instead, the dean proposed moving me up to fourth year, skipping a year. It was tough, but I pulled through and actually found myself enjoying school. The new priest was a hard pusher but had a wry sense of humor, and my new classmates were mature and sophisticated, in my eyes, and accepted me like a little brother. No reason was ever given for my move. The next year, Father Kelly had been transferred back across the border.

By then we had moved to a more pleasant neighborhood, dominated by English Canadians. It was a friendlier place. Reserved, but people did at least greet you, and the neighbors next door didn't threaten to call the police when I stepped across the midpoint of the common driveway. Irish Catholics were at the bottom of the socioeconomic ladder in Montreal, just above French Canadians. Why did so many of them seem to want to take it out on German Catholics? Why did some of their most educated people harbor such a grudge? It was the slashing prejudicial remarks of teachers, from Mrs. Brawley to Father Kelly, that hurt the most and that still resonate with me today.

A final incident of another kind rounds out these examples of my

Canadian experience. In a third-year history course at McGill University I had been getting straight "firsts" (As), when suddenly I got a "third" on my class paper. It was on Roman history, and, significantly, I can't remember my reasons for believing that this was another case of ethnic prejudice. But shaken, I went to the professor and complained, implying that I received that grade because I was a German. Sorrowfully he looked at me and then explained quietly why my paper had missed the mark. I was terribly embarrassed, and I still feel red in the face about it today. But I began to recognize that I was obsessed with victimization and was becoming paranoid. It proved to be an important step in growing up, in snapping out of that mind-set.

That same embarrassment helped me a decade later, when I was a young instructor at the University of Wisconsin. Three Jewish students, I heard by mail, had gone to the dean while I was away on research leave, attributing the Bs and Cs they had received in my course to my being a Nazi. Considering my life experience, it hurt me deeply. But I eventually saw the connection with my Roman history course. Those students, too, had been fighting prejudice all their lives, and they were vulnerable and suspicious. From then on, I made an extra effort when grading papers by minority students of any kind to spell out my criticisms in full and to do so gently. I have also reflected on what can happen to minority students who lack either the confidence or the articulacy to speak up and complain: that obsession, that cloud of suspicion can sap their will to succeed, because they believe that merit has nothing to do with it; the system isn't fair; they haven't got a chance. Prejudice works like a poison on children and teens. Small but regular doses can also blind you about what is positive and well intended; they can take over your life and turn it into a nightmare.

After Canada

At twenty-one, master's degree in hand from McGill, I went back to Germany with a national scholarship to work on my Ph.D. It took me a while to match up the Germany of 1955 with the images recalled by my parents. The doctoral students I interacted with, some of whom had served in the military, were enthusiasts for a united Europe, without borders. Others were from Spain, Sri Lanka, Iran, and Japan, and all were given warm welcomes and genuine support. Up to two hundred students from all over faithfully attended several long slide shows on Japanese rural landscapes by our Japanese friend. Six hundred to nine hundred citizens of Bonn could be expected to attend any popular lecture at the university on a foreign country. African Americans, who could not sing in U.S. opera performances, starred in the town opera and were enthusiastically applauded. Whatever unreconstructed thoughts lurked somewhere among an older generation, those were heady times not only to be in Germany but to be anywhere in continental Europe. The era of obsessive consumerism and "guest workers" had not yet dawned, and it seemed as if everyone had just come up for pure oxygen after the years of repression, war, or occupation. This all stood in contrast with the grim parochialism I had experienced in Montreal.

I continued to cherish memories of the incomparable natural environment of my country home in the Laurentians, and I seriously thought about going back to study the failed farming venture of my French Canadian friends, whose families had moved into that inhospitable area in the 1840s. But in the end I became a specialist on the Near East. I began to value my Canadian passport as a Commonwealth identification, in those two decades when the Commonwealth symbolized international cooperation rather than special-interest bickering. In 1959 I accepted a university appointment in the United States and married a German woman.

The state of Wisconsin proved to be another felicitous choice. It was a friendly place with multicultural roots. After a month, the elevator operator in my university building asked me whether I was going to stay in Wisconsin. I said yes, a little hesitantly because I remembered in another life being sarcastically asked when I would be leaving. But the woman smiled at my answer and said, "Good!" That welcome never seemed to fade, and the four children that my German wife and I raised grew up without ostracism as authentic Americans, proud of their Old World roots. That is the healthy way for children to come to maturity.

Looking Back

Recalling and recording these events and emotions has not been done easily, if only because I am a private person. My generation was conditioned to be tight lipped about personal matters and had little tolerance for what might be perceived as whining or complaining. Add to that the relatively benign ethnic prejudice that my family was exposed to, for I have never considered myself a victim. Yet over the years, despite my repression of the more painful memories, I found myself drawing intuitively upon these experiences in reaching out to "others" and in dealing with prejudice. Later, I found that these same experiences had come to dominate the issues central to my most important university courses.

Immersing myself in recalling and sorting out the more salient memories, the very fact of rearranging them in linear time with reference to occasional family or external happenings, brought back details I thought forgotten. Many such events had been captured by Father's camera and preserved in the photographic albums that he assembled, with dates, from the 1920s to 1952. In 1981 he also provided me with a chronology of his life between 1907 and 1941. Some missing details were supplied by my brother, who, six years my senior, did have a sequential memory bank for our years in England. For our parents' recounting of the flight from Germany and its antecedents, we pooled our recollections.[9] I was surprised to reexperience emotions long forgotten and recalled some naive attempts to make sense of what was happening around me.

As I began to write I found myself being more candid and explicit than I had intended to be, but only then did it become apparent to me that none of the literature I had read provided personal accounts of how commonplace prejudicial words or actions can impact a child. There seems to be silence about the countless "little" things that hurt, humiliate, or provoke mute anger; the thoughtless or spiteful ways in which educators can make a mockery of their own vocations. If others with such power at their disposition are to learn what not to do, I had to spell out what it was like to be at the receiving end.

My father had resisted the pressures to conform, as a matter of conscience. Unwilling to compromise, he had taken us abroad, as refugees from Nazi intolerance. But there we had found ourselves in an increasingly hostile world, unjustly branded as Nazis and for ten years subject to most of the gamut of biased behavior. Perhaps worst of all, our fellow Catholics and even some of the priests had rushed to judgment, scapegoating us—as children—for the tragedy unfolding thousands of miles from Canada's shores. It was only very much later that I would try to explain such behavior as the displaced aggression of a once-marginalized group, barely emerged from the ghettos of Montreal, Toronto, or Boston. For some, God was reduced to a tribal deity, but this did not shake my anchoring as a Catholic, and although I include several Jesuits among my early role models, it did leave a mixed taste in my mouth for that order.

More difficult to explain was our almost total ostracism by virtually all the people who thought they knew who we were, specifically the Catholic community of St. Ignatius parish. For years, the four of us remained almost totally isolated, our own reactions to rejection probably reinforcing that rejection. The vital importance of support groups became apparent when European immigrants and visitors began to arrive in Montreal around 1950 and we also first met earlier immigrants from other parts of the city. At last we could compare experiences and talk things out. My brother went on to study at the University of Toronto in 1948, and we traveled more widely as the restrictions on foreigners were lifted. Our morale picked up rapidly once we transcended the confines of the parish community, literally and figuratively.

The lack of overt ethnic prejudice that I had discovered as an undergraduate at McGill, and the warm reception my brother had experienced as a graduate student at the University of Toronto, impressed all of us that socioeconomic background had a lot to do with it. These were elite institutions, where many of the best (and most gentlemanly) professors at the time were British. But as a graduate student, I also became aware of the other side of that coin—the favoritism displayed for students fresh from Britain, some of whom were less than gracious.

The preferential treatment of British immigrants at some Canadian universities was not too popular among the Canadian students. I now befriended Canadians for the first time, as well as two West Indian students, preferring the company of a novel group of "outsiders." But the geography department at McGill provided my first institutional home, and I felt comfortable. I was competing on my own ground, in my own microcommunity, and I had full confidence in my own ability to do so. Unable to get a Canadian government fellowship for my doctoral studies, I simply moved on to Germany. Four years later, unable to get a position in Canada, I joined countless others among the brain drain from Canada to the United States. But an attachment did persist, and I waited until 1991 to take out U.S. citizenship.

Over the years I revisited Canada on various professional occasions and was surprised at how rapidly it had changed. Toronto and Vancouver had moved from post-Victorian provincial towns to multiethnic metropoles. Friendly, open young people had replaced their dour parents of Scottish heritage in the small towns of central Ontario. Canada had indeed opened itself up to the outside world. It had managed to become cosmopolitan without losing its distinctiveness. But Montreal had changed into a somewhat sad place, riven by ethnic hostility. The French Canadians, who so long had been reduced to hewers of wood and drawers of water by a dominant, anglophone minority, had turned the tables, but the outcome seemed ambiguous. At a faculty cocktail party at McGill I heard francophone universities reviled and was then exposed to a French Canadian faculty member being ridiculed to his face with ethnic clichés by an English-speaking colleague. Small wonder, it seemed, that the Quebec legislature had curtailed funding for McGill University. On the subways, I found that people looked sullen, as if they had lost rather than won a majority voice in their own affairs. In victory, French Canadians seemed to have lost some of their graciousness.

There seem to be no winners when ethnicity degenerates from positive solidarity to the corrosive pathologies of resentment and conflict. Perhaps that is because the generosity of spirit, which gives us confidence in a shared humanity, is its first victim.

Full Circle

Dislocation, prejudice, and a partial awareness of international events during my early years influenced the decisions I made in graduate school. My home environment certainly whetted my interest in foreign countries and history. But my favorite childhood book was Richard Halliburton's *Complete Book of Marvels,* and I remember the sense of escape from a hostile environment as I read and reread it to lose myself in the past or in remote places. This was not some world of the imagination but was written about real events and places. During my teens that interest became increasingly directed, and I taught myself how to read German in Gothic type, giving me access to the wealth of historical and geographical information in our twenty-volume Meyer encyclopedia of 1897. During the summer that I turned nineteen I read Arnold Toynbee's *Study of History* in the abridged edition, fascinated by the normative approach to macrohistory and especially the notion of challenge and response as a prime mover. As a master's degree student I wrote a term paper on the problem of ethnicities in the Hapsburg Empire, and by then I had decided I would not do my doctorate on a Canadian topic.

A growing fascination with the Near East was combined with a curiosity about how people adapted their lifeways to a marginal, arid environment that was unpredictable and prone to frequent change. To avoid the trap of determinism I would need a great deal of sophistication in the social sciences, so that the matter of interaction could only be tackled incrementally. In regard to environmental history, short or long term, there were next to no reliable data. The first priority became to generate such hard data. To meet both objectives I regularly collaborated with archaeologists, most of them grounded in anthropology. Together, we formulated, discussed, and argued interdisciplinary questions. My technical expertise derived from the natural sciences. Nominally addressed to environmental reconstruction, the more intriguing questions for me concerned the patterning of human settlement and subsistence in environmental mosaics that changed over time.[10]

Eventually I devised the term *geo-archaeology* for such cross-disciplinary research and was drawn into a variety of projects from Spain and Egypt to eastern and southern Africa. Depending on the area and issues, I worked on sites or in settings in a wide range of topographic and environmental settings, from architectural features and cemeteries to rock art, stone artifact horizons, and fossil beds. Observational skills are best honed not by endless repetition under similar parameters but by comparing and contrasting. Paleolithic caves in Spain shed light on the formation of Pliocene cave breccias in South Africa. The big river valleys and their modern indigenous settlements in Ethiopia helped explicate the mechanisms of the Egyptian flood cycle and early floodplain settlement along the Nile. The deserts of North Africa were both similar to and different from the arid plains of South Africa and Namibia. These complex data came together in a mental matrix that was turned into a number of regional and thematic articles and systematized in successive books.

My audience was among anthropologists, human paleontologists, and Near Eastern specialists, rather than among the ranks of earth scientists, and for over a decade I mainly participated in anthropology and archaeology meetings. Research for a book directed primarily to social questions in ancient Egypt first convinced me that historical documentation is a great deal more insightful and nuanced, and hence more intellectually satisfying, than the somewhat normative procedures typical of a "hard" science methodology. My lectures on earth processes and landforms refocused on people as geologic agents, emphasizing human impacts on the environment. A course on human geography was added, and I wrote an early article on the potential implications of global climatic change. To gain greater freedom to develop a new curriculum, I accepted a position in Switzerland in 1981. There I developed a course sequence that emphasized historical human ecology, including such themes as demography, long-term population cycles, famines, the Industrial Revolution, social justice, war and genocide, and Third World exploitation. Such an agenda was unprecedented in the conservative framework of Swiss geography.

Twenty-five years of hands-on field experience with different peoples, in so many places, had become an inestimable resource. Anthropological sensitivities developed across eighteen years of close, collaborative work could now be put to full use. The command of scientific technologies was an asset, and my penchant for comparative reflection, complexities, and diachronic thinking could be readily transferred. This was what I had once chosen to do, and at midlife I was consciously coming full circle.

As I sensed the stimulus of new intellectual challenges, my research changed radically. My wife had been working on Islamic Spain, and together we had explored the layouts of medieval Islamic cities and countrysides on earlier occasions. In 1980 she and I began a long-term project to study several Islamic hill villages north of Valencia. She alternated between research in the main historical archives, to ferret out and decipher medieval documents about "our towns," and direct observations as a "participant observer" in the village where we stayed. At the same time, I excavated in an abandoned Muslim hamlet, destroyed after a revolt in 1526, and later in two Islamic castles, one of which had been ravaged after another Muslim rising in the 1270s, shortly after the Christian Reconquest.

Halfway through our six seasons in the sierra I was also doing semistructured interviews, using local informants to interpret the function of medieval features. I was impressed by the continuity of adaptations, despite ethnic replacement, and eventually privileged to hear the inner feelings of some of the young people on their rootedness in the frugal environment that they considered home.[11] The monographic publication that ensued relied heavily on medieval documents to bring to light the travails of a cluster of minority communities, chafing against cultural domination, subject to forced conversion, massacred after their unsuccessful rising in 1526 (for which we had uncovered the fired timbers in collapsed houses), and finally driven into exile in 1609.[12] We began to grasp, emotionally, the scope of the tragedy of the Muslim minority, made accessible to us by being allowed to sense the nostalgic loyalty to "home" shared by modern émigrés from a dying mountain community.

It became increasingly evident to me that I was tapping directly into my earlier life experiences, even as the recurrent theme of human response to climatic change and environmental stress revealed a subconscious fascination with resistance and adaptation in the face of adversity (see also Peter Suedfeld's chapter, "A Generalist in Search of a Specialty," in this volume).[13] I also believe that my lifelong penchant for crossing disciplinary boundaries and seeking other points of view owes much to early experiences where other "outsiders" were presumed to be interesting people and possible allies. Both my lectures and research began to resonate with concerns about social responsibility and values, and I grew conscious of a deep-seated relativism, an unwillingness to reach premature closure, and a comfort with ambiguity.

In deciding to take a new position in Texas, my wife and I were both strongly attracted by the vibrantly bicultural Hispanic world that began a few miles south of Austin and by the prospect of continuing our research in colonial Mexico. I remember standing in front of the Spanish governor's house in San Antonio, wondering about how a young military conscript from our Valencian village would have felt, arriving on this former colonial frontier. Appropriate or not, that reflection somehow guided my next research focus, to try to understand nonstereotypic Spanish impressions of the New World.

Sixteenth-century letters written by Spanish emigrants to relatives back home give no hint of obsessive greed or ambition. Instead the letters display everyday human concerns, apprehensions, and tenderness, as their writers attempt to rationalize family events within deeper cultural values. These ordinary people express the same emotions, hopes, sensitivities, and biases as do modern North Americans. Of course there were conquistadors who, beyond government oversight, were just as inhuman as the colonialist villains of Joseph Conrad's "Heart of Darkness," set in the Belgian Congo of the 1890s. But the contemporary writer Oviedo did distinguish between brutal and upright conquistadors. That does not excuse or legitimize wars of conquest and human subordination, but the "burden" of "civilizing" other peoples was still misconstructed a century ago by Rudyard Kipling, whom I read in school. Hindsight is a convenient tool for stigmatizing other people, as people, while forgetting the endless litany of horrors perpetrated by one's own nation. The polemic about the Columbian quincentenary largely missed its opportunity to *reflect* on prejudices, insensitivity, and intolerance toward the other,[14] by simplistically condemning Spain and implicitly whitewashing the Anglo-American pursuit of Manifest Destiny.

The "critical theorists" have had a field day twisting the words of early writings on the "New" World, and even the faculty of departments of English have rushed out fearlessly to deconstruct history. But the observations of the sixteenth century are instructive about the complexity of human emotions and intellectual processes of articulate writers, many with nonacademic backgrounds, when confronted with a new paradigm of *two* world hemispheres. Their efforts to comprehend differences and similarities, to devise logical explanations, and to learn to appreciate unfamiliar historical trajectories and cultural behaviors are illuminating—if only because they mirror the life experiences of every individual at any time.

It is also productive to look at documents such as indigenous artists' sculpture or maps as more than evidence of "resistance." There are over a thousand informal maps from sixteenth-century Mexico drawn locally for litigation purposes that reveal a continuous transition between indigenous and European conventions as used to represent physical and cultural topographies. These suggest efforts by both parties to find common ground in representing the visible world. They point to "communication" that, although incomplete and difficult to interpret, suggests how individual Spaniards and Indians might sporadically recognize each others' cognitive processes as comparable and hence grasp their shared humanity. Much the same can be argued for naturalists or missionaries who employed indigenous artists to paint zoological, botanical, or medicinal specimens; or for the master stonemason who carved European iconographic images on a church facade and gave them a distinctive indigenous imprint or added indigenous symbols as an expression of a personal search for a coherent synthesis of worldviews.

At the same time, second and third generation European settlers were learning to see the biotic landscape through indigenous eyes, judging by the rapid expansion of Nahuatl nomenclature in early Spanish documents to describe the native flora, even as Nahuatl speakers adapted their own language to accommodate Old World livestock. The voluntary exchange of crops is particularly tangible, with indigenous peoples adapting Old World fruit trees, while Spanish settlers preferred Mexican peppers to their own spices and shifted from wheat bread to maize tortillas. By the late 1700s, all ethnoracial classes in Mexico were formally intermarrying. These are examples of the complexities of the transculturation, the process by which different peoples learn from each other and become more alike.

Reaching Out

In trying to understand the finer grain of transculturation, we can recognize a creativity of the human spirit and perhaps even a sense of pleasure or optimism in new aesthetic or intellectual accomplishments. Colonial domination and alienation clouded that process in Mexico, but we cannot let the ideologues reduce its complexity to an unmitigated saga of suppression, pain, and injustice. "Resistance" is a multifaceted thing, its motives and vitality probably more positive than negative. Then, and now, mutual respect and collaboration can potentially draw upon sufficient goodwill among sullen minority groups to allow constructive engagement. Surely there must be better solutions than more "circumscribing" legislation to deal with the seemingly "indigestible" minorities created by culturally distinctive immigrants within the industrialized nations of today.

Raised in the tradition of national states, westerners have long been prone to the assumption that nationality and ethnicity are synonymous. Painfully, we have begun to learn that they are not, even when the standard language is the same. The nation-state came together, often by manipulation or force, at the expense of vibrantly rich and distinctive regional traditions that represent centuries of cultural and historical experience. The attempted suppression or reduction of regional traditions or ethnicities to folkloric curiosities, as in the case of the *petit pays* of France,[15] would be a great cultural loss. "Conservative clerical nationalism" helped save the Catholics of Ireland, the French Canadians, and the Belgian Flemings from cultural submersion. Beyond "mere" regionalism, it was the application of the same arbitrary concept of national state that has brought a heightened level of ethnic tension or conflict to the Balkans, culminating in ethnic cleansing in Turkey and Greece during the 1920s, various forced expatriations in the 1940s, and incredibly bloody conflict in Bosnia in 1941–45 and again in the 1990s.

Beginning with the introduction of single-language public education in Europe during the 1850s, the national state has sought to homogenize its peoples directly or indirectly through centralization.[16] Whereas, in an earlier era, many cities or rural districts had thrived with interdigitated linguistic, religious, or ethnic tapestries,[17] the nation-state insisted on standardizing one national language and based itself on a monoreligious (read: cultural) establishment. "Others" were increasingly marginalized, accentuating tensions and enforcing conformity at the price of ridicule or suppression.[18] Among a dominant people conditioned to an unhealthy awareness of "difference," demagogic politicians and community leaders incited bigotry or violence, especially in times of crisis.[19] That is what led to the pogroms of Russian Poland and eventually opened the door to the Holocaust as well as to other atrocities on a grand scale in Europe and Asia throughout that frightful decade of the 1940s.

There is an urgent message here: that intolerance of diversity is nothing new and that we must find more equitable and constructive ways to demarginalize minorities, without requiring them to sacrifice their identities or the cultural heritages that they embody. Traditional customs and values are seriously at risk when minority individuals reject their own society, without grasping the complexity of the majority culture, leaving themselves increasingly rootless. Such deculturation is accompanied by confusion and a spiritual anomie that threatens the social contract. It is not by accident that within the immigrant population of Texas the number of teenage pregnancies is highest in the third and fourth generations. The United States has yet to confront the reality that 9 percent of its population is of foreign birth and that 26 percent of the total is of non-European background, with that percentage increasing rapidly. Can the charter society accept a reasonable level of cultural pluralism within the ever changing quilt of an immigrant nation?

That will be a daunting task, especially in the face of hardening militancy, hypersensitivity, and mutual distrust. Education is critical here, and parents and teachers must instill respect for others at an early age. We see others through a filter of perception, learned from our parents, our teachers, our age cohorts, our media, as well as our religious congregations and secular leaders. Ethnic *circumscription* comes easily to humans, as they seek psychological comfort and find support in a familiar universe, particularly on those occasions on which they are confronted with difference. But ethnic *behavior* towards the other is learned at an early age, implicitly and explicitly, from our peers and elders. Whether that behavior emerges as pejorative and hostile depends largely on the innumerable signals we pick up as children, adolescents, and young adults. Such signals will eventually govern our innermost thoughts and spontaneous reactions, and will substantially affect how we deal with difference.

Teachers at all levels have an open mandate to study our immigrant communities and their heritages so as to educate the dominant group, influence policy-making, and ultimately help build transethnic bridges. The scale of crisis in failed integration continues to build, with superficial acculturation more than offset by a disintegration of traditional values among immigrant populations. The resulting social problems and insecurity exacerbate ethnic friction, setting in motion feedback patterns (all too familiar from the faltering accommodation of African Americans into the mainstream) that tacitly institutionalize stratification. The challenge is to find ways to enable immigrant communities to hold on to their own cultural values, to reinforce their informal institutions, and to retain their self-esteem as they seek acceptance rather than rejection by the dominant group. Once a minority has been totally deculturated—and before it can properly embrace the value system of the dominant group—the social problems become almost intractable. If nothing else, the very scale of finding a new multicultural accommodation between *old* minorities and *new* minorities, who will make up almost half of the American population within thirty or forty years, is a compelling reason for dealing constructively with the issues today rather than paying the incalculable costs of failure tomorrow.

Most universities now offer broad curricula and ample options for a "multicultural" education, even if that tends to be inadequate in practice. But rather than try to impose multicultural study from above, universities should first of all support those scholars in ethnic studies who may be willing to offer constructive, quality courses aimed at mainstream students rather than "insiders." They should also identify the large, existing menu of courses in other departments that have substantial multicultural content and provide students with appropriate incentives to sample some of them. Finally, they should encourage those departments that now offer the basic courses in "Western" history or civilization to bring in guest lecturers specializing in non-Western or "minority" fields, so as to broaden the agenda—on a regular basis. Above all, this task should not simply be turned over to militant polemicists.

Cultural and other prejudices continue to play an unfortunate role on the international stage. Edward Said's *Orientalism*,[20] argues that colonialism and its representation of other cultures—specifically the Middle East—continue to pervade intellectual, political, and social circles. While Said's indictment of political policies and popular attitudes is fairly close to the mark, his sweeping condemnation of Western scholarship on the Middle East is unfair and counterproductive. Through a rather selective study of a vast database, Said allowed himself to stereotype scholarship and then, inexcusably, treated politics and research as the interchangeable but reinforcing points of a polemic argument. His underlying purpose may well be to challenge Western cultural stereotyping of the Middle East. But in the process he rejects the hand reached out by countless genuine Orientalists to find common ground and make "the East" accessible to well-meaning readers among the educated and influential middle class.

One of the more compelling international problems today is how to deal constructively with the Islamic world. That world is just as diverse as the entity we label "the West," and for over a century its many different peoples have been in turmoil over roughshod colonial intrusion and cultural westernization. In combination with the excesses of Islamic fundamentalism, Said's rejectionism reinforces those sympathetic with Samuel

Huntington's *The Clash of Civilizations*,[21] a trove of recipes for a new, cultural fascism. A Harvard historian, Huntington paints the Islamic world as the post-Soviet enemy of Western civilization and recommends not only strict cultural containment but a purification of Western culture from within.[22] To the contrary, I would argue that we must learn to understand the Islamic world and its historical experience. On seeing the traumatized faces of the Muslim children in Bosnia and Kosovo, I am reminded of how much we need to discover and explain the shared roots and values that "East" and "West" hold in common. And we must build many different bridges of communication, based on mutual respect. Above all the academy must be drawn into the political process, at the highest levels of long-term policy making, focusing not on expediency, but on reconciliation and a shared vision for the future.

In sum, these examples serve to illustrate applications of my childhood experiences in my professional life. I deeply despise the arrogant and categorical Nazi ideology that caused so much human suffering, and for that reason I am fundamentally opposed to contemporary ideologues who stereotype with a broad brush and believe that a righteous cause justifies any means. Instead I persist in trying to promote understanding of others and so to find common ground. I see my childhood experiences with ethnic prejudice as indispensable, even as a privilege that allows me to feel some of the anguish and anger of those who have truly been marginalized. That is what drives my efforts to link my research to a real but flawed world, in which there are many shades of gray and where pain is all too often inflicted carelessly. While I try to learn from the past, I am concerned about the future and hope that all our children may be able to grow up with dignity and equal opportunites.

NOTES

My brother, Paul, shared his recollections with me, just as he once instructed me about a larger world, and later inspired me with his willingness to speak up, as a mathematician and historian of science. My wife, Elisabeth, taught me much about anthropological practice as she led me to appreciate that people are fascinating in and of themselves. Our daughter Kieke provided helpful suggestions in regard to education. A number of students have stimulated me through their own insights or experiences: Pavel Kraus, Karl Offen, Natasha Barsotti, Adriana Olivares, and especially Christine Drennon. To all, my gratitude. This chapter was written for my children, and theirs, so that they will not forget why we didn't go with the flow. Perhaps it will also offer insight and understanding to the children of other émigrés of conscience. It is dedicated to the memory of my parents, who through their example pointed me to a good path.

1. J. O'Loughlin, C. Flint, and L. Anselin, "The Geography of the Nazi Vote: Context, Confession, and Class in the Reichstag Election of 1930," *Annals, Association of American Geographers* 84 (1994): 351–80.

2. H. Hürten, *Deutsche Katholiken 1918–1945* (Paderborn: F. Schöningh, 1992); P. Steinbach and J. Tuchel, eds. *Lexikon des Widerstandes 1933–1945* (Munich, 1994); U. von Hehl, C. Kösters, P. Stenz-Maur, and E. Zimmermann, *Priester unter Hitlers Terror: Eine biographische und Statistische Erhebung* (Paderborn: F. Schöningh, 1996). I am indebted to A. Brecher and D. Wynands (both from Aachen) and especially C. Kösters (Kommission für Zeitgeschichte, Bonn) for kindly supplying information in this matter.

3. K. Macrakis, *Surviving the Swastika: Scientific Research in Nazi Germany* (New York: Oxford University Press, 1993).

4. D. J. K. Peukert, *Inside Nazi Germany: Conformity, Opposition, and Racism in Everyday Life*, trans. R. Deveson (New Haven: Yale University Press, 1987).

5. E. Zeller, *The Flame of Freedom: The German Struggle against Hitler*, 368–81 and notes (Boulder, CO: Westview Press, 1994).

6. For a parallel but better documented example of this process, see E. Weber, *Peasants into Frenchmen: The Modernization of Rural France, 1870–1914* (Stanford: Stanford University Press, 1996).

7. Militant Nazism in part derived from recurrent, open violence between right- and left-wing toughs that began in 1918. This polarization played itself out in the industrialized areas. In the Ruhr Valley, for example, the Hitler Youth held Sunday parades, which sometimes spilled out into brawls, as early as 1930. But the Nazis also sponsored hypernationalist associations for various professional groups, which permeated less polarized towns to some degree or other, and exerted less visible but equally insidious pressures after 1933.

8. Although with the exception of the French Canadian boy, all the other children were at least partly Irish, in a Catholic, public, and English-language school (a Quebec anomaly), many of the children identified themselves as "English" or "Scottish," although that varied slightly over time.

9. My brother, Paul L. Butzer, returned to Germany permanently in 1955 and has long been active in applying the lessons from our family experience. Despite considerable opposition, as editor of the German Mathematical Society's journal, he insisted upon the publication of Maximilian Pinl's commemoration of the 188 German mathematicians who were forced into exile or died in concentration camps in 1933–45: M. Pinl, "Kollegen in einer dunklen Zeit," *Jarhresbericht der deutschen Mathematiker Vereinigung* 71 (1969): 167–228 and four additional parts. This comprehensive work was subsequently republished in English translation by the Leo Baeck Institute. More recently he saw to the inclusion of the twelve Jewish professors expelled from the Technical University of Aachen in a jubilee volume: "Vertriebene Professoren. In Rhenisch-Westfälische Technische Hochschule Aachen," in *Wissenschaft zwischen technischer und gesellschaftlicher Herausforderung 1970–1995* (Aachen: Einhard, 1995), 181–274. Paul L. Butzer assembled the article on Otto Blumenthal, from whom both of our parents took lectures.

10. K. Butzer, "Environment, Culture, and Human Evolution," *American Scientist* 65 (1977): 572–84.

11. K. Butzer, "The Realm of Cultural-Human Ecology: Adaptation and Change in Historical Perspective," in *The Earth as Transformed by Human Action*, edited by B. L. Turner II et al. (New York: Cambridge University Press, 1990), 685–701.

12. K. W. Butzer, E. K. Butzer, and J. F. Mateu, "Medieval Muslim Communities of the Sierra de Espadán, Kingdom of Valencia," *Viator* 17 (1986): 339–443.

13. K. W. Butzer, "Sociopolitical Discontinuity in the Near East c. 2200 B.C.E.: Scenarios from Palestine and Egypt," in *Third Millennium B.C. Climate Changes and Old World Collapse*, edited by H. N. Dalfes, G. Kukla, and H. Weiss, NATO ASI Series (Berlin: Springer, 1997), 245–96.

14. K. Butzer, "Judgment or Understanding? Reflections on 1492," *Queen's Quarterly* 99 (1992): 581–600.

15. Weber, *Peasants into Frenchmen*. On the suppression of North Italian vernaculars after Italian unification by a national school system propagating only Tuscan Italian, see G. Sobiela-Caanitz, "Ecole et langue locale," in *Languages in Contact and Conflict*, edited by P. H. Nelde (Wiesbaden: Franz Steiner, 1980), 173–80. Standard versus vernacular languages in historical context are examined by P. S. Ureland, "Sprachkontakt und Glottogenese in Europe," in *Entsteheng von Sprachen und Völkern*, edited by P. S. Ureland (Tübingen: Max Niemeyer, 1985), 7–43.

16. On "linguistic imperialism" by Denmark, see B. Sondergaard, "Vom Sprachenkampf zur sprachlichen Koexistenz im deutsch-dänischen Grenzraum," in *Languages in Contact and Conflict*, edited by P. H. Nelde (Wiesbaden: Franz Steiner, 1980), 297–306; similar Prussian legislation against non-German school instruction or "official" use in minority areas dates to 1872–88, notably coincident with the religious culture war: K. Pabst, "Das preussische Geschäftssprachengesetz von 1876: Sprachwechsel nationaler Minderheiten als Mittel politischer Integration," in *Languages in Contact and Conflict*, edited by P. H. Nelde (Wiesbaden: Franz Steiner, 1980), 191–200.

17. For example, C. J. Halperin, "The Ideology of Silence: Prejudice and Pragmatism on the Medieval Religious Frontier," *Comparative Studies of Society and History* 26 (1984): 442–66; A. C. Hess, *The Forgotten Frontier: A History of the Sixteenth-Century Ibero-African Frontier* (Chicago: University of Chicago Press, 1978), esp. chaps. 9–10; also S. F. Bloom, "The Peoples of my Home Town before Nationalism crushed Rumania's Design for Living," *Commentary* 3, no. 4 (1947): 329–35.

18. The travails of Slavo-Macedonian speakers in Greece illustrate the problem: A. Karakasidou, "Politicizing Culture: Negating Identity in Greek Macedonia," *Journal of Modern Greek Studies* 11 (1993): 1–28. Except of course for the police intervention, there are instructive analogues in regard to how social pressures affect Spanish-speaking Americans.

19. S. J. Tambiah, "Ethnic Conflict in the World Today," *American Ethnologist* 16 (1989): 335–49.

20. E. W. Said, *Orientalism* (New York: Pantheon Books, 1978).

21. S. P. Huntington, *The Clash of Civilizations and the Remaking of the World Order* (New York: Simon and Schuster, 1996).

22. The seeds of bigotry are remarkably pervasive. On May 6, 1997, national newspapers reported that the publisher Simon and Schuster recalled all copies of a children's book by reputedly serious historian W. J. Jacobs, entitled *Great Lives: World Religions,* agreeing that the book unfairly portrays the prophet Mohammed as a bloodthirsty hatemonger.

The Impact of a Childhood in Nazi Germany

Siegfried Streufert

Biographical Note

Siegfried Streufert received his B.A. and M.A. from Southern Methodist University and his Ph.D. in experimental (social) psychology from Princeton University. He has taught at Princeton, Rutgers, and Purdue Universities. He has also held appointments as chair professor of social psychology at the University of Bielefeld, visiting professor at the University of Mannheim, and resident scholar at the National Institutes of Health. Since 1979, he has been professor of behavioral sciences at Pennsylvania State University (College of Medicine). He is founding editor of the Journal of Applied Social Psychology, *among other editorial positions.*

    Dr. Streufert's research, which deals with decision making, managerial effectiveness, behavioral medicine (including the effects of drugs), and complexity theory, has been published in twelve books and over three hundred other publications in both English and German. He is the recipient of an award from the Advanced Research Projects Agency and a fellow of the American Psychological Association, American Psychological Society, Society of Behavioral Medicine, and other professional organizations and academies.

Introduction

The biological, psychological, and social sciences frequently find it difficult to agree. How much of what we do, what we think, how we live is due to nature, and how much is due to nurture? We may quibble over fine distinctions, yet all of us, whether biologists on one end of the spectrum or cultural anthropologists on the other, would give at least some credence to environment, to experience, to whatever happened to shape us at some point in the past. Maybe past events made only slight modifications in whatever nature had decreed. Maybe experience was the primary determiner of what we are today. Maybe nurture had a limited, yet quite powerful, impact. Whatever the views of the reader might be, let me trace the environment of my past, the dream that emerged, and the reality that did not quite realize the dream. How much of it is nature, and how much is nurture? The reader is free to decide.

Experiences

It happens again and again. People persecute people. Sometimes the persecution is subtle, the denial of privileges, the spreading of rumors. Sometimes it ends in genocide. Think of the killing fields of the Khmer Rouge, the murder of natives in the Amazon. Think of the recent ethnic cleansing in former Yugoslavia. And think of the at least eleven million people who were murdered by the Nazi regime. My father was one of those eleven plus millions.

While people are dying, life continues. Individuals go along. They may be afraid to object, or they may see no reason to object. Martin Niemöller, famous Protestant clergyman, tells of his response to the persecution. He said:

> When Hitler attacked the Jews I was not a Jew, therefore I was not concerned. And when Hitler attacked the Catholics, I was not a Catholic, and therefore, I was not concerned. And when Hitler attacked the unions and the industrialists, I was not a member of the unions and I was not concerned. Then Hitler attacked me and the Protestant church—and there was nobody left to be concerned.[1]

It seems strange, but we can learn to accept the unacceptable when it happens every day. We can learn to live with cancer. We can learn to live with bombs, as I did during World War II in Germany. We can learn to live with artillery shells raining down upon us, as we have recently seen in Sarajevo. Even death and destruction become something "normal" if they happen every day. What is worse, experiences, if they are repeated over and over again, tend to distort reality. Let me tell you about Elke, one of the stories from my book *Arch of Fire: A Child in Nazi Germany*. That story will tell you how strange our view of the world can become.

———⊷∘⊶———

There was more than one way to get from our house to my school. Sometimes I would walk along the main street, meeting some of my friends, finally following a small path downhill. For some unknown reason, that path was known to everyone as the "Coffee Bean Way." I liked chatting with classmates along Coffee Bean Way, but on other days, I wanted to be alone. I would take an old unpaved road, past fields and past rows of hedges that are common in that part of northern Germany. At first, the road would take me south, mostly downhill. But when I reached the house of the baker, the road turned sharply to the right, traversed a ravine, and, after a while, continued past the house where Elke lived. On summer mornings, even before eight o'clock, the time when I had to be in school, I often saw her playing in their front yard.

Elke must have been three or four years old. She seemed to enjoy it when I passed by; she would walk up to the fence and talk to me. Of course, Elke did not tell me anything fascinating; after all I was about five years older than she. But she was so nice, so full of life! I enjoyed stopping and talking to her, no matter what she had to say. I simply liked her! There were even days when I was disappointed that Elke was not playing in the front yard, that she was not waiting for me to pass by.

Then, one day, I was told that Elke had died. It had been evening when she had suddenly developed a very high fever. Our suburb was too small to have its own physician. Most of the medical personnel in nearby towns had been drafted for the military. It was difficult to obtain quick medical aid. Elke had not survived the night.

Now her front yard was empty. No nice, alive little girl! No smiling eyes! No eager talk!

If a bomb had hit Elke's house, I would have understood. Bombs were normal; they were everyday occurrences. Of course people died of bombs. Somehow I could have accepted her death. I would have been sad, of course. Yes, a bomb would have made sense! But a sudden fever?

———⊷∘⊶———

How can death in an air attack be more real, more reasonable, than illness and death? Strangely enough, it can. Day-to-day events, repeated over and over again, become very real. And daily propaganda, repeated over and over again, becomes credible to people who don't think on their own. Enough, though by no means all, people living in Germany at that time eventually believed Goebbels and his Nazi propaganda.

I would like to discuss a family that did think independently, a family that did not go along with the Nazi system, for that matter, a family that fought the system. I was the only child of that family, a child that survived the Nazi years. They were years—and I will only provide a few examples, again taken from the book *Arch of Fire*—that will show how those experiences influenced what I did, how I felt, and probably how I thought in my teen and adult years since.

My father had been a member of the *Reichstag*, the single-house legislature of the Weimar Republic. It was more of a senate than a house of representatives. It was also a failure in democracy. Too many parties made governing impossible and allowed Hitler—who gained only one-third of the votes—to overthrow the republic. My father fought the Nazis before they took over. They tried to kill him then, but through luck he survived. Once Hitler was in power, my parents and other family members were considered "enemies of the state." No German company was allowed to hire us. My father finally found a job with the Dutch Van-Houten chocolate manufacturer in the northernmost province of Germany. There I grew up. We lived in a carefully selected suburb, full of socialists and communists who, in more cases than not, had little appreciation for Adolf Hitler. It was a lovely suburb with trees and hills and lakes—and a Nazi flag above City Hall. One of my first very clear memories is of a day when, once again, the Nazis came to search through our house. . . .

It was Sunday, about twenty minutes before ten in the morning. One of the radio stations played classical music until eleven; I liked that music. A finch sang in the quince tree outside of my window. I imagined the bird appreciated my music and was just singing along. The window was wide open and fresh spring air was gently moving the lace window curtains back and forth.

Suddenly, there was a harsh pounding on the front door. The doorbell rang insistently at the same time. My mother opened the door. Three men pushed her out of the way and forced themselves into our hallway. Even though I was only wearing a nightshirt, I ran to see what was happening. As a five year old, one could still run around without being fully dressed—it did not matter.

I knew one of those three men: the local policeman. He seemed just a bit embarrassed. The second intruder also seemed a bit familiar. But I was not sure. Maybe all of those who wore brown Nazi shirts and black boots looked the same. But the third one—I knew I had never seen him before. He was wearing a suit, and he stared at me with angry, unpleasant eyes. "We are going to search the house!" he barked at nobody in specific.

My father had finished dressing and emerged from the bedroom. "Can I help you?" he said. "What are you doing here on a Sunday morning?"

"We are going to search your house!" the important one barked again. He reminded me of that angry hound that had torn off a piece of my playmate's ear. This man would do something like that!

He stared at my father and said in a sarcastic tone: "We are going to get you!" His hand moved horizontally across his neck as though he was cutting off his own head. A triumphant look crept over his face.

They started. Books were flying off our shelves. They found nothing except bare walls. Drawers were ripped out of my fathers desk. They found only supplies and some papers related to my father's work. Nothing of interest to them. Now they marched into my bedroom. The radio was still playing.

The man in the suit looked suspiciously. "That is a big radio" he said. "You can listen to foreign stations. You know that is forbidden. You must trade it for a 'People's Radio,' one that receives only German stations!"

Just then I remembered a few books on the shelf. The dust covers had been changed! The books inside were forbidden. It was funny, the Nazis had searched our house several times; they had just been through the bookshelves all over again, yet they never thought that the books might be different than their jackets. "They must be pretty stupid," I thought.

The one object that I knew could displease them was that sad picture in the hallway. It was a lithograph, an old painting that had recently become a protest picture against Hitler. Actually, I had never liked the picture: it was too sad. An old woman was sitting on a park bench, in Vienna I think, crying bitterly. Her husband had put his arm around her shoulders and was staring into the distance. He didn't look happy either. He did not try to comfort her. The whole scene was so unpleasant!

Just the previous week, I had asked my mother about the picture. "Why do we have to have such a sad picture?"

"Those are people who used to live in South Tirol. At the end of the world war, southern Tirol was given to the Italians. And now Hitler has finally given their home away forever, because he wants Mussolini to be his friend. Now the old woman and that old man are sitting in a park in Vienna. They don't have a home anymore. But, don't tell the story of that picture to anyone," my mother reminded me. "We are not supposed to have such a picture." I got the message. I had learned long ago that anything we would say at home was not to be repeated anywhere else.

The angry man in the suit had come into the kitchen and moved very close to my mother, nearly pushing her into the wall. His eyes were hard, yet mocking. "Where are you hiding everything?" he wanted to know.

"What are you looking for?"

Now he yelled, "You know perfectly well what we are looking for! Don't pretend innocence!"

"Nearly like Kafka," she mentioned under her breath as he turned away.

"Nearly like what?" he screamed. I guess he had never heard of Kafka. Actually, at my age, I had not heard of him either. The civilian's face had turned bright red. He looked intently at the walls in the room. His eyes stopped when he saw the sad picture through the open kitchen door. I was scared and started to tremble a little. I had a funny feeling in my stomach.

"What kind of picture is that?" he demanded.

"A lithograph."

"I know that!" He seemed in thought for a minute. "That is such nonsense," he continued with sharp anger in his voice. "We are living in Germany's finest hour. Our armies will conquer the world. Adolf Hitler has made all that possible. His picture should hang there, not such sad nonsense! If you had the sense to hang up a beautiful picture of Adolf Hitler, instead of that kind of garbage, we probably would not have to search your house! But that is something you will probably never learn!"

He turned, and the other two followed him. As he opened the front door on the way out, he looked back: "Next time we will surely get you! Then you've all had it! Heil Hitler!"

⇒◦⇐

Not much later, I entered first grade. My first teacher made an unfriendly comment about the Nazis and was drafted and "killed in combat" in Norway only a couple of days later. To say the least, his death in combat was unlikely. The next teacher was a true believer. A Nazi. Let me include short excerpts from two *Arch of Fire* recollections that deal with him:

⇒◦⇐

It was during a break between classes. We used a soccer ball, throwing and kicking it from kid to kid. Some of us yelled and screamed; it was all part of the game. Suddenly the teacher came storming out of the building: "Shut up," he yelled even louder than we had been screaming. "You are acting like little Jews! This is not a Jew School!"

That evening, I told my father. His face became very hard. His large steel blue eyes stared beyond me, seemingly far into the past. Finally he spoke, not in a loud voice but with anger: "That kind of thing is a great injustice. My best buddy in the last war was Jewish. He fought just as hard for Germany as I did. He was injured on the same day as I. He was and is a German. He loved Germany. It is unjust that our country no longer returns that love. A teacher who does not understand that is incompetent."

He was quiet and seemed to be deep in thought for a while. And then, he turned toward me and spoke more gently. "But you know that you can't repeat that in school."

One day, our teacher spent the morning talking to all four grades in our classroom. We should listen carefully, he insisted. He had something very important to tell us!

He began by glorifying Hitler and his "victories." He spent much time explaining how the Nazi government had "saved Germany from ruin." "But you know all about that," he continued. "I have told you about Hitler and his great deeds many times. You know about the fabulous future of our country under Hitler's leadership."

"But some of your parents have not had the opportunity to learn as much as you have. It is not their fault. They don't go to school any more. They can't hear what I am telling you!"

He looked at us intently: "You must help them. If your parents say that they don't like Adolf Hitler or the party, you should tell me right away! Tell me all the things your parents have said. That way we will know what to teach them. You see, I want to make sure that your parents will understand everything as well as all of you do!"

He let the message sink in. He looked around the classroom: "Is there any one of you who wants to tell me something right now?"

Not one child raised a hand. The teacher seemed disappointed. Again, he urged us to speak. Nobody did.

"Well, you don't have to talk about it now. Come to me after school is over. Remember, I want to help your parents. Make sure to tell me everything you have heard!"

It was hardly surprising that none of us volunteered our parents' views. Most children had no idea how adults in their world felt. Only kids whose parents had accepted the Nazi point of view had heard their parents speak about politics. Any adult who disagreed was very quiet about it. Children might inadvertently repeat something their parents said. It was much too dangerous to speak to anyone, unless one absolutely knew that this person was anti-Nazi. And, if one did know someone to whom one could speak freely, one had to do it far away from possible listeners—somewhere deep in a forest or quietly at night in one's bedroom.

Of course, I would not tell the teacher about my parents' attitudes. Any information that they did not support the Nazis would have amounted to a death sentence for them. I *knew* they would be taken away and killed. For me, it could also mean death or, more likely, full-time residence in a Nazi school.

Several times, the Nazis came to arrest my father. They would pound on the door, early in the morning. They would not let him out of their sight while he dressed. He would be taken to Gestapo headquarters, questioned, threatened, and finally released. But it would be different that day in 1944, shortly after an attempt on Hitler's life by the military and the intelligentsia had failed. The Nazi government was scared. Anyone who was part of the attempted coup was immediately killed. Anyone who might be involved was arrested, murdered, or placed in a concentration camp. I remember that day quite well. . . .

———————

August 1944. He pounded on the door. He kept ringing the bell. It was about five in the morning. We had been sleeping.

We all knew the meaning of the early morning hour and the serious demeanor of the policeman. Only a couple of weeks ago, there had been an attempt on Hitler's life. Military officers, politicians, and members of the intelligentsia had united to kill him. They failed. The Nazis were scared. It was not likely that they knew of my father's association with the underground movement. But even without such knowledge, his past as a senator of the Social Democratic Party and his early activities against the Nazis made him a suspect.

Once more I was scared. I hid in my parents' bedroom and did not want to leave. I heard the policeman's boots in the hallway. He was following my father. Step by step. There was no time for breakfast. "We have to be there before six-thirty," the uniformed man announced.

The policeman was kind enough to allow my parents to say a private good-bye in the bedroom. For a minute they were alone, except for me. We put our arms around each other.

My father looked at the open window. It would have been simple for him to jump and run. They never would have found him—he had enough connections in the underground.

He looked at the window. Then he looked at my mother. And at me. No, he would not risk his family. He knew the Nazis would avenge his disappearance; they would arrest and possibly torture or kill his wife and child. Once more he kissed my mother and returned to the waiting policeman. They left.

My mother was pale. She looked almost dead.

I was still afraid. "Should we hide?" I asked. She tried to calm my fears: "We must be here when Daddy comes back."

I waited. He was not back when I came home from school. I waited all evening. Finally, it was time to go to sleep. I promised myself to wake up if the doorbell rang. It never did.

He did not come back the following day. Or the next. My mother took the train downtown and inquired at the state offices of the Nazi Party. When she returned, she told me that she had to wait a long time before anyone would speak with her. They sent her to the headquarters of the secret police, the Gestapo. There they interrogated her. Finally, she was allowed to tell them why she had come: she wanted information about my father's fate. She was told that he had been placed into the concentration camp "Dragon Lake." Yes, she might get a visitor's pass. However, such a pass could be issued only if there were important nonpersonal reasons for a visit. For example, she could see him once if she and my father had to resolve financial matters. There would only be one visit. Never any more.

She obtained a pass for Thursday. "You must leave now," the official ordered after issuing the pass. "Heil Hitler."

There was nothing more my mother could have done. Security systems were everywhere. Armed men in Nazi uniform stood close by. If she had not left, she, too, would have disappeared. That she could not risk: there was still a child to raise. And she could hope that the war would end soon, that the Nazi regime might collapse. Considering the state of the war, it could not last much longer. Maybe not even a year. . . .

When Thursday came, I wanted to go to Dragon Lake. It seemed such an appropriate name! But I was not allowed to go. The visitor's pass was registered to my mother alone. I had to stay home. I waited and waited for her return. What would she have seen? What would she tell me? What was a concentration camp? I asked my friends in school. I asked my best friend's parents after school. Nobody knew of such a thing. "A concentration camp? Are you sure you got that name right? Maybe it is something new."

My mother returned in the late afternoon. She had been allowed to speak with my father for fifteen minutes. The conversation with him had had a major emo-

tional impact on her. The sights she had seen at the Dragon Lake camp seemed to have changed her. She told me of the guards with submachine guns. She spoke of the careful attention those guards paid to anything that was said, to any slight movement. It looked as though they were ready to aim and fire their guns immediately; they seemed so willing to kill anyone who might say or do something that would displease them. And she told me about the inmates she saw, scared and skinny, held back by electrified barbed wire.

As she left the camp, she was told that it was forbidden to mention the existence of this concentration camp to anyone. Providing information about anything she had seen would be considered "treason" and would be punished by death. "This installation is a secret operation by the SS for the protection of the country."

Upon leaving, she was supposed to turn in her visitor's pass. But the guard at the gate said, "Why don't you keep it? It is issued for Thursday. There is no date. Come back next week—you can see your husband again." My mother thanked him. What strange kindness in the middle of vicious horror. . . .

She repeated her trip to Dragon Lake the following week. But my father was no longer there. "Gone," said the administrator. "He was sent somewhere else. You have to leave now. Heil Hitler."

"But where was he sent?"

The answer was curt: "We cannot provide any information."

Yet, as my mother was leaving, one of the guards handed her a small torn piece of wrapping paper. "From your husband."

After leaving the camp she read:

My love,

I am sorry that we cannot see each other again. Try everything to attain my freedom. I cannot do anything from where I am or will be. I don't know where they are sending us. Please keep our love alive—and thank you for all the wonderful things you have done. Have courage, God will be with us. All my love and kisses to you and to our son.

My father had been taken to another concentration camp: Neuengamme near Hamburg. Months of frantic activity designed to persuade the authorities to free my father passed. Nothing. Nobody, even devout Nazis who tried, had any impact on the system. We got a short letter each month, with the censor's initials clearly visible. Yet my parents had long ago agreed on words that had secret meaning only to them. But then the letters stopped coming.

My father's last letter from Neuengamme arrived in mid-December. There was no letter in January. Packages we sent were returned. No reason was given. The same in February. One of the returned February packages was marked with a design that could have been a swastika, except that the lines at the ends of the cross were drawn through in both directions. My mother suspected the worst but wanted to hope. She asked several experts about the meaning of the design.

"It looks like a Kukenkreuz," she was told. Such a design was once used by an Austrian movement that had been quite similar to the Nazis.

She contacted the Nazi Party at the county and at the state levels. Nobody would speak with her. Letters addressed to the commander of the concentration camp were returned unopened. February and March passed. Still nothing. More packages kept coming back. Letters to my father were returned.

In April we received a package. The return address was "The Commander of the Concentration Camp Hamburg-Neuengamme." My mother opened it. She found my father's clothes, the suit and underwear he had worn on the day he had been arrested. And there was a letter.

> Concentration Camp
> Hamburg-Neuengamme
> The Commander
> Enclosed you will find the clothing of August Streufert who died on 27 December 1944 of pneumonia.
> Heil Hitler!

My mother collapsed. I did not know whether I should cry or try to comfort her. I did both. I touched her. Her heart was beating incredibly fast. I could feel it all over her body. It frightened me. I ran across the street to get our neighbors: I was sure that she would die. The neighbors sent me away. I walked across the meadows in back of our house. The grass was still there, and so were the trees. Spring flowers were in bloom. But all that meant nothing. The world seemed so empty. The sun was shining, but it was gray. It was spring, but it could as well have been winter. Would life go on? Was it worth continuing? Why? Why?

A few weeks later we received another package. It was an urn with ashes. Whose ashes? According to the attached brief note, the urn supposedly contained the remains of my father. But, after all this time, how could it be? I wondered how many bodies had contributed to the dust in that urn. But, whatever it might be, we had something that we could bury, something that represented my father, even if only in spirit. It was the dust of all those people who suffered with him.

Very few of our neighbors came to the burial. They were too afraid to come. The Jansens came. The farmer next door. My best friend's family. And a few others. Most of the neighbors, in contrast, secretly shook my mother's hand—some time, somewhere, in some dark corner. We had joined the world of outcasts. It was dangerous to be seen talking with us: now it was known that my father had been arrested and killed by the Nazi government. They did not know how or where he had died. Most did not know about concentration camps. We were not allowed to mention that term. But people in town did know that he had been killed as an "enemy of the Nazi state." That was enough.

Except for an entry in the death book of the concentration camp, there was no proof, no witness who could confirm that my father had died on December 27, 1944. There were some who said that he had lived beyond that day. Whatever the day or the cause of his death may have been, he would forever be lost to us—and to the democratic Germany that emerged afterward. The Nazis had won another temporary victory. They had destroyed the life of another person who dared to fight them—even though they had never found out that my father had been active in the underground. They did not know about the VanHouten van that picked up people who had been hidden by a dentist, my best friend's father *and* a registered member of the Nazi party. They did not know that the van transported those people during the early dark morning hours. They did not see that those people were taken to boats anchored in nearby fishing villages. They could not know that those boats would meet Swedish fishing boats somewhere on the Baltic Sea.

Nevertheless, the Nazis were sure that my father could be dangerous to them. Even the chance that he might have been part of the last attempted coup or that he might participate in another was enough: anyone opposing the regime was not to live. All who might be dangerous were arrested in *Aktion Gitter*, a roundup that placed thousands into concentration camps. Little did it matter that Nazi Germany needed workers, no matter how old or how weak. If victory would be possible, if defeat should be delayed, the government needed anyone who might be able to contribute something to the "war effort." In retrospect it seems an absurdity, a paradox: if those more than eleven million people had not been killed, the outcome of the war could have been different. Possibly the Nazis defeated themselves!

Impact

Fortunately, the Nazis lost their war. They lost their hold on the people of Europe. Once the occupation troops had taken power, the process of "de-Nazification" classified party members as *Mitläufer,* those that had gone along without committing crimes, and those that had been guilty of transgressions. Many who should have been grouped among the guilty were let off easy. Even the local party leader who was in some part guilty of my father's death in the concentration camp was listed as a *Mitläufer.* As a result, he could run in the first democratic election after the war. When he tried to become mayor of our city, people wrote "Nazi" and drew swastikas on his posters. He lost badly.

For years yet we would be hungry. Our city was more than 95 percent rubble. The stores remained empty. Black markets flourished. But we were safe: Allied soldiers patrolled the streets. No more Nazi uniforms. No more dead people lying in the streets. No more early morning arrests. Very slowly life began to return to normal. But what was normal? I had never known "normality" before. What would it be like? What *should* it be like? Would it last? How could one be sure that the horror of fascism, the fear and destruction of war would not return? What was it about people that led them to hate, to destroy? What could anyone do, what could I do to create a better, a safer world, a world where love would win over hatred, where happiness would prevail over misery? I asked that question many times.

In 1951 I was selected to become an exchange student in the United States. It was a different world. Hunger did not exist in the United States. I had my first milkshake, my first hamburger. I met people to whom democracy and safety from persecution were normal. How could it be that this other world, this United States, was so different? Were the people different? Was it chance? Had it been the Versailles Treaty that created the opportunity for Naziism? Why would Germany, a country that produced a "Frederick the Great," bring someone like Hitler to power? (Frederick's minister of the interior once said to the king, "Your Majesty, it has come to our attention that there are people in Your country that do not practice Your religion! What do You want us to do with these people?" During that time period, European monarchs were not tolerating freedom of religion. But Frederick the Great responded, "In my country everyone becomes a saint in his own fashion!")

After my exchange year in the United States I once more lived in Germany. Five years later, however, I returned to the United States to attend college. What profession should I seek? It had to be something that would allow me to make a contribution to people's lives! The final choice was between medicine and psychology. I was accepted in both graduate school and medical school. The decision was influenced by three phone calls on one single day. Three times Princeton University called and asked whether I had decided. The calls made the difference. I went to Princeton and obtained a doctorate in psychology.

Graduate school was a transition period. For the first time I had choices. I could focus my own research questions. My dissertation research returned to concerns I had expressed over the years: how could the Nazis inflict such horror on other people, even though they, as individuals, seemed to love and care for their own families? Was it normal to make such strong distinctions among one's own and others? Why, for example, did that Nazi teacher hold such derogatory views about Jewish people? How did prejudices (Allport 1954) develop? Were some minds truly "closed" (Rokeach 1960)? I turned to research on attitudes (Heider 1958; Kelman 1959) and social distance (Bogardus 1925). Would the degree to which people held similar or different views impact on how those people felt about others? Would the level at which people interacted, their familiarity with each other, color their resulting likes and dislikes? Would their capacity to view others on just one (evaluative) versus on more than one dimension determine whether they would accept or reject dissimilar views?

My subjects were college students and high school students in Texas, New Jersey, and Missouri. The data confirmed my fears. Prejudices emerged easily: especially students who primarily used an evaluative dimension rejected anyone with a different point of view. That rejection was even stronger if they might have to interact closely with someone who was "different" (Streufert 1965, 1966). At least on paper, at least in my research studies, U.S. students seemed to display the same prejudiced views that I had observed in Nazi Germany. The strength of their rejections reminded me of that Nazi civilian who had searched our house. He viewed us as dissimilar. He knew we did not believe the "greatness" of Hitler. If we had had a picture of Hitler hanging in the house, he pointed out, they would not have needed to search our home in the future. If we had not had dissimilar views, they would not have rejected us!

What was it about people that generated prejudice against anyone who might be dissimilar? What was different about people who did *not* succumb to negative prejudicial attitudes? When I arrived in Princeton, Harry Schroder, my major professor, had asked me to read the draft manuscript of a book he had written with two colleagues (Harvey, Hunt, and Schroder 1961). It spoke about four kinds (systems) of people who had developed into (or had been "arrested" at) four different stages of development and, consequently, would process information differently. It seemed that those described as "System I" were the "bad guys," biased, prejudiced, simpleminded (even if intelligent). "System II" people were rebels; "System III" individuals were described as interpersonally oriented and nice. Finally, "System IV" individuals had developed to function optimally and multidimensionally (Bieri 1957): they were the "good guys."

I had frequent and lengthy discussions with Mike Driver, another graduate student. Our debates were influenced by our early data (e.g., Driver 1962) as well as those of Peter Suedfeld (1964). We concluded that the "systems approach" was not viable, that it was "tainted" by a kind of prejudice. We proposed a new theory to Harry Schroder that found its way into Schroder, Driver, and Streufert (1967). It argued for an interplay between environmental stressors (similar to those that existed in Germany before the Nazis came to power) and for an effect of cognitive complexity. More complex people would not simply reject those who thought differently. They would be more empathic.

Yet high stress would lead to some decrements in functioning for anyone. In contrast, comfortable, that is, optimal (intermediate) environments should generate the most effective functioning of which any one individual might be capable. This "interactive complexity theory" could explain why fascism would emerge. It could explain how that destructive ideology could take hold of people who were under severe stress: those who were unemployed and hungry, those with little hope. The many data collected over the years (e.g., Streufert 1970) supported such a view: even people who were able to think in a more complex fashion would show serious decrements in cognitive functioning as stress became excessive.

Indeed, stress can have its impact. Yet the Nazis' obvious initial success in alleviating hunger, in rebuilding industry, in putting people back to work should have reduced the stress. Why did the German population fail to rebel once the stressful period had ended? Was it merely the favorable comparison of the misery during the late 1920s with the more comfortable life in the late 1930s that had generated an unwillingness to object? Was it the "obedience" that was demonstrated by Milgram's (1963) experiment with U.S. students? Was it fear of discovery, the knowledge that anyone might be a government spy, something that the Nazi teacher was recruiting us to be? Of course, any overt objection to the Nazi government would have been extremely risky. Those who objected, even gently, tended to pay for their "disloyalty," their different views, with their lives. My first teacher had been a good example.

What kind of people would nonetheless engage in such risks, would put their own lives and the lives of their families into danger? Our research suggested that risk taking was associated with overload stress and physiological arousal. In other words, it did not emerge when things seemed comfortable and normal (Streufert, Streufert, and Denson 1983). In addition, risk taking is subject to considerable individual differences but, on a possibly encouraging note, may respond to training programs (Streufert 1986).

However, part of the motivation to take risks, in this case the risk of fighting the Nazis—as my father had done until he was arrested and killed by the regime—depends on one's feeling of responsibility. My father took risks for himself, yet he decided against escape during his final arrest, even though he could have continued in the underground. He would not take the risk of sacrificing his family. To what degree, then, will a concern with responsibility lead to risks? We investigated attributions (Weiner and Kukla 1970) and found that people are more likely to take credit for "good" (success) events but refuse to accept responsibility for "bad" (failure) events (Streufert and Streufert 1969). This is an easy way out! If the situation is not to one's liking, one is not responsible! Such a view would allow people to close their eyes to events that are not acceptable to them.

Moreover, people tend to switch back and forth between seeing themselves as "causal" versus "responsible" (Nogami and Streufert 1983). If one can be causal without being responsible, then one is free to engage in destructive behavior, yet one need not feel responsible and/or guilty for that behavior! When they were tried after the war, many Nazis claimed that they were not responsible for their atrocities: the orders had come from above. Causal they were, yes—but not responsible!

If people are capable of abhorrent behavior without feeling responsible, then it is not surprising that the Nazis killed at least eleven and a half million people. Yet there still is a paradox: they needed the efforts of all these individuals to support their war effort, their attempts to win World War II. Of course, we are relieved that the Nazis did not become the rulers of the world. Yet, we can ask ourselves, why would Hitler and his fascists be so self-destructive? True, Hitler believed that Jews, Gypsies, and many other groups were *Untermenschen,* that is, less than human. He felt they did not deserve to live. Yet, was it not entirely unstrategic to kill them, for example, to initiate the "Final Solution" for Jews, just as his war machine needed them most? Indeed it was!

Complexity theory (Streufert and Streufert 1978; Streufert and Swezey 1986; Streufert 1997b) may provide an explanation for that unstrategic behavior of the Nazi leadership. Strategy involves the ability to integrate information, to process problems broadly, to plan sequentially and to carry plans toward future goals. Strategic thought is aided by optimal task settings that are relatively devoid of stress. Especially after the loss at Stalingrad, Hitler had to be afraid of losing the war (and his own life). Stress was at hand. That stress may have defeated any strategic capacity that could have been there. But how much ability to be strategic did Hitler and his cohorts possess in the first place? The Nazi leadership, while in some cases rather intelligent (Göring, Goebbels, Speer) was, with some exceptions, not very cognitively complex. It suffered from the same lack of dimensionality that my early research had discovered in an analysis of social distance and attitudes. Consequently, strategic thinking was not one of their strong points, not even in the best of times. Killing all those that were not part of the "master race" became an obsession for the Nazis. In Hitler's mind, the obsession with death became paramount. At one point he said that all Germans should die if Germany should lose the war. If Germany could not win, Germans would not be the "master race" after all! They, too, would not deserve to live!

The many interrelated findings of my research over a period of some thirty-five years do not justify Nazi behavior, but, to some extent, they may help to explain certain events and the sources of some people's actions. Unfortunately, our data suggest that the behaviors of people in Nazi Germany are not unique. U.S. research subjects—students, managers, and adults of various professions—seem to display the same dangerous characteristics. Since the Third Reich we have seen humankind's inhumanity to other human beings in many other places, for example, in Cambodia in the East and Yugoslavia in the Western world. Will it ever end? What can we do to diminish persecution? To some extent we can change attitudes. To some extent we can train people in responsibility. Sometimes we can prevent stressful situations that decrease the capacity to function multidimensionally. Most of all, however, we may be able to train individuals and groups toward broader thinking, toward more use of strategy and with it toward greater tolerance. Much of my present research focuses on those efforts (e.g., Streufert 1993).

Afterthoughts

Were my varied approaches to behavioral science influenced by early experiences in Nazi Germany? On the surface it certainly seems that they were. In retrospect, the connection seems obvious. Did I think about Nazi Germany when I designed my research? In many cases I did not. I tried to keep the horrors of that time—the Nazi teachers, my father's death, the bombs, the rubble, and the dead people lying in the streets—out of my mind. It was too painful to remember. But, I believe, the underlying desire to understand and the desire to contribute to a better future remained. When I asked questions about people's aberrant actions or thoughts I did not always say, "Why did the Nazis do this or that?" I observed the same kind of behavior, typically at a lesser degree of intensity and horror, in other settings in the United States: the prejudice against minorities among them. Still, I asked the same question, "Why?" I obtained the same answers.

It took a request of the mayor of the town in Germany where I had grown up to make me once again focus on the Nazi period. The mayor was writing a book about my father (Ohl 1994). He needed letters, documents, remembrances. It was my effort to go through all that material nearly fifty years later that brought all of it back. It was that effort that persuaded me to write the books *Arch of Fire* (1995) and *Drachenwind* (1997). It was that effort, as unpleasant as it was, that tied everything together. But I shall not insist that my work as a scientist was determined by experiences in Nazi Germany. To me, it appears that it was. Let the reader be the judge.

NOTES

Excerpts from the book *Arch of Fire* by the author of this chapter are reprinted with permission from Aina Kai Books, 4615 Custer Drive, Harrisburg, Pennsylvania 17110.
    1. Qtd. in *Congressional Record,* October 14, 1968, 31636. <http://www.magnet.ch/serendipity/cda/niemoll.html> (September 13, 2000).

REFERENCES

Allport, G. W. 1954. *The nature of prejudice.* Cambridge, MA: Addison-Wesley.
Bieri, J. 1957. Cognitive complexity-simplicity and predictive behavior. *Journal of Abnormal and Social Psychology* 51:263–68.

Bogardus, E. S. 1925. Measuring social distance. *Journal of Applied Sociology* 9:299–308.

Driver, M. J. 1962. *Conceptual structure and group processes in an internation simulation: The perception of simulated nations.* Office of Naval Research Technical Report 9, NR 177-055, Princeton, NJ.

Harvey, O. J., D. E. Hunt, and H. M. Schroder. 1961. *Conceptual systems and personality organization.* New York: Wiley.

Heider, F. 1958. *The psychology of interpersonal relations.* New York: Wiley.

Kelman, H. C. 1959. Compliance, identification, and internalization: Three processes of attitude change. *Journal of Conflict Resolution* 11:51–60.

Milgram, S. 1963. Behavioral study of obedience. *Journal of Abnormal and Social Psychology* 67:371–78.

Nogami, G. Y., and S. Streufert. 1983. The dimensionality of attributions of causality and responsibility for an accident. *European Journal of Social Psychology* 13:433–36.

Ohl, H. 1994. *Aktion Gitter: Der Reichstagsabgeordnete August Streufert-ein deutsches Schicksal.* Raisdorf, Germany: Ostsee Verlag.

Rokeach, M. 1960. *The open and closed mind.* New York: Basic Books.

Schroder, H. M., M. J. Driver, and S. Streufert. 1967. *Human information processing.* New York: Holt, Rinehart and Winston.

Streufert, S. 1965. Communicator importance and interpersonal attitudes toward conforming and deviant group members. *Journal of Personality and Social Psychology* 2:242–46.

———. 1966. Conceptual structure, communicator importance, and interpersonal attitudes toward conforming and deviant group members. *Journal of Personality and Social Psychology* 4:100–103.

———. 1970. Complexity and complex decision making: Convergences between differentiation and integration approaches to task performance. *Journal of Experimental Social Psychology* 6:494–509.

———. 1986. Individual differences in risk taking. *Journal of Applied Social Psychology* 16:482–97.

———. 1993. Assessment/training of senior personnel with the strategic management simulations. In *Thirty-fifth conference of the International Military Testing Association,* 429–33.

———. 1995. *Arch of fire: A child in Nazi Germany.* Harrisburg, PA: Aina Kai Books.

———. 1997a. *Drachenwind.* Harrisburg, PA, and Raisdorf, Germany: Aina Kai Books and Ostsee Verlag.

———. 1997b. Complexity: An integration of theories. *Journal of Applied Social Psychology* 27: 2068–95.

Streufert, S., and S. C. Streufert. 1969. Effects of conceptual structure, failure, and success on attribution of causality and interpersonal attitudes. *Journal of Personality and Social Psychology* 11:138–47.

———. 1978. *Behavior in the complex environment.* New York: Wiley.

Streufert, S., S. C. Streufert, and A. L. Denson. 1983. Information load stress, risk taking, and physiological responsibility in a visual–motor task. *Journal of Applied Social Psychology* 13:145–63.

Streufert, S., and R. Swezey. 1986. *Complexity, managers, and organizations.* London and Orlando: Academic Press.

Suedfeld, P. 1964. Attitude manipulation in restricted environments: Conceptual structure and response to propaganda. *Journal of Abnormal and Social Psychology* 68:242–47.

Weiner, B., and A. Kukla. 1970. An attributional analysis of achievement motivation. *Journal of Personality and Social Psychology* 15:1–20.

Part 4

Reflections

Loss and Renewal

Paul Marcus

Biographical Note

*Paul Marcus, Ph.D., a practicing psycho-
analyst, is a member of the National Psychological Association for Psychoanalysis
and the founder of its Center for the Psychoanalytic Study of Social Trauma. He is the
author of* Autonomy in the Extreme Situation: Bruno Bettelheim, the Nazi
Concentration Camps, and the Mass
Society *and coeditor of* Psychoanalytic
Reflections on the Holocaust: Selected
Essays *and* Healing Their Wounds: Psychotherapy with Holocaust Survivors
and Their Families, *among other books.*

All of the chapters contained in this extraordinary volume are painful
reading for they describe the horror of life immediately before, during,
and after the Shoah. Whether the subject is a hidden child, a refugee, or
a member of a non-Jewish family that opposed the Nazis, all of these
poignant stories to some extent reflect the traumatic impact of having
one's childhood world radically assaulted. Themes of separation, loss,
and incomplete mourning are especially evident in these narratives.

Yet, all of these stories also reflect the authors' tremendous strength, their courage, and the capacity for renewal—to love, to work, and to live reasonably satisfying lives. These testimonials further support recent research, such as Helmreich's (1992) pathbreaking study of Holocaust survivors who came to the United States to live after the war. As a group survivors were more able to achieve a substantial degree of psychic integration after their ordeal as reflected in their capacity to generate more "successful" lives, based on a number of sociological measures, than a comparable control group of U.S. Jews. Indeed, without minimizing the current discomfort and lack of integration that some of the authors insinuate they feel in terms of their Holocaust past, one is struck by the degree to which they have not allowed their heartrending losses of family members, stable childhood and parental care, countries and native tongues to foreclose their ability to live loving, productive, and creative lives. To quote the last line of Helmreich's book: "It is not a story of remarkable people. It is a story of just how remarkable people can be" (276).

It is to the last point that this volume makes a significant contribution, namely, it addresses the issue of "how early trauma and adult career meshed with each other" (preface). That is, this book attempts to shed some light on how the authors' wartime experiences influenced their choice of career and, in particular, their research and scholarly work in the social and behavioral sciences. Because scholars who have largely focused on Holocaust studies and clinical work with survivors are excluded, the connections between wartime experience and scholarly research are more subtle, though by no means obscure.

Rather than discuss each of the contributions to this volume, a task that I could not do justice to in this epilogue, I will comment on what I think are two of the key questions that for me link all of the chapters.

(1) Why did the contributors choose scholarly research and writing as their career path?

(2) What is the relationship between personal loss of one's home world—of one's stable and secure childhood, parents and parental care, country and native tongue—and the choice of particular research themes in the social and behavioral sciences?

Obviously, to adequately answer these questions on an individual level would require much more personal information than the contributors have provided. That is, each contributor's choice of career path and particular research interest, like anyone else's life, has been an idiosyncratic trajectory and is psychodynamically multidetermined. Therefore, since I do not know the "inside story" of each contributor, I will offer some provisional, general answers to the questions raised previously that I hope will, to some extent, illuminate each contributor's particular life story. However, before doing so, I want to briefly contextualize my comments in a framework for conceptualizing trauma.

Having a World, Losing a World, Replacing a World

In my view, an illuminating way of understanding the contributors' lives in terms of their choice of scholarly careers is to contextualize their lives in terms of "having a world, losing a world and replacing a world" (Marcus 1999, 73–74). That is, nearly all of the contributors during the Shoah were either children in hiding and/or refugees who had, prior to their ordeal, what Erving Goffman has called "a 'home world'— a way of life and a round of activities taken for granted" (Goffman 1961, 12). This "home world" gave a sense of safety, security, and direction to their lives. It was this routinized world, of parents and stable parental care, of friends and community, and of country and language that gave them a secure sense of having a rich and satisfying personal and social existence.

As Anthony Giddens has pointed out, to fashion a world that one feels safe and secure in requires a high degree of comfortable routinization. These routines are "vital to the psychological mechanisms whereby a sense of trust and ontological security is sustained in the daily activities of social life" and are "integral to the continuity of the personality of the agent, as he or she moves along the paths of daily activities" (Giddens 1984, 376). Routines, in other words, foster a sense that the world can be controlled and understood and, most important, that effective decisions and interventions can be made. Moreover, there is usually a deep, generalized affective involvement in the routines of daily life that ties the adult and child to routines. That is, routine allows the person to move relatively smoothly and comfortably in the world without being overwhelmed by disorganizing and stressful affects. Routinization also minimizes the unconscious sources of anxiety, and it strengthens a person's "confidence or trust that the natural and social worlds are as they appear to be, including the basic existential parameters of self and social identity" (Giddens 1984, 376). This confidence and this trust are rooted in a person's capacity to predict events and to control both him- or herself and immediate circumstances. This sense of one's presence in the world as real, alive, whole, and continuous emanates from one's home world in that it is developed early in life by parents who establish predictable and caring routines that generate adequate anxiety-controlling mechanisms in the child.

It is precisely this "home world" that many of the contributors, especially the hidden children, either lost or had severely assaulted during their Holocaust ordeal. In other words, their pre-Holocaust routines that underpinned their ontological security, self-concept, self-esteem, and self-continuity were significantly compromised. In many instances, this made the individual feel as if he or she were trapped in a maze of grotesque happenings. Such an experience of "losing one's world" had a shattering impact on the individual for which he or she was totally unprepared.

In a certain sense, the trajectories of the contributors' lives can be understood as an attempt to generate a "replacement world" in light of their losing their home worlds. That is, when a child's world—including the sense of continuity, self-control, efficacy, and perhaps sanity—was drastically threatened as it was with many of the contributors, he or she felt compelled to acquire or develop a new round of routines that helped to some extent to regularize life and provide a sense of self-efficacy, control, and self-esteem. The contributors' lives after the war in part were a response to their need to diminish anxiety and foster a sense of security. Fashioning themselves as scholars in the social and behavioral sciences may thus be viewed as part of their attempt to regularize their Holocaust-generated disordered and terrifying world. Their career choice was part of the process of creating a meaningful and effective replacement world. As I will suggest, writing was, and is, central to this process.

Writing as a Spiritual Exercise

All of the contributors to this volume have chosen scholarly research in the social and behavioral sciences as their career paths. None of them decided, for example, to be dentists, doctors, lawyers, social workers, accountants, or businesspeople. In my view, one way to perhaps shed some light on why this occurred is to reflect on the general psychological function and personal meaning of writing in a person's life. For regardless of what a contributor researched, his or her aim was to write about it, to publish it usually in either a professional journal or in book form. Why, then, do people write? To answer this question, it is, I think, most helpful to briefly go back to Greek and Hellenistic times.

As Michel Foucault (1984) and Pierre Hadot (1998) have pointed out, in Greek and Hellenistic times, intellectual and personal transformation was achieved in part through writing. Writing was used as a practice of self-regulation such as in Marcus Aurelius's magisterial *Meditations*. Hadot points out, for example, that "the goal [e.g., in writing the *Meditations*] is to reactualize, rekindle, and ceaselessly reawaken an inner state which is in constant danger of being numbed or extinguished. The task—ever renewed—is to bring back to order an inner discourse which becomes dispersed and diluted in the futility of routine"[1] [or in the horror of wartime trauma?] (Hadot 1998, 51).

That purpose of writing for the ancient Greeks and Hellenists was the internal transformation of one's way of seeing and the reestablishment of oneself as an integral and integrated part of the cosmos (Hadot 1995, 283). Writing can thus be described as a "spiritual exercise." It is a technique for self-transformation, a way of constituting oneself as a personality and fashioning one's subjectivity. It is important that, according to Foucault, this includes writing as a form of resistance to normative modes of subjectification. For example, many survivors viewed themselves as pathological, based on the normative judgments of the psychiatric "experts" (Marcus 1988). Writing thus gives one the means to resist the definitions of and limits to our being imposed on us by powerful others and to choose and create who we want to be according to our own views and wishes.

I think the preceding conceptualization of writing as a spiritual exercise, as a technique of self-transformation, is a helpful way of understanding possibly why the contributors chose to be scholars and researchers involved in publishing. Regardless of the particular research subjects, including the seeming unrelatedness of their chosen research topics to their Holocaust past, I believe that the general function of their research and writing, as with the ancient Greeks and Hellenists, was self-transfiguration on the way to self-mastery (especially of their traumatic past), self-realization, and personal improvement. Put somewhat differently, it was part of creating a replacement world. In a certain sense, one can view the contributors' lifetimes of writing and scholarship as a form of camouflaged confessional writing that has probably given them a degree of therapeutic benefit as well as helping others who read their writings. It is to this subject that I now turn.

Loss and the Therapeutic Value of Writing

I have suggested that writing is, in part, a spiritual means to sustain one's psychic equilibrium and to create a replacement world after traumatic assault on one's personal world as was the case with the contributors to this volume. As D. H. Lawrence wrote after finishing *Sons and Lovers,* "one sheds one's sicknesses in books, repeats and presents again one's emotions to be master of them." And Franz Kafka wrote, "a book is an axe to crack the frozen sea within us." These perceptive comments suggest to what extent the act of writing and the author's personal struggles are connected. In the case of the contributors to this volume, the personal struggles they have been attempting to "work through" over a lifetime of scholarship have, I think, been related to the anguish and heaviness of their past, specifically to themes of early loss and bereavement.

Loss, especially loss of parental care, has been shown to be an extremely important early influence on the creative writing and lives of a number of well-known thinkers. For example, as Maurice Friedman (1981) has pointed out, Buber's insight into the nature of meeting and dialogue is entwined with the childhood traumas that they are based on. When Buber was age three, his mother "disappeared without leaving a trace" (4). He saw her only once afterward, many years later, says Friedman. It was "the decisive experience of Martin Buber's life, the one without which neither his early seeking for unity nor his later focus on dialogue and on the meeting with the 'eternal Thou' is understandable" (15). Buber was raised by his grandparents, and clearly his parents' breakup severely traumatized him and influenced the direction not only of his scholarly and creative writing but of his whole life (Aberbach 1989, 122).

As Aberbach has claimed, many of the greatest philosophers, such as Spinoza, Pascal, and Sartre, suffered loss in childhood, and the development of their thinking and writing was affected by their losses. The same could probably be said of many of the great thinkers in the social and behavioral sciences who have decisively influenced their disciplines. As with these philosophers and social scientists, the contributors to the present volume probably use writing and scholarship as a way to master the pain of their past associated with their Holocaust losses of significant others, loss of childhood stability and parental care, and loss of country and language. John Bowlby, who wrote the foreword to Aberbach's interesting book, *Surviving Trauma: Loss, Literature, and Psychoanalysis,* aptly summarizes the many ways that creative writing can help the author master his or her past.

Creative writing . . . can attempt many things—to express feelings that are almost inexpressible, to understand what is almost unintelligible, to accept what is at the limit of the bearable, or to restore in symbolic form what cannot be restored in another way. Even in its expression of despair creative writing expresses a search for a way forward. (vii)

I believe that for the contributors to this volume, their lifetimes of writing and researching served one or more of the preceding purposes. Indeed, judging from the titles of some of the articles and books they have written, one gets the impression this is true: *Meaning and Void: Inner Experience and the Incentives in People's Lives;* "Born Unwanted: Long Term Developmental Effects of Denied Abortion"; "The Effect of Hope on Coping with Stress"; *Between Peace and War: The Nature of International Crisis;* and "Violence without Moral Restraint: Reflections on the Dehumanization of Victims and Victimizers." The evocative list of titles could be considerably extended; thus, it would seem that the authors were trying, to some extent, to master aspects of their horrendous Holocaust-related experiences through their writing. As Sartre said, "All books are attempts to improve one's biography."

Loss, Self-Transformation, and the Other

As I have already said, most of the authors in this volume were subjected to severe childhood loss and trauma. Frequently, from my professional experience as a psychoanalyst, I have noted that people who have been so traumatized have a numbing of their imagination and affectivity that impairs their ability to be creative and to live reasonably satisfying lives. This has not been the case with the contributors to this volume, and it supports the claim that loss can simultaneously be a force and a subject of creativity (Aberbach 1989).

However, what I find even more exceptional is the fact that as far as I can tell, the moral lives of the contributors, their attitudes toward others, have been transformed toward a Levinasian ethic of "responsibility to the Other." That is, one of the recurrent themes of most of the chapters is the author's commitment to helping others, to preventing similar crimes against humanity, and to engaging in a variety of forms of social activism meant to improve the world. I believe that the authors' writing and lecturing are not only a partly narcissistically driven phenomenon as those activities are with all authors. Rather, as survivors in the most general sense, they view themselves as bearing witness in their work to the horror of the Holocaust. All of the authors strike me as deeply committed to observing, to remembering, and to transmitting to others what they have seen and experienced. To do so, as Tzevetan Todorov has pointed out, is to take a stand against inhumanity (Todorov 1996, 98, 99). In other words, for most of the authors to know and to let others know is a way of contributing to the world's perfection, to the betterment of humanity.

I believe that it has in part been through their writing, scholarship, and social activism that the contributors have fulfilled what Hadot said was the main goal of writing in Greek and Hellenistic times: "to restore [oneself] as an integral and integrated part of the cosmos." That is, to become a more fully developed human being involves a kind of cosmic consciousness: striving to give one's life a positive and enduring meaning beyond one's mere transient existence through a strong commitment to the betterment of the human community in accordance with justice (Hadot 1995, 270, 274). In this sense, despite, or more accurately and compellingly, because of their painful experiences the contributors to this important volume have all managed to teach us something hugely important about the art of living in the face of, and after, terrible childhood suffering.

NOTE

1. Routines can potentially be both enabling (as Giddens emphasizes) and deadening (as Hadot emphasizes). Obviously, routines can impact on a person in both ways depending on a number of contextual and other variables.

REFERENCES

Aberbach, D. 1989. *Surviving trauma: Loss, literature, and psychoanalysis.* New Haven: Yale University Press.
Foucault, M. 1984. On the genealogy of ethics: An overview of work in progress. In *The Foucault reader,* edited by Paul Rabinow. New York: Pantheon.
Friedman, M. 1981. *Martin Buber's life and work.* Vol. 1. New York: E. P. Dutton. Quoted in D. Aberbach, *Surviving trauma: Loss, literature, and psychoanalysis* (New Haven: Yale University Press, 1989), 122–23.
Giddens, A. 1984. *The constitution of society.* Berkeley: University of California Press.
Goffman, E. 1961. *Asylums.* Garden City, NY: Anchor Books.

Hadot, P. 1995. *Philosophy as a way of life.* Oxford: Blackwell Publishers.
———. 1998. *The inner citadel. The Meditations of Marcus Aurelius.* Cambridge: Harvard University Press.
Helmreich, W. B. 1992. *Against all odds: Holocaust survivors and the successful lives they made in America.* New York: Simon and Schuster.
Marcus, P. 1999. *Autonomy in the extreme situation: Bruno Bettelheim, the Nazi concentration camps, and the mass society.* Westport: Praeger.
Marcus, P., and A. Rosenberg. 1988. *Healing their wounds: Psychotherapy with Holocaust survivors and their families.* Westport: Praeger.
Todorov, T. 1996. *Facing the extreme: Moral life in the concentration camps.* New York: Henry Holt.

Afterthoughts

Peter Suedfeld

This collection of essays was finished approximately four years after it was conceived. It was only recently that I fully realized some of the special things about it and some of the things I learned (or relearned, or was confirmed or disconfirmed in believing) while editing it.

Reflections on the Contributions

For most of us writing these essays was a highly unusual, if not unique, exercise. All of the contributors to the book are highly prolific in research and publication (a point I shall return to later). Our many articles, chapters, and books reflect our training as social scientists: our writing is usually objective, dispassionate, and distanced. We are careful to separate our personality from our work. But the autobiographical chapters to be prepared for this volume explicitly required the opposite: bringing our personal self into written conjunction with our professional self. Although a few of the authors had previously written autobiographies—formal or informal; for publication or not; and varying in openness, detail, and length—for most this requirement was a first.

The contributors met the challenge in different ways. Some made their chapter as much like a scientific paper as possible. They delved into their memory for facts and developed a theoretical framework to connect those facts (in particular, the early personal facts and the later professional ones). The result is a primarily intellectual autobiography. Others opened sealed doors, sometimes to their own serious discomfort, and let "hot" cognition—thought permeated by emotion—take them to an unknown destination. The result is high diversity in how revealing the chapters are. I don't find this objectionable, nor do I believe that either approach is in any way "better" than the other; the differences reflect strong and real differences in how my colleagues and fellow child survivors face their past, present, and future. As far as I am concerned, whatever works for the individual is good, and I am pleased that the book shows this lack of consensus.

It would be interesting to examine how writing the chapters influenced the feelings and thoughts of the authors. I know that some of us found the exercise very stressful. It brought into focus many painful memories, not only from the Nazi years but also regarding the difficulties of readjustment after the war, which were sometimes more severe than the physical survival issues of the years just before liberation, and the disappointments and tragedies that mark all people who reach the age of sixty or so. In the course of writing their chapters, some of our contributors thought deeply about these events for the first time. Consequently, they suffered through changing insights and comprehensions about themselves and others. We can hope that on balance the experience will have positive long-term outcomes (Pennebaker 1997).

The different childhood backgrounds of the contributors, which I mentioned in the introduction and which are very obvious from the individual chapters, raise difficult questions. Intuitively, it makes sense that there would be very different consequences of, for example, escaping to a safe haven early versus living in a ghetto or in hiding; or between the degrading treatment meted out to Jews as contrasted with the dangers of being in a family known to be political enemies of the regime. Yet, the only pattern I have noticed is that the contributors in the "refugee" category seem to be especially able to differentiate between Germany as it behaved during the war on the one hand and German culture before and since the war on the other. It would be interesting to examine to what extent this is a function of their age (this category includes some of our oldest contributors), their greater prewar exposure to non-Nazi aspects of German society, or their having been removed from the sites of the eventual Nazi massacres.

Aside from this tendency, the chapters do not show obvious long-term differences in how our authors coped with their diverse situations or in their life paths afterward. Of course, our roster is not a representative nor a very large sample of our total cohort, and we cannot tell how typical the pattern is of child survivors and refugees in general. This uncertainty also applies more broadly to the issue of generalizability: how similar are the histories in this book to the later lives of children who have lived through other horrendous events (Elder 1995)?

On another topic, I have thought about those colleagues who turned down my invitation to write a chapter. Some pleaded too much to do and not enough time. I can well believe that; after all, the contributors were selected partly because they are highly active, involved, and therefore busy people. Anyone trying to edit a book encounters such demurrers, as I certainly have in previous projects. However, some of the negative responses in this case were explicit refusals to remember those times or to expose one's feelings about them. These were poignant reminders that most child survivors stayed hidden, in a sense, until decades after the war ended. We did not tell people about our experiences and tried our very best to become indistinguishable from native-born children in our country of refuge.

That some of our colleagues are still not ready to speak or write publicly (and perhaps not even to think privately) about the connections between their early experiences and the later trajectory of their life does not surprise me. In fact, it reveals an aspect of the long-term aftermath of the Holocaust, and possibly of persecution in general, whose significance is frequently overlooked. Social scientists, and perhaps especially psychologists, tend to be introspective people. I would guess that it is unusual and dissonant for them to avoid thinking about what is surely a significant portion of autobiographical memory. Child survivors and refugees have overcome this resistance at different ages and to different degrees; it would be interesting to study the relevant personality factors, motives, or experiences that influence whether, when, and to what extent people can face this aspect of their past, integrate it into their present, and communicate the results to others.

Reflections on the Contributors

In his thoughtful comments about the chapters, Paul Marcus makes some very intriguing points concerning the reasons why people write. I would like to add some others for the consideration of those who are interested in motivational questions of this sort.[1] These suggestions also move the focus from particularism and idiographic foci to looking at how our behavior fits with broader psychological theories.

Without hard data, I nevertheless have the feeling that the contributors as a group, and survivor social scientists more generally, have reached levels of productivity and recognition that are well above the average for their disciplines. This impression is compatible with a look through the biographies of the recipients of various honors in the social sciences, such as the American Psychological Association's annual awards. The same is probably true when one looks at involvement in administrative and executive positions, both within scientific and professional associations and on university campuses or in research institutes. Without excessively elaborating the point, and bearing in mind the appropriate qualifications for the actual diversity of the contributors' wartime experiences, I offer the following nonexclusive possibilities to explain these high levels of activity and productivity.

1. In several contexts, child survivors demonstrate a desire to make the most of every moment. My impression is that this is true in leisure activities as well as vocational ones: child survivor gatherings, for example, consistently offer programs from early morning to late in the evening. This high level of activity may be interpreted as evidence of high achievement motivation, compulsiveness, or an attempt to distract oneself from unpleasant memories. Which explanation to select is a matter for theoretical and perhaps empirical exploration.

2. Jews in Nazi-influenced Europe were incessantly told that they were worthless, antisocial, and parasitic upon society. To a somewhat lesser degree, the same was said of political opponents of the regime. Such propaganda may have had little effect on adults, who knew what they and other Jews or opposition activists had accomplished; but it may have made more impression on children. Youngsters did not have the same protective knowledge as grownups and may have been more persuaded by messages emanating from authority figures such as government officials, newspaper columnists, radio commentators, teachers, youth group leaders, and the like. Some of the striving of former child survivors may be a desire to prove that those who characterized us in this way were wrong.

This hypothesis is the direct opposite of "stereotype threat" theory, which holds that children's performance is impaired by the knowledge that their demographic group is believed to do badly on the particular task (Steele 1997). That explanation has puzzled me since I first encountered it: it seems to me that such a negative stereotype would be more likely to serve as a challenge to prove it wrong. Perhaps members of different subcultures react differently in such a situation, an interesting empirical question.

3. As noted previously, work has been seen as an escape for many child survivors, a way to avoid thinking about our past. The busier we were, the less time we had to reflect on painful memories. Conversely, the fact that our age cohort is reaching the age of retirement and "empty

nests," as well as of somewhat diminishing physical energy, may help to explain the relatively recent emergence and current flood of child survivor groups, gatherings, oral histories, and autobiographical publications. In late middle age and onward, "life review" becomes a particularly common activity (Birren 1993; Butler 1963), and "ego integrity"—the search for wisdom, balancing despair with acceptance—becomes an important focus (Erikson 1982). In that area, we seem to fit the prevalent theories.

4. We have probably had closer brushes with death than most children, certainly than most children in the societies where we eventually settled. We lost more of our family members, at an earlier age; and many of us lived through events that threatened our own life. Terror management theory (Solomon, Greenberg, and Pyszczynski 1991), which argues that the cognitive and emotional salience of mortality leads to existential terror, provides two relevant predictions. The first is related to the avoidance of wartime memories, discussed earlier. Arndt et al. (1998) reported that when mortality was made salient by the administration of a death anxiety questionnaire, experimental participants avoided thoughts focusing on themselves. A fortiori, one would expect that memories of life events in which the threat of death was high would be even more aversive.

The second prediction is that people managing high levels of death salience might be unusually concerned about leaving posthumous traces of their existence. Such "mementos" for our contributors can include not only our children and grandchildren but also our impact on students, our own publications and the references colleagues make to those publications (e.g., citations), autobiographical videotapes, our names in lists of officeholders and award recipients or engraved on plaques and memorials, and so on.

Our identification with causes greater than ourselves can also be interpreted in this way. Viewing oneself as part of an important, numerous, and long-lasting movement, group, or cause can help avoid the impact of knowing that the self is evanescent. The intense involvement of many child survivors in educational, scientific, political, and charitable organizations may reflect some of this motivation. This hypothesis is a major leap from existing data (e.g., Nelson et al. 1997), but I think not an unreasonable one.

5. Still another factor may be the disruption of early attachments that many child survivors and emigrés experienced. Separation from parents, other relatives, and friends often led to deprivation of close relationships

that institutions and even affectionate foster parents could not replace. The need to be loved is probably especially high early in life, and deprivation may strengthen the motivation to compensate. In the motivational theories of both Maslow (1962) and Foa (e.g., 1993), the need for love and affection and the need for status and prestige are neighbors; as Foa wrote, "When an individual is denied the most needed resource he tends to choose the resource which is nearest in the order to the preferred one" (Foa 1993, 27). Thus, the search for status (which for Foa subsumes prestige, regard, and esteem) may be a substitute for the frustrated need for love.

All of the preceding explanations are, of course, speculative. They may apply to various degrees and in different combinations to all, some, or none of the contributors. Still, if we are to make progress toward a nomothetic science of trauma survival and resilience—topics that seem to me of great importance, not only personally but in view of the continuing and perhaps proliferating instances of mass violence in the world— we need to start integrating our individual stories into broader theoretical and empirical questions.

NOTE

1. I am grateful to Phyllis J. Johnson for her insights and suggestions on this topic.

REFERENCES

Arndt, J., J. Greenberg, L. Simon, T. Pyszczynski, and S. Solomon. 1998. Terror management and self-awareness: Evidence that mortality salience provokes avoidance of the self-focussed state. *Personality and Social Psychology Bulletin* 24:1216–27.

Birren, J. E. 1993. Understanding life backwards: Reminiscing for a better old age. In *Who is responsible for my old age?* edited by R. N. Butler and K. Kiikuni, 18–32. New York: Springer.

Butler, R. N. 1963. The life review: An interpretation of reminiscence in the aged. *Psychiatry* 26:65–76.

Elder, G. H. Jr. 1995. The life course paradigm: Social change and individual development. In *Examining lives in context: Perspectives on the ecology of human development,* edited by P. Moen, G. H. Elder Jr., and K. Lüscher, 101–39. Washington, DC: American Psychological Association.

Erikson, E. H. 1982. *The life cycle completed: A review.* New York: Norton.

Foa, U. G. 1993. Interpersonal and economic resources. In *Resource theory: Explo-*

rations and applications, edited by U. G. Foa, J. Converse Jr., K. Y. Törnblom, and E. B. Foa, 13–30. San Diego: Academic Press.

Maslow, A. H. 1962. *Toward a psychology of being.* Princeton: Van Nostrand.

Nelson, L. J., D. L. Moore, J. Olivetti, and T. Scott. 1997. General and personal mortality salience and nationalistic bias. *Personality and Social Psychology Bulletin* 23:884–92.

Pennebaker, J. W. 1997. *Opening up: The healing power of expressing emotion.* Rev. ed. New York: Guilford.

Solomon, S., J. Greenberg, and T. Pyszczynksi. 1991. A terror management theory of social behavior: The psychological functions of self-esteem and cultural worldviews. In *Advances in experimental social psychology,* edited by P. M. Zanna, 24:93–159. San Diego, CA: Academic Press.

Steele, C. M. 1997. A threat in the air: How stereotypes shape the intellectual identities and performance of women and African-Americans. *American Psychologist* 52:613–29.

Index